ALSO BY MARC EGNAL

*New World Economies: The Growth of the
Thirteen Colonies and Early Canada*

*Divergent Paths: How Culture and Institutions
Have Shaped North American Growth*

*A Mighty Empire: The Origins of the American Revolution*

# CLASH OF EXTREMES

# CLASH

## — OF —

# EXTREMES

*The Economic Origins of the Civil War*

MARC EGNAL

HILL AND WANG
*A division of Farrar, Straus and Giroux*
NEW YORK

Hill and Wang
A division of Farrar, Straus and Giroux
18 West 18th Street, New York 10011

Grateful acknowledgment is made for permission to
reprint parts of the text and selected maps from
*Civil War History* and *Ohio History*:
"The Beards Were Right: Political Parties in the North, 1840–1860,"
*Civil War History* 47 (2001): 30–56. Copyright © 2001 The Kent State University Press.
"Rethinking the Secession of the Lower South: The Clash of Two Groups,"
*Civil War History* 50 (2004): 261–90. Copyright © 2004 The Kent State University Press.
"Explaining John Sherman: Leader of the Second American Revolution,"
*Ohio History* 114 (2007): 105–17. Copyright © 2007 The Kent State University Press.
Reprinted with permission.

Library of Congress Cataloging-in-Publication Data
Egnal, Marc.
    Clash of extremes : the economic orgins of the Civil War / Marc
Egnal.
        p.   cm.
    Includes bibliographical references and index.
    ISBN-13: 978-0-8090-9536-0 (hardcover : alk. paper)
    ISBN-10: 0-8090-9536-X (hardcover : alk. paper)
        1. United States—History—Civil War, 1861–1865—Economic aspects.
    2. Republican Party (U.S. : 1854– )    I. Title.
HC105.6.E35 2009
973.7'11—dc22

                                                              2008028740

*Designed by Jennifer Ann Daddio*

www.fsgbooks.com

1   3   5   7   9   10   8   6   4   2

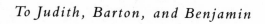

*To Judith, Barton, and Benjamin*

# CONTENTS

CONTENTS

# MAPS

# TABLES

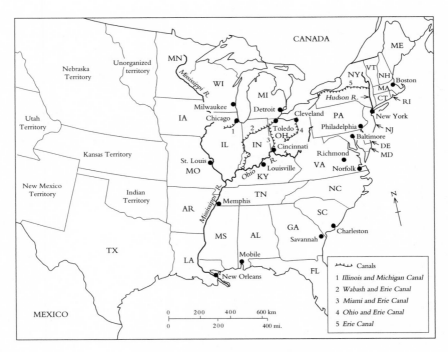

*Map 1. Eastern United States, 1860*

# CLASH OF EXTREMES

# INTRODUCTION

*Rethinking the Origins of the Civil War*

The Civil War will not go away. The outpouring of books about the causes of the conflict, Abraham Lincoln, and the war itself continues unabated. And for good reason. Whether the issue is race, region, or industrialization, the Civil War has left a deep imprint on modern America. You would think that after all these years historians would agree on why the country came to blows. But they do not. In many ways, to be sure, our knowledge of the era has advanced remarkably, particularly since the 1960s, when I attended graduate school. During the past decades there has been an outpouring of works on politics, the economy, and ideology. Bookshelves fill with biographies and studies of secession, as well as works on the role of African Americans, women, and the less wealthy. Printed volumes of papers and new sources on the Internet have proved a marvelous boon for researchers. So what is the problem? Why cannot historians explain the origins of the Civil War—or at least agree on the general outlines of an interpretation? Part of the difficulty lies with the very abundance of material. No one individual could come close to mastering the relevant secondary and primary sources. Even those who work on a single state can spend decades understanding events in one commonwealth. Part of the problem lies in the nature of what historians do. Despite the dreams of a few theorists, writing history remains as much an art as a science.

Still, there is no reason to abandon the question or succumb to an "anything goes" relativism. The Civil War is too important to leave alone. It haunts anyone who wonders how the United States came to be the country it is today. Moreover, professional scholars agree on a great deal before they begin to disagree. Almost all acknowledge the widespread racism in the North. Very few see African Americans as docile, childlike creatures. Most historians recognize the dynamic nature of the Northern economy at least from the 1820s onward—even as they argue about the pace of change in the South. Debates among scholars tend to be exchanges among the well informed. They are clashes between two lawyers who agree about certain facts but differ markedly in the way they interpret those facts.

*Clash of Extremes* is presented in that spirit. It is written, in part, because of the importance of the topic and the new vistas opened by the literature of the past decades. It is also written because of the problems that beset recent interpretations. If there is a leading explanation today, it is one that harkens back to earlier views. Many historians now affirm the traditional wisdom that slavery caused the Civil War. The North, led by the Republican Party, attacked the institution, the South defended it, and war was the result. James McPherson, the best-known scholar writing today on the Civil War, entitled his great work *Battle Cry of Freedom* and labeled Lincoln's victory "the revolution of 1860." He quotes approvingly a Southern newspaper that in 1860 described the triumphant Republicans as a "party founded on the single sentiment . . . of hatred of African slavery." Southerners, according to McPherson, had no choice but to respond to this threat and did so in "the counterrevolution of 1861." Reviewing a book by Maury Klein, McPherson notes: "If anyone still has doubts about the salience of slavery as the root of secession, Klein's evidence should remove them." In short, according to McPherson and the historians who agree with him, the North's passionate opposition to slavery and the equally fervent Southern defense of the institution caused the sectional clash.[1]

There are, however, difficulties with this "idealistic" explanation. To begin with, an emphasis on strongly held views about slavery sheds little light on the sequence of events that led to the Civil War. At least since the beginning of the nineteenth century, Northerners had resolutely condemned slavery, even if few advocated immediate abolition. This hostility to bondage, however, marked both the era of compromise, 1820 to 1850, as well as the increasingly bitter clashes of the 1850s, culminating in war. A persuasive interpretation must look elsewhere to explain why a lengthy period of cooperation gave way to one of conflict.

A focus on slavery also explains little about the divisions within the North and the South. It assumes unity in each of these regions when in fact there was fragmentation. Southerners who deemed the Republican victory so threatening that they called for secession comprised a distinct minority within their section. Of the fifteen slave states only seven, located in the Deep South, left the Union before fighting broke out. And many people in those seven states resisted immediate secession. At least 40 percent of voters, and in some cases half, opposed immediate secession in Georgia, Alabama, Mississippi, and Louisiana. The Border States—Delaware, Maryland, Kentucky, and Missouri—remained in the Union, while the Upper South states—Virginia, North Carolina, Tennessee, and Arkansas—joined the Confederacy only after Lincoln's call for troops forced them to choose sides. One hundred thousand whites (along with a larger number of blacks) from the Confederate states fought for the Union. There is no question that *some* individuals in the South felt that Lincoln's election posed a mortal threat to slavery, but more did not.[2]

Similarly, the North was divided in the years before the war, with only the Republicans rejecting compromise. In 1856 most Northerners backed the Republicans' opponents, and even in 1860 45 percent of the North voted for a candidate other than Lincoln. A convincing explanation must shed light on all groups and not simply focus on those whose outlook fits the interpretation.

Finally, the idealistic interpretation distorts the policies and positions of the Republican Party. Unquestionably Republicans, like virtually all free state residents, condemned slavery. But for most Republicans, opposition to bondage was limited to battling its extension into the West. Few Republicans advocated ending slavery—except in the distant future. Party members roundly rejected abolitionist demands for immediate action. Moreover, most Republicans (like most Northerners) were racists and had little interest in expanding the rights of free blacks. Indeed, many Republicans advocated free soil and a prohibition on the emigration to the West of all African Americans, free and slave. Blocking the spread of slavery was an important stance and one that frightened many in the South. But this position must not be equated with a humanitarian concern for the plight of African Americans. For most Republicans nonextension was more an economic policy designed to secure Northern domination of Western lands than the initial step in a broad plan to end slavery.

Nor does a celebration of the "battle cry of freedom" fairly characterize Republican goals once fighting began: the party initially rejected emancipation. Freedom became a war aim only once the North saw its utility in hastening a Confederate defeat. Had the conflict been brought to a quick close, as most Northerners and Southerners confidently assumed it would, slavery would have survived. Even after a year of war, with pressure for emancipation building, Lincoln told the editor Horace Greeley: "My paramount object in this struggle *is* to save the Union, and is *not* either to save or destroy slavery. If I could save the Union without freeing *any* slave I would do it, and if I could save it by freeing *all* the slaves I would do it; and if I could save it by freeing some and leaving others alone I would also do that."[3] The Emancipation Proclamation of January 1, 1863, conformed to that third option: freeing some of the slaves. It liberated those in the rebel states without threatening the property of Border State slaveholders.

The prevailing interpretation creates an odd dichotomy in explaining the first decades of the Republican Party. Before the war, according to this idealistic approach, the Republicans were humanitarians, driven by their concern for free farmers and African Americans. However, this portrayal of the Republican Party quietly yields to a very different picture in the years after the war. Most accounts depict the postwar Republicans as the corrupt servants of big business. The result is a striking discontinuity. The noble crusaders of the antebellum years become the spoilsmen of the Gilded Age. Of course, parties change. But it is striking how many of the leaders of the 1850s continued to guide the party in the 1870s and later. Idealism existed before the war. But making it the key to understanding the Republicans distorts the record. It fails to explain the actions of a party that, as soon as it took power in 1861, introduced a bold, coherent program to build a national economy and strengthen the dominance of Northern producers.

In sum, the current emphasis on slavery as the cause of the Civil War is fraught with problems. It does not clarify the sequence of events, the divisions within the sections, or the policies and actions of the Republican Party. It is these problems that a new interpretation must address.


*Clash of Extremes* responds to these concerns. It argues that more than any other reason, the evolution of the Northern and Southern economies explains the Civil War. This interpretation may strike some students of the Civil War as unfashionable, or, even worse, old-fashioned. But then in the well-trod field of Civil War historiography, most explanations have their antecedents. The best-known proponents of an economic interpretation of the Civil War are Charles and Mary Beard, who wrote during the first decades of the twentieth century. Their work, which is well known to historians, is badly flawed. They ignored local politics, overlooked the role of ideology, downplayed the impact of individuals, and more generally provided a creaky, mechanistic analysis of sectional conflict. But these faults, which generations of historians have rehearsed, should not discredit an entire approach.[4]

The story set forth in *Clash of Extremes* begins with the era from 1820 to 1850 and the unifying influence of the national economy. Business activity during these decades brought together the North and South for five reasons. First, trade along the Mississippi and its tributaries gave the Northwest and Southwest a shared outlook and a common set of interests. Second, the Border States, which comprised the northern reaches of the slave regime, had strong and growing ties with the North. These commonwealths saw few benefits and many drawbacks to clashes with the free states. Third, the growth of textile manufacturing and the cotton trade linked the mill owners and merchants of the North with the planters of the South. This alliance, complained Massachusetts senator Charles Sumner, joined the "lords of the lash and the lords of the loom." Fourth, the buoyant economy of the Southwest reinforced the case for the Union. The region boasted fresh soils and high returns, as well as a deep appreciation for the role the federal government played in pushing back natives, Spaniards, and Mexicans. Finally, the burgeoning economy fostered similar divisions in every state, creating the foundation for two national parties. Throughout the United States prosperous farmers, planters, and businessmen came together to support the Whigs. At the same time urban workers and poorer farmers, individuals who felt excluded by the new exchanges, backed the Democratic Party. While the two parties battled each other vigorously over economic issues, both had adherents throughout the country, and shared a common belief in a unified nation.

By midcentury new patterns of commerce and new attitudes had emerged, shattering the unities of the earlier era and providing the basis for a decade of increasingly bitter sectional politics. In the North the rise of the Great Lakes economy changed the outlook of many in the region from western New York to Wisconsin. Producers in the Northwest now conducted most of their business along an east–west axis that began with the lakes and included the Erie Canal and New York City. The booming lake economy required extensive spending on the waterways, higher tariffs to pay for those improvements, and an active federal government to oversee these programs. Using the language of nationalism, individuals in this region demanded the federal government assist the growth of the Northern economy.

A second development helped reorient the North, reinforcing the changes that emerged from the new patterns of trade. Militant antislavery grew from a handful of abolitionists in the early 1830s to a powerful movement at midcentury. Perhaps 15 percent of the Northern population came to affirm radical doctrines, including the abolition of bondage in the District of Columbia and the repeal of federal fugitive slave laws. Most of these individuals lived in New England and in the areas of Yankee settlement around the lakes. Together the rise of the lake economy and the spread of antislavery sentiment transformed the North and created the basis for the Republican Party, an organization that had little interest in compromising with the South. The new party was remarkably successful, winning much of the North in its first national contest in 1856 and electing the president in 1860.

Reflecting their roots, Republicans enunciated both antislavery and economic policies, but their clear priority was Northern growth rather than helping African Americans. Even more fervently than other Northerners, Republicans condemned slavery, citing the Declaration of Independence and its affirmation that "all men are created equal." But the only significant initiative Republicans advocated to assist blacks was free soil, a program that furthered both economic and humanitarian goals. Declaring the new territories off-limits to slaveholders, this policy assisted Northern farmers at the same time that it struck a blow against slavery by limiting its expansion. Mainstream Republicans pointedly refused to condemn the Fugitive Slave Act, the interstate slave trade, or slavery in the District of Columbia and federal shipyards. The party acquiesced in the racism that defined Northern society. Although eschewing programs to help blacks, Republicans vigorously supported economic initiatives including higher tariffs, free homesteads, internal improvements, land grant colleges, and a transcontinental railroad.

Not all areas of the North were swept up in these changes; nor did all Northerners rush to the Republican standard. The most outspoken opponents of the new party came from the lower North, an area that included the Ohio Valley, as well as New Jersey and much of Pennsylvania. These districts lay farthest from the lakes and stood apart from the fires of antislavery agitation. Only in 1860 did Republicans win over former Whigs in this region. These partisans responded not to antislavery rhetoric but to the economic measures that were at the heart of the Republican program. Democrats in the lower North, however, did not care for the Republicans' economic and antislavery planks and remained firm in their opposition to the party of Lincoln.

By 1850 the South too had been transformed by economic change, leading many individuals to become more ardent defenders of states' rights. The most striking turn toward sectionalism appeared in the southern reaches of the Deep South. Planters in these districts displayed little interest in manufacturing or diversified agriculture. Instead, they hitched their future to slavery, a single cash crop, and fresh land. Their determination to expand was intensified in the 1840s by depleted soils, the need for new states to preserve the balance in the Senate, and mounting fears about rebellious slaves in a static society. Unfortunately for these planters, the demand for new lands coincided with the growing opposition in the North to further expansion of the slave regime. The result of this collision of interests was the emergence of an outspoken states' rights group and the "first secession crisis" of 1849–51. Across the cotton states prominent politicians, like John C. Calhoun, called for separation. At midcentury, however, unlike in 1861, lawmakers in Washington hammered out a compromise, staving off disunion.

Even in the Deep South not all planters and small farmers cheered the turn toward states' rights. Residents in the northern districts of these states had ties of kinship and trade with the Upper South and were reluctant to go along with the plans of sectional politicians. Many in these areas favored a more diversified economy and believed the South could continue to prosper, even if its expansion was checked. These divergent views led to clashes during the debates over the Compromise of 1850.

The evolution of the national economy also shaped the response of the Border States and Upper South to the midcentury crisis. Thanks to expanding trade and the declining importance of slavery, the Border States—Missouri, Kentucky, Maryland, and Delaware—gradually drew closer to the North and shunned the protests led by states' rights politicians. The Upper South—Virginia, Tennessee, North Carolina, and Arkansas—also boasted many unionists. They included city dwellers, individuals involved in the expanding exchanges with the free states, and many small farmers, particularly those residing in the Ozark Mountains of Arkansas and the Appalachian highlands. However, unlike the Border States, the Upper South claimed a militant group of slaveholders, who echoed the disunionists' views.

During the winter of 1860–61 the cotton states seceded. Leading the campaign for separation were the planters and smaller farmers in the southern districts of the commonwealths from South Carolina to Mississippi, and kindred spirits in Texas, Louisiana, and Florida. The arguments put forth echoed those raised in 1849–51. Only now the case was immeasurably stronger with the Republicans triumphant, slavery still weaker along the "Great Border," and more free states in the Union. For those championing disunion, the logic of their position was clear: Republican pronouncements about the "ultimate extinction" of slavery and references to the Declaration of Independence signaled the inevitable destruction of Southern society. Dire foreboding about rebellious slaves, restless lower-class whites, and subversive factions nursed by Republican patronage sealed this analysis. Separation was the only answer.

Thus the secession of the Lower South emerged from what seemed to be a glaring asymmetry. States' rights leaders in the cotton states feared for the survival of slavery and regarded the Republicans as abolitionists. Republicans swore they would not interfere with the "peculiar institution" where it existed and affirmed that bondage might last another hundred years. Secessionists accused Republicans of seeking equality. Republicans replied they had no intention, for the foreseeable future, of disturbing race relations in either section. Both sides were right. The Republicans' short-term agenda, as party members repeatedly protested, was a cautious one; it focused on economics rather than on race. But over the long run, which might have meant decades or even a century, Republican policies would accelerate the end of slavery. Initiatives that boosted Northern industry and the spread of free labor inevitably undermined bondage.

A different calculus governed actions in the Border States and Upper South. Few in the Border States and only a minority in the Upper South agreed with the fire-eaters of the cotton states. Overwhelmingly, the citizenry of this northerly part of the South rejected the notion that the mere election of a Republican president was cause for secession. In these states plantations were smaller, slaveholding less important, economic activities more diversified, and ties with the North stronger. Secession came only once war began, and Lincoln's call for troops forced Southerners to choose sides. Led by the larger slave-owners, the Upper South joined the Confederacy. The Border States, with their smaller, less influential planting communities, remained with the Union. Class lines, at least as they were reflected by regions within states, were a more important determinant of loyalties in these two tiers of states than in the Deep South. The free districts of western Virginia split from Virginia, while many small farmers in eastern Tennessee, western North Carolina, and northwestern Arkansas fought for the Union.

The policies adopted by the Republicans after 1861 confirm and illuminate the nature of the prewar party. As in earlier years, party members pursued two priorities—assisting African Americans and developing the Northern economy—but not with equal determination. Republicans did not enter the war with any intention of transforming the South's institutions. But after a year of fighting and the prospect of a prolonged conflict, party members became more open to proposals for emancipation and the recruitment of black soldiers. Military necessity coupled with long-standing Republican beliefs in freedom and black rights argued for such daring initiatives. Still more fully in keeping with party ideology were the economic measures adopted between 1861 and 1865. Guided by their self-serving ideology of "nationalism," lawmakers passed legislation for internal improvements, higher tariffs, a national banking system, a uniform currency, a homestead act, and a transcontinental railroad.

After the war Republicans again hoped to make progress on both fronts: defending the basic rights of blacks and fostering economic activity in the North. Faced with the intransigence of white Southerners, who refused to accept the moderate program advocated by mainstream party members, Republicans adopted strong measures. They divided the South into military districts, enfranchised blacks, and took the vote away from former Confederates. However, Republican support for these measures was short-lived. State by state they abandoned their African American allies and the progressive regimes in the South. By contrast, Republican determination to assist Northern business continued undiminished. Currency policies, lucrative subsidies to corporations, regressive taxation, and the use of troops to suppress strikers and relocate Indians helped the rich get richer and made possible the rise of monopolies and oligopolies. The Republican Party also changed. The leavening of idealism, which had attracted many to its ranks, disappeared by the early 1870s. Radical politicians left an organization they now felt was misguided. More than ever, the party focused on its prime directive: developing the North.

That is a bare-bones outline of the argument of the book. This interpretation explains the sequence of events leading up to the war, the divisions within the North and South, and the goals and evolution of the Republican Party. It indicates why before 1861 the most defiant positions were taken in the northern part of the North and the southern part of the South, making the Civil War—as the book's title suggests—a clash of extremes.

But this plot summary is not enough. It is also important to suggest the larger dimensions of this "economic interpretation." To begin with, this explanation values the role of individuals. There is no contradiction between a focus on particular people and an emphasis on the importance of broader developments. Indeed, the two approaches complement each other. Understanding the evolution of society in the North and South provides a context for individual actions. Often the most successful politicians were those who grasped the dynamics of change and harnessed these energies to their own ends. Few individuals were more adept in responding to shifting conditions than Abraham Lincoln. In 1864 Lincoln explained to Kentucky editor Albert Hodges why he had come to support emancipation. "When, early in the war, Gen[eral] Fremont attempted military emancipation, I forbade it," Lincoln remarked, "because I did not then think it an indispensable necessity." But conditions changed, Lincoln noted: "[In] 1862 I made earnest, and successive appeals to the Border States to favor compensated emancipation. . . . They declined the proposition; and I was, in my best judgment, driven to the alternative of either surrendering the Union, and with it, the Constitution, or of laying strong hand upon the colored element. I chose the latter." Lincoln concluded: "In telling this tale I attempt no compliment to my own sagacity. I claim not to have controlled events, but confess plainly that events have controlled me."[5]

Individuals not only responded to broader trends, but they also shaped history. Andrew Jackson's entry into national politics helped realign voting patterns. John C. Calhoun's forthright defense of Southern rights influenced his many followers. Stephen A. Douglas's Kansas-Nebraska Act precipitated divisions within the North and the formation of new parties. The far-reaching influence of particular people does not undercut an economic interpretation. Rather, a focus on individuals helps illuminate the society in which they functioned and the conditions that made their accomplishments possible. Jackson had such a significant impact on voting because tensions already existed between employees and employers, poorer farmers and wealthier ones. Many in the Deep South eagerly embraced Calhoun's wisdom because they too feared that the cotton economy could not secure new soils within a Union dominated by the North. Douglas's Kansas-Nebraska Act brought into the open divisions within the North that had been evident for several years. Understanding the pattern of change requires looking at both leaders and society.

Second, this study introduces no abstract, disembodied Larger Forces. Historians are justly wary of concepts emblazoned in capital letters or ones that enter the stage with an aura of inevitability. The Beards called Northern politicians "statesmen of the invincible forces recorded in the census returns" and labeled their chapters on events leading to the war "The Sweep of Economic Forces" and "The Politics of the Economic Drift."[6] Such concepts obscure more than they clarify. Students of this era cannot do away with collective nouns. New Englanders voted together on some issues, as did people living around the Great Lakes. But aggregates must emerge from a close analysis of the data. That is the approach taken in *Clash of Extremes*.

Third, ideology serves as the link between interest and action. Few people chose sides in the sectional conflict simply to put dollars in their purses. Rather, beliefs—which had strong roots in self-interest—guided their behavior. Some individuals developed their worldview after poring over book-length treatises or writing eloquent disquisitions. But for most people the power of partisan ideologies came from the succinct, forceful way these ideas were communicated and the relevance of these ideas to their lives. Thus in the 1830s the poorer farmers of northern Illinois and Indiana endorsed Democratic doctrines. These landowners applauded politicians who denounced high tariffs and railed against government spending. In the 1850s these same farmers embraced the ideology of the Republican Party. Their trade had shifted, and they now viewed themselves in a different light—as members of a lake economy that needed outlays on harbors, higher tariffs to pay for those improvements, and a stronger government to administer these programs.

Fourth, if economics was most important, it was never the only influence on the political process. The growth of antislavery reshaped Northern politics—even if economic concerns remained more important in forming parties and determining their platforms. People's origins made a difference, as did their religion. New Englanders who settled in the Midwest carried their beliefs with them, helping to lead the anti-Southern movement in their new states. Quakers took a similar, critical view of slavery wherever they settled and were in the forefront of the reform movement. By contrast, Irish Catholics, who tended to be poor and often competed with blacks for jobs, mocked the abolitionists and opposed the Republicans. Residents of the Upper South who migrated to the Deep South were usually more moderate than their neighbors. All these influences helped shape the politics of the antebellum period.

This work presents an economic interpretation of the origins of the Civil War. It contends that the evolution of the Northern and Southern economies, more than any other factor, explains the conflict. This argument, however, is never simplistic or reductive. Individuals, religion, and ideologies also shape the story. Chapter 1 examines the foundations for the era of compromise, 1820–50, and the prominent role played during these years by Henry Clay, Andrew Jackson, and Martin Van Buren.

# PART ONE

# AN ERA
# OF
# COMPROMISE

—— 1 ——

# FOUNDATIONS

T he Compromise of 1850 was the last hurrah for the Second
Party System,* which had emerged in the 1820s. For almost
three decades Democratic and Whig politicians had stood
shoulder to shoulder on national unity, while fighting each other over
economic policies. Now that system was breaking down, as the voices
of sectional spokesmen grew ever louder. With so much at stake the
old guard, who had created and steered the two national parties, came
together to rally the troops one last time. Henry Clay of Kentucky,
founder and revered leader of the Whig Party, urged his fellow congressmen "solemnly to pause—at the edge of the precipice, before the
fearful and disastrous leap is taken in the yawing abyss below."[1]
Stephen Douglas of Illinois, a leading Democrat and so often Clay's
opponent, joined with the Kentuckian in supporting the Compro-

*The First Party System of Jeffersonian Democratic-Republicans and Federalists began in the 1790s
and disappeared by 1820.

mise. Douglas concluded his remarks with a note of cautious optimism: "The excitement is subsiding, and reason resuming its supremacy. The question is rapidly settling itself, in spite of the efforts of the extremes at both ends of the Union to keep up the agitation. The people of the whole country . . . will not consent that this question shall be kept open for the benefit of politicians, who are endeavoring to organize parties on geographical lines."[2]

Events would prove Douglas's optimism unfounded. Even though the Compromise of 1850 was adopted, "parties on geographical lines" soon replaced the national organizations of the Second Party System. In little more than a decade the "efforts of the extremes" drove the nation into that abyss Clay so feared. That was the end of the era of compromises. But how did it all begin? It started with the unifying impact of the American economy in the 1820s, 1830s, and 1840s and with a remarkable set of party builders: Clay, Andrew Jackson, and Martin Van Buren.

I.

The economy of the young republic provided the foundations for an era of sectional compromise and resilient national parties. To begin with, in the West the Mississippi River formed a powerful North-South axis, bringing together the Northwest and Southwest. In October 1811 the steamboat *New Orleans* made a historic voyage, traveling from Pittsburgh to the Crescent City. In New Orleans this first steamboat to appear on the "Western waters" took on cargo and made the trip back upriver to Natchez. Robert Fulton, the artist and inventor who had helped design and finance the vessel, was delighted. "The Mississippi . . . is conquered," he exclaimed to his friend Joel Barlow, and added, "These are conquests perhaps as valuable as those [of Napoleon] at Jena." Before the voyage of the *New Orleans*, rafts and keelboats had brought goods down the Mississippi, but the return voyage had been slow, arduous, and expensive. The steamboat changed all that. The cost of goods imported through New Orleans fell precipitously, as did traveling times in both directions.[3]

Despite the voyage of the *New Orleans*, the age of the steamboat on Western waters did not arrive until the 1820s, when trade along the "Father of Waters" began to grow rapidly. As late as 1818 only thirty steamboats operated in the West. By 1830 more than 150 steamboats plied the Mississippi and its tributaries. That number increased to nearly 500 in 1840 and over 600 in 1850. Trade expanded still more rapidly than these numbers suggest, as steady technological advances (at least until the 1840s) allowed vessels to carry more cargo, more quickly, more safely, and for more days each year.[4]

The expansion of trade on the Mississippi and its tributaries had far-reaching ramifications. It tied the Western states together and defined, for many Americans, a capacious, fertile region that transcended North-South divisions. Many politicians extolled the unity and power of the Great Valley. Among them was John C. Calhoun, the South Carolina leader who hoped support from the Valley along with his popularity in the South would propel him into the presidency. In 1845 he traveled to Memphis to chair the Southwestern Convention. At a gathering in New Orleans, he offered a toast: "*The Valley of the Mississip[p]i.*—The greatest in the world, take it all in all. Situated as it is, between the two oceans, it will yet command the commerce of the world, and that commerce may be centred in New Orleans." At Memphis Calhoun promoted a rail network to connect the Mississippi River with Charleston.[5]

Many others shared this belief in the greatness of the Valley. Stephen Douglas built his career on the assumption of Western unity. In the late 1840s he pushed for aid to the Illinois Central Railroad and the construction of a railroad linking Mobile and Chicago as a complement to river-borne traffic. In his speech defending the Compromise of 1850 Douglas pointed to the Valley as the heart of the country. He told his fellow senators: "There is a power in this nation greater than either the North or South—a growing, increasing, swelling power, that will be able to speak the law to this nation, and to execute the law as spoken. That power is the country known as the great West—the Valley of the Mississippi, one and indivisible from the gulf to the great lakes . . . There, sir, is the hope of this nation."[6]

Lewis Cass of Michigan was another politician who trumpeted the unity of the Great Valley—and he clung to that belief long after sectional conflict had divided the Northwest from Southwest. Born in New Hampshire in 1782, Cass moved to the Northwest Territory with his family in 1801. He stood out in the newly settled West for his education (he graduated from Phillips Exeter Academy and read law in Ohio) and his ability. During the War of 1812 he was appointed colonel of an Ohio regiment and rose to be major general of volunteers. President Madison rewarded Cass for his wartime services by naming him Governor of Michigan Territory, a post he held until 1831. Cass was a strong defender of Western interests, an outspoken expansionist, and by the 1830s a loyal Democrat. He became secretary of war under Jackson, ambassador to France, Democratic presidential candidate in 1848, Michigan senator, and secretary of state under James Buchanan. In the 1850s as sectional tension mounted, Cass, who was now well into his seventies, reaffirmed his lifelong faith in the importance of the Great Valley. "I have descended its mighty river two thousand miles in a birch canoe," he told his fellow senators in 1856, "when there was hardly a white man above St. Louis." He continued: "The destinies of this Republic, in the event of internal dissensions, will be found in the hearts and heads and hands of the people of the West, and there they will, I trust, be safe."[7]

The movement of population within the Mississippi Valley reinforced these unities. During the first three decades of the nineteenth century the Northwest was settled largely by Southern migrants who were drawn to the fertile soils on the north side of the Ohio River. Fully 58 percent of the delegates who wrote the first constitution for Indiana were born in the South. After Illinois was admitted to the Union in 1819, its first two senators, its single representative, and its governor were all Southern born. Not everyone leaving the South applauded the practices of their native region. Kentucky-born Abraham Lincoln, who moved with his family to Indiana before settling in Illinois, abhorred slavery. But most of these migrants remained far more sympathetic than other Northerners to the arguments put forth by the states' rights leaders.

The Border States, with their increasingly close ties to the North, comprised a second force for national unity. These commonwealths—Delaware, Maryland, Kentucky, and Missouri—were the march lands of the slave regime and gradually were drawn into the Northern commercial orbit. The Great Compromiser, Henry Clay, hailed from this region. After Clay's death in 1852, another Kentuckian, John J. Crittenden, assumed his mantle. Even as economic change after mid-century transformed the North and the cotton South, deepening the hostility between the sections, Border State politicians remained peace weavers.

A third set of economic ties—the links between the manufacturers and merchants of the North and the cotton planters of the South—also drew together the sections. Northern mills, which expanded rapidly after the War of 1812, consumed perhaps a fifth of the cotton crop. Shipments of this raw material to the North amounted to nearly $20 million a year and encouraged the mill owners to look favorably upon ties with the South. This relationship culminated in the election of a prominent "cotton Whig," Robert C. Winthrop of Massachusetts, as Speaker of the U.S. House of Representatives in 1847. The *Boston Whig* harrumphed: "Mr. Winthrop is elected as the favorite candidate of the slaveholding section of the party of South Carolina."[9]

Ties between New Yorkers and cotton planters were equally

strong. New York merchants, working with their representatives in the Southern ports and smaller towns, purchased and shipped most of the cotton crop. Manhattan's position as the nation's financial capital meant that New York traders could offer their correspondents favorable terms, ousting other competitors from this commerce. Brokers were able to extend to landowners the year's credit they needed to finance their crop and to continue acquiring slaves and land. Typically, New York vessels carried the cotton directly from the South to Europe, although some of the bales were brought to docks along the East River for reshipment. New Yorkers profited from shipping, insuring, and financing the crop, as well as selling it. Manhattan traders also supplied manufactures and other finished goods to the South, and here New York's role as entrepot was unmistakable; the cloth and hardware that the planters needed arrived first in New York and then were reshipped to the South. Many New Yorkers, rich and poor, were involved in these exchanges and came to sympathize with the South and its view of national issues.[10]

A fourth aspect of the national economy contributed to this era of cooperation: the South, *with the assistance of the federal government*, grew rapidly during the 1820s, 1830s, and 1840s. The new soils of the Southwest delivered high returns, creating a series of land rushes and waves of speculation. Virginian Joseph Baldwin, who visited Alabama and Mississippi in the mid-1830s, reported, "This country was just settling up. Marvellous accounts had gone forth of the fertility of its virgin lands; and the productions of the soil were commanding a price remunerating to slave labor as it had never been remunerated before. Emigrants came flocking in from all quarters of the Union, especially from the slaveholding States. The new country seemed to be a reservoir, and every road leading to it a vagrant stream of enterprise and adventure."[11] Such returns were less notable in the older states of the South; by the 1820s landowners in Maryland, Virginia, and the Carolinas complained of falling yields. But Tennessee, Kentucky, and the new states of the Southwest had rich lands to offer settlers.

Until the late 1840s the federal government played a crucial role in promoting Southern growth. With Andrew Jackson's victory at Horseshoe Bend, Alabama, in 1814 and the expulsion of the Cherokee from Georgia in 1838, the federal government drove the Indians from the fertile soils they had long occupied. Washington also pressured Spain to give up Florida in 1819 and forced Mexico to relinquish all claims to territory north of the Rio Grande in 1848. The national government provided other benefits to Dixie. French traveler Alexis de Tocqueville, who toured the United States in the early 1830s, remarked that the South was "bound to wish the Union to have a strong fleet" to protect its exports, and noted that "southerners must wish to preserve the Union so that they should not face the blacks alone." Tocqueville observed that such advantages made Southerners strong supporters of the Union but added ominously, "I have no confidence in that calculated patriotism which is founded on interest and which a change of interests may destroy."[12]

## II.

The economy of the young republic helped unify Americans in still another way. It provided the basis for national parties by fostering common sets of interests and similar conflicts in every state. The growth that quickened in the 1820s divided Americans within each town and state as never before. The United States always had rich and poor people. What was new after the War of 1812 was the dramatic expansion of opportunities to rise or fall in the world. In the colonial era the standard of living rose about 0.5 percent a year; by the 1820s the pace had quickened to 1.5 percent. What these numbers mean is that, unlike the stately pace of change in colonial times, growth now was jarring and spectacular and filled with possibilities for those who dared to seize them. Americans for the first time witnessed dramatic changes in material conditions. A woman born in 1820 saw, by the time she was thirty, machine-made fabrics replace homespun, horse-drawn carriages give way to locomotives, and postal riders yield to the telegraph.[13]

A diverse class of driven entrepreneurs emerged with this era of quickening growth. This group included merchants, manufacturers, and wealthy farmers. Visitors were struck by the American passion for making money. Tocqueville remarked, "It is odd to watch with what feverish ardor the Americans pursue prosperity, and how they are ever tormented by the shadowy suspicion that they may not have chosen the shortest route to get it."[14] Harriet Martineau sketched in a similar picture. Martineau was a well-known English popularizer; her books brought the ideas of Jeremy Bentham and John Stuart Mill to a large audience. From 1834 to 1836 she tackled the breadth of America with the same gusto she brought to the intricacies of political economy. An intrepid traveler despite her physical problems—she had a weak heart and carried an ear trumpet to hear better—Martineau ventured from the east coast to the frontier and from Canada to New Orleans. The wealthy traders in the Eastern cities, Martineau felt, fully embodied the qualities that characterized Americans. "The spirit of enterprise is very remarkable in the American merchants," she noted. "Beginning life, as all Americans do, with the world all open before them . . . a passionate desire to overcome difficulties arises in them."[15]

These men on the make (few women ran businesses or farms) were not uniformly distributed: they clustered in cities and near trans-portation routes where goods were more readily available. Using window glass as an illustration, Martineau compared the lives of those near canals with homeowners in more remote areas. "Persons who happen to live near a canal, or other quiet watery road, have baskets of glass of various sizes sent to them from the towns, and glaze their own windows," she observed. "But there is no bringing glass over a corduroy, or mud, or rough limestone road."[16]

The spirit of gain pervaded the South as well as the North, though the two sections were not mirror images of each other. Eventually, a deep commitment to the "peculiar institution" would lead planters to make decisions that showed more concern for protecting their way of life than for maximizing profits. But in the 1820s and 1830s there was no need to face such difficult choices. Fresh soils made slavery exceptionally profitable, particularly in the Southwest.

These successful individuals, including Southern planters, prosperous Northern farmers, as well as merchants and manufacturers in both sections, shared common interests, despite their geographical diversity. They praised government support for roads, river improvements, schools, and banks. They accepted the need for higher tariffs to pay for such programs, and they favored an expanding though not inflationary currency. Eventually, these individuals would come together in a national organization, the Whig Party.

The burgeoning economy also produced a large class of individuals who were less successful, less involved in the market economy, and more critical of government policies that promoted growth. Many farmers were poor and worked land far removed from the major arteries of transportation. Tocqueville came to know the isolated farms of Tennessee well since he stayed at such a homestead while recovering from a bout of illness. "The interior of these dwellings attests the indolence of the master even more than his poverty," he noted in his journal. "You find a clean enough bed, some chairs, a good gun, often books, and almost always a newspaper, but the walls are so full of chinks that the outside air enters from all sides. . . . You are hardly better sheltered than in a cabin of leaves." Homes on the Michigan frontier, Tocqueville observed, were similarly crude if better insulated.[17]

Conditions on many of the smaller farms of the Southwest were still more primitive. Joseph Ingraham, a New England traveler, described the poorer landowners in Mississippi. This "peculiar class," he noted, "include the majority of the inhabitants on the east part of this state." He added: "They are in general uneducated, and their apparel consists of a coarse linsey-woolsey, of a dingy yellow or blue, with broad-brimmed hats; though they usually follow their teams bare-footed and bareheaded, with their long locks hanging over their eyes and shoulders, giving them a wild appearance . . . At home, they live in log-houses on partially cleared lands, labour hard in their fields, sometimes owning a few slaves, but more generally with but one or none."[18]

Working men and women in the towns shared many of the same attitudes as the poorer farmers; both groups felt themselves outsiders in an expanding economy. These decades were marked by a widening gulf between employer and employees. In the colonial period master craftsmen and journeymen had labored and often lived together. They marched side by side in parades and perceived no conflict of interests. However, during the first decades of the nineteenth century the structure of work and the outlook of workers changed. Shoemaking and the men's clothing industry, for example, were transformed by the increasing division of labor. Where a single individual had once crafted a pair of shoes or stitched a complete shirt, now the tasks were more narrowly defined. One individual might only attach soles or sew on collars. Merchant capitalists financed and oversaw the work of many. In other industries, such as cotton textiles and iron making, capitalists erected large establishments and hired many employees. Working people now came together in unions, even if many of these efforts were short-lived, and defined themselves in opposition to their bosses.[19]

These workers and less wealthy farmers shared a common view-point, often called an "Old Republican" outlook. This ideology pointed back to an idealized early Republic where hardworking farmers and skilled artisans lived comfortable lives untroubled by banks, paper money, monopolies, speculators, or the oppressive hand of government. Just as the wealthier farmers and merchants came together under the Whig banner, so these laborers and poorer farmers became the mainstay of a competing national organization, the Democratic Party.

## III.

Although clashing interests within each state provided the basis for competing groups, national parties did not form themselves. It took politicians with vision and determination to build upon those possibilities and form long-lived organizations. During the 1820s three men—Henry Clay, Andrew Jackson, and Martin Van Buren—began the process of creating durable parties. More than any other single individual, Henry Clay brought together the affluent and the entrepreneurial in every state and formed them into a national organization. This party, which by the 1830s was called the Whig Party, demanded an active government that promoted growth.

But who was Henry Clay? He was tall for the time, nearly six feet, homely, with a high forehead, a long straight nose, and small blue eyes. A contemporary humorously observed that his face was a "compromise" assembled by a committee. He was also a bundle of contradictions. Clay often reminded listeners of his lack of education: "I know my deficiencies . . . from my father I inherited only infancy, ignorance, and indigence. I feel my defects."[20] But he was a trained lawyer, and his speeches show a good grasp of the intricacies of political economy. He was a high-minded nationalist, who focused on policy questions more consistently and more passionately than most public figures. At the same time, his immoral behavior was public knowledge; the press and his opponents castigated him for his drinking and flagrant womanizing. And all too often desperate ambition rather than policy or principles dictated Clay's actions.[21]

Although Clay had been active in politics since the first years of the century, only in 1824 did he formulate the economic program that he would defend throughout the rest of his long career. This program, the "American System," gave the federal government a central role in promoting development. His plan included a protective tariff, internal improvements, a national bank, and revenue from the sale of Western lands. The American System reflected Clay's keen awareness of the new economic realities that emerged in the 1820s: the rise of a restless, entrepreneurial population; the success of manufacturing; and the need to revive the country after the Panic of 1819. He spelled out his views in a series of speeches delivered to Congress early in 1824. Clay explained that the older approach (the "European System"), which emphasized exports and the carrying trade, no longer could help the United States. "Our system is anomalous," he noted. "It can succeed only in the rare occurrence of a general state of war throughout Europe."[22]

For Clay the growing importance of manufacturing demonstrated the need for a protective tariff. While acknowledging that "our agricultural is our greatest interest," he argued that industry must be the engine of development. Clay illustrated his point with a colorful metaphor: "The difference between a nation with, and without the [manufacturing] arts, may be conceived, by the difference between a keelboat and a steamboat, combating the rapid torrent of the Mississippi. How slow does the former ascend. . . . With what ease is she not passed by the steamboat, laden with the riches of all quarters of the world, with a crowd of gay, cheerful and protected passengers, now dashing into the midst of the current, or gliding through the eddies near the shore!" The success of cotton textile production in the North, Clay noted, fully demonstrated the wisdom of protection.[23]

Clay regarded the American System as the embodiment of the nationalism he had long espoused. He had been a "War Hawk" during the War of 1812 and had engineered the first of his great sectional compromises with the admission of Missouri in 1821. The American

System, he asserted, would give Americans a common set of interests. Southern cotton would be sent to the North rather than to England, and finished goods would come from American mills, not European ones. A network of roads, canals, and deepened rivers would bind the regions together. "All the powers of this Government should be interpreted in reference to its first, its best, its greatest object, the Union of these States," he observed. "And is not that union best invigorated by an intimate, social, and commercial connexion between all the parts of the Confederacy?"[24]

Clay hoped that his economic policies would gain him support throughout the country and pave the way to the presidency in the 1824 elections. But these hopes were dashed. Although many supporters revered him, he never generated the popular excitement his rival Jackson could claim. Clay finished a distant fourth, behind Jackson, John Quincy Adams, and William Crawford, and the election had to be settled in the House of Representatives. Driven by his desire for high office, Clay struck the infamous "corrupt bargain" with Adams. He agreed to support Adams in return for the position of secretary of state. The deal enraged Jackson's supporters, who noted the general had finished first in popular and electoral votes. It angered voters in Kentucky, who made clear Jackson was their second choice. And the deal was odd on another level. Judged by their stated positions on economic matters, Clay stood closer to Jackson than to Adams in 1824.[25]

In response to his electoral setback in 1824 and the broadening support for Jackson, Clay resolved to build, state by state, a national party to promote the American System. Clay urged his correspondents to focus on a common set of economic priorities. "I have sketched a plan of co-operation," he told a Philadelphia leader in 1827. "Let all persons (friends of D[omestic] M[anufactures &] I[nternal] I[mprovements] and the Admin.), without regard to party denominations heretofore existing, be brought out."[26] He asked Edward Everett of Massachusetts: "Can you not find time to prepare such a pamphlet . . .

as I suggested on I[nternal] Improvements and D[omestic] M[anufactures] intended for the meridian of Pennsa.? . . . The developements [*sic*] every day shew that those are the two great subjects which divide the parties." Clay regarded John Quincy Adams, who now endorsed an expansive program of government measures to encourage growth, as a suitable leader for the new party.[27]

Clay's correspondents responded eagerly to these appeals, and their replies demonstrated that they fully shared his commitment to an economic agenda. A Pittsburgh politician told the Kentuckian: "Our interests, public and private, are identified with those of the friends of *'domestic manufactures and internal improvement'* throughout the Union— and the next battle to be fought in good old Pennsylvania, will be between the friends of those measures and their opponents."[28]

In the face of Jackson's remarkable popularity, Clay succeeded in creating a national party with a clear focus and strength in both sections. Clay's "National Republicans" had a firm base in New England, particularly in the wealthier states of Massachusetts, Connecticut, and Rhode Island. In 1828 his party also received electoral support from New York, Maryland, and Delaware and in 1832 triumphed in three slave states: Delaware, Maryland, and Kentucky. The party polled over 35 percent of the votes in Louisiana, where the sugar interests favored tariff support.

Clay was not the only successful party builder in the 1820s and 1830s. Andrew Jackson and Martin Van Buren together helped form the Democratic Party, bringing together a coalition of those who felt rebuffed by the new economy. The Democrats believed the powers of the federal government should be sharply circumscribed. Tariffs, they argued, helped rich manufacturers at the expense of ordinary people. Internal improvements and a national bank catered to the needs of special interests. Jackson and Van Buren, however, played very different roles in creating this party.

In 1824 Jackson seemed—in some respects—an unlikely person to champion a party that advocated less government and more power for the common folk. During his brief tenure in the U.S. Senate, 1823–24, he favored internal improvements as well as the protective tariff of 1824, arguing that American workers must "stand on a footing of fair competition with the labourers of Europe."[29] In Tennessee politics Jackson— a wealthy planter with more than 150 slaves—stood on the side of the elite. After the Panic of 1819 he opposed laws to ease the burden on poorer farmers, and in the 1821 race for governor he backed the conservative Edward Ward against the popular William Carroll.[30]

Many contemporaries contended that General Jackson was no frontier democrat but a ruthless, untutored autocrat who cared little for the rule of law. These charges, widely circulated during the 1824 and 1828 campaigns, were exaggerated but contained an element of substance. Critics noted his duel with Charles Dickinson. (Jackson took a bullet but killed Dickinson, who had called him "a worthless scoundrel, a poltroon and a coward.") They pointed to his execution of six militiamen, his harsh enforcement of martial law in New Orleans, his incursion into Florida, and the hanging of two British subjects there.[31] In 1824 after his return from Washington, Jackson confided to his friend John Coffee: "Great pains had been taken to represent me as a savage disposition; who allways carried a Scalping Knife in one hand, & a tomahawk in the other; allways ready to knock down, & scalp, any & every person who differed with me in opinion—instead of this they as they expressed found a man of even temper—firm in his opinions advanced, and allways allowing others to enjoy theirs, untill reason convinced them that they were in error."[32] Daniel Webster was among those surprised—and charmed—by the general. The Massachusetts congressman told his brother: "General Jackson's manners are more presidential than those of any of the candidates. He is grave, mild and reserved."[33]

But in other ways Jackson *was* the right man to head a broad-based democratic movement. He was a folk hero, more widely acclaimed than any American since George Washington. His duels illustrated his remarkable force of will. Jackson was not a quick shot, and in his contest with Dickinson he allowed his opponent to shoot first. Jackson was wounded and bleeding badly, but he kept his composure. He carefully took aim and hit Dickinson squarely. "Oh, I believe that he pinked me," Jackson told his second, Thomas Overton, "but I don't want those people to know," pointing to the group around the stricken Dickinson. "I should have hit him," Jackson pronounced, "if he had shot me through the brain."[34]

The many Americans who pored over the lengthy newspaper reports of the victory over the Creeks in Alabama and the triumph over the British at New Orleans recognized that Jackson was an exceptional military commander. In defeating the native Americans, Jackson had to contend with raw recruits, volunteers who were all too eager to return home, a lack of supplies, his own illness, and fierce opponents who were fighting in defense of their homes. Other commanders had given up or been defeated. The British were an even more formidable foe. Sir Edward Packenham commanded more than 11,000 battle-hardened troops, many of them veterans of the Napoleonic Wars. Jackson had fewer than 5,000 soldiers to oppose these forces. Packenham also had the advantage of having innumerable routes to choose among in his march on New Orleans. But Jackson, through a combination of a stout defense and bold offensive forays, dealt the British a crushing defeat.

Jackson also viewed himself in 1824 as a popular leader. Although he had aggressively sought the presidency, he cast his run for high office in a different light. "Being brought forward by the people," he told a correspondent, "I rest my pretensions with them, & in their decision I will be content."[35] He frequently characterized the contest as a struggle between an autocratic caucus, which had selected William Crawford, and the common folk, who backed him. He told John Coffee: "It is now a contest between a few demagogues and the people and it is to be seen whether a minority of less than one fourth of the whole members of Congress, can coerce the people to follow them."[36]

Outside New England and the "Old Republican" states of Georgia and Virginia, Jackson ran strongly, with his greatest support coming from the common folk. A Pittsburgh editor summarized the division in Pennsylvania and, indeed, in much of the nation. "You have, to be sure," John McFarland told Jackson, "a vast number of friends ardently attached to your interest and admirers of your character, but confined to the lower and middle classes of society, all they can do is to give you their votes. The leading men in Pennsylvania, with very few exceptions, are opposed to you."[37] In 1827 a Kentucky politician (and friend of Clay's) described Jackson's support in similar if less flattering terms: "The presidential question is much discussed by our back woods politicians at this time. . . . I find that the illiterate or unthinking part of mankind are easily led away by sounding names; the brave warrior the hero of N. Orleans, &c pass very current with that class of mankind."[38] Exclaimed an Ohio politician, "It is an infatuation passing all measure, and one which can only be accounted for by their blind and heedless devotion to Military glory."[39]

But "infatuation" is too facile an explanation for Jackson's popularity. More to the point, the sudden, remarkable acclaim for the general reflected the divisions created by the new economy. Many of those who resented the newly wealthy merchants, manufacturers, and planters voted for the Hero of New Orleans. His image as a brave frontier leader, who was at ease with ordinary folk, was argument enough for the less affluent, particularly in the West.

While Jackson helped transform American politics, the demands of the political world transformed Jackson. The general soon found that the economic program he espoused in 1824 was out of step with his constituency. The less wealthy farmers and urbanites who huzzahed him had mixed feelings about banks, internal improvements, and high tariffs. Some of the poorer farmers, particularly in the West, welcomed assistance from Washington. But many believed in a hard money economy where self-reliance rather than government intervention determined a person's well-being. The truly enthusiastic supporters of activist policies were the professionals, merchants, manufacturers, affluent farmers, and planters who cheered Clay, not Jackson.

At this juncture Martin Van Buren, who had backed Crawford in 1824, reached out to Jackson. In return for electoral support that would almost certainly make Jackson president, Van Buren asked the general to endorse the economic views of the Old Republicans. In November 1826 Van Buren explained his strategy to a Virginia friend: "If Gen Jackson & his friends will put his election on old party grounds, preserve the old systems, avoid if not condemn the practices of the last campaign we can by adding his personal popularity to the yet remaining force of old party feeling, not only succeed in electing him but our success when achieved will be worth something."[40]

Jackson responded to this appeal, and quietly but unmistakably moved closer to the Old Republican orthodoxy. He backed away from his earlier stand on economic issues. "My real friends," he informed a correspondent, "want no information from me on the subject of internal improvements and manufactories, but what my public acts has afforded."[41] He now affirmed his belief in states' rights and enunciated his new thinking on economic issues. In a "Memorandum of Points to be considered in the administration of government," the general noted: "The Public debt paid off, the Tariff modified and no power usurped over internal improvements."[42]

By 1827 political observers throughout the United States recognized that Jackson had become leader of the party demanding less government. Edward Ingersoll reported to Clay from Philadelphia: "The anti-American, anti-improvement, anti-manufacturing principles of South Carolina are now fixed upon the Jackson party."[43] Sidney Breese noted the same transformation of the Jackson party in Illinois. He commented: "The opposition come out openly for the Virginia doctrines, with some little modifications, they are disciples of Van Beuren [sic], and will if they can *Vanbeurenize* the state."[44]

During his presidency Jackson promoted a laissez-faire approach to the economy. His Maysville Road veto in 1830 was a sharp rebuke to the advocates of internal improvements. His veto of Clay's bill to recharter the Bank of the United States dealt a lethal blow to the "American System." His appointment of Roger Taney to head the Supreme Court created a judiciary that moved away from the restrictive policies of John Marshall's court. Jackson, however, was never a doctrinaire opponent of government involvement in the economy. Unlike the Democratic presidents of the 1840s and 1850s he accepted many internal improvement bills and a protective tariff. Nor was he single-minded in his defense of states' rights. Jackson's vigorous opposition to South Carolina's efforts to nullify the tariff shows the strong strain of nationalism that always remained part of his outlook.

Martin Van Buren, the third individual who helped shape the national parties, was in many respects the mirror image of Henry Clay. Like Clay, Van Buren was committed to an ideology of development. For Clay, the American System was the key to growth. For Van Buren, the government that governed least contributed the most to prosperity. Like Clay, Van Buren was a party builder with a vision that transcended sections and regions. Finally, like Clay, Van Buren was extraordinarily ambitious and willing to engage in stratagems that all too often undercut the principles he held so dearly.

For many contemporaries, Van Buren was the ultimate schemer. "He is an artful, cunning, intriguing, selfish, speculating lawyer," frontiersman and politician Davy Crockett remarked. New Yorker Henry Wheaton commented, "Van B's intrigues will not cease, so long as there is the slightest glimmering of hope."[45] There was substance to these charges. Many politicians, including John Calhoun, were certain that Van Buren piled duty upon duty in the highly protective "Tariff of Abominations" in 1828 so it would be defeated. A defeat would allow Van Buren to assure both opponents and supporters of the tariff that he had their interests at heart. The explanations the Little Magician (as the New Yorker was sometimes called) offered for his actions were wildly contradictory. In fact, the measure passed, angering the South, and historians continue to debate Van Buren's role.[46]

But despite such scheming and vacillation, a core set of principles—dedication to Old Republican values—guided Van Buren. Thomas Jefferson was his beau ideal of a statesman, and in 1824 a lengthy visit with the aging president reaffirmed Van Buren's faith in orthodox Republican principles. These beliefs included an affirmation of states' rights, as well as opposition to tariffs, the national bank, and federally supported internal improvements. In 1825 Van Buren, who served as senator from 1821 to 1828, introduced a constitutional amendment "that Congress does not possess the power to make Roads and Canals within the respective States." He also instructed Jackson not to affirm *"any opinion upon Constitutional questions at war with the doctrines of the Jeffersonian School."*[47]

Van Buren initially hoped that the election of William Crawford would allow Republican principles once more to shape national policies. But in campaigning for Crawford, the Little Magician confronted insuperable obstacles. In September 1823 Crawford fell seriously ill and could barely speak, see, or write. He slowly recovered but never fully regained his faculties. Crawford also bore the stigma of being selected by the congressional caucus. Van Buren defended the procedure, but the other candidates condemned nomination by caucus as highly undemocratic.[48]

Recovering from the setbacks of 1824, Van Buren realized, as had Clay, that success required more than the right candidate and platform—it demanded the creation of a national party with a strong base in every state. Van Buren now saw that Jackson was the man to head this organization, and after receiving tacit assurances from the general, he set out to form that broad coalition. In December 1826 he met with Calhoun and persuaded him to back the new party. Van Buren then turned his attention to Thomas Ritchie, editor of the *Richmond Enquirer* and leader of the powerful coterie of Old Republicans in Virginia. Van Buren explained his plan "to combine Genl Jacksons personal popularity with the portion of old party feeling yet remaining." The New Yorker continued: "Political combinations between the inhabitants of the different states are unavoidable & the most natural & beneficial to the country is that between the planters of the South and the plain Republicans of the North." Ritchie agreed to back Jackson as did Crawford, whom Van Buren also courted.[49]

While Van Buren extolled his Jeffersonian ideals, he showed flexibility in implementing this credo. A concern for his constituents and a desire to build coalitions led the New Yorker repeatedly to temper principles with practicality. He voted for most provisions of the protectionist tariff of 1824. When he introduced his constitutional amendments on internal improvements, he softened the impact of his resolves by noting that he (as the *Register of Debates* reported) "did not, of course, wish to press their immediate consideration."[50] Later as one of the chief advisers to President Jackson, he cautioned Jackson against vetoing the recharter of the Bank of the United States, and later he told the general that removing government deposits from the Bank would be "both injudicious and impolitic." But Jackson, often a braver politician than Van Buren, forged ahead with his plans.[51]

## IV.

The two parties, which would play a vital role in holding the country together, gradually took shape during the course of the four presidential elections between 1828 and 1840. It was one thing for party leaders to create organizations defined by economic issues and class lines; it was another for the citizenry, unaccustomed to party loyalty or even regularly voting, to join these groups. The parties that Clay and Van Buren dreamed about in the 1820s did not coalesce fully until 1840.

After the "no-party" era of the early 1820s, the 1828 election marked the initial battle between two coherent organizations that sought votes everywhere. The two parties, however, were truly competitive in less than half the twenty-two commonwealths. In nine states, mostly in the South and West, Jackson won 60 percent or more of the vote, while in four others, all in New England, Adams led by the same margin. Close contests marked states such as New York, Ohio, and New Jersey, while Jackson's strong but unsuccessful campaigns in the two poorest New England commonwealths, Maine and New Hampshire, suggested the beginnings of a two-party system in New England. In still other ways, the 1828 election was an important step in the development of two national parties. With its vigorous, often vicious campaigning, the election brought more voters to the polls. Only 27 percent of adult white males had voted in 1824, while 56 percent took part in the 1828 contest.

The 1832 election, which pitted Clay against Jackson, indicated that party allegiances were gradually superseding personal and regional loyalties. Pennsylvania, for example, which had been a Democratic stronghold in 1828, now became a partisan battleground. Democrats won signal victories in two New England states, New Hampshire and Maine, while the National Republicans recorded gains in the South, winning three slave states, Delaware, Maryland, and Kentucky. In 1828 Adams had taken only Delaware. Jackson, however, easily won the election and received over 60 percent of the vote in eight states of the South and West. If wealth divided voters in some states, loyalty to Jackson continued to unite a broad swath of the electorate and kept parties from forming in many other commonwealths.

Party development advanced still another step with the 1836 election, the first presidential contest in which Jackson's opponents called themselves "Whigs." Once Van Buren replaced Old Hickory as Democratic leader, opposition politicians grew bolder. Democrats now could point to only three states, Arkansas, Missouri, and New Hampshire, where they enjoyed overwhelming support, and nowhere did Whigs receive 60 percent or more. Still, 1836 was another Democratic victory, and the proportion of voters going to the polls did not rise, reflecting in large part the failure of the Whigs to mobilize their supporters. They ran three presidential candidates—William Henry Harrison in the West, Hugh Lawson White in the South, and Daniel Webster in New England—but gave strong encouragement to none of them. Whigs failed in their effort to deny Van Buren a victory in the electoral college and throw the election into the House of Representatives.

Finally, two fully formed, opposing, national parties coalesced in 1840. The Whigs selected a single nominee, William Henry Harrison of Ohio, and supported him with a vigorous campaign. They took a leaf from the Democratic campaign book, portraying Harrison as a man of the people and his opponent, Martin Van Buren, as an aristocrat. Whigs organized huge rallies, including one at Tippecanoe battleground in Indiana to remind voters of Harrison's success in defeating the native Americans in 1811. Chanting "Down with Martin Van Ruin," they placed the blame for the depression afflicting the country on the shoulders of the Democratic incumbent. Everywhere Whigs celebrated Harrison's humble origins, singing log cabin songs, handing out "log cabin" cider, and using log cabins for campaign headquarters. The result was not only a Whig victory but also the establishment of two broad-based, competitive parties in virtually every state. The proportion of eligible voters casting ballots soared to 78 percent, a sharp rise over the 55 or 56 percent that had taken part in elections from 1828 to 1836.

Throughout the country partisan loyalties were now fixed and would remain relatively constant for the next dozen years. With some exceptions (chiefly in the South) the parties formed along the lines of class and interest envisaged by their founders. Throughout the Union prosperous farmers, merchants, and manufacturers supported the Whigs, while the poorer farmers and workers backed the Democrats. The bitter sectional disputes that emerged in the 1840s gravely tested these organizations. That these parties would survive as long as they did, despite such strains, testifies to their deep roots in American society.[52]

The national economy provided the basis for an era of compromise. The expansion of trade on the Mississippi; the links between the Border States and the North; the burgeoning commerce that connected the cotton lords and Northern capitalists; the South's reliance on the federal government to foster its expansion; and the emergence of two national parties with supporters in every state—all helped unify the country and lay the foundations for three decades of sectional cooperation. Democrats and Whigs played a particularly important role in keeping diverse regions together. A closer look at the mature parties of the 1840s, the constituencies that supported them, and the issues they fought for reveals how these organizations defended the Union during an increasingly troubled decade.

—— 2 ——

# RICH MAN, POOR MAN

Seventeen-year-old Varina Howell was struck by the tall, slender, intense planter she had just met. "I do not know whether this Mr. Jefferson Davis is young or old," she wrote her mother in December 1843. "He looks both at times. . . . He impresses me as a remarkable kind of man, but of uncertain temper, and has a way of taking for granted that everybody agrees with him when he expresses an opinion, which offends me; yet is most agreeable and has a peculiarly sweet voice and a winning manner of asserting himself." But Howell was puzzled by Davis's politics. She told her mother: "Would you believe it, he is refined and cultivated, and yet he is a Democrat!" Her parents and (as she later recollected) "most of the gentlefolk of Natchez," where she was raised, were Whigs.[1]

Neither their difference in politics nor their disparity in age (Davis was thirty-five when they met) proved an insurmountable obstacle. Davis proposed a month later, and they were wed in 1845. The two remained close as Davis's career progressed from congressman to senator to, eventually, president of the Confederacy. Still, Howell's initial surprise at Davis's political loyalties was understandable. In Mississippi in the mid-1840s most planters and lawyers were Whigs, while the poorer folk were Democrats. The exceptions, such as Jefferson Davis, stood out in Mississippi as they did in many Southern states.

The two great parties—Whigs and Democrats—were the products of the expanding economy, and together these organizations helped unify the country. Although there were notable exceptions like Davis, in most states poorer men gravitated to the Democrats while the wealthier favored the Whigs. Analysis of the parties in their heyday sheds light on the glue that held the Union together and allowed slave and free states to negotiate a series of compromises.

## I.

Throughout the North the more affluent and commercially minded joined the Whigs, while those left behind by the burgeoning economy backed the Democrats. The family of wealthy Nathaniel Appleton provides a window into the divisions in Boston. In September 1840 Nathan traveled to a Whig convention in Boston, leaving his twenty-three-year-old daughter Fanny in Newport, Rhode Island, where the family had rented a large house for the summer. Fanny, who was in the throes of courtship with the poet Henry Wadsworth Longfellow (whom she later would marry), was an effusive letter writer. She told one of her friends about the upcoming Whig meeting and the houses the delegates would stay in: "This famous Whig gathering . . . is working like a tempest in a teapot in that quiet city of Boston," she noted. "Beds and boards are supplied for this Whig army. Some patriotic ladies had their garrets hospital-like with beds—some, though absent from town, give keys to their servants to open their houses."[2] In the Northern cities the links between wealth and Whiggery were strong. Boston, to be sure, was a Whig town, typically giving the party 60 to 65 percent of its vote. But affluent Bostonians were even firmer in their partisan loyalties. A remarkable 89 percent of the five hundred wealthiest men were Whigs. The top stratum was still more consistent in its loyalties. Virtually all of the fifty-nine men, including Nathaniel Appleton, with estates worth over $500,000 were Whigs.[3]

Similar loyalties were evident in New York, a strongly Democratic city. In the 1840s fully 86 percent of those with holdings of $200,000 or more were Whigs. The greater the wealth, the stronger the allegiance to Whiggery. Loyalty to the Whigs stood at over 90 percent in the group with more than $400,000. One observer remarked: "The Democratic merchants could have easily been stowed in a large Eighth avenue railroad car." Within the elite, religion, national origins, and ancestry had little impact on partisanship. Methodists and Baptists, New Englanders, Southerners, British, and Dutch were all strong Whigs. Poorer citizens in New York (as in Boston), however, cheered the Democrats.[4]

Clearly, wealth was not the only determinant of political affiliations, or the percentage adhering to each party in the two cities would have been similar. New Englanders had long been more partial to the party of John Quincy Adams and Henry Clay, making Boston a Whiggish town while New York remained Democratic. But in every Northern city the economic lines separating Whigs and Democrats were unmistakable.[5]

The reasons for this polarization are not hard to find: each party had its own distinct appeal, dating back to the efforts of Clay, Jackson, and Adams to attract voters. Poor city folk regarded Jackson as the hero of the common man and saw his opponents as standard-bearers for the elite. In 1828 fifteen-year-old Stephen A. Douglas, who would later become a powerful Illinois senator, left the small Vermont town where he had grown up and went to Middlebury to learn cabinetry. He recalled: "At this time politics ran high in the presidential election. . . .

My associate apprentices and myself, were warm advocates of Gen. Jackson's claims, whilst our employer was an ardent supporter of Mr. Adams and Mr. Clay. From this moment my politics became fixed, and all subsequent reading, reflection and observation but confirmed my early attachment to the cause of Democracy."[6]

The divisions Douglas sketched were evident in the smaller towns as well as in the large coastal cities of the North. In Wayne County, Michigan, where Detroit was located, 65 percent of the elite supported the Whigs, while the less wealthy backed the Jacksonians. Economic activities correlated still more fully. Eighty percent of the merchants, manufacturers, and other entrepreneurs voted Whig. Similarly, in Springfield, Illinois, Whigs were wealthier than Democrats. In 1850 Springfield Whigs were worth an average of $1,918 compared to $1,456 for Democrats. Again occupational differences are more striking. Four-fifths of professionals supported the Whigs, while almost two-thirds of unskilled workers backed the Democrats. In Rochester, New York, Whigs commanded the loyalty of 60 percent or more of the businessmen, master craftsmen, and those drawn from the top 10 percent of taxpayers. Democrats drew comparable levels of support from journeymen craftsmen, clerical employees, and laborers.[7]

Voting patterns in the countryside present the same picture: the affluent and commercially minded favored the Whigs, while those less wealthy and less involved in the market backed the Democrats. In Greene County, a solidly Democratic locale in southern Illinois, the average Whig owned $1,030 worth of property compared to $738 for the average Democrat. Occupations in Greene County also correlated with loyalties, with less wealthy farmers solidly in the Democratic camp, while nonfarmers and professionals strongly favored Clay's party. In Genesee County, a district in western New York, Whig leaders were wealthier than their opponents. While 55 percent of Democrats held less than $5,000 in real property, only 35 percent of Whigs were in that group. A similar correlation, albeit a modest one, emerges from a study of eighteen New England communities. Democrats comprised 59 percent of those with assets valued at $1 to $500 but only 43 percent of the wealthiest townsfolk, those with real wealth of more than $5,000.[8]

What of ethnicity, birthplace, and religion? Take Mike Walsh, a charismatic Irish politician. In the early 1840s Walsh was a well-known speaker in New York's Bowery district. He strode onto the stage, jaw jutting, clothed in workingman's garb, his voice marked by a lilt that reflected both his birth in County Cork and his Irish audience. Cries of "That's right Mike, go ahead," greeted him. Walsh, who served as assemblyman, editor, and congressman, seemed to embody the links between the Irish and the Democrats. He was a darling of the Irish poor, the Bowery B'hoys, who applauded his flowery speeches and sarcastic attacks on rival politicians. At home in the city's rough-and-tumble politics, Walsh was founder of the Spartan Association, a mix of street rowdies and loyal Democrats. The Spartans would as soon break jaws as vote, and they did both. Walsh's speeches trumpeted his Anglophobia, his defense of Irish freedom, and his condemnation of nativists. Walsh, like his Irish constituents, was a passionate Democrat. Congressman Walsh told his fellow lawmakers: "In using the word 'Democracy,' I of course meant to be understood as alone referring to that patriotic, chivalrous, and self-sacrificing party which . . . preserved the Constitution in the purity and unshaken integrity of its letter and its spirit."[9]

But ethnicity was not the only explanation for Walsh's political loyalties or for the allegiances of his Irish followers. The Irish immigrants of New York not only shared a common birthplace and religion, but they were also poor and working class. Walsh not only sang paeans to a liberated Ireland, but he also spoke the language of class conflict. In the 1840s he challenged his readers in a series of fiery newspaper columns. "What is capital," he asked, "but that all-grasping power which has been wrung, by fraud, avarice, and malice from the labor of this and all ages past?" Were Walsh and his followers ardent Democrats because they were Irish or because they were poor? The obvious answer is both. But what's significant is that ethnicity was rarely an independent variable. In almost all cases it strongly correlated with class. How did *wealthy* Irish Catholics vote? There's no concrete answer, since there were so few of them. The study of New York City's richest individuals in the 1840s found only one Irish Catholic (who happened to be a Democrat) in a group of 571 men.[10]

Clashes in the North between Northern-born and Southern-born individuals also underscore the importance of economic concerns. In Greene County, Illinois, most of those born in the Southern states favored the Democrats, and their preponderance in the district helped keep Greene County in the Democratic column. By contrast, most individuals from the North, including an overwhelming 86 percent of New Englanders, favored the Whigs. But in fact these correlations involve more than geography. Northerners in Greene County were wealthier than Southerners, and those born in New England comprised the wealthiest subgroup.[11]

Northern-born settlers (and more particularly New Englanders) and Southern-born migrants had distinct work habits and their own approaches to entrepreneurial activities. Michel Chevalier, a French official who came to America in the 1830s to study public works, remarked upon the differences: "In a village in Missouri, by the side of a house with broken windows, dirty in its outward appearance, around the door of which a parcel of ragged children are quarreling and fighting, you may see another, freshly painted, surrounded by a simple, but neat and nicely whitewashed fence, with a dozen of carefully trimmed trees about it, and through the windows in a small room shining with cleanliness you may espy some nicely combed little boys and some young girls dressed in almost the last Paris fashion. Both houses belong to farmers, but one of them is from North Carolina and the other from New England."[12] Other observers decried New

Englanders as "sly, grinding, selfish, and tricking," and "devoted to the pursuits of gain." Everywhere outside their home states Yankees tended to be wealthier than their neighbors. In contrast, contemporaries regarded the Southern-born residents of the Midwest as less enterprising. Governor Thomas Ford of Illinois noted that the Southerners who filled the southern part of his state were mostly "poor white folks." They were, Ford continued, "a very good, honest, kind, hospitable people, unambitious of wealth, and great lovers of ease and social enjoyment."[13]

Similarly, differences in the partisan leanings of religious groups often reflected differences in wealth. In Greene County, Presbyterians were the most Whiggish group, and the wealthiest. By contrast, Methodists and Baptists were more Democratic—and poorer. Significantly, in Greene County the small group of Methodists and Baptists who engaged in business and professional activities voted Whig. In eighteen New England communities a majority of Congregationalists favored the Whigs. But these communicants were also wealthier than the members of other churches or the nonchurched. The poorest Congregationalists favored the Democrats. Studies of other Northern communities confirm this pattern. The two most important sects—Baptists and Methodists—divided between the two parties according to wealth, not denomination.[14]

## II.

Aggregate data also help explain voting in the North and underscore the links between wealth and party. If individual statistics (of the sort used above) allow us to walk down the streets of a village or wander by isolated farms and recognize people by name, county data let us soar at the height of an eagle and see the broader patterns that linked together groups of villages and counties. They indicate how districts voted and make possible comparisons with measures such as farm values and manufactures. This analysis shows that the wealthier counties, notably those along lines of transportation and those most involved in industry, supported the Whigs, while the poorer, more isolated districts backed the Democrats.

West of the Appalachians the largest concentration of Whig counties lay along the National Road in Ohio and Indiana, and in the Illinois counties just to the west of those districts. These are the areas identified as the Whig midstate belt in Map 2. These counties comprised the safest Whig districts in the Old Northwest. In a request for patronage, Abraham Lincoln in 1849 reviewed for President Zachary Taylor the merits of claimants from northern and southern Illinois. Then he observed: "I am in the center. Is the center nothing?—that center which alone has ever given you a Whig representative?"[15] The Whig midstate belt was wealthier and more commercially oriented than the Democratic counties to the south or north. It was also more affluent than Michigan, which was solidly in the Democratic column. As Tables 2.1 and 2.2 show, these Whig counties had higher per capita farm values and higher per capita values of animals slaughtered than either of the Democratic belts to the south or north.

### TABLE 2.1: FARM VALUES FOR WHIG AND DEMOCRATIC REGIONS IN THE MIDWEST, 1850

|  | *Illinois* | *Indiana* | *Ohio* | *Michigan* |
|---|---|---|---|---|
| Whig midstate belt | $160.19 | $175.17 | $205.54 |  |
| Democratic northern belt | 97.26 | 153.16 | 193.15 | 130.67 |
| Democratic Ohio Valley belt | 82.72 | 114.78 | 168.24 |  |

*Source:* Map 2 depicts the belts. The notes for Map 2 discuss the identification of "Whig" and "Democratic" counties. All voting and census data used in these tables are taken from *The Great American History Machine* (CD-ROM produced by Academic Software Development Group, College Park, Md.), version 2.0.

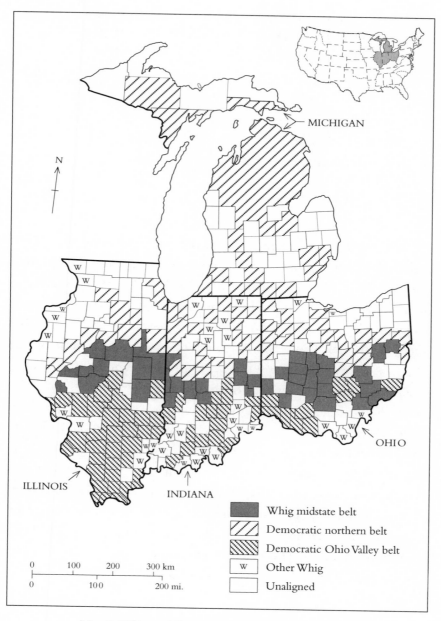

N

MICHIGAN

ILLINOIS

INDIANA

OHIO

Whig midstate belt
Democratic northern belt
Democratic Ohio Valley belt
W  Other Whig
Unaligned

0      100      200      300 km
0            100          200 mi.

*Map 2. Whigs and Democrats in the Midwest, 1840–52*

## TABLE 2.2: VALUE OF ANIMALS
## SLAUGHTERED IN WHIG AND DEMOCRATIC
## REGIONS IN THE MIDWEST, 1850

|  | Illinois | Indiana | Ohio | Michigan |
|---|---|---|---|---|
| Whig midstate belt | $6.65 | $8.70 | $4.37 |  |
| Democratic northern belt | 4.59 | 5.06 | 3.83 | 3.20 |
| Democratic Ohio Valley belt | 4.90 | 5.58 | 2.92 |  |

*Source:* See note to Table 2.1.

Two other smaller Whig belts in the Midwest* were also distinguished by their commercial activities. Counties in both these clusters are labeled on Map 2 with the letter *W*. Most of these districts lay along waterways. The northern Whig belt consists of 12 counties, 8 of which border either a Great Lake or the Mississippi River. The Ohio Valley Whig belt comprises 20 counties, 12 of which front on the Ohio or Mississippi River. Data for farm values and animals slaughtered documents the affluence of these districts.[16]

In the Northeast, manufacturing was more important than it was in the Midwest and (along with agricultural prosperity) defined party lines. Generally, the counties in Pennsylvania, New Jersey, and New England with the most industry voted Whig. The clusters of Whig-manufacturing districts included the group of counties running from the iron and textile centers of northern New Jersey and stretching across southern Pennsylvania, to the iron foundries of Allegheny County (Pittsburgh). This reach of industrial counties, with its insistent demands for higher tariffs, was an important stronghold of the

---

*Throughout this work *Midwest* refers to Ohio, Indiana, and Michigan (all in the Union by 1840), as well as Iowa (1846), Wisconsin (1848), and Minnesota (1858). *Midwest* and *Northwest* are used interchangeably.

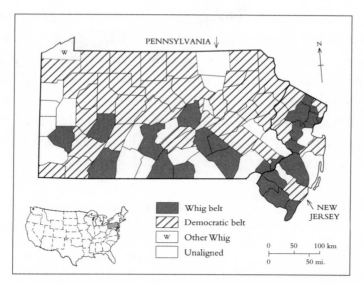

Map 3. *Whigs and Democrats in Pennsylvania and New Jersey, 1840–52*

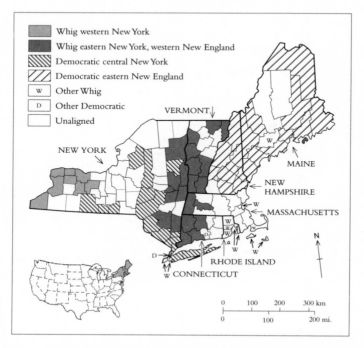

Map 4. *Whigs and Democrats in New England and New York, 1840–52*

Whig Party and would eventually be a crucial addition to the Republican Party. The manufacturing centers of New England, including districts in Rhode Island, Connecticut, western Massachusetts, and Suffolk County (Boston), were also Whiggish. The major exception to the rule linking high manufacturing to Whiggery was New York City. In that metropolis the wealthier citizens were overwhelmingly Whig, but the less wealthy kept the city loyal to the Democracy. (See Maps 3 and 4, and Table 2.3.)

## TABLE 2.3: MANUFACTURING IN WHIG AND DEMOCRATIC REGIONS IN THE NORTHEAST, 1850

This table for the New England and Middle States lists all groups with per capita value of manufacturing exceeding $100.00

(N = NUMBER OF COUNTIES IN GROUP)

| | |
|---|---|
| Eastern Massachusetts Whigs (4) | $177.47 |
| Democratic New York City (1) | 175.31 |
| Whig Rhode Island (5) | 149.74 |
| Whig Western Connecticut (4) | 132.63 |
| Pennsylvania Whig belt (12) | 105.19 |
| New Jersey Whig belt (11) | 103.33 |
| Whig Richmond & Kings counties (2) | 100.87 |

*Source:* These groups can be identified using Maps 3 and 4. The number of counties listed for each group helps confirm that identification. The notes to Maps 3 and 4 explain how counties were classified as Whig or Democrat. Note that the value of manufacturing for each group is an average, dividing total output by total population of all the counties in a group. In the Democratic regions production was usually much lower. For example, per capita manufacturing averaged $45.51 in Democratic Pennsylvania and $40.07 in Democratic New Jersey. All data for population and economic variables are taken from *Great American History Machine* (CD-ROM produced by Academic Software Development Group, College Park, Md.), version 2.0.

As in the Midwest, the richer farming districts in the Northeast were Whig while the poorer regions were Democratic. In northern

New England, for example, Whig Vermont was better off than its Democratic neighbors, New Hampshire and Maine. The most significant exception to this pattern lay in the Hudson Valley, where these

## TABLE 2.4: FARM VALUES FOR WHIG AND DEMOCRATIC REGIONS OF NEW ENGLAND, 1850

| (N = NUMBER OF COUNTIES IN GROUP) | Per Capita Value of Animals Slaughtered | Per Capita Farm Value |
|---|---|---|
| Whig Vermont (8) | $5.96 | $219.30 |
| Whig western Connecticut (4) | 5.92 | 204.57 |
| Whig western Massachusetts (2) | 4.85 | 194.22 |
| Democratic New Hampshire (9) | 4.66 | 171.78 |
| Democratic Maine (10) | 2.63 | 90.71 |

*Source:* See note for Table 2.3.

## TABLE 2.5: FARM VALUES FOR WHIG AND DEMOCRATIC REGIONS OF NEW YORK, 1850

| (N = NUMBER OF COUNTIES IN GROUP) | Per Capita Value of Animals Slaughtered | Per Capita Farm Value |
|---|---|---|
| Democratic central New York (13) | $5.59 | $256.30 |
| Whig Hudson River counties (8) | 5.08 | 222.45 |
| Whig western New York (8) | 4.59 | 220.97 |
| Democratic western New York (3) | 4.38 | 211.00 |

*Source:* See note for Table 2.3.

prosperous farming counties remained true to the Democratic Party. The Democratic loyalties of this upstate region date back to the 1790s, when Thomas Jefferson gained a cadre of strong supporters along the Hudson. In the 1820s these "plain farmers" comprised the northern end of the New York–Virginia axis that lay at the heart of the newly formed Democratic Party. But with the exception of these upstate districts, farmers divided between the two parties in the Northeast along class lines, as was the case in the Midwest. Tables 2.4 and 2.5 indicate the wealth of the rural areas.[17]

## III.

Divisions in much of the South resembled those in the North, providing the basis for strong national parties. John Claiborne, a Virginia Democrat whose political career began in the 1850s, later reflected on the composition of the Whig Party before its "final defeat" in 1855. He observed that the Whig Party "had undoubtedly represented the conservative element of Virginia. It was the party that had always represented the culture and wealth of the State. It was the party of the cities and of the older and eastern sections of the State, the party of the low grounds on the big rivers, and the party of the old colonial mansions." He added that the old party members "knew each other by the instincts of gentlemen."[18] In the South, as Claiborne suggests, wealthy city folk and prosperous planters often backed the Whigs while poorer farmers favored the Democrats. These alignments echoed those in the North and provided a Southern foundation for the two national parties.

Still, there were far more exceptions to the rules defining constituencies in the South than in the North. This is not surprising: the two sections were not mirror images of each other. Differences in political culture were noteworthy and reflected the opposing labor systems. Southern states lacked the bustling commercial regions that supported the Whig Party in the North. Few Southerners engaged in manufacturing. The cloth produced in Middlesex, a single Massachusetts county, was worth more than the output of all Southern mills combined. The South had fewer urban places. In 1850 fully 20 percent of Northerners lived in towns of over 2,500, compared to only 8 percent in the South. Five Southern states—North Carolina, Arkansas, Florida, Mississippi, and Tennessee—had less than 2.5 percent of their population in towns. The South also lacked the hundreds of thousands of small, prosperous farmers who formed the backbone of the Whig Party in the Midwest and parts of the Northeast.

A very different sense of community characterized the South—and this too was reflected in voting patterns. Southern communities were more close-knit and deferential than were districts in the North. Strong-minded outsiders rarely settled in Southern neighborhoods. Southern society fostered fewer religious sectarians and welcomed fewer foreigners. In 1850 only 3 percent of the Southern population was foreign-born, compared to 14 percent in the North. Northern communities were marked by inequalities, but not by deference. A few servants may have voted as their wealthier Whig masters did, but most Northerners were "atoms of self-interest" not cowed by their wealthier neighbors.[19]

In the South the slave lords stood atop the social pyramid and their views shaped the outlook of their less affluent neighbors. Deference and hierarchy were the order of the day. An observer in Randolph County, North Carolina, singled out William Long for "largely controlling as he always did the vote of his county."[20] In Lowndes County, Mississippi, John Gilmer was particularly influential. In response to several requests, Gilmer wrote the local newspaper: "I have been so often asked how I intended to vote . . . that there seems to be no mistake that many, who have not had the pleasure of seeing, would like to know where I stand."[21] To be sure, some candidates actively campaigned for office; treating was common on election day. But most polls turned on local ties rather than rhetoric or last-minute appeals. Detailed studies of counties in several Southern states make clear the importance of voting by neighborhoods. At each polling station the votes of the less wealthy typically reflected the outlook of the leading magnate in the community. The result was a remarkable degree of local consensus.[22]

Despite these differences between the two sections, an analysis of Southern voting must emphasize the similarities with the North. To begin with, in the South, as in the North, townsfolk, professionals, and those involved in commercial activities favored the Whigs. These loyalties were abundantly evident in both the Upper South and Border States. In Virginia, a Democratic state, all but one of the nineteen towns with a white population over one thousand backed the Whigs. In North Carolina too Whigs were far stronger in the county seats than in the rural precincts. Studies of Caldwell County in Kentucky, Cumberland County in North Carolina, and Prince Edward and Southampton counties in Virginia also illustrate this urban-rural split.[23]

The same definite (if moderate) correlation between commerce and Whiggery was evident in the Lower South. Four of the five counties containing the largest towns in Texas gave the Whigs a much higher percentage than their statewide average. New Orleans party divisions resembled those in many Northern cities. The commercial classes voted Whig, while many of the working people, especially the Irish, cheered the Democrats. What little support the Whig Party garnered in South Carolina came from the cities of Charleston and Columbia. Similarly, Arkansas towns favored the Whigs. In Mississippi the Whigs found more support among those involved in commerce than the Democrats. The nonfarm group accounted for 36 percent of the Whigs and only 27 percent of the Democrats.[24]

The key to Southern voting, however, was the response of the rural citizenry—and much of the South was marked by the familiar pattern of wealthier Whigs and poorer Democrats. More particularly, this split shaped politics in a broad arc of states, beginning with Georgia, and continuing through Alabama, Mississippi, Arkansas, and ending with Missouri. In these commonwealths the slaveholding areas, located on the richer soils of the great river valleys, were Whig, while the poorer nonslaveholding districts remained Democratic. County returns underscore the division. In 1844 these states had eighty-seven counties where less than 15 percent of the population was slave. Over 90 percent of these districts voted Democratic. By contrast, Whigs won a majority in more than three-fourths of the districts where slaves made up 60 percent or more of the population.

Why did these states embody the split between wealthy Whigs and poorer Democrats when in the rest of the South the divisions were less clear? These were the "Jacksonian states," commonwealths whose political culture had been molded in the 1820s and 1830s. During these decades Democratic politicians declared from stumps and from courthouse steps that society was divided between the common folk (whom they represented) and aristocrats. The Democrats depicted a battle between the "people" and the capitalists and asked the new voters to choose sides. The formative years for these states are suggested by the dates they entered the Union: Mississippi in 1817, Alabama in 1819, Missouri in 1821, and Arkansas in 1836. Georgia, to be sure, had been one of the original states, but Jackson's success in expelling the Indians and opening much of the state to white settlement reshaped allegiances.

In these states the small farmers and tradesmen regarded Jackson as more than an iron-willed general; they saw him as a symbol of popular democracy, a defender of the poor against the elite. In Alabama Ben Sherrod, a Whig politician, asked Woodson May, a shingle maker, what May had thought of Sherrod's speech. May responded with a telling story about Jackson: "Colonel, I don't understand much of what you have been saying, but one thing I knew; when the war came to an end, and the boys had all marched toward home, except such as were in the hospital, we were started under an officer, who was riding on a horse, and I was very weak and staggered as I walked. General Jackson and his staff overtook us, and seeing my condition he said roughly to the officer: 'Why don't you get down and put that man for awhile on your horse? Don't you see he can hardly drag himself along? By the eternal! You ought to be cashiered!' This plain talk saved my life, and enabled me to see my wife and child once more, and if I ever forget General Jackson, may God Almighty forget me."[25] These poorer farmers, who often lived in neighborhoods where there were few slave lords, were loyal Democrats and proud of their local autonomy. "I have been battling for the Democracy in Bibb County 25 years," one Georgia Democrat noted. "We primitive folk never heard of . . . great men amongst us (they had all come in, or found the party since) to tell us who to send to conventions."[26]

Wealthy planters, along with merchants and many city folk in these five states, favored the Whigs, particularly once Jackson left office. Partisan battles in the 1820s and 1830s shaped the views of the affluent much as they molded the outlook of the less wealthy. Traders and slave lords disliked Democrats who trumpeted, as did one Alabama editorialist, the "incessant war . . . between the moneyed interests and the rights of labor." The merchants and large landowners applauded the plans for economic and social development that Clay's party set forth.[27]

Outside the five "Jacksonian states," loyalties in the rural South were less constant. For example, in the older states of Maryland, Virginia, North Carolina, Kentucky, and Tennessee, tradition was often more important than interest in shaping the voters' choices. All of these commonwealths had entered the Union before the Jacksonian era, and loyalties were often passed from father to son. For example, Maryland politician Henry Winter Davis, who became a Whig, respected his Federalist father's advice, "My son, beware of follies of Jacksonism!"[28] In these states partisan divisions cut across lines of wealth. The 131 counties where slaves comprised less than 15 percent of the population were split almost evenly between Democratic and Whig districts in 1844. Similarly, in the areas where slaves were the majority, Whigs held only a slight edge. Henry Clay won 53 percent of those districts, James Polk 47 percent.

Long-established patterns provide a better explanation for voters' choices in these Upper South and Border States. For example, in Maryland and Virginia the election of 1800 foreshadowed the divisions of the 1830s and 1840s. Most of the areas that supported the Federalists in 1800 later backed the Whigs, while Democratic-Republican districts became Democratic. To be sure, these results suggest a grain of truth in John Claiborne's quote, which opens this section of the chapter. Whigs *did* fare best in the towns and were strong in some of the wealthier river valleys, such as the counties on both sides of the Potomac. But the pattern seems less tied to interest than Claiborne indicates. Democrats captured the planting counties of "Southside" Virginia, while western Virginia was a patchwork of Whig and Democratic districts. [29]

A study of planters in Southampton County, Virginia, hints at still another dimension of the Whig-Democratic divide—one not measured by the number of slaves or acres owned. In Southampton, it appears, Whig landowners were more likely to invest in railroads, canals, and manufacturing; Democrats were more likely to focus solely on agriculture. These different activities may help explain the remarkable tenacity of party lines in the Upper South. Even during the first months of 1861 Whig planters refused to join Democratic slaveowners in applauding the new Confederacy. [30]

Rural voters in the three remaining states in the Lower South—South Carolina, Texas, and Florida—also do not fit easily into the rich Whig/poor Democrat mold. South Carolina was a world unto itself, largely controlled during the 1830s and 1840s by one man: John C. Calhoun. The Whig Party was small and limited chiefly to older, commercial families in Charleston and Columbia. Calhoun, however, was never entirely happy with the national Democrats and in the 1830s had bitterly opposed Jackson and Van Buren. Texas, which achieved statehood in 1845, was strongly Democratic, an outlook shared by planters and small farmers alike. These loyalties were no surprise. Nationally, Democrats had favored, and Whigs had criticized, the acquisition of this new slave state. Of these three commonwealths, Florida most resembled the "Jacksonian states." When Florida entered the Union in 1845, the state already had a nucleus of Whig cotton planters in "Middle Florida," as the Panhandle counties between the Suwannee and Apalachicola rivers were called. The small farmers who flooded into the new state from Georgia and South Carolina brought with them their Democratic sympathies. Still, the parallels are limited: Florida also had wealthy Democratic planters, and most of the influx of Democratic farmers came after 1850 when the Whig Party was in disarray.[31]

Within the South, it is clear, were many exceptions to the rule that the Whigs were the party of the wealthy and commercially minded, while the less affluent flocked to the Democratic standard. In some areas, such as the Appalachian highlands of Virginia, Kentucky, and Tennessee, counties seemed to be assigned to one party or another at random. Planting districts, particularly in the Upper South, stood on both sides of the partisan fence. Even in the Deep South, an important coterie of planters, those who supported states' rights leaders such as Jefferson Davis in Mississippi and Dixon Lewis in Alabama, defied the norm and voted Democratic.

The exceptions to the rules defining the Whigs and Democrats demonstrate that party membership was never rigidly defined. At the same time the exceptions do not overturn the broader generalizations. The North contained 70 percent of the country's white population, and in most Northern districts the market economy divided the citizenry. Even in much of the South townsfolk and well-off planters were Whigs, while the poorer farmers cheered the party of Jackson.

The result was two long-lived, unified national parties. Within each party Northerners and Southerners shared an ideology developed in response to a broad range of economic issues. More broadly, citizens across the country gave primacy to party and nation rather than to section or the divisive issue of slavery.


# IV.


The soaring (and sometimes crashing) national economy did more than shape the constituencies and ideologies of the two parties. It also left its imprint on the battles in the state legislatures. The Whigs, so often the beneficiaries of the market revolution, championed banks, corporations, internal improvements, and education. The Democrats, frequently outsiders in the new business order, were far more likely to vote for debtor relief, hard currency, and the acquisition of new territory. In almost every state Whigs and Democrats glowered at each other from opposite sides of a divide defined by approaches to the economy.

Studies of assembly votes in a variety of states, from New Hampshire in the North to Mississippi in the South, illuminate these differences. To be sure, the chasm separating the parties in each commonwealth was never uniform. Depending on the time and issue, this gap widened or narrowed and at times disappeared. Despite such variations, roll call votes make clear that in every state the two organizations voted as they spoke—taking distinct stances on a series of issues. Data for Pennsylvania and North Carolina, presented in Tables 2.6 and 2.7, illustrate this clash. In the 1840s members of the two parties cast opposing ballots on internal improvements, banking, currency, education, and humanitarian institutions.[32]

## TABLE 2.6: PENNSYLVANIA LEGISLATURE: PERCENT OF AFFIRMATIVE VOTES ON SELECTED ISSUES, 1841–42

| Issue and Year | Democrats | Whigs |
|---|---|---|
| SUPPORT FOR STATE BANKS | | |
| 1841 | 0 | 100 |
| 1842 | 28 | 75 |
| LIMITING THE CIRCULATION OF SMALL BILLS | | |
| 1841 | 98 | 9 |
| 1842 | 94 | 3 |
| SUPPORT FOR INTERNAL IMPROVEMENTS | | |
| 1841 | 42 | 89 |
| 1842 | 52 | 100 |

*Source:* Herbert Ershkowitz and William G. Shade, "Consensus of Conflict? Political Behavior in the State Legislatures During the Jacksonian Era," *Journal of American History* 58 (1971): 600, 602, 607.

## TABLE 2.7: NORTH CAROLINA SENATE: PERCENT OF AFFIRMATIVE VOTES ON SELECTED ISSUES, 1840–49

| Issue and Year | Democrats | Whigs |
|---|---|---|
| SUPPORT FOR STATE BANKS | | |
| 1840–41 | 11 | 86 |
| 1842–43 | 19 | 93 |
| APPOINTMENT OF SUPERINTENDENT OF COMMON SCHOOLS | | |
| 1844–45 | 30 | 76 |
| 1848–49 | 14 | 91 |

| Issue and Year | Democrats | Whigs |
|---|---|---|
| SCHOOL FOR DEAF & DUMB/INSANE ASYLUM | | |
| 1844–45 | 14 | 90 |
| 1848–49 | 14 | 91 |
| SUPPORT FOR INTERNAL IMPROVEMENTS | | |
| 1840–41 | 11 | 85 |
| 1842–43 | 10 | 65 |

Source: Marc Kruman, *Parties and Politics in North Carolina, 1836–1865* (Baton Rouge, La., 1983), 58, 61.

# V.

Not only on the state level but also nationally the two parties displayed a remarkable coherence across a range of issues—as well as a willingness to bridge the sectional divide. The typical politician in the 1830s and 1840s considered himself a Whig or a Democrat, not a Northerner or a Southerner. Most congressmen had cut their teeth on state politics. Democrats had battled in their state legislatures against internal improvements, banks and small bills, and excessive spending on education and charitable institutions, while Whigs had supported these causes. In Washington these politicians confronted similar issues and gravitated to those men who shared the same outlook—regardless of where they came from. The two parties were marked by striking internal unity as they battled their opponents over a variety of economic questions. Table 2.8, which details the divisions on the Independent Treasury, tariff, preemption (the right of settlers to purchase public lands), and graduation (lowering the price of public lands), underscores the strength of party identity.

## TABLE 2.8: U.S. HOUSE OF REPRESENTATIVES: PERCENT OF AFFIRMATIVE VOTES ON SELECTED ISSUES, 1840–46

| Issue and Year | Democrats | Whigs |
|---|---|---|
| INDEPENDENT TREASURY | | |
| 1840 | 98% | 0% |
| 1841 | 99 | 1 |
| TARIFF | | |
| 1842 | 23 | 69 |
| 1844 | 22 | 99 |
| PREEMPTION (RIGHT OF SETTLERS TO PURCHASE PUBLIC LANDS) | | |
| 1840 | 88 | 35 |
| 1846 | 88 | 24 |
| GRADUATION (LOWERING PRICE OF PUBLIC LANDS) | | |
| 1845 | 70 | 7 |
| 1846 | 79 | 0 |

Source: John Ashworth, *"Agrarians" and "Aristocrats": Party Ideology in the United States, 1837–1846* (Cambridge, Eng., 1987), 272, 277, 278.

During the decades before 1850 the decision to put party first and section second shaped the activities of most politicians, even those with strong views about slavery. The career of William Seward, a prominent New York Whig and vocal opponent of the "peculiar institution," is a case in point. Seward served as state senator from 1830 to 1834, New York governor from 1838 to 1842, and U.S. senator from 1849 to 1861, when Lincoln appointed him secretary of state. Extraordinarily convivial, Seward liked nothing better than a glass of brandy, a cigar, an impromptu dinner party, and a chance to swap stories with friends. His dislike of slavery emerged only gradually. His father, a prosperous farmer and speculator, had owned several household servants. But William's views changed after he married a pious Christian, Frances Miller, and moved to Auburn, a town in the heart of western New York's "burned over district," where reform sentiments ran high. By the mid-1840s vigorous opposition to bondage made good moral and political sense in western New York, and Seward always remained an astute politician. At times Seward's rhetoric made him appear not far removed from the abolitionists. "Friends of emancipation! advocates of the rights of man! I am one of you," he told a Syracuse gathering in 1844. In 1850 he criticized proposals to open western territories to slavery. Seward intoned: "There is a higher law than the Constitution."[33]

Despite such passionate statements, Seward's first loyalty was to the Whig Party. Like Whigs in the North and South, he believed in Clay's American System with its emphasis on a national bank, protective tariffs, internal improvements, and domestic sources of growth. He was an outspoken advocate of schools and asylums—also good Whig doctrine. And while he condemned slavery, his plan for achieving freedom was barely more radical than the program advocated by Henry Clay. Seward felt freedom could come only at a distant date, peacefully, with full compensation—and within the framework of the existing two-party system. "How is it to be prosecuted?" he asked in 1844. "I think by firm decisive urgent advocacy in the North, tempered nevertheless by moderation, in making it collateral and if need be subordinate to other questions of Administration raised by the two great parties, and above all tempered by conciliation."[34]

The full measure of Seward's dedication to party came in 1844 and 1848, when he campaigned ardently for the Whig presidential candidates, Henry Clay and Zachary Taylor, both of whom were wealthy slaveholders. In 1844 he insisted that the Whigs were a better choice than either the Democrats or the fledgling Liberty Party, whose platform called for abolition and equal rights. Seward emphasized Clay's reluctance to admit Texas, a new slave state. "You say Henry Clay disavows abolition," he told a Syracuse audience. "Let him do so. What care you and I for that? He is opposed to the coming in of Texas. He is the candidate of the whig party. They are opposed to the coming in of Texas."[35] Votes given to the Liberty Party, Seward argued, were wasted: "To attach ourselves to a third party, which has not and can not, while the others last, have a representation in the public councils, is to renounce, for the present at least, the right of interference in public affairs."[36] Seward's approach in 1848 was similar. He argued that ballots cast for the Free Soil Party were wasted and that support of Democrat Lewis Cass was foolish. Voters, he remarked, should choose the party, not the man. Speaking in Ohio's Western Reserve, Seward explained, "The slaveholding of the candidate [Taylor] is a personal matter, an ephemeral one; the error, if it be one, can be corrected; the principles of the whig party are national and eternal."[37]

Most Southern Whigs also put party before section. Alexander Hamilton Stephens, congressman from Georgia, well illustrates these priorities. Stephens was an unusual figure: sickly and tiny, he weighed only about ninety pounds and once described himself as "a malformed ill-shaped half finished thing." Stephens was also a brilliant lawyer and debater; his northern Georgia constituents applauded his outspoken ways, sending him to Congress in 1843 and reelecting him seven more times. Stephens was as firmly opposed to the Wilmot Proviso, which limited the spread of slavery, as Seward was determined to adopt it. He told Congress in 1848, "I shall never give my sanction, while I have a seat upon this floor, to any legislation on the part of Congress by which the rights of the southern people to an equal and just participation in these Territories, while they remain as territories, shall be endangered."[38] Despite such strong, sectional views, Stephens remained a loyal Whig and vigorously campaigned to elect Taylor and defeat his opponent, Lewis Cass. Remarkably, not even rumors that Taylor would accept the Wilmot Proviso put off Stephens. The *Congressional Globe* reported Stephens's remarks: "He (Mr. S.) said he would prefer an out-and-out Wilmot proviso man to one who would undertake to cheat him, to deceive him, as the letter [from Lewis Cass] to which he had referred indicated the attempt to deceive the people of the South. He would rather have an open enemy than a pretended deceitful friend. General Taylor would write no such letters."[39]

Democrats similarly joined together across sectional boundaries, despite different views of slavery. Howell Cobb, whose district in northern Georgia adjoined Stephens's, was one of the wealthiest Democrats in an area where most voters were poor farmers. A successful lawyer who had married well, Cobb was the master of several plantations and about two hundred slaves. Like Stephens, he was committed to the defense of Southern rights. "No truth is more plainly written in the history of our country," Cobb remarked in 1848, "than the one which teaches us of the continued inroads which northern fanaticism has unceasingly attempted upon our peculiar institutions." But Cobb was also a resolute party member and a firm believer that Democrats, North and South, defended the slaveholders' interests. "The course which the two political parties of the North have pursued towards the South is widely different," he told a Charleston audience in 1848.[40] Cobb rejected Calhoun's call in 1849 for an alliance of all Southerners against Northern encroachments. In his public rejoinder Cobb stated: "So long as we contemplate the continuance of the Union, so long will we look to the preservation of the integrity of the Democratic party of the Union, as an element of our greatest strength and security."[41]

Northern Democrats reciprocated Cobb's affection. Regardless of their views of slavery, Democratic congressmen from the Northern states backed Cobb for Speaker, and their ballots assured his victory in 1849. Ten of the forty Northern Democrats who voted for Cobb condemned the slave trade in the District of Columbia. Fourteen of the forty denounced the Fugitive Slave Act. Despite their views of slavery, these men stood by Cobb during the course of the fifty-nine ballots it took to elect a Speaker, delighting observers like James Buchanan of Pennsylvania. "A Southern Speaker at the present moment," Buchanan remarked, "elected by Northern Democratic votes, is an event of the most propitious character." Indeed, the 1849 election for Speaker was marked by a striking symmetry. While most Northern Democrats backed Cobb, Southern Whigs remained loyal to Massachusetts Congressman Robert C. Winthrop, who opposed the expansion of slavery.[42]

In sum, during the 1820s, 1830s, and 1840s the two great parties comprised the cement of the Union. Their existence reflected the unities of the national economy, which drew people together across sectional lines while dividing them by class and occupation. Parties fostered a spirit of compromise and contributed to the resolution of a series of disputes that might have driven the North and South apart. When the economy changed at midcentury, the Whig and Democratic parties, which had taken years to build, crumbled with remarkable speed, thereby removing a powerful force for cooperation.

# DEAL MAKING

W hen James Tallmadge addressed the House of Representatives about slavery in Missouri, it seemed the United
States was teetering on the brink of a horrific civil war.
The New York congressman, who had done so much to provoke this
sectional clash, was shaken but unbowed. A military man, he refused to
back down in face of Southern threats. "Sir, if a dissolution of the
Union must take place, let it be so!" he told his fellow representatives.
"If civil war, which gentlemen so much threaten, must come, I can
only say, let it come!" He added sternly, "If blood is necessary to extin-
guish any fire which I have assisted to kindle, I can assure gentlemen,
while I regret the necessity, I shall not forbear to contribute my mite."[1]

That was bold talk, but the year was 1819, not 1860. And the aftermath of the Missouri Controversy was not civil war but an era of
accommodation that endured to midcentury. Between 1820 and 1850
there was no shortage of contentious issues that could have sparked a
sectional conflagration. They did not, because leaders in both sections

were willing to hammer out a series of compromises. The successes of these years, however, were not simply the triumphs of able politicians. The deals struck also reflected the outlook of key groups, North and South, drawn together by the unifying force of the national economy. Hence the country was able to withstand the angry exchanges and threats leveled during four conflicts: the Missouri Controversy of 1819–21; the tariff debate that led to the Nullification Crisis of 1833; the battles in Congress over the "gag rule" blocking abolitionist petitions, 1835–44; and the clashes over the territory gained from Mexico, 1846–50.

## I.

Strong economic ties helped hold the country together during the bitter disputes over the admission of Missouri. The debate over whether Missouri should enter the Union as a slave state or a free state began with two propositions that James Tallmadge set forth in February 1819. Tallmadge was accustomed to thinking boldly. He had commanded the New York militia during the War of 1812 and organized the defense of New York City. As a politician he dared to snub Tammany Hall, the political "machine" already shaping voting in Manhattan, and instead cultivated supporters among the blacks and Quakers. Tallmadge, who was determined to see Missouri enter the Union as a free state, proposed that no new slaves be allowed to enter the territory and that those present be gradually emancipated.[2]

Reactions on both sides of the Mason-Dixon line were intense. Northerners endorsed Tallmadge's bill and denounced bondage. "The free people I have the honor to represent," declared Clifton Clagett of New Hampshire, "have, by their constitution, excluded slavery, and believe it *malum in se* [an evil in itself], and my own sentiments sincerely accord with theirs."[3] Pennsylvanian William Darlington was one of many echoing these thoughts. "The existence of slavery," he remarked, "seems to be universally considered a great moral and political evil."[4] Northerners argued that the nation would prosper only if freemen populated the West. New Yorker John W. Taylor underscored the incompatibility of slave and free labor. "If slavery shall be tolerated, the country will be settled by rich planters, with their slaves," he noted. "If it shall be rejected, the emigrants will chiefly consist of the poorer and more laborious classes of society." The choice for Taylor, as for most Northerners, was self-evident: free labor must rule the new territories. Northern lawmakers pointedly compared the wealth of the free states with the backwardness of the South.[5]

Southern congressmen counterattacked, arguing that slavery was sanctioned by the Constitution, by the treaty governing the Louisiana Purchase, by the Bible, as well as by the practices of past civilizations. Foreshadowing arguments that would be common at midcentury, several politicians also contended slavery benefited African Americans. Prominent among these defenders of bondage was South Carolinian Charles Pinckney, a wealthy rice planter and slave lord. Pinckney spoke with great authority; he had been a leading member of the 1787 Constitutional Convention and in 1803 had helped secure the Louisiana Purchase. "The great body of slaves," he pronounced, "are happier in their present situation than they could be in any other, and the man or men who would attempt to give them freedom, would be their greatest enemies."[6] Most Southerners in 1820, however, conceded that slavery was wrong but asserted that good or evil was not the question at hand.

Southerners blustered and swore and threatened secession if the North blocked the expansion of slavery. No blood was shed, but the prose flowed purple. "I perceive a brother's sword crimsoned with a brother's blood," Congressman Freeman Walker of Georgia exclaimed. "I perceive our houses wrapt in flames, and our wives and infant children driven from their homes. . . . I trust in God, that this creature of the imagination may never be realized. But if Congress persist in the determination to impose the restriction contemplated, I fear there is too much cause to apprehend, that consequences fatal to the peace and harmony of the Union will be the inevitable result."[7]

Despite the anger evident in the North and South, strong economic ties provided the basis for a broad compromise. To begin with, politicians in the Mississippi Valley states of Ohio, Indiana, and Illinois were sympathetic to Southern demands that slavery continue in Missouri. Residency in this expansive region gave individuals a frame of reference that transcended sections. "We inhabit the great valley of the West," Ohio senator Benjamin Ruggles explained. "We belong to the family of the Mississippi. Our latitude, pursuits, productions, and markets are the same."[8] Many of the politicians whose states bordered the Ohio River (a tributary of the Mississippi) were Southern born, including Illinois senators Jesse Thomas and Ninian Edwards, Indiana senator Waller Taylor, and several congressmen.[9]

The two Southern-born Illinois senators were key figures in crafting the Missouri Compromise. At first, lawmakers had discussed a deal with two components: the admission of Missouri as a slave state and the admission of Maine, which was part of Massachusetts, as a free state. But that proposal would not pass the House of Representatives, where the North held a decided majority. Most Northern lawmakers demanded a free Missouri and felt Maine deserved statehood apart from any deal. In February 1820 Illinois senator Thomas proposed a third component: dividing Louisiana territory (which included Missouri) at the 36° 30' parallel, with the larger northern area free and the smaller southern region open to slavery. The Thomas amendment essentially said to the North: give up something in the present (a slave Missouri) to gain a lot in the future (free soil in most of Louisiana). Broadly viewed, Thomas's initiative was a pro-Southern move, facilitating the introduction of a new slave state. Southerners, at least in the rapidly growing Southwest and Border States, backed the measure.

Ninian Edwards, the other Illinois senator, who had long accepted slavery in Missouri, applauded Thomas's proposal, as did Taylor of Indiana. Other congressmen from the Northwestern states generally took a conciliatory stance in the debates, with several Southern-born lawmakers—including Illinoisan John McLean and Ohioan (and future president) William Henry Harrison—endorsing a slave Missouri.[10]

Ties of trade and investment encouraged a second Northern group, Massachusetts politicians, to back compromise in 1819–21. Although few in the Bay State had any love for slavery, the puritan commonwealth had strong commercial links with the South. Manufacturers depended on the cotton planters for raw materials, while wealthy merchants agreed with Southerners on the need for low tariffs. Massachusetts senator Harrison Gray Otis, who was connected to both the shippers and the manufacturers, initially opposed the Tallmadge amendments, which called for an end to slavery in Missouri. He changed his mind but still cautioned his colleagues against "intemperate expressions."[11] Four Bay State congressmen—including Jonathan Mason, who represented Boston—voted with the South in key divisions. Mason blandly observed that "not a Man in New England cares one farthing" about slavery in Missouri. He was wrong; many opposed the extension of bondage. But significantly, the state legislature was slow to endorse freedom in the new territory, leading one politician to complain that "Massachusetts cowers under the arrogant Pretentions of Virginia."[12]

Not only key leaders in the North but also important slave state politicians and groups, buoyed by economic growth, favored compromise in 1820. No Southern figure embodied nationalism during these years more fully than John C. Calhoun of South Carolina. Calhoun's rise to eminence within his state and section was remarkable and reflected his nationalism, ambition, and extraordinary intellect. Born in 1782, John received no formal education as a child. At age thirteen he briefly attended an academy run by his brother-in-law Moses Waddel.

Then his father died, and John returned home for the next four years to help manage the family plantation. But a desire for an education burned in him, as did a sense of his own destiny. At age eighteen he persuaded his older brothers to support him for seven years while he pursued the best schooling he could find. After two years back at Waddel's academy, Calhoun applied to Yale University and was admitted with junior standing. Although every other student had more formal education, Calhoun soon rose to the top of his class and delivered the Phi Beta Kappa address at commencement. His topic, "The Qualifications Necessary to Make Statesman," revealed his growing interest in public service. After Yale he read law with two exceptional mentors: Charleston lawyer Henry W. DeSaussure and Judge Tapping Reeve of Litchfield, Connecticut. At each turn the Carolinian impressed classmates and professors. Yale president Timothy Dwight remarked that Calhoun had the ability "to be President of the United States" and one day might hold that office.[13]

Calhoun's nationalism reflected sentiments in the cotton South and more particularly in South Carolina's Upcountry region, where he was born and where he made his home after he finished the study of law. A local meeting in 1807 to protest the British attack on the American frigate *Chesapeake* launched the young lawyer's political career. At the request of his neighbors, Calhoun spoke at the gathering and prepared a set of resolutions. Impressed by his abilities, voters sent him to the state assembly the next year and to the U.S. House of Representatives in 1810. Calhoun arrived in Washington, along with Langdon Cheves and William Lowndes, as one of three South Carolina "War Hawks" eager to beard the British lion. Speaker Henry Clay awarded him the number-two position on the Foreign Relations Committee, and Calhoun became a leader in attacking those who, like John Randolph of Virginia, criticized firm measures.

After the war Calhoun's nationalism continued unabated, and he pushed for a program that included higher tariffs, internal improvements, and a national bank. "Let us direct our attention," he declared in 1816, "to the objects calculated to accomplish the prosperity and greatness of the nation, and we shall certainly create a national spirit."[14] Calhoun mirrored not just the views of his immediate neighbors but also the optimism of the cotton planters who were expanding into new territories across the Gulf region. Although South Carolina had the oldest soils in the Deep South, cotton prices averaging twenty-six cents a pound (as they did from 1816 to 1819) spelled prosperity for most growers.[15]

Calhoun was a formidable member of the nationalist camp. He was an affluent cotton planter. Born to a family of moderate wealth (his father had owned about thirty slaves), Calhoun joined the planter elite with his marriage in 1811 to his second cousin, Floride Colhoun. Floride's widowed mother was generous, and with her help he came to own two plantations and about two hundred slaves. Calhoun was also an imposing speaker. Standing six feet two inches, with angular features, piercing eyes, and a shock of black hair that he combed straight up, he commanded attention in Congress and on the stump. His strength as a speaker lay not in an eloquent delivery; he spoke rapidly and in language lacking adornment. Rather, his intensity and the penetrating logic of his arguments made his speeches resonate. And in 1819 he held national office: two years earlier President James Monroe had appointed him secretary of war.[16]

During the Missouri Controversy Calhoun's advocacy of compromise placed him with the majority in the South. "I cannot but think," he told an Alabama friend in 1820, "that the impression, which exist[s] on the minds of many of our virtuous and well informed citizens to the South, . . . that there had commenced between the North and the South a premeditated struggle for superiority, is not correct." He continued: "Our true system is to look to the country; and to support such measures and such men, without regard to sections, as are best calculated to advance the general interest."[17] Most in the region agreed.

The New Orleans *Gazette* remarked that Louisiana was "deeply, vitally interested in conserving the union of the states entire," while Alabama senator John Walker applauded the Compromise, remarking, "It was a wise and *necessary* measure—and has saved the Republic." Furthermore, Southerners convened no public meetings to condemn the compromise; only in the halls of Congress did a few firebrands voice their bellicose sentiments. "Our people do not petition much," North Carolina senator Nathaniel Macon lamented; "we plume ourselves on not pestering the General Government with our prayers."[18]

Most Southerners in 1820 felt optimistic about their future within the Union and even judged that the coming years would solve the knotty problem of slavery. For many this faith in the future was embodied in the "diffusion" argument. These Southerners argued that if slavery were allowed to spread into the West, the condition of blacks would improve and eventually freedom would prevail. "Slaves, divided among many masters," Congressman Robert Reid of Georgia explained, "will enjoy greater privileges and comfort than those who [are] cooped within a narrow sphere. . . . Emancipations will become common."[19] Northern speakers pointed out the flaws in this argument. Extending slavery, they noted, would no more weaken the institution than spreading a fire or pestilence could lessen that scourge. Whatever its validity, diffusion was an optimistic, expansionist argument that assumed that new soils would take care of the region's economic and moral problems.[20]

Not all Southerners, to be sure, favored compromise, and as a rule the most vocal opponents came from the oldest districts where the soils were worn out and the prospects for growth the least. The strongest dissent against the Thomas amendment (dividing Louisiana territory at 36° 30') came from Virginia congressmen, who voted 18–4 against this provision. Senators John Randolph of Virginia, Nathaniel Macon of North Carolina, and (much to Calhoun's chagrin) William Smith of South Carolina opposed making any concessions to the

North. These hard-liners were also the ones most likely to broach the new argument that slavery was a positive good. In 1821 Randolph, Macon, and Smith opposed the fourth component, which was now added to the other parts of the Missouri Compromise. The constitution that Missouri drafted in 1820 had banned the immigration of free blacks and mulattoes, a clause that reignited Northern anger. In the last part of this deal, Missouri agreed not to exclude U.S. citizens and in return was admitted to the Union.[21]

Finally, one aspect of national politics remained constant from the 1820s to the 1850s: the determination of representatives from the Border States to maintain sectional harmony. Congressmen from Maryland and Kentucky voted 15–2 for the amendment dividing Louisiana territory. By 1820 Maryland was relying more and more on free labor and clearly was following a different path of development than Virginia or the cotton South. Kentucky also had strong ties of trade and kinship with the North, and its politicians favored sectional cooperation. No single individual worked harder to bring together all the parts of the deals struck in 1820 and 1821 than Kentuckian Henry Clay, who served as Speaker of the House.[22]

Thus shared economic interests fostered a climate of sectional cooperation and contributed to the satisfactory resolution of the Missouri Controversy. Despite its heated, sometimes apocalyptic rhetoric, the Missouri conflict ushered in not civil war but three decades of compromise.

## II.

The patterns of the national economy, and more particularly, favorable conditions in most of the cotton South, allowed for a peaceful resolution of the next great sectional clash: the Nullification Crisis. This conflict began in the mid-1820s and culminated in a deal worked out in 1833. The clash was provoked by increasingly higher tariffs, and by South Carolina's determination to disobey ("nullify") these imposts. Tariffs protecting manufacturers, planters argued, unfairly favored the North while punishing their agrarian commonwealth.

For several reasons South Carolinians took the lead in opposing the federal government during this conflict—just as they would during later clashes. To begin with, the downturn of the 1820s hit the state harder than any of the commonwealths to the west because South Carolina's soils were older and less fertile. Cotton prices fell precipitously during these years, from an average of 26 cents a pound in 1816–19, to 14.6 cents in 1820–25, to 9.3 cents in 1826–32. Fresh lands in states such as Alabama and Mississippi allowed planters to thrive even with these lower prices. Hard times, however, oppressed the Palmetto State, where the courts were clogged with debt cases and hundreds of farms were lost to foreclosures. In 1828 Calhoun lamented, "Our staples can hardly return the cost of cultivation, and land and Negroes have fallen to the lowest prices and can hardly be sold."[23]

South Carolina's leadership in this clash also reflected its unusual politics: it was more unified and more thoroughly dominated by the planter class than any other Southern state. The South Carolina constitution gave disproportionate power to the coastal aristocracy—a dominance reinforced by the spread of planting culture into the Upcountry. By 1830 blacks comprised at least 40 percent of the population in every county, except in those near the North Carolina border. Marriages between Lowcountry heiresses and Upcountry planters, involving such well-known figures as John Calhoun, George McDuffie, and James Hammond, further helped unify the state. South Carolina did have economic and political divisions; in most instances, the districts with the fewest slaves opposed nullification. But compared with their counterparts in other Southern states, dissenters in South Carolina were fewer and less influential.[24]

Furthermore, the extraordinary concentration of wealth and slave-holding in the Lowcountry parishes created a set of planters who were among the most outspoken defenders of slavery in the South. In coastal districts from the Georgia border to the Santee River, slaves comprised over 80 percent of the population. Nowhere else in the South was there such a concentration of slaves or so many estates with more than a hundred bondspeople. In the 1820s an exceptional concern for the fate of slavery, more than hard times, spurred these planters. Because the primary crop in the coastal region was rice, supplemented by sea island cotton, a different economic calculus prevailed in the parishes than in the Upcountry. Though quotations for rice declined in the 1820s, the value fell less than that of short-staple cotton, and profits remained steady. One planter justly observed that rice was "a much more certain crop than Cotton, liable to few diseases, less likely to be seriously affected by physical causes, and but seldom subject to ruinous fluctuations in price." Sea island cotton, which commanded premium prices, also helped shield planters from the chill of the downturn. Still the Lowcountry's extraordinary dependence on slavery fostered radicalism, and most landowners in the parishes applauded the fiery rhetoric of politicians such as Robert Barnwell Rhett.[25]

The steep rise in tariffs during the 1820s, coupled with the downturn in the local economy, led more and more Carolinians to espouse states' rights—and eventually demand nullification. In the decade after the War of 1812 most of South Carolina's congressmen and senators, including Robert Hayne, George McDuffie, and James Hamilton, were nationalists and Calhoun loyalists. But higher duties in 1824 and the "Tariff of Abominations" of 1828 gradually changed the outlook of these individuals. By the late 1820s Hayne, McDuffie, and Hamilton had become ardent defenders of Southern rights, joining those politicians who long had criticized Calhoun's moderation. These men urged Calhoun to add his voice to theirs and publicly demand nullification. Calhoun sympathized but at first made his views known only privately. His presidential ambitions and the high public office he held (he was elected vice president in 1824 and again in 1828) made him circumspect. Keeping his authorship a secret, Calhoun in 1828 wrote a lengthy document, *Exposition and Protest*, that provided a theoretical basis for nullification. The pressure on Calhoun to declare himself increased, and in 1831 he announced his support for defiance. His public stance and the series of carefully reasoned tracts he penned helped persuade many wavering South Carolinians.[26]

The Nullification Crisis was as much about defending slavery as it was about resisting an oppressive federal tax. In this respect the conflict of 1832–33 was a true precursor of secession; both clashes reflected the determination of members of the planting class to resist steps that might lead to the end of their way of life. Since the Missouri Controversy, slavery had been kept at the top of the national agenda by a series of events: the Denmark Vesey slave conspiracy that shook Charleston in 1822; the proposals of the Ohio legislature in 1824 for gradual emancipation; the appearance of William Lloyd Garrison's abolitionist newspaper, *The Liberator*, in January 1831; Nat Turner's rebellion in Virginia later that year; and the Virginia debate over abolition in 1832. Looking through this lens, many Carolinians viewed their struggle with the federal government as a battle to preserve Southern institutions. Calhoun explained, "I consider the Tariff, but as the occasion, rather than the real cause of the present unhappy state of things." He continued, "The states . . . must in the end be forced to rebel, or submit to have . . . their domestick institutions exhausted by Colonization and other schemes, and themselves & children reduced to wretchedness."[27] James Hamilton, who became governor in 1830, emphasized the same point: "I have always looked to the present contest with the government, on the part of the Southern States, as a battle at the out-posts, by which, if we succeeded in repulsing the enemy, *the citadel would be safe.*"[28]

The conflict with the federal government came to a head in 1832 and 1833. In October 1832, after months of agitation, nullifiers swept the state elections and dominated the new House and Senate. The legislature promptly called a convention, which declared the tariffs of 1828 and 1832 null and void in South Carolina and announced that after February 1, 1833, no duties would be collected in the state. Most but not all South Carolinians supported this protest. Dissent came from three groups: wealthy Charleston merchants, whose national and international ties gave them a broader perspective; some of the old, established Lowcountry families; and small farmers in districts where the proportion of slaves was lowest. But most Carolinians were eager to defend their state. Calhoun now resigned from the vice presidency and was promptly elected to the Senate. Hayne, who had left the Senate to provide a place for Calhoun, became governor. The new governor issued a call for volunteers and urged a state of preparedness. An observer listening to Hayne's inaugural address observed: "It made *me* feel solemn, for it seemed as if that awful scourge—civil war must *soon* come."[29]

But favorable conditions elsewhere in the South, along with Henry Clay's skill in bringing all sides together, helped resolve this dispute. Much as he had during the Missouri Controversy, Clay took a leadership role in Congress. President Jackson, always an ardent nationalist, strongly condemned South Carolina's actions and threatened the use of force. In December 1832 he issued the Nullification Proclamation, which declared the protest an "impracticable absurdity." In January Jackson asked Congress to authorize additional powers so he could ensure that U.S. customs laws were obeyed. The lawmakers responded by enacting the Force Bill. But already Clay was working on a compromise that would have South Carolina repeal its ordinance of nullification and Congress commit to lowering tariffs over the next nine years. Calhoun, who was more moderate than some of his compatriots, approved the deal, arguing that with lower tariffs his state gained much of what it sought. Congress heeded Clay's pleas and also endorsed the compromise. Following Calhoun's lead, South Carolina rescinded the nullification ordinance, and the crisis was defused.[30]

Equally significant in the peaceful resolution of this conflict was the refusal of the other slave states, which were faring better than South Carolina, to support nullification. South Carolinians recognized that any show of force would isolate them. To be sure, most Southerners disliked the tariffs of the 1820s. A few prominent individuals, such as Senator George Poindexter of Mississippi and Congressman Dixon Lewis of Alabama, applauded South Carolina's defiance. A Richmond newspaper, *The Jeffersonian and Virginia Times*, several state senators in Mississippi, and a handful of politicians in Louisiana took a similar stance. But overwhelmingly, Southern lawmakers condemned South Carolina's protest. Favorable conditions in the cotton states to the west made a strong case for the value of Union. Rejecting nullification, Mississippi governor Abram Scott told the legislature that theirs was a "youthful and enterprising state" that was growing in "glory and prosperity." The lawmakers agreed and charged that South Carolina had acted with "reckless precipitancy." They denounced the "unwarrantable attitude assumed by a sister of the South."[31] The Alabama assembly called the scheme "unsound in practice and dangerous in theory." Louisiana governor André Roman noted, "Such doctrines find no advocates in Louisiana." The Georgia legislature condemned South Carolina, contending that its "mischievous policy" was "rash and revolutionary."[32]

Politicians in the Upper South also rejected nullification. "However much we might all deplore the necessity of coercing [South Carolina] to do her duty," Tennessee governor William Carroll remarked, "no hesitation should take place in adopting such a course if the emergency requires it."[33] Even Virginia and North Carolina politicians, who often espoused states' rights doctrines, did not support South Carolina. Because the planting elite in those tobacco states had long wrestled with worn-out soils, the downturn of the 1820s was less of a shock to them. Nor did these wealthy slaveholders dominate state politics to the same degree that their counterparts in South Carolina did. Hence their response to the high tariffs and to the Nullification Crisis was restrained. The Virginia legislature called on both parties to "abstain from any and all acts, whatever, which may be calculated to disturb the tranquility of the country, or endanger the existence of the Union."[34]

In short, thanks to the buoyant economy of the cotton South, unionism in the Upper South, and Clay's efforts, nullification gained little support. Cooperation rather than armed confrontation remained the hallmark of American politics.

## III.

The unifying force of the national economy was also evident in the series of accords that helped Congress muddle through the clashes over the gag rule between 1835 and 1844. The conflict over the proper response to the abolitionist petitions pouring into Congress after 1835 was more subdued than the battles over the admission of Missouri or nullification. No Southern state threatened disunion; no Northern leader called for military action. But the conflict stretched over many years; provoked heated exchanges in Congress; and demonstrated how the newly formed political parties, which coalesced around economic issues, promoted sectional peace.

The controversy began in December 1835 when Congressman James Henry Hammond of South Carolina proposed that the House of Representatives close its doors to antislavery petitions that were now arriving in the thousands. Up to that time the House had no formal procedure for handling such memorials, although the result of its deliberations was not far removed from the goal Hammond desired. Congress received these petitions and directed them to a standing committee, where invariably they died. Hence the battle that continued for the next nine years was more over form than substance.

Northern Democrats led by Martin Van Buren sought a compromise that would defuse the furor ignited by Hammond's proposal. Northern Democrats disliked abolition but also judged unacceptable any measure that blatantly trampled on the right to petition. Van Buren also recognized that a sectional rift among Democrats might derail his plans to succeed Jackson in 1836. So the Little Magician persuaded Charleston representative Henry L. Pinckney to propose a middle course. In February 1836 Pinckney urged that petitions be received and referred to a select committee bound by strict instructions. The panel was told that Congress could not constitutionally interfere with slavery in the states and "ought not" interfere with slavery in Washington, D.C. In May the House voted, 117–68, to adopt Pinckney's resolution as a standing rule.[35]

The vote illustrated the strength of the Democrats, who on this issue, as others, put party before section. Whigs divided, with Southern Whigs favoring the gag and Northern members opposing it. Hence the crucial votes came from the Northern Democrats who joined their Southern colleagues in backing the measure. These pro-compromise Northern Democrats typically represented poorer farming districts in Maine, New Hampshire, northeastern New York, northeastern Pennsylvania, and Illinois. These individuals wanted smaller government, disdained reforms including antislavery, and respected the need for party unity.[36]

Undaunted by the strength of forces supporting the gag, the opponents of this rule united behind a remarkable champion: the ex-president John Quincy Adams. The son of a president, Adams had been a distinguished diplomat and a successful secretary of state, although an ineffective chief executive. But his greatest role came after 1830 when at age sixty-three he entered the House of Representatives. While he opposed abolition, he adamantly defended the right of abolitionists to submit their memorials. Day after day, and year after year, he attacked the gag rule with wit and incisive arguments. Physically unimposing, short and bald, and considered by some to be cold and austere, Adams became a widely respected figure in the North, "Old Man Eloquence." He forced Southerners to debate the limits of debate and quoted the Declaration of Independence when they tried to silence him. A Southern effort to censure Adams failed, 105–21.

Adams gained more support after 1840, when the Southern representatives overreached themselves and pushed through a stricter gag, similar to the total ban that Hammond had urged. The House voted three times in 1841 to repeal this harsh rule, although in each case the vote was reversed. Finally, in December 1844, by the decisive margin of 108–80, the gag was repealed. Northern Democrats now joined Northern Whigs in voting overwhelmingly against the ban. Southern representatives, recognizing the futility of continuing the campaign, shifted their focus to other issues. The parties were not shattered; that would occur a decade later. But some of the internal cohesion, evident among Democrats in the 1830s, had weakened.[37]

# IV.

The final sectional dispute of the era of compromises lasted from 1846 to 1850 and came to involve the settlement of the West, fugitive slaves, and slavery in the District of Columbia. This clash was peacefully settled thanks to constituencies, North and South, whose self-interest suggested that cooperation was better than conflict. Still, it was clear that the unities fostered by the national economy were crumbling. The strength of the Great Valley; the Southern sympathies of the Northern entrepôts; the optimism of the cotton South; the importance of the Border States; and the roles of the two great parties in bringing together Northerners and Southerners were still evident. But by 1850 powerful centrifugal forces were supplanting the cohesion that had marked the preceding decades.

The clash began with a debate over the future of the West: Was the territory gained in the Mexican War, which began in April 1846, to be slave or free? In August 1846 David Wilmot introduced his Proviso banning slavery from soils the United States might acquire. A large man, who loved his food and drink and cared little about his dress, Wilmot had been known as a faithful Democrat. Representing a hard-scrabble region in northeastern Pennsylvania, well removed from the lakes and the Erie Canal, Wilmot had applauded Polk's economic program. He praised Polk's veto of the rivers and harbors bill and approved the Democratic-sponsored Walker tariff, which lowered rates. Other Pennsylvania Democrats, with more manufacturing in their districts, defected from the party line on tariff policy. Hence the Speaker readily called on Wilmot in a heated debate on financing the Mexican War. And hence the shock many Democrats felt when Wilmot introduced his rider, boldly claiming the West for free soil.[38]

Support for the Proviso throughout the North was immediate and widespread. In August 1846 Northern representatives voted 88–8 for the measure. The Proviso never became law because Southerners blocked it in the Senate. But thanks to the near unanimity of Northern lawmakers, the House approved it several times between 1846 and 1849. Moreover, thirteen Northern states adopted resolutions opposing the extension of slavery. Northerners also demanded that Oregon be organized as a free territory. Unlike California and New Mexico, Oregon was not part of the expanse gained from Mexico. But the United States had recently secured clear title to this area, settling a long-standing dispute with Britain, and the lawmakers debated the status of this territory as well.[39]

In the clashes over the Proviso, Northerners once again made clear their distaste for slavery. "The people of the North," Jacob Collamer of Vermont stated, "regard slavery as a great moral and political evil, and its introduction into these territories would be not only an injury to them but also to the nation."[40] Advocates of the Proviso, like their counterparts decades earlier, pointedly compared the prosperity of the North with the backwardness of the South. "Your lands are worn out," Senator Thomas Corwin of Ohio stated, "because the slave has turned pale the land wherever he has set down his black foot! . . . Must we then extend to these Territories that which produces sterility whenever it is found, till barren desolation shall cover the whole land?"[41] Speakers emphasized the incompatibility of slave and free labor. Remarked Senator James Bradbury of Maine, "The free laborers of the North have a repugnance to labor by the side of the slave."[42]

Southerners vehemently attacked the Proviso, rehearsing the same constitutional and historical arguments they had put forth during the Missouri debate. Noting the predominance of the North in Congress, Senator James Mason of Virginia concluded: "In such a struggle, our only hope is in the Constitution. We appeal to its guarantees. We invite a fair and rigid scrutiny of its provisions."[43] "At every stage of our progress," South Carolina congressman Daniel Wallace explained, "the South has appealed to the great conservative principles of the Constitution." Speakers also noted the prevalence of slavery in Biblical times and throughout recorded history.[44]

In 1850 the divisions were deeper and the threat to the Union more serious than thirty years earlier. Far-reaching forces for change were evident at midcentury, weakening the bonds forged during the 1820s and 1830s. In the North the rise of the Great Lakes economy gave many citizens—Democrat, Whig, and Free Soiler alike—a new set of loyalties. The growing importance of antislavery sentiment fostered doubts about the value of compromise. In the South the declining fertility of once-rich soils and the waning prospects for expansion led many planters to take a new, more skeptical view of their future within the Union.

At midcentury, unlike in 1820, calls for secession were widespread and went far beyond the halls of Congress. In both crises Southern senators and congressmen threatened disunion if the North persisted in its efforts to limit the spread of slavery. What was new in the late 1840s was the anger vented in county and state conventions and the willingness of common folk to contemplate separation. If the majority in the South continued to support the Union, the minority was militant and outspoken. Meeting at the local courthouse, the citizenry of Orangeburg County, South Carolina, declared their "fixed and unswerving determination to resist aggression and maintain our equality at every cost and hazard."[45] Voters in neighboring Sumter District similarly announced their readiness to support "any measure necessary for the preservation of our common institutions."[46] In Accomack County, Virginia, those gathered resolved to defend their "*Sovereign Equality* . . . to the last extremity of argument, . . . and finally, if compelled to do so, *by force of arms.*"[47]

State conventions held during 1849 took similarly strong stands. A meeting at Columbia, South Carolina, resolved to resist the Wilmot Proviso "at every hazard." The Mississippi convention declared that if the Proviso was adopted or slavery abolished in the District of Columbia, the Southern states would have "to take care of their own safety, and to treat the nonslaveholding States as enemies to the slaveholding States and their domestic institutions."[48]

John C. Calhoun's correspondents reported the growing numbers who considered secession. Richard Crallé wrote from Virginia that "many men here speak openly in favor of *dissolution*; for the course of the northern States has goaded them on to this."[49] South Carolinian James Hammond remarked that "the value of the Union is now calculated hourly in every corner in the South."[50] Many were unperturbed by the thought of armed conflict. "Virginia has an immense store of arms," William Duval noted from Florida, "and she will distribute them to sustain the South. When the time shall come (and I fear it is near) I will return to my native State, and leave nothing undone to procure 1200 stand or arms for a corps that I will raise & command in this State and hold ready to march to any point where their services may be required." Calhoun was among those urging that armed resistance was preferable to submission to Northern demands.[51]

In the North too the voices opposing compromise were far louder than they had been in earlier decades. In 1848, for the first time, a significant Northern party declared itself against all deals with the South. The Free Soil Party, which received almost 15 percent of Northern votes, declared: "There must be no more compromises with Slavery: if made, they must be repealed." Abolitionists were more numerous and vocal than ever before.[52]

Despite the vehemence of sectional politicians, the long-standing ties forged in the preceding decades held and accommodation prevailed in 1850. While patterns of commerce and party loyalties made the compromise possible, astute politicians had to fashion the deal. Henry Clay, after consultation with other senators, proposed a far-reaching compromise. He embodied his proposals in an omnibus bill, which lawmakers were asked to vote up or down. When this approach failed, Stephen Douglas took the lead and gained acceptance for a set of measures adopted one by one. The Compromise of 1850 as finally approved had five parts. It admitted California as a free state. It ended the slave trade (but not slavery) in the District of Columbia. It enacted a stricter fugitive slave law. It left New Mexico and Utah territories open to slavery. It reduced the size of Texas, while affirming that the federal government would assume the state's debt.

Although militant Southerners opposed some measures (admission of a free California; end of the D.C. slave trade) and antislavery Northerners denounced others (tougher fugitive slave law; slavery in the Southwestern territories), a familiar set of interests rallied behind the compromise and made possible a shifting series of coalitions that passed all five parts. In the North, representatives of the Great Valley demonstrated once again their sympathy for the South. Illinois congressmen had stood out in their opposition to the Wilmot Proviso; four of the eight Northern votes against the Wilmot Proviso in August 1846 came from Illinois, the only Northern delegation to oppose the measure. The other four also came from the Midwest, including a southern Ohio congressman, who was the lone Northern Whig opposed to the measure. These congressmen helped pass the Compromise of 1850. For example, a bloc of fourteen representatives from the southern reaches of Illinois, Indiana, and Ohio comprised the largest free state group backing the fugitive slave law, which Northern representatives opposed, 73–27. Stephen Douglas, leader of the campaign for these measures, spoke for the Ohio Valley settlers, many of whom had Southern roots.[53]

The great commercial cities and their representatives comprised a second group sympathetic to the South. Most businessmen in Boston, New York, and Philadelphia shared the Northern distaste for slavery and its extension. But they benefited greatly from Southern commerce and found threats of boycotts and secession unnerving. New York, whose traders dominated the South's seaborne commerce, took the lead in agitating for conciliatory measures. In February 1850 more than two thousand New York merchants and businesspeople signed a call for a public meeting for "sustaining Mr. Clay's compromise." A group of businessmen contributed nearly $10,000 to establish a pro-Compromise newspaper in Albany. And when the debates over Clay's proposals dragged on, New York merchants launched a petition campaign. They collected 25,000 signatures for a memorial calling for "a proper spirit of concession." Boston and Philadelphia merchants also organized pro-Compromise rallies, including a large gathering in July at the Chinese Museum in Philadelphia.[54]

No individual articulated the views of the business community so forcefully or with greater impact than Daniel Webster. Webster was born in New Hampshire in 1782, the same year as Calhoun. Like Calhoun, Webster got his start in the world thanks to a keen intellect, a powerful ambition, and a supportive family. Son of a prosperous farmer, young Daniel was far more at home poring over books than walking behind a plow. His parents sent him to Phillips Exeter Academy, where he soon ascended from the bottom of the class to the top, and then to Dartmouth College. Webster became a successful lawyer, a rising politician in the Federalist Party, and a powerful orator. His craggy features made him a striking figure. An observer remarked, "He was a black, raven-haired fellow, with an eye as black as death, and as heavy as a lion's—and no lion in Africa ever had a voice like him."

From his earliest years in public life, Webster was closely connected with the business elite. His law practice first flourished in Portsmouth, New Hampshire, where Federalists sent the talented newcomer to Congress in 1813. Three years later Webster moved to Boston, at the urging of the merchant-industrialist Francis Cabot Lowell. Webster would serve the Boston business community both in the courts and in Congress, and by 1819 had a princely annual income of more than $15,000. Webster lived well, with a fashionable home on Beacon Hill, a farm south of Boston at Marshfield, and various speculative properties in the West. His income, sizable though it was, was never enough to cover his expenses. So more than any other figure in this era, Webster came to depend on the largesse of the business community. Contemporaries testified that his "good fat client," the Second Bank of the United States, paid him $50,000 in fees. In the 1840s members of the Whig elite in New York and Boston raised over $60,000 to supplement his income, while other merchants extended "loans" to help him maintain his lifestyle.

Webster provided good value for his backers. Before the mid-1820s he defended free trade, but once manufacturing soared in New England, he became a high tariff man. Along with Clay, Webster worked to recharter the Bank of the United States. In the Massachusetts state constitutional convention he led the forces urging that property, not population, be the basis for representation. Webster smoothly changed his party allegiance, matching the loyalties of his supporters. He began as a Federalist in the 1810s and became a National Republican in the 1820s and a Whig in the 1830s.

Reflecting both the needs of his constituents and his larger vision, Webster stood forth as an ardent nationalist. The American System of tariff, bank, internal improvements, and expanded domestic trade, Webster asserted, strengthened the country and benefited everyone. (These policies, not incidentally, helped the wealthy Whigs he served.) Webster's fame was established by his exchange in 1830 with Senator Robert Y. Hayne of South Carolina. Hayne launched a broad attack on New England, abolitionists, high tariffs, and the doctrine of "consolidation," which Hayne declared rode roughshod over the rights of states. Webster responded with a peroration to the Union, finishing, "Liberty *and* Union, now and forever, one and inseparable!" No speech was so widely celebrated in the era before the Civil War as the Reply to Hayne. Contemporaries who came to know Webster well remarked his two sides: "Godlike Daniel," the gifted orator and nationalist, and "Black Dan," the venal, self-serving politician.

Webster's Senate speech in March 1850 defending the Compromise measures was an eloquent statement of views widely shared in the Northeastern business community. "I wish to speak today," he began, "not as a Massachusetts man, nor as a northern man, but as an American. . . . I speak today for the preservation of the Union." Webster was remarkably conciliatory to the South. He argued there was no reason to adopt the Wilmot Proviso: "The law of nature—of physical geography"—would keep slavery out of California and New Mexico. He criticized Northern extremists, remarking that "abolitionist societies . . . have produced nothing good or valuable." And he urged all lawmakers to honor the fugitive slave law as a "constitutional obligation."[55]

Predictably, Webster's remarks delighted the merchants. One trader declared the address would "live side by side with the Constitution."

A group of "sons of New England and merchants of New York" presented him with a gift, while Washington banker William W. Corcoran, who had lent Webster over $5,000, canceled his debt. Several hundred New York businessmen sent Webster a memorial thanking him for his speech. However, abolitionists in the North and fire-eaters in the South condemned his remarks.[56]

The Compromise received support in the North not only from the Mississippi Valley and the major cities but also from those who still put party before section. Many Northern Democrats and a few Northern Whigs continued to favor cooperation over conflict. Typically, these individuals—both constituents and lawmakers—came from districts relatively untouched by the flames of antislavery fervor. Democratic congressmen from northern Maine and northern New Hampshire, as well as from several districts in Pennsylvania, Ohio, and Iowa, backed the fugitive slave law. So did two senators from Iowa and one from Pennsylvania. Equally striking were the abstentions on that vote. Democratic Senators Cass of Michigan, Douglas of Illinois, and Daniel Dickinson of New York cast no votes, although they were active in the debates. Nor did cotton Whig Robert Winthrop of Massachusetts, or the erratic Whig William Seward. Those abstentions allowed a solid South to push the measure through. Only after 1854 did party lines crumble in the North and were most compromise-prone individuals voted out of office.

In the South too the forces for accommodation, if weakened, remained visible. As in earlier crises, representatives of the Border States applauded moderation. For example, both senators from Kentucky (Clay and Joseph Underwood), Thomas Hart Benton of Missouri, and both senators from Delaware, which was nominally part of the South, supported the ban on trading slaves in the District of Columbia. John Bell of Tennessee voted for admitting California. Apart from the Border State lawmakers, however, few Southerners broke ranks to support the pro-Northern compromise measures: California statehood and ending the D.C. slave trade.

In the Southwest, Texas senator Sam Houston stood as a remnant of the nationalism that had once characterized that region. Houston's life was a saga of high adventure and accomplishment. He was born in Virginia, moved to Tennessee, and fought with Jackson at Horseshoe Bend in 1814. He then became a lawyer, congressman, and governor of Tennessee—all before moving to Texas in 1832. In Texas Houston led the army that in 1835 defeated the Mexicans under Santa Anna. Grateful Texans chose him to be president of the Lone Star Republic, and after the state was admitted to the Union, made him its first senator. Texans and Sam Houston had good reason to support the Union in 1850. The United States had just successfully concluded a costly war to keep Mexico at bay, while the 1850 Compromise included a generous provision to pay the state debt. Moreover, unlike the states to the east, Texas still had rich expanses of virgin soil. Houston embodied this unionism and was one of few senators to vote for all the Compromise measures. He told his fellow lawmakers: "I deny the power of all the ultras on earth to dissolve this Union, or to rend it in twain."[57]

Houston, the Border State congressmen, many Northern Democrats, Ohio Valley representatives, and the business interests of the Northeast all came together to push through the Compromise of 1850 and to demonstrate one last time the unities that had marked the earlier decades. But the sectional peace these votes achieved was a fragile one. New patterns of trade and new political loyalties were emerging, and those developments would lead to ever more bitter conflicts and, ultimately, war.

# PART TWO

# ROOTS OF CONFLICT

## 4

# RISE OF THE
# LAKE ECONOMY

T
hey poured into Chicago, a gathering of angry people. Perhaps ten thousand individuals, including more than two
thousand convention delegates, arrived, almost doubling the
population of the small, muddy town. The vast majority of those attending the Northwestern Rivers and Harbors Convention in July
1847 came from the Great Lakes region. Apart from the Missouri delegation, only six individuals hailed from the South. What angered
those assembling in Chicago was President James Polk's veto of the
1846 rivers and harbors bill, a step that blocked funds desperately
needed for the improvement of lake harbors. In the aftermath of the
president's action, irate Chicagoans nicknamed sandbars "Polk bars"
and snags "Polk stalks." A reporter for a Chicago newspaper defiantly
suggested that a long hickory pole should be placed "upon the Polk
bar at the mouth of our harbor." He wrote: With "Polk's breeches
pocket containing the Harbor and River Bill attached, it would make
an excellent beacon for both steamboat pilots and politicians."[1] The

convention was unabashedly a regional gathering. James DeBow, the states' rights editor of *DeBow's Review*, contrasted the Chicago meeting with the recent conference in Memphis. "The Memphis Convention sought to conciliate all parties," he remarked. But the Chicago convention limited itself to the "necessities of the North-west and the Lakes."[2]

The Northwestern Rivers and Harbors Convention signaled the emergence of a new regional power: the Great Lakes economy. The convention resolves announced what many in the area knew well: that the trade of much of the Northwest now flowed east through the lakes and Erie Canal rather than south down the Mississippi. The political consequences of the gathering were even more important. Democrats from the lake region showed they could no longer support a party line that condemned internal improvements. Rather, they began to make common cause with Whigs and Free Soilers in demanding outlays for the lakes. The foundations for a powerful Northern party were being laid. The lake representatives, along with their allies in New England, also began developing a new, self-serving credo of nationalism, which insisted the federal government take the lead in promoting growth.

I.

Few individuals were more qualified to chronicle the growth of the lake economy than Joshua Giddings, who grew up near these waterways and went on to serve as an Ohio congressman for twenty years. Giddings spent his early childhood in western New York, but in 1805, when he was ten, he moved with his family to a homestead in Ohio's Western Reserve, an area near Lake Erie settled by New Englanders. He cleared fields and tended horses on the family's farm. By the time he was eighteen, he was six feet two inches, two hundred pounds, and renowned for his prowess as a wrestler. His size and courage would serve him well in Congress when he stood up to the taunts and threats of Southern opponents. Though unschooled in his early years, he became an avid reader and eventually a lawyer. He served in the Ohio legislature in the 1820s and entered the U.S. House of Representatives as a Whig in 1838. Giddings witnessed the beginnings of trade on the lakes in the 1830s and the rapid expansion of this commerce in the 1840s. When an Illinois congressman spoke against appropriating funds for Cunningham's Bay on Lake Erie, commenting it "was a place he had not heard of," Giddings immediately replied, "The harbor was commenced around 1832. . . . This harbor was the first landing-place on the northwestern lake border—the first landing-place of the old Western Reserve."[3]

During the 1840s Giddings called on the lawmakers to recognize the greatly expanded trade on the lakes and provide funds for harbor improvement. "While we cheerfully contribute our wealth and influence to support . . . our Atlantic friends," he remarked in 1844, "we demand of them in return the same generous support of our lake commerce." He continued: "I am, however, aware that our friends at the East and at the South are not conscious of the importance of that commerce. . . . That vast country, extending from western New York to Wisconsin, which our eastern and southern friends have been accustomed to regard as an almost unbroken wilderness, contains millions of people, whose whole commercial transactions are effected by the aid of lake navigation." Like other spokesmen for the lakes, Giddings paraded figures demonstrating the expansion of this commerce. He noted that trade on these waterways amounted to more than $65 million in 1841 and over $100 million in 1844. Giddings added, "This commerce has come into existence so suddenly that I do not wonder that gentlemen are unconscious of its extent."[4]

Chicago's Democratic congressman, John Wentworth, was among the lawmakers seconding Giddings's statements. Born in New Hampshire in 1815, Wentworth attended Dartmouth College, where he had his own room because he was too tall to share a bed with any of the other boys. His classmates called him "Long John," a name that stuck with him for the rest of his days. After graduating in 1836, he headed west to seek his fortune, arriving in Chicago that fall. He jumped at the chance to run a local newspaper, the *Chicago Democrat*, and began a long and successful career in journalism. At six feet six inches and slender (although later he would grow portly), Wentworth turned heads when he walked the streets. Beyond a striking height, Wentworth shared with Giddings a growing interest in politics and a commitment to the lake economy. But in other ways the two men were very different. Wentworth was a Democrat; Giddings a Whig and later a Free Soiler. Wentworth was a savvy land speculator, a political wheeler-dealer, and a powerful local boss whose principles wavered at times. Giddings, by contrast, never rebuilt his fortune after the Panic of 1837 and was often naïve in his political maneuvering. Increasingly, he was also regarded as the principled voice of the antislavery opposition in Congress.[5]

Despite their differences, Wentworth was no less dedicated to the lake economy than Giddings, and Wentworth's speeches in Congress (which he entered in 1843) sounded the same note of boosterism as those of his Ohio compatriot. In a lengthy address delivered in 1846, Wentworth trumpeted the vitality of trade on these waterways. He provided figures for the growth of Chicago, the sale of public lands, the exports of Kalamazoo ("6,000,000 feet lumber . . . 1,500,000 shingles"), and the vessels built on the lakes. He pointedly compared exchanges on these inland seas to America's foreign trade: "The commerce of the lakes the past season has been $125,000,000, employing 6,000 active seamen. The large amount of lake commerce will be best appreciated when it is known that the whole export commerce of the United States is but $114,000,000."[6]

Wentworth and Giddings were right: the lake economy was soaring. Canals, funded by the states, and railroads, built with a mix of public and private money, made these burgeoning exchanges possible. The Erie Canal served as the linchpin for the new system of trade. Construction of this impressive 363-mile-long ditch began in 1817 and was completed in 1825. Eighty-three locks raised boats 675 feet. Aqueducts carried the canal over rivers, while innumerable bridges tied together farms severed by the waterway. Although the Erie Canal reached Buffalo in 1825, not until the mid-1830s did significant traffic arrive from the West. Before that time perilous overland transportation within the Midwest, sparse population, and obstructed harbors kept lake shipping to a minimum.

During the 1830s and 1840s three canal systems in the Midwest linked inland counties to the lakes, greatly boosting east-west commerce. (See Map 1.) The first of these waterways, the Ohio and Erie Canal, served Cleveland and was completed in the 1830s. It provided a lake outlet for the farmers of eastern Ohio and helped make Cleveland the top port in the Midwest for produce from the 1830s to the late 1850s. The second system had its terminus in Toledo and was opened in the 1840s. These waterways, which included the Wabash and Erie Canal as well as the Miami and Erie Canal, aided farmers in Indiana and western Ohio. Thanks to its rich hinterland, Toledo replaced Cleveland in the late 1850s as the leading entrepot for grain. The third system, the Illinois and Michigan Canal, connected Chicago to the Illinois River in 1848 and helped transform the small town into a bustling metropolis. The population of Chicago rose from 12,000 in 1845 to 30,000 in 1850. Trade increased even more dramatically. "In the year 1847," Congressman Richard Yates explained, "before the completion of the canal, the imports and exports of the city were only $4,500,000; while in the year 1848, the first year after its completion, they amounted to $20,000,000."[7]

Railroads supplemented the canal systems and further bolstered trade at the lake ports. During the late 1840s and on into the 1850s tracks were laid at breakneck speed throughout the Midwest. In 1845 Ohio had only 45 miles of railroads. By 1852 it had more than 1,400, and in 1860 it led the nation with more than 2,900 miles of track. Illinois had only 95 miles of railroad in 1852; by 1860 it had 2,790 miles and stood second to Ohio. Track mileage in Wisconsin soared from 20 miles in 1850 to 905 miles a decade later. Milwaukee's rise as a lake port was based on the strength of its rail connections. Although by the mid-1850s railroads emerged as interregional carriers, for the most part these lines expanded rather than competed with lake traffic.[8]

The rise of the lakes reoriented the economy of the Midwest. Reflecting the influx of settlers from New England and western New York, more and more of the regional population lived around the lakes rather than in the Ohio Valley. An ever larger portion of shipments from these states flowed east rather than south. In 1835 the volume of freight forwarded from the Midwest to New York and other eastern destinations amounted to only 5 percent of the total sent to New Orleans. By 1840 that percentage rose to almost 40 percent, and by midcentury eastbound freight surpassed shipments south. Up until 1855, these goods overwhelmingly moved on the Erie Canal, with only a few percent of the total shipped down the St. Lawrence or on the Pennsylvania canals. After 1855 east-west railroads grew in importance and, on the eve of the Civil War, accounted for over 20 percent of the greatly expanded interregional shipments. Whether goods moved in canal boats or railroad cars, the lake economy had come of age and was tied firmly to the Northeast.[9]

## II.

It was a dark and stormy day in 1813. American Commodore Oliver Hazard Perry and his fleet were stuck in the harbor of Erie, Pennsylvania. Indeed, doubly stuck: a sandbar kept Perry's newly constructed vessels from getting into the lake, and beyond that obstruction lay a British fleet waiting to attack. Fortunately for Perry, as Senator Lewis Cass recounted in 1854, the storm "drove [the British] off, and he had time to get his vessels out empty, careening them on one side to get over the bar." Cass told the story to make a point: "The expenditure of a few hundred dollars beforehand upon that harbor of Erie would have been sufficient to enable Commodore Perry's fleet to get out into the lake under any circumstances."[10]

The Great Lakes had extensive, pressing needs for government outlays, and these needs shaped the outlook of those who lived in the region. To begin with, the lakes had no natural harbors and required dredging and lengthy piers to open ports to vessels. Jacob Brinkerhoff, a Democratic congressman from northern Ohio, noted in 1844 that every river mouth was clogged by a sandbar, and it was "only by the erection of piers, cutting those sand-bars, and extending into deep water, that any harbor can be obtained, or any commerce can be carried on."[11] The process of dredging harbors and building piers was endless, a fact emphasized by opponents of lake improvements. "The truth about the Chicago harbor," Senator Robert Toombs of Georgia observed in 1858, "seems to be that if you run your pier out into the lake three hundred yards this year, you must run it out five hundred next year, and seven hundred the next year, and so on until you run it across the lake."[12] Illinois senator Stephen A. Douglas agreed with Toombs, arguing that no appropriation was ever going to complete the Chicago harbor. "Money is to be expended there each year," he remarked, "as long as it is a city, and the world lasts."[13]

Lake representatives demanded the government create "harbors of refuge" for vessels caught in the violent storms that often swept across these inland seas. Many called for the creation of these ports on the eastern shore of Lake Michigan, where there were few large cities. "For twenty years, every fall," Michigan senator Charles Stuart remarked in 1854, "I have seen scores of my fellow-citizens go to the bottom of

Lake Michigan, and hundreds of thousands of dollars worth of property sunk . . . simply because there are not proper appropriations made."[14] But the need for such harbors was evident on all the lakes. "I never was nearer losing my life than I was at the harbor of Cleveland," Lewis Cass observed. "I was driven ashore, and my salvation was a mere matter of accident. There was no harbor into which we could go."[15]

Fearing another conflict with the British, these congressmen also sought assistance in bolstering the defenses of the lakes. In the mid-1840s a clash seemed possible, as American and British leaders exchanged harsh words over Texas and Oregon. The War of 1812, which had been fought on the lakes, was still fresh in the minds of many. Lake representatives argued that better harbors were as important as forts in defending the northern border. For example, James Thompson, a Pennsylvania Democrat whose district included the port of Erie, argued that "improving the harbors on the lakes for the protection of our marine . . . was an efficient substitute for fortification."[16]

Senator Benjamin Franklin Wade of Ohio also underscored the importance of lake defenses. Wade was born in 1800 to a poor family in western Massachusetts, and his upbringing gave little hint that he would become one of the country's most powerful senators. Wade followed his older brothers to Ohio, joining them in the Western Reserve. He farmed, herded cattle, worked as a laborer, and taught school, though he had little formal education. Then in 1826, with encouragement from his family, he began to study law. His ability attracted the attention of Joshua Giddings, and in 1831 the two formed a successful partnership. Although their friendship would be short-lived, the two men shared much: strong roots in the Ohio's Western Reserve, opposition to slavery, and a commitment to the development of the lake economy.

In 1852 in his maiden Senate speech Wade emphasized the link between improving lake harbors and bolstering national defense. The occasion for his remarks was a proposal to subsidize an Atlantic steamship line. Its proponents billed the vessels "as an arm of the national defenses in times of war with England." Wade argued the money would be better spent along the exposed Northern border. He remarked, "Sir, it is of infinitely more importance to us that we build up and maintain our harbors on Lake Erie and the other lakes, which divide us from the shore of the British provinces. What should we do in case of war now, when our sailors on the lakes have to combat the elements as well as an enemy, and have no harbor—no place of safety to fly to in case of storms?"[17]

Advocates for the lakes also insisted that improvements be made at two choke points: the Falls of the St. Marys River and the St. Clair Flats. The St. Marys River, which flows past the town of Sault Ste. Marie, connects lakes Superior and Huron. "The expenses of transhipment," Michigan congressman Alexander Buel claimed, "amounted in a single instance to $1,500, independently of loss from detention of hands, which might have been saved by a canal of less than a mile in length."[18] Thanks to intense lobbying, a canal was dug around the falls in 1855. But that improvement only put more pressure on the St. Clair Flats, which were part of the waterways connecting Lake Huron and Lake Erie. In 1856 Lewis Cass noted the problems at the flats: "The channel is very narrow; so that when a vessel gets aground there is a total obstruction, and no other can pass until the first is removed."[19]

For all these reasons—the lack of natural harbors, the need for "harbors of refuge," national defense, and the obstructions at two choke points—lake representatives insistently and repeatedly demanded federal support for their region. Those requests would have serious political repercussions.


## III.


The demands of Great Lakes congressmen for government outlays led to a realignment of Northern voters. These changes were first evident in the deep fissures that emerged in the Democratic Party in the late 1840s and early 1850s. Calls for internal improvements proved less of a challenge to Whigs and Free Soilers. Whigs had long been receptive to such requests, as were the Free Soilers, who held their first convention in 1848. But Democratic orthodoxy, dating back to the 1820s when Martin Van Buren helped organize the party, celebrated small government. These policies had never been consistently implemented. But by the 1840s many Democrats, particularly in the South, rediscovered their fundamental principles and pushed them with a vengeance. That pressure put Democrats from lake districts in a tight spot. They had to reconcile the demands of their constituents for harbor improvements with their party's increasingly strident opposition to such spending.

Democrats outside the lake region grew ever more shrill in their denunciations of party members who backed federal outlays for internal improvements. Many Democrats had long mistrusted government spending but had accepted the need to assist the growing nation. In the 1840s the crescendo of requests from the lake region provided a new, powerful argument for opposing such bills. Earlier subsidies, which were devoted to ocean ports or the Mississippi Valley, seemed less avowedly sectional. Unsurprisingly, many of the loudest voices affirming Democratic orthodoxy came from the South. South Carolina senator George McDuffie was in the forefront of those attacking Democratic spendthrifts. McDuffie had a long career in politics, dating back to his election to the state legislature in 1818. Like Calhoun, he began as a nationalist and then reinvented himself as a states' rights leader. But the most dramatic change in McDuffie's life came in 1821 when he fought two duels with Colonel William Cumming, an expert shot and also an acerbic critic of McDuffie's nationalist views. McDuffie, who was braver than he was skilled in combat, received the worst in both exchanges. In the first a bullet struck near his spine; the second duel shattered his arm. Observers agreed that the injuries changed not only his bearing but his personality. He became an angry, brooding individual with an awkward gait, and he developed an odd but peculiarly captivating manner of speaking. One commentator noted: "He hesitates and stammers; he screams and bawls; he thumps and stumps like a mad man in Bedlam." South Carolinians delighted in his rhetoric and flourishes, particularly when he emerged as an advocate of nullification.[20]

McDuffie damned the legislation funding river and harbor improvements. In March 1845 he declared, "Here was a bill which combined not two, but more than two hundred different objects, not one of which could stand alone on its own merits. . . . It was neither more nor less than a combination to plunder the public treasury." McDuffie emphasized that spending on internal improvements violated Democratic principles. The Democratic Party, he intoned, "had, from the days of Gen. Jackson downward, been distinguished by its uncompromising opposition to the whole system" of internal improvements.[21]

Jefferson Davis seconded these sentiments, disowning those party members who dared support such appropriations. In spring 1846 Davis, newly married and newly arrived in Washington, established himself as an outspoken defender of the South and an opponent of outlays for the lakes. Although his stay in Washington was short (he left in the summer to serve as colonel of the First Mississippi Regiment and would return from the Mexican War a hero), he helped lead the attack on apostate Democrats and their allies. "The people have recently entrusted the Government to the hands of those who always have avowed the faith of strict construction," he declared, noting the elevation of James Polk to the presidency.[22]

Polk's vetoes of internal improvement bills in August and December 1846 delighted Davis and other Southern Democrats. Polk declared the acts sectional measures, at odds with Democratic precedents. The president's opposition to these appropriations was no surprise. Since 1825, when his Tennessee district had first sent him to Congress, Polk had railed against tariffs, internal improvements, and the national bank. His veto messages offered a pointed history lesson. "The policy of embarking the Federal Government in a general system of internal improvements had its origin but little more than twenty years ago," he noted in December 1846. "In this alarming crisis, President Jackson refused to approve and sign the Maysville road bill, the Wabash river bill, and other bills of similar character. His interposition put a check upon the new policy of throwing the cost of local improvements upon the national treasury."[23] Polk's depiction of Jackson, as critics would point out, was not wholly accurate. But Polk's statement made clear the direction in which he wanted to take the country, and lake improvements were not part of that plan.

Other Southern Democrats added a final, powerful argument against internal improvements: these outlays inevitably led to higher tariffs. Virginian Fayette McMullen put it most bluntly: "Disguise it as you may, if you take this money out of the treasury for appropriations for the rivers and harbors of the country you will have to fill up the vacuum by a tariff."[24]

Overwhelmingly, Southern Democrats toed the party line, despite their local needs and despite the funds directed to Southern rivers and harbors in the omnibus bills that Congress passed. In August 1846, for example, Southern Democrats in the House voted 43–1 to uphold Polk's veto of an internal improvements act. In February 1851 by a margin of 36–3 these partisans opposed a rivers and harbors bill that was approved by the House (and would become the basis for the 1852 act signed by Whig President Millard Fillmore).[25]

Northern Democrats who came from districts outside the lake region generally joined their Southern counterparts in condemning internal improvements. John A. McClernand, congressman from southern Illinois, typified those applauding Polk's vetoes. He lauded the "bold and patriotic stand taken by the President upon the subject of internal improvements" and declared: "All who profess to be Democrats should now prove their faith by their works."[26] New Yorker Samuel Gordon, who spoke for the farmers in the upper Hudson Valley, agreed. If improvements were needed, Gordon argued, then local rather than federal governments should fund them. "New York had made her own canals, roads, and railways," he declared. "Let other States do the same."[27] These Democrats resented appropriations that catered to one region within the North. Indiana Democrat John Robinson labeled the 1851 rivers and harbors bill "a sectional measure." Lawmakers, he observed, are called on to "vote away millions for the Atlantic and the northern lakes, but nothing for the Ohio river."[28]

Few Northern Democrats residing outside the lake districts responded more fully and thoughtfully to the changing climate of opinion within the party than Illinois lawmaker Stephen Douglas. Despite a strong commitment to the Democratic Party, Douglas backed internal improvements in the 1830s and 1840s. Douglas had flourished along with the West. As a young man of twenty he moved from Vermont to Illinois, settling in Jacksonville, a small town near Springfield. He was admitted to the bar, served in the state legislature, helped organize the Jacksonian party in the state, and in 1843 was elected to Congress. In those pioneer days both Democrats and Whigs gladly accepted assistance from all levels of government, relying on those funds (since local tax revenues were sparse) to build roads and clear rivers. When Democratic orthodoxy stiffened, Douglas at first denounced the remarks of Southerners like William Lowndes Yancey, who labeled him and other such party members "'pretended' Democrats."[29] Douglas squirmed but was not ready to abandon all support for internal improvements. In August 1846, after Polk's veto, Douglas remarked that he favored "the good old Democratic doctrine of strict construction . . . but he was not willing to rush on extremes, to deprive government of its usefulness."[30]

Gradually, Douglas soured on federal support for internal improvements as the major bills became increasingly devoted to the needs of the lakes. In 1854 he announced his change of heart to the Senate. "I came here eleven years ago," he explained, "zealous for all these appropriations, believing that I was serving my country and my own section by it, and never having fully investigated the subject. We succeeded in getting appropriations. I see the manner in which they are expended. My conviction is, that nine out of every ten has been squandered."[31]

Despite the disapproval of Southern party members and many fellow partisans in the North, most lake-district Democrats firmly supported internal improvements. They rejected the reasoning and conclusions of their critics. Given the outlook of their constituents, lake Democrats had little choice. Charles Stuart, Democratic representative from Michigan, remarked, "I tell you here to-day that the man who shall start in the State of Michigan with the declaration that he is opposed to all harbor improvements cannot get one hundred votes, however great, however popular he otherwise might be."[32]

Lake Democrats, with considerable justice, questioned the party history elaborated by the critics of internal improvements. Men such as Stuart, "Long John" Wentworth, and Lewis Cass pointed out that Jackson's vetoes of such bills were the exception, while the general's sustained support for roads, rivers, and harbors was the rule. Stuart was one of several representatives who reminded lawmakers of the high levels of spending on internal improvements under earlier Democratic administrations. The fact that Jackson topped the list of spenders underscored Stuart's point. The Michigan congressman provided this tally of appropriations:

|  |  | [Party affiliation] |
|---|---|---|
| Under Mr. Jefferson | [$]48,400 | [Dem-Repub.] |
| "    "    Madison | 250,800 | [Dem-Repub.] |
| "    "    Monroe | 707,621 | [Nonpartisan] |
| "    "    J.Q. Adams | 2,310,475 | [Nonpartisan] |

| | | | | |
|---|---|---|---|---|
| " | " | Jackson | 10,582,882 | [Democrat] |
| " | " | Van Buren | 2,222,544 | [Democrat] |
| " | " | Tyler | 1,076,500 | [Whig] |

Cass noted that in the very session when Jackson vetoed the Maysville Road, he approved other outlays for internal improvements totaling over $650,000.[33]

The lake representatives were right: the real change in Democratic policies arrived not with Jackson but with Polk. As long as the demand for spending came from a familiar mix of Atlantic ports (time-honored recipients of federal largesse), Western roads and rivers, and the occasional lake harbor, presidents from all parties were willing to spend, and most lawmakers, regardless of political allegiance, were eager to accept these funds. The rise of the lake economy, with its seemingly insatiable demands and its peculiarly regional nature, upset this familiar pattern and with it the long-standing practices of the Democratic Party.[34]

Being right about past Democratic support for internal improvements was hardly a satisfactory defense; the new realities put lake Democrats in an uncomfortable position. Other Democrats attacked them as apostates, while Whigs labeled them hypocrites. The conflicted positions taken by "Long John" Wentworth and Lewis Cass illustrate the challenges these politicians faced. Wentworth, like many lake Democrats, defended his actions by noting that he distinguished between good and bad public works. The rule, he remarked in 1846, was "to make improvements where the benefits would be 'general, and not local—national, and not State.'"[35] But separating "national" improvements from "local" ones was never easy. Georgian Robert Toombs wryly observed, "To build a road from my cotton gin house to the river, on one principle, is national, because it will help me to get my cotton to market, and make me a richer man, and as I am part of the community, it will benefit the whole nation. It is upon that logic that these appropriations are national."[36]

Whigs excoriated Wentworth for remaining a party loyalist while campaigning for internal improvements. Caleb Smith, an Indiana Whig, caustically observed, "You always vote for these [improvement] bills and then you are always sure to vote for a man for President who will veto them. How long will it take for your constituents to get their harbors completed under this system of having a Representative to vote for the bills in Congress and a President to veto them after they are passed?"[37] Wentworth resolved his dilemma only in the mid-1850s when he left the Democrats and joined the Republicans with their strong pro-development platform.

Lewis Cass, Democratic senator from Michigan, was also a man caught between his Democratic loyalties and his support for lake improvements. Cass refused to attend the 1847 Rivers and Harbors Convention and conveyed his refusal in a perfunctory note, his so-called Chicago letter. Roundly criticized by politicians from the lake districts, Cass struggled to explain his decision. "I declined to go for two reasons," he noted in 1852. "1st, because I considered such assemblages for mere local purposes worse than useless. . . . And 2d, I was satisfied then, and am still more satisfied now, that it was got up for the purpose of injuring Mr. Polk, and through him the Democratic party."[38] Cass, who was the 1848 Democratic presidential nominee, had good political reasons for affirming his loyalty to the party. Still, he sought to assure lawmakers in the lake region of his devotion to their cause. He emphasized that "while the [rivers and harbors] bill was pending before Mr. Polk for his signature, I went myself to him and tried to urge considerations to induce him to sign the bill—the 'Chicago letter' . . . to the contrary notwithstanding." Cass, who had long been part of the inner councils of the Democratic Party, was among the minority of lake representatives who remained with the party after the mid-1850s.[39]

## IV.

By the late 1840s farsighted observers could see that the pressing demands of the lakes for federal funds might reorient Northern politics. The Democratic Party was dividing over the issue. Significantly, many of the same constituencies that backed rivers and harbors bills also supported measures to check the spread of slavery. Both causes drew support from Whigs and Free Soilers in New England, and from all parties in the lake region. Western New York, particularly along the route of the Erie Canal, was strongly committed to the two issues. To be sure, the backing for antislavery and internal improvements was not identical. Democratic New Hampshire and Maine wanted to check slavery, but questioned the value of government outlays for the lakes. Whigs in the Upper South and Ohio Valley favored internal improvements but not strong measures against the slavocracy. Still the majority of representatives who favored helping the lakes also wanted limitations on slavery. And therein lay the foundations for a new, purely Northern party.

Few observers were more prescient than Duff Green, who in 1847 warned John C. Calhoun about the dangerous consequences of these developments. Green and Calhoun were old friends. Born in Kentucky, Green had fought in the War of 1812, serving under William Henry Harrison. He migrated to Missouri, where he became wealthy as a merchant, lawyer, land speculator, and stagecoach operator. In 1823 he purchased a newspaper, the *St. Louis Enquirer*, which in the election of 1824 first threw its support to Calhoun's campaign for the presidency, then Jackson's. In 1825 Green moved to Washington, where he bought another newspaper, the *United States Telegraph*, which warmly endorsed Jackson. After Jackson's election, the Democratic Congress rewarded Green for his partisanship by making him its official printer. Green's ties with Calhoun, however, remained stronger than his links to Jackson. (Their bonds were reinforced by the marriage of Calhoun's son to one of Green's daughters.) When Jackson and Calhoun quarreled, Green took Calhoun's side and as a result lost his job as government printer. Thereafter Green pursued a number of activities, including pro-Southern politics, business ventures, and on occasion international diplomacy.

In 1847 Green drew Calhoun's attention to the Northwestern Rivers and Harbors Convention planned for Chicago. "My opinion," Green remarked, "is that the deliberations of that body will do much to control the future destiny of this country." Green urged Calhoun to attend the gathering and make internal improvements a Southern issue. Green tellingly prophesied, "If the South oppose all appropriations for Harbors and Internal Improvements, the Great West will unite with the East, and carry the measures against the South. In that case Abolition and Internal Improvements go together & strengthen each other."[40] Calhoun, however, would have nothing to do with proposals to aid the lakes. Although the two men remained friends, a gap yawned between the entrepreneurially minded Green and Calhoun, the stiff-backed defender of slavery and planter society.[41]

Green's comments were prophetic: "Abolition and Internal Improvements" would be the basis for a new Northern party—one that brought together New England and the Great Lakes. Viewing Green's terms more broadly, many in the North came to share a common aversion to slavery and support for economic development. But of the two issues, economic development was unquestionably the more important. And that, it may be noted, is one of the tragedies of American history. Few Northerners, including those who became Republicans, had a deep concern for African Americans. Few believed blacks were equal to whites. Few favored abolition, except at some distant date in the future. In the early 1850s Northerners from the lakes and New England were more likely to share a commitment to the idea of a rapidly growing nation developed by free, white farmers.

## V.

Beginning in the late 1840s lake representatives and their allies in New England enunciated a nationalist ideology that reflected their self-interested goals. *Nationalism* had a very specific meaning for congressmen from the lakes. To be sure, the term conjured up the idea of policies that benefited the entire country. Henry Clay's American System had been such a program. And at first glance the new Northern ideology, with its emphasis on government activism to help grow the economy, seemed to resemble older Whig doctrines. But the two agendas were very different, reflecting the transformation of the economy between the 1820s and midcentury. Clay's program appealed to men on the make and wealthy individuals throughout the country. In its heyday the plan enjoyed the backing of townsfolk and planters in the South as well as successful farmers and merchants in the North. The nationalism that emerged at midcentury was peculiarly regional. It was the ideology of the newly ascendant Great Lakes and their New England supporters. It rested on the assumption of "What's good for the lakes is good for the country."

Democrats, as well as Whigs and Free Soilers from the lake region, spelled out this credo. Their pronouncements provided a broad justification for their campaign to secure federal money for the northern waterways. "Let gentlemen consider how many States are interested in this commerce," Democrat Robert McClelland of Michigan remarked in 1846, "and they will no longer doubt the policy of such appropriations. Some ten or twelve States are now deeply, and sometimes profitably engaged in it, and from seven to eight millions of people are benefitted by it. And what objects can, then, partake more of a national character, and what can interest more the entire Union?"[42] "Long John" Wentworth enunciated a similar, expansive vision. "I am a national man in every sense of the word, a National Democrat," he announced in 1854, "and am growing stronger and stronger in the faith every day I live. The commerce of my constituents is that of the whole nation."[43]

Other lake representatives agreed with these statements, emphasizing the equation between lake commerce and the national interest. These politicians ignored what most Southern observers considered obvious: that this lofty nationalism cloaked self-serving localism. The lake districts would not entertain such skepticism. Congressman Henry Goodwin of New York noted in 1858, "The commerce of the lakes is a national commerce."[44] Michigan senator Zachariah Chandler agreed, remarking, "If there is any work which is national, and truly national, it is the channel over the St. Clair flats."[45]

Many New Englanders affirmed the same doctrine. If nationalism represented self-interest writ large for the lake region, then it reflected enlightened self-interest for New England. By the mid-1840s internal improvement bills offered few outlays for New England. But these "eastern" states had become (along with the middle states) the center of manufacturing and banking, and what helped their customers helped them. Most New England Whigs, like Connecticut senator Truman Smith, backed the demands of the lakes. "The people of the Northwest," Smith remarked in 1852, "must stand up resolutely for their rights, and hold to a severe responsibility every man who falters in the least." Smith continued, "Can we not look over our own country—over this great Republic, and rejoice in its prosperity? And can we not believe that the prosperity of each part is the prosperity of the whole?"[46] Massachusetts senator John Davis agreed. After Lewis Cass finished a Senate speech in August 1852 on the need for a canal around the Falls of St. Marys, Davis rose to his feet. "I am rejoiced to hear the remarks of the Senator from Michigan," he stated. "He uses exactly the right word when he applies the term 'national' to the work for which the appropriation of land was made yesterday."[47] New Hampshire senator John Hale, a Free Soiler, set his support for the appropriations bill on the same broad foundation. "I will not shut up my sympathies, nor confine my action here by any such miserable consideration as might arise or . . . from the fact, that not a dollar has ever been, or probably ever will be, appropriated to the little State which I have the honor in part to represent on this floor," he remarked. "No, sir, I will remember here, however I may forget it elsewhere, that I am a citizen of the United States."[48]

Southerners rejected such nationalism in any form along with (in their minds) its synonyms "consolidation" and "centralization." To many in the South, nationalism signified an all-powerful government that might seize the West for Free Soilers or threaten slavery where it existed. Calhoun told a Charleston meeting in 1847: "Ours is a Federal, and not a National, or Consolidated Government—a distinction essential to correct understanding of the Constitution, and our safety."[49] Jefferson Davis concurred. "That such a doctrine [as abolition] ever had disciples," he observed in 1849, "is only to be accounted for by the political heresy that ours is a union of the people, the formation of a nation, and a supreme government charged with providing for the general welfare."[50] Occasionally Southerners claimed that the Mississippi and Ohio rivers were "national" waterways and worthy of federal largesse. But such references were rare. More common were the sentiments expressed by a Southern politician who longed for a new set of parties: "In our government, it seems to me, the only sensible & legitimate division of parties is by the line which separates the State rights doctrine from that of consolidation."[51]

The nationalism of the lakes was a doctrine with singular importance. It embodied the aggressive approach that the lake representatives (and their New England allies) took to economic development, and it demonstrated their eagerness to rely on the federal government. This ideology would shape the views and actions of the Republican Party that coalesced in 1856 and controlled the government after 1861.

More broadly, the rise of the Great Lakes economy had a far-reaching impact on the fabric of American politics. The new patterns of trade weakened old political allegiances. Rather than battle lines that set rich against poor in every state, regional loyalties would define politics in the 1850s. The rise of the lakes laid the foundation for a new, purely Northern party that joined together two overlapping groups: the strongest critics of slavery and the advocates of federal programs to develop the North. The new party, the Republicans, had no ties with the South and little interest in compromise. Thus the reorientation of Northern commerce made for an explosive situation as planters in the Deep South increasingly questioned the value of union—and as antislavery sentiment strengthened in the free states.

# 5

# THE CAMPAIGN
# AGAINST SLAVERY

Harrisburg did not welcome abolitionists, particularly not black ones. In August 1847 William Lloyd Garrison, the best-known white abolitionist in the country, and Frederick Douglass, the most famous African American opponent of slavery, arrived in the Pennsylvania capital. Garrison addressed a small crowd at the courthouse and then turned the stage over to Douglass. As soon as Douglass began to speak, the townsfolk milling outside hurled rotten eggs, pepper, and snuff through the open windows. "I could occasionally hear amid the tumult, fierce and bloody cries, '*throw out the n———r*, THROW OUT THE N———R,'" Douglass recounted. As the mob's rage increased, Garrison, Douglass recorded, rose and calmly announced, "Our mission to Harrisburg is ended. If there be not sufficient love of liberty, and self respect in this place, to protect the right of assembling, and the freedom of speech, he would not degrade himself by attempting to speak under such circumstances." Garrison and Douglass left

Harrisburg and traveled to the Western Reserve of Ohio, where they received a far friendlier welcome.[1]

Along with the rise of the Great Lakes economy, the campaign against slavery transformed the North, helping to end the era of compromise. Although few in number, abolitionists gradually gained a hearing for their views. By the late 1840s, despite the ill behavior exhibited in towns like Harrisburg, Northerners had become more tolerant of these reformers. Most citizens agreed they had a right to speak and petition, even if no more than 5 percent of the Northern population approved of the abolitionists' demands for an immediate end to bondage and an extension of full rights to free blacks. More numerous were the "Radicals." These individuals, such as Charles Sumner, Salmon Chase, and their supporters, urged steps to accelerate the demise of slavery but made clear that they would not disturb the "peculiar institution" where it existed. The Radicals too remained a relatively small group. At midcentury they embraced perhaps another 10 percent of the Northern citizenry. Most Northerners and both major parties disdained abolition and rejected the array of reforms that Radicals advocated.

Any consideration of antislavery agitation in the North demands a careful assessment of its strengths and weaknesses. On the one hand, during the 1830s and 1840s the movement grew in both size and influence. In particular areas—such as the Western Reserve of Ohio and northern New England—reformers became a powerful force. On the other hand, the limitations of militant antislavery must be underscored. Before the mid-1850s antislavery parties fared poorly, while racism remained pervasive. Northerners condemned forced labor and opposed its spread, but their votes did not reflect those views. Piecing together this picture helps explain why antislavery remained a secondary concern and economics was primary in the formation of a strong Northern party in the 1850s.

## I.

Even though only a small group fully supported their goals, abolition-ists had a far-reaching impact on the North. The most important antislav-ery crusader was a slight, bespectacled newspaper editor, William Lloyd Garrison. Born in Newburyport, Massachusetts, Garrison was the child of a pious Baptist mother and an alcoholic father who abandoned his wife and four children. At age thirteen William was apprenticed to a local printer. He was also a scrapper and a proud member of the South-end Boys, joining them in their regular clashes with the rival North-enders. By his teenage years his course seemed set. He would pursue printing, and guided by his religious faith, he would speak out against injustice, including the intemperance that led his father to ruin. He would also remain a scrapper, not cowed by seemingly invincible foes.

After serving brief stints as editor of several reform publications, Garrison on January 1, 1831, founded his own abolitionist paper, *The Liberator*. "I *will be* as harsh as truth, and as uncompromising as justice," the twenty-five-year-old editor thundered in the first issue. "On this subject [abolition] I do not wish to think, or speak, or write, with moderation."[2] What Garrison introduced to his Boston newspaper and to the movement against slavery was the demand for immediate aboli-tion. While denunciations of bondage predated the American Revolu-tion, earlier advocates viewed emancipation as a distant goal. Garrison rejected such moderation as well as colonization, the campaign to send freed African Americans "back" to Africa or to another location outside the United States. Garrison also labored to secure equal rights for free blacks. Typically the leaders of the movement to end slavery in the South spearheaded the fight against discrimination in the North.[3]

Garrison, like most abolitionists, was a proselytizer, determined to convert others to the doctrine of immediate abolitionism. In January

1832 he helped found the New-England Anti-Slavery Society, and the following year he traveled to Philadelphia, where a group of sixty-two abolitionists, including four women and four black men, established the American Anti-Slavery Society. Along with Garrison's New England circle, the most important people in the national organization were the New Yorkers, led by two brothers, Arthur and Lewis Tappan. Born to a devout Calvinist family in western Massachusetts, the Tappans had become wealthy Manhattan dry goods merchants and committed evangelical reformers. Before focusing their attention on slavery, they had labored for a broad range of causes, including temperance, the American Bible Society, and colonization. Persuaded by Garrison, among others, the Tappans abandoned colonization and devoted their abundant energies and resources to promoting immediate abolition.[4]

The American Anti-Slavery Society launched its campaign to change minds, North and South, with three initiatives: public speeches, mass mailings, and petitions. Addresses to local groups proved the most effective method for winning converts. Garrison spoke in nearby churches and meetinghouses, while speakers, supported by the national organization, carried the same message to a wider audience. The Tappans helped support Theodore Dwight Weld, a convert to abolition and a powerful orator who in the 1820s had worked closely with the great revivalist Charles Grandison Finney. Weld first won over the students at Cincinnati's Lane Seminary, where he was studying. Then in 1834, 1835, and 1836 he went from town to town in eastern Ohio, western New York, and western Pennsylvania, making the case for immediate emancipation. Many of the "Lane Rebels" (as his fellow students were now called) undertook similar campaigns. In 1836 the national society recruited the Seventy, a cadre of young reform-minded men typically drawn from Northern seminaries. The group, whose task was to broadcast the antislavery message, was named after the seventy disciples chosen to convey Christ's gospel. Weld coached them in New York during three weeks of twelve-hour days. They learned the economics, history, and philosophy of slavery and listened to African American speakers who related "truly affecting" accounts of slavery and prejudice. Once prepared, the Seventy fanned out across the North, campaigning in New England, Pennsylvania, New York, Ohio, Indiana, and Michigan.[5]

It is hard to overstate the hostility these speakers encountered in the 1830s or, as they persisted, the success they had. Violence was not limited to any one region; mobs were nearly as common in New England or upstate New York as in the Midwestern districts where Southerners had settled. In October 1835 angry citizens accosted Garrison in Boston, put a rope around his neck, and dragged him through the streets. In virtually every town Weld visited, as his journal makes clear, he encountered hostile crowds. Typically, his visit to Zanesville, Ohio, did not begin well. "Zanesville was locked up," he recorded. "Could get no place to lecture, not a shanty even. Putnam, on the other side of the river, was a little better, and I could get *one* public room. Lectured. A mob from Zanesville came, broke the windows, doors, tore off the gate, and attacked me, when I came out, with stones and clubs. This continued until the trustees of the room shut it up. Then adjourned to a private room. In short every kind of outrage was committed."

But in Zanesville, as in almost every town he visited, Weld refused to be intimidated and persisted until he triumphed. He preached night after night in Putnam, and the citizenry, impressed by his courage and conviction, curious to hear what he was so determined to share with them, began coming to his meetings. He was invited to move his lectures back to Zanesville from Putnam, and when on the last (and sixteenth) night he asked, as he always did, for those converted to immediate abolition to rise, hundreds did. He moved on to the next town, and the next mob, leaving the newly converted to build the local chapter of the American Anti-Slavery Society.[6]

The result was a remarkable growth in antislavery organizations and in the number of abolitionists. The figures collected by the American Anti-Slavery Society give an approximation of this growth. The total number of local and state antislavery organizations grew from perhaps 200 in mid-1835, to 1,000 by 1836, to more than 1,300 in 1838. By 1840 these societies had about 250,000 members. These organizations were not uniformly distributed. Outside of New England, areas of Yankee settlement provided the most fertile soil. A New Yorker remarked, "Wherever the New Englanders, either in the old States or new States are settled, there Abolitionism in some form or other takes root."[7] In New York, which had the largest number of societies, abolitionists were concentrated in the "burned over district." These were the western counties, usually near the Erie Canal, where Yankee settlement was most prominent and the fires of revivalism had burned the brightest. Ohio's Western Reserve, another area populated by New Englanders, boasted many antislavery societies. Massachusetts and Vermont stood forth as leaders in New England. In New England, where the Congregational church was often a conservative institution, two-thirds of abolitionists were either Methodists or Baptists.[8]

The second initiative was the postal campaign, launched by the American Anti-Slavery Society in 1835. The goal was "to sow the good seed of abolition thoroughly over the whole country." While public speaking was limited to the North and the petition campaign focused on Congress, these mailings were directed to clergy, editors, and elected officials in both the North and the South. Antislavery societies placed more than twenty thousand Southerners on their mailing lists and distributed more than a million pamphlets and speeches. But hopes of converting slaveholders were quickly dashed. Southerners responded with anger and violence: mobs in South Carolina burned sacks of mail and hanged Garrison and Arthur Tappan in effigy. Jackson's postmaster general, Amos Kendall, a Kentucky slaveholder, let Southern postmasters know they could refuse to deliver the abolitionist tracts. "We owe an obligation to the laws," Kendall remarked, "but a higher one to the communities in which we live."[9]

While mailings continued in the North, Southern postmasters and lawmakers ended the influx of these tracts in 1836.

Abolitionists undertook a third tactic: a massive petition campaign. The memorials sent to Congress dealt with areas where the federal government plausibly had jurisdiction. Most of these documents focused on slavery in the District of Columbia, but some discussed abolition in Florida (which was still a territory), the interstate slave trade, and the three-fifths compromise, which was enshrined in the Constitution. Before this campaign began in 1833 Congress had received no more than a few dozen antislavery memorials in any year. But by 1836 more than 30,000 petitions were sent, and by 1838 well over 400,000 had been forwarded to Washington. In May 1836 Congress adopted a gag rule, which made certain the petitions would be tabled and not considered.[10]

The abolitionist movement was further strengthened in its early years by the involvement of women, although their participation was the source of bitter controversy. Female antislavery societies had emerged alongside the male organizations, a development encouraged by the American Anti-Slavery Society, which "respectfully and earnestly invited the ladies of the land" to form separate organizations. The activities of the Female Societies, however, were sharply circumscribed. Women could help raise money with sewing bees and fairs; they could discuss tracts among themselves and listen attentively to male lecturers. But they were not to be speakers nor to direct activities properly left to men. Many women, as letters to *The Liberator* revealed, found themselves pressed to defend even those limited roles. Increasingly the Cult of True Womanhood, which dictated that a woman's place was in the home, shaped the views of middle-class Americans.[11]

Abigail Kelley's career is a good illustration of the importance of women to the abolitionist movement—and the impact that that movement had on women. Kelley was born into a Quaker farm family in western Massachusetts in 1811. Trained to be a schoolteacher, she moved to the shoemaking town of Lynn in 1835 to instruct in a Quaker academy. Soon after settling in, she joined the recently founded Lynn Female Anti-Slavery Society. Many of the other members were also Quakers, a sect that had long testified against slaveholding. In summer 1836 Boston women proposed that female antislavery societies be allowed to circulate petitions. When this suggestion was approved, Kelley agreed to take the memorials door to door in Lynn. An attractive woman, dressed in Quaker gray, Kelley showed considerable courage encountering angry homeowners. People said to her, "I hope you get a nigger husband," and men reproached her, "Women are meddling with that that's none of their business." She persisted, carrying about her pen and inkhorn, and in 1836 sent Boston four memorials with nearly fifteen hundred signatures. Almost half the women in Lynn had put their names to one of these documents.[12]

Once brought into the abolitionist movement, Kelley, like many other women, refused to play a limited role. She attended the national meetings of antislavery women in 1837 and 1838, experiencing both the comradeship of other reformers and the hostility of the local populace. (After the 1838 Philadelphia convention ended, a mob burned down the building.) Kelley was also inspired by the public speaking of Angelina Grimké. Angelina and her sister Sarah had left their privileged life in Charleston, South Carolina, because of their dislike of slavery, and had joined the female antislavery movement in the North. Angelina spoke, as was permitted, to women's groups but soon found that men also wanted to hear her—and to the consternation of many, she broke down gender barriers in a series of public addresses. When Angelina came to Lynn, Kelley introduced her, and in those introductory remarks urged other women to overcome the "diffidence" that kept them "from coming forward and communicating thoughts unreservedly." In 1838, after vigorous debate, the New England Anti-Slavery Society accepted Kelley and sixty-four other women as full members. That same year Kelley made a momentous decision: she would give up teaching and become a public lecturer like Angelina Grimké. In 1840 Kelley was nominated along with Garrison and Lewis Tappan to the executive committee of the American Anti-Slavery Society. Garrison enthusiastically supported this move, but the Tappans and other New Yorkers did not. And after the convention voted 557–451 in favor of Kelley's nomination, the dissidents marched out and founded their own organization, the American and Foreign Anti-Slavery Society.[13]

Remarkably, the split in the national society in 1840 was a sign of strength: the abolitionist movement had become too broad and diverse to be governed by any one leader or organization. Garrison and the American Anti-Slavery Society remained important, but many abolitionists took exception to some or many of Garrison's strongly held principles: his encouragement of women; his opposition to political action; his calls for cutting ties with the sinful, slaveholding South (he put "No Union with Slaveholders!" on the masthead of *The Liberator*); and his emphasis on nonviolence. Despite the split, most of the activities begun in the 1830s continued and expanded. Garrison, for example, regularly gave public talks, as did an increasing number of women, and more and more African Americans. Among the former slaves who lectured during these years were William Wells Brown, Henry Highland Garnet, Sojourner Truth, and Frederick Douglass. While the actions of Southern postmasters discouraged mass mailings, abolitionists continued to circulate petitions and denounce the congressional ban on these memorials. In fact, Theodore Dwight Weld (who married Angelina Grimké in 1838) served as an assistant to John Quincy Adams in the early 1840s and helped him win the battle to end the gag rule.[14]

The lectures, petitions, mailings, and other abolitionist campaigns had an unmistakable impact on Northern opinion. In many locales, crowds demanding the release of a captured slave became more common than those attacking reformers. In 1842 enraged citizens forced

Boston authorities to free a jailed fugitive, and later that year Massachusetts adopted a "personal liberty law," declaring that state authorities would give the federal government no assistance in capturing fugitives. By 1847 Vermont, Ohio, Connecticut, and Pennsylvania had passed similar statutes. On particular issues abolitionists enjoyed broad support. Most Northerners concurred with reformers that petitions should be heard and mail delivered, even if the content criticized slavery. And gradually abolitionist lecturers became more welcome visitors. Hostility never ceased in some parts of the North, but other regions were "abolitionized." Local congressmen, whether Whig or Democrat, had at least to pay lip service to antislavery sentiments in order to be reelected.[15]

Perhaps the most acute observations about the growth of antislavery came from those with the most to lose from these developments. Southerners registered shock at the spread of abolitionism. "Whilst this warfare upon our institutions was confined to the few fanatical madmen with whom it originated, the people of the South looked upon it with feelings of contempt only," noted South Carolina congressman Daniel Wallace in 1848. "But it cannot be longer disguised, that the association and union which this fanatical spirit has formed with the political parties of the North, has placed the whole matter before us in a much more imposing attitude."[16] Representative Alfred Iverson of Georgia was equally upset: "We have witnessed the steady and rapid march of the foul fiend of abolitionism, until it is already in sight of our very threshold. Where will it stop? Who can say that it will not enter?"[17]

The most significant departure for abolitionists in the 1840s was their entry into electoral politics. Gerrit Smith, the wealthiest abolitionist in the nation and the only one who would be elected to Congress, was in the forefront of this campaign. A remarkable inheritance shaped Gerrit Smith's life. His father, Peter Smith, was a land baron who accumulated holdings of nearly one million acres in upstate New

York. In 1819, when Gerrit was twenty-two, his father decided to re-
tire and asked Gerrit to manage the estate. The request came as a
shock to Gerrit—a young man who drank, adored the poetry of Lord
Byron, and imagined that a literary career lay ahead of him. "With
feelings of great reluctance," he accepted his father's request. Gerrit
would prove surprisingly adept at overseeing and expanding his inheritance. At the same time, encouraged by his devout wife and local reformers, he underwent a spiritual transformation that changed him
from a self-indulgent young man into a pious adult and eventually a
committed reformer. By 1827 he had joined the Presbyterian church,
quit drinking, sold off the distilleries he owned, and taken his first step
toward reform by supporting the American Temperance Society and
the American Colonization Society. His spiritual journey, however,
had only begun. By the mid-1830s he had become more interested in
millennial religion, abandoned temperance for total abstention, and
moved from colonization to immediate abolition.

Unlike Garrison, Smith believed that politics could be a proper vehicle for reform, and in 1840 he helped found the Liberty Party. Dedicated to ending slavery, the party attracted only 7,000 votes for its
presidential candidate, James G. Birney, but it did better in the 1843
congressional vote. In the 1844 presidential contest Birney garnered
almost 66,000 votes, or just over 3 percent of the total cast in the
North. The Liberty Party demanded not only the immediate "overthrow of Slavery" but also the removal of "any inequality of rights
and privileges . . . on account of color" in the North.[18] The party
drew its votes largely from a far-flung Yankee constituency. Its strength
lay in northern New England and in the areas of Yankee settlement in
the West, including western New York, the Western Reserve in Ohio,
scattered Michigan districts, and the northern tier counties in Illinois.
Another pocket of votes came from Indiana's Whitewater Valley, an
area of Quaker settlement.[19]

Smith's militancy only intensified in the late 1840s, leading him down pathways where most abolitionists dared not tread. Unlike most antislavery crusaders, Smith rejected the Free Soil Party, which superseded the more radical Liberty Party in 1848; he formed a new group, the National Liberty Party, to carry on the campaign for immediate emancipation and black civil rights. His splinter group garnered only a few thousand votes in the 1848 and 1852 elections. He also ran for Congress from his New York district, where he was respected as a reformer and wealthy landowner, even by those who questioned his views on slavery. He won, becoming in 1853 the only abolitionist to serve in the national legislature. Smith did not last long in the hurly-burly of Washington, resigning before his term was over. He viewed politics, however, as only one means of achieving his goals. Unlike Garrison's followers, Smith believed in righteous violence. In 1851 he broke into a Syracuse police station and helped free an escaped slave, Jerry McHenry, who would have been sent back to the South. He financed free-state guerrillas in Kansas and was one of the "Secret Six" supporting John Brown's raid on Harpers Ferry. He also used his wealth to purchase freedom for several slaves, setting aside 120,000 acres of his land in the Adirondacks to provide homesteads for poor New York blacks.[20]

The abolitionist movement, which hewed more to religious perfectionism than to Smith's strain of violence, had by midcentury grown dramatically in numbers and influence. Still, the dimensions of this crusade must be kept in perspective. The several hundred thousand members of the abolitionist societies comprised only a small percentage of a Northern population that exceeded fourteen million in 1850, and many in these societies were blacks and women who were barred from voting. There is no reason to dispute the conclusions of South Carolinian John Calhoun, who remarked in 1847: "The Abolitionists proper—the rabid fanatics . . . constitute one class. It is a small one, not probably exceeding five per cent of the population of those States."[21] To be sure, they made a crucial contribution to the dialogue over slavery and discrimination. But they were not a major factor in the downfall of the Whigs and Democrats and the formation of a new party system in the North.


## II.


More numerous, influential, and likely to hold office than the abolitionists were the Radicals, militant antislavery reformers who took the "sensible" position of renouncing immediate emancipation. Their ranks included senators, congressmen, and governors. Yet despite the prominence of particular leaders, the Radicals too remained a small minority within the North.

Charles Sumner, who served as senator from Massachusetts from 1851 until his death in 1874, was the best-known Radical. Fervent convictions and a passion for ideas, rather than religious beliefs, drove Sumner. Sumner was loosely connected with the Unitarian Church but confessed that he was "without religious feeling." Rather he was an intellectual strongly committed to carefully elaborated principles. Born in 1811, Sumner was a tall, awkward, bookish child who surprised his father by learning Latin when he was ten. As an adult he retained some of those traits. He was uncomfortable with small talk and had little sense of humor. A strikingly handsome man, who caught the eye of several women, Sumner was nonetheless ill at ease in their company and remained a bachelor until late in life. But he charmed his friends, who delighted in his erudition and keen mind.

Graduating from Harvard Law School with a distinguished record, Sumner seemed to be on track to become a leading member of the Massachusetts bar as well as a pillar of the Whig establishment that ran Boston and the state. But he was bored by the duties of a lawyer. "Though I earn my daily bread," he observed, "I lay up none of the bread of life." Nor did local politics interest Sumner. While he de-

scribed himself as a "silent and passive Whig," he had no burning political ambitions.[22]

His life changed in 1845 with his newfound public commitment
to antislavery. The annexation of Texas, which dramatically expanded
the area open to forced labor, galvanized him to action. Sumner, like
most Massachusetts Whigs, disapproved of slavery, but before 1845 he
had never expressed those sentiments publicly. An anti-annexation
meeting in January stirred him, ending his years of quiescence and
giving focus to his powerful intellect. Sumner broadcast his convictions when he delivered Boston's 1845 Fourth of July address, condemning all wars and particularly the prospect of a clash with Mexico.
Sumner warned, "By an act of unjust legislation, extending our
power over Texas, peace with Mexico is endangered."[23] The address
upset Boston's Whig establishment, which hitherto had considered
Sumner as one of its own. Whigs like Massachusetts senator Daniel
Webster and Boston representative Robert C. Winthrop walked a fine
line. They often denounced slavery, but they also remained party loyalists and were careful not to anger either the conservative merchant
community or Southern Whigs. In a dinner that followed Sumner's
address, Winthrop rebuked the young lawyer.[24]

In response, Sumner broadened his attack and reached out to new
allies, helping to realign Bay State parties. Caustically noting the
hypocrisy of the leading Massachusetts Whigs, he told Winthrop that
the congressman's silence on Texas was "so strangely inconsistent
with your recent avowal of 'uncompromising hostility to all measures
for introducing new Slave States and new Slave Territories into our
Union.' "[25]

By 1848 Sumner had turned his sights on a larger target: the
Yankee upper class, with its deep involvement in cotton manufacturing and its strong ties to the South. The Whig nomination of Zachary
Taylor for president, Sumner noted, "was brought about by an unhal-
lowed union—conspiracy let it be called—between two remote sec-

tions: between the politicians of the Southwest and the politicians of the Northeast,—between the cotton-planters and flesh mongers of Louisiana and Mississippi and the cotton spinners and traffickers of New England,—between the lords of the lash and the lords of the loom."[26] Sumner's rhetoric may have been excessive and his charge of conspiracy overblown, but his contention that wealthy New Englanders favored the South and opposed the antislavery crusade had much substance. The upper classes of Boston, New York, and Philadelphia were indeed reluctant to jeopardize their ties with the planters.[27]

Sumner drew closer to a group that first was called the "Young Whigs" but increasingly was referred to as the "Conscience Whigs," in distinction to their opponents, the "Cotton Whigs." This coterie included individuals such as Charles Francis Adams, who was the son and grandson of presidents, and Henry Wilson, an able politician who had begun his career humbly as a farm laborer and shoemaker. Sumner also found a broad base of support for his position among the residents of the rural areas and small towns of Massachusetts.[28]

Paralleling efforts in other states, Sumner helped establish the Free Soil Party in Massachusetts. In 1848 the party ran a national ticket, headed by Martin Van Buren and Charles Francis Adams. The party platform emphasized the nonextension of slavery but also advocated river and harbor improvements and a homestead act. However, Sumner, like many Radicals, passed lightly over economic questions, considering them secondary to the crusade against the "Slave Power." On key issues, the party platform was more moderate than that of the Liberty Party. Free Soilers eschewed abolition, declaring "we . . . propose no interference by Congress with Slavery within the limits of any State," and they did not mention equal rights for free blacks.[29]

Despite its moderation, the Free Soil Party achieved only modest success. The 14.5 percent of the Northern vote it received lagged far behind the totals for the Whigs and Democrats, but represented a notable advance beyond the 3.4 percent that the Liberty Party garnered in 1844. Much to Sumner's delight, the Free Soilers fared best in Massachusetts and the neighboring state of Vermont; in both states they received about 29 percent of the vote and ran second to the Whigs. While the Free Soil vote fell off everywhere in the 1850 congressional elections and in the 1852 presidential contest, the new party remained a force to be reckoned with, particularly in closely divided state elections. In Massachusetts Henry Wilson, working with the Democrats, brokered a deal that made Sumner senator in 1851. Free Soilers helped the Democrats elect a governor and organize the legislature, and in return Democratic lawmakers sent Sumner to Washington.[30]

Salmon Chase was Sumner's counterpart in Ohio. In one important respect—the role of religion—Chase rather than Sumner typified the Northerners who applauded the Radical attack on slavery. To be sure, Chase never asserted (like Garrison) that he was following in Christ's footsteps; nor did he (like Gerrit Smith) espouse millennialism. But he taught Sunday school, read the Bible every day, and like thousands of reform-minded Yankees who settled in the West was profoundly affected by the revivals of the Second Great Awakening. Chase was born in 1808 in Cornish, New Hampshire, to a comfortable family that fell on hard times. When he was twelve, he was sent for a year to live with his uncle, Philander Chase, who was the Episcopal bishop of Ohio. Chase's spiritual education continued after he returned to New Hampshire and entered Dartmouth College. He was caught up in the wave of revivalism that swept through the college and the nearby community of Hanover. Not every Yankee who sang hosannas became a reformer, but the compounding of revivalism with New England traditions created a potent amalgam: individuals left revival meetings acutely aware of the need to perfect the world and help other men and women.[31]

Despite his religious awakening, Chase only gradually assumed the mantle of leadership in the antislavery movement. After college he went to Washington, where another uncle, Dudley Chase, was a U.S.

senator from Vermont. After briefly teaching school in the capital, Salmon decided to become a lawyer and studied in the office of William Wirt, attorney general under John Quincy Adams. Already Chase's antislavery leanings were evident; he helped a Quaker mechanic draw up a petition (which would be widely circulated) for the abolition of slavery in the District of Columbia. In 1830 the twenty-two-year-old lawyer went to Cincinnati to seek his fortune. He included abolitionists as well as affluent businessmen in his circle of friends, but during his first years in the Queen City he focused on building his practice. Then in 1835 his life changed when he was caught up in the middle of an anti-abolitionist riot. Chase intervened when a crowd pursued the outspoken Kentucky-born reformer James Birney.

Six feet two inches tall and large-boned, Chase stood in the doorway of the Franklin House (where many thought Birney was staying) and would not let the rioters pass. One of the crowd asked who he was. "Salmon P. Chase" was the firm reply. A grateful Birney soon called on Chase to help in the defense of fugitive slaves, and the young lawyer agreed. Taking on a series of high-profile cases defending fugitives and those who harbored them, the deeply ambitious Chase did more than combat slavery: he made his name known nationally.[32]

In the 1840s Chase joined the Liberty Party to moderate its doctrines, make it a national party, and not incidentally provide himself with a springboard to higher office. While opposing immediate emancipation, he urged a broad set of measures: "Abolish Slavery in the District [of Columbia], on the seas, in all places of exclusive national jurisdiction—employ no Slaves on public works—give a clear preference to anti slavery men in public appointments." Chase's approach did not sit well with many of the Eastern Liberty Party men who demanded abolition rather than simply limitations on slavery. But it fairly reflected the more moderate nature of the antislavery crusade in the West. Chase also hoped, perhaps naïvely, that these doctrines could be the basis for reforming the Democratic Party. As a young man, Chase had supported the Whigs, but he gradually shifted his sympathies. He now regarded the Democratic attack on the Money Power as a crucial complement to the war against the Slave Power.[33]

The success of the Ohio Free Soil Party, which Chase joined soon after its formation in 1848, made possible his elevation to the U.S. Senate. The party, with its eight representatives in a lower house of about seventy members, held the balance of power between the Whigs and Democrats. The deal that Chase struck with Ohio's Democrats in 1849 was similar to the one that Wilson and Sumner concluded in Massachusetts. The Free Soilers allowed the Democrats to organize the legislature in return for Chase's elevation to the Senate. In addition, Chase demanded that the Democrats join in the repeal of the most objectionable of the Black Laws. The acts in question restricted the entry of blacks into the state, prohibited them from testifying against whites in court, and prevented the state from funding African American schools, including segregated ones.

The deal was fraught with tension. Most Free Soilers hailed from the Western Reserve (far removed from Chase's home in southern Ohio) and had Whiggish leanings. Many of the Democrats came from Southern families and held profoundly racist views. "My location is unacceptable to some of the Free Soilers, all of whom are from the Reserve," Chase explained to his wife, "and my political position is unacceptable to many of the Democrats, who, naturally enough, prefer a man acting fully with themselves. Still as neither can elect alone, and as I am perhaps more acceptable to both though not to each, than any other individual, I may be elected." Chase succeeded, but Whigs both inside Ohio and out resented his maneuvers.[34]

While Sumner and Chase were genuine antislavery Radicals, New York's Martin Van Buren was not. Even though Van Buren was the Free Soil candidate for president in 1848, his actions before, during, and after the campaign undercut his commitment to the cause. If there was any consistency in the behavior of the wily New Yorker before the mid-1840s, it lay in his dedication to Democratic ideals of small government and his determination to preserve the New York–Virginia axis that lay at the heart of the Jacksonian party. Repeatedly, the "Little Magician" had affirmed pro-Southern policies. He opposed the campaign to grant freedom to the mutinous slaves on the *Amistad*; he upheld the ban on the delivery of "incendiary" pamphlets in the South; he denounced John Quincy Adams's efforts to end the gag rule on abolitionist petitions; and he resisted emancipation in the District of Columbia.[35]

Critics suggested with some validity that Van Buren cast his lot with Free Soilers in 1848 not from any belief in their cause but out of anger at the Democratic politicians who had denied him the presidential nomination in 1844 and who had refused patronage appointments to his New York faction, the Barnburners. Many abolitionists and Radicals questioned the decision to place Van Buren at the head of the new party. Van Buren's acceptance of slavery in D.C. was particularly galling. Chase remarked, "Mr. Van Buren has some sins to answer for, which will greatly affect his reception as a Candidate among antislavery men."[36] Still both Sumner and Chase, along with most other Radicals, campaigned for Van Buren. As Sumner noted, "His name gives our movement a national character."[37]

Van Buren's behavior after the election only confirmed the suspicions that many antislavery activists had about his true colors. Just weeks after the vote the leaders of Van Buren's faction, the Barnburners, sought reconciliation with their opponents, the Hunkers, and an accord was reached by 1849. Van Buren also soon ended his flirtation with Free Soil. He backed Franklin Pierce, the Southern-leaning Democratic candidate, in 1852, and despite pleas from Republicans, he remained a loyal Democrat until his death in 1862.[38]

The New Yorker's place at the head of a Free Soil ticket had a far-reaching impact on support for the new party. His presence undercut the platform, which declared that river and harbor improvements were "objects of *national concern.*" A party led by Van Buren was unlikely to use the central government to encourage growth. The great electoral strength of the Republican Party, which was in some respects the successor to the Free Soil Party, came from its ability to join antislavery militants with economic nationalists determined to foster Northern development. As a long-term Jacksonian Democrat, Van Buren made such an alliance unlikely. The decision of the party in 1852 to nominate John Hale, another former Democrat, only confirmed this perception.[39]

Van Buren also attracted an exceptional number of Democratic votes, particularly in New York, suggesting that antislavery sentiment was weaker in 1848 than the balloting might indicate. Van Buren's total of 14.5 percent of the Northern vote was the high-water mark for any antislavery party before 1856. However, fully 123,000 (or 42 percent) of his total of 290,000 votes came from New York. Most of these New Yorkers were Van Burenites rather than true Free Soilers, and their support melted away soon after the election. In no state did support for the third party plummet more rapidly between 1848 and 1852 than in New York. Free Soil candidate John Hale received only 25,000 New York votes in 1852, a decline of 80 percent, while in most states the falling-off was less than 33 percent. If the New York vote is adjusted (using the 1852 returns as a benchmark), a truer picture of Free Soil strength in 1848 might have been 10 percent of the Northern ballot.

The weakness of antislavery forces is also suggested by the limited number of Radicals elected. Before 1854 Northern legislatures anointed only four Radical senators—Sumner, Chase, John Hale of New Hampshire, and Benjamin Wade of Ohio—out of thirty possible seats. In each case these elections reflected the astute bargaining of a Free Soil minority that held the balance of power. Senators William Seward of New York and Hannibal Hamlin of Maine were kindred spirits, but their dedication to the cause was less than absolute. Seward's fiery speeches earned him the reputation of an antislavery zealot. But he remained a staunch Whig, condemned third parties (before joining the Republicans), and muted his views so he could influence President Taylor. Hamlin remained even more moderate than Chase and Sumner. He did not support the Free Soil Party and stayed a Democrat until the Kansas-Nebraska Act in 1854. Only about a dozen representatives espoused strong antislavery views. That group included Joshua Giddings; Gerrit Smith (for part of a term); George Julian of Indiana; and about nine or ten others—out of a total of 139 seats from the free states. These representatives came from northern New England, Western districts where Yankees predominated, and some of the Quaker settlements.[40]

In sum, voting returns and the success of antislavery candidates make clear that militant opponents of slavery did not comprise much over 15 percent of the Northern population. This percentage, to be sure, was much higher in Greater New England, where often more than a fourth of voters applauded the antislavery program. But it stood lower in states such as New Jersey, Pennsylvania, Indiana, and Illinois. Three out of twenty voters comprises a significant minority, but that bloc by itself could never become the majority party in the North or elect a president. Nor did this Radical group set the tone for racial politics in the North.

## III.

"The American people are emphatically a *negro-hating* people," remarked Indiana congressman George Julian. "By their actions, politically, socially, and ecclesiastically, they declare that 'the negro is not a man.'"[41] Overwhelmingly, white Northerners felt that blacks were inferior and not deserving of equal treatment. The pervasiveness of racism provides a crucial context for analysis of the antislavery movement.

Suffrage laws were one indication of Northern attitudes. In most states of the Northwest and Far West, African American suffrage was simply not an issue; whites agreed that blacks were not entitled to take part in politics. In Indiana the 1850 state constitutional convention rejected a clause enfranchising blacks, 122 to 1. The issue was more hotly contested in Wisconsin, where the Free Soil Party, reflecting the views of New England settlers, endorsed suffrage. In an 1847 referendum 34 percent of voters backed suffrage, and in a poll held in 1849 a majority of those voting favored enfranchising blacks. But the turnout for this suffrage initiative was low, falling below the threshold set by the Board of Canvassers, and so the measure failed.[42]

In several of the Eastern states Jacksonian democracy disenfranchised blacks. In Pennsylvania, where previously some African Americans had voted, Democrats at the 1837 state constitutional convention sought a total prohibition. They achieved this goal despite the best efforts of Thaddeus Stevens, the sharp-tongued lawmaker from Gettysburg, who stood out at the convention for both his appearance and his vehemence. Stevens, crippled with clubfoot and sporting a red wig that covered up his bald head, vigorously opposed disenfranchisement. However, Stevens gained the support of only a portion of the Whigs, and the convention adopted the ban on black suffrage, 77 to 44.[43]

Other Eastern states also restricted African American voting. New Jersey and Connecticut barred blacks from the polls, while New York limited their participation. In New York a state convention in 1821 and laws adopted five years later opened suffrage to virtually all white males but excluded blacks with estates worth less than $250. New York held a referendum in 1846 to end this property qualification and give all blacks the vote. Upstate Whigs, including Seward and Thurlow Weed; Liberty Party advocates; and many future Free Soilers supported the cause, although the circle around Van Buren did not. In a vote that reflected both party and patterns of Yankee settlement, the pro-suffrage side garnered only 28 percent of the total. Only the states of northern

New England granted the vote to all black males. In 1842 Rhode Island joined Massachusetts, Vermont, New Hampshire, and Maine in enfranchising African Americans. These states, however, accounted for only 8 percent of Northern blacks.[44]

Voting was not the only legal restriction on African Americans. Ohio, Illinois, Indiana, and Oregon banned the immigration of blacks. These laws were never consistently enforced, but their presence was a chilling reminder of the views of the white community. Illinois, Ohio, Indiana, Iowa, and California forbade blacks from testifying in court against whites. Everywhere outside of Massachusetts blacks were excluded from juries, and they gained that right in the Bay State only in 1860. Laws, customs, and court decisions kept black schooling (outside of New England) segregated and badly underfunded or simply nonexistent.[45]

Oppression of free blacks went beyond the bounds of any statute. Insults were common. Trains, steamships, and omnibuses as well as hospitals, theaters, churches, and cemeteries segregated African Americans. Mob violence was endemic in the larger cities. In 1829 angry whites attacked the black quarters in Cincinnati, demanding the enforcement of the laws restricting immigration. In response, about half the African American community, perhaps 2,000 people, fled to Canada. Vigilantes filled the streets of Cincinnati again in 1841, while Philadelphia experienced five antiblack riots between 1832 and 1849. New York City and several smaller centers were the sites of similar actions. Blacks also faced discrimination in the workplace and typically were relegated to menial jobs. The influx of Irish immigrants after 1845 only intensified the competition at the bottom of the ladder. Jobs that blacks had traditionally held, such as barber and servant, now were frequently filled by poor whites.[46]

Only in Massachusetts (and to a lesser degree other New England states) was any progress recorded. There antislavery militants emphasized the hypocrisy of fighting slavery while oppressing free blacks. In

1849 Sumner concluded his legal brief for integrating Boston schools by stating, "Slavery, in one of its enormities, is now before you for judgment. Hesitate not, I pray you, to strike it down."[47] Such appeals succeeded. The legislature ended the ban on mixed marriages in 1843, pressured railroads during the 1840s to end segregation, and integrated Boston schools in 1855. Many hotels and restaurants continued to discriminate, but progress was unmistakable. Still, if northern New England was an island of hope for Northern blacks, it was a sparsely populated one. In 1850 the states of Massachusetts, Rhode Island, Vermont, New Hampshire, and Maine were home to only 16,000 blacks out of the total of 200,000 in the North. Over 90 percent of African Americans in the North lived in states where deep-rooted racism created an oppressive society.[48]

## IV.

The pervasiveness of racism, as well as the low levels of support for abolitionists and Radicals, suggest the complexity of Northern antislavery sentiment. If Northerners overwhelmingly condemned slavery and overwhelmingly opposed its expansion, why were they so reluctant before the mid-1850s to join parties that espoused those views? Why were they so hesitant to endorse the strong measures that would hasten the demise of the peculiar institution? The answers to those questions shed light on the subordinate role that antislavery played in Northern politics during the era of compromise.

Several reasons help explain the gap between the antislavery sentiments of Northerners and their actions. To begin with, most individuals in the North revered property rights more than they loathed slavery. Consequently, battles with the slavocracy were fought at distant outposts. Northerners eventually rallied behind the right of petition and (as part of the Compromise of 1850) legislation to end the slave trade in the District of Columbia. But in other skirmishes, the free state citizenry proved remarkably timid. Few endorsed Radical demands for abolition in the capital and in federal dockyards, or ending the interstate slave trade, let alone attacking the "peculiar institution" in the Southern states. Those daring steps would have taken property from its rightful owners. Indeed, in the 1830s and 1840s Northerners seemed more upset by the demands of the abolitionists than by the persistence of servitude.[49]

Second, at least until midcentury, economic ties between the two sections led many in the North to overlook their antislavery scruples and accept compromises that allowed the spread of slavery. Despite divisions in Congress that showed nearly solid Northern opposition to slavery extension, many lawmakers acceded to Southern demands. Northern votes in Congress made possible the admission of Missouri, Arkansas, and Texas and for many years the persistence of the gag rule. Typically, sympathetic Northern congressmen hailed from the Ohio Valley, the large commercial centers, poorer rural communities, and the New York half of the New York–Virginia axis that lay at the heart of the Democratic Party.

These economic bonds strengthened loyalties to the two national parties and discouraged individuals from jumping to any new organization, such as the Free Soil Party. For many in the North, votes on slavery reflected a temporary alignment; divisions on economic issues a longer-lasting one. In evaluating the antislavery movement, Caleb Smith of Indiana spoke for many. "So far as the movement has for its object the preserving of 'free soil' unstained with slavery, I am with it in heart and soul," he observed in 1848, "although I cannot see the propriety of a separate and independent party organization upon that question alone."[50] Only a small portion of those who declared for nonextension rushed to the banner of the Free Soil Party, even though it was the only national party opposed to the spread of slavery. "I have now waited twelve days," New York editor Horace Greeley wrote

Joshua Giddings in 1848, "for such demonstrations of free soil sentiment as ought to have followed the Baltimore [Democratic] and Philadelphia [Whig] nominations. The truth is there is no deep devotion to principle among any large portion of the American people."[51] When the Republicans coalesced around the free soil issue in the 1850s, their opposition to expansion was never simply a matter of principle. It was part of a broad economic agenda to promote the development of the North.

Finally, racism kept white Northerners from endorsing the broader goals of the abolitionists and Radicals. Even some Free Soil leaders made clear that their intention was to help whites, not blacks. "The negro race already occupy enough of this fair continent," David Wilmot, originator of the Proviso, told a political rally. "Let us keep what remains for ourselves, and our children—for the emigrant that seeks our shores—for the poor man, that wealth shall oppress—for the free white laborer, who shall desire to hew him out a home of happiness and peace, on the distant shores of the mighty Pacific." Lyman Trumbull, who became Republican senator from Illinois, concurred. "I want to have nothing to do, either with the free negro or the slave negro," he remarked. "We wish to settle the Territories with free white men." Many Northerners, with justice, called the Proviso the "White Man's Resolution."[52]

Despite the near universal dislike of slavery, moral arguments for assisting African Americans had a limited appeal in the North—as Southerners were well aware. Jefferson Davis reflected on why the North raised such a hue and cry about slavery. "Is it love for the African?" he asked in 1848. "No! His civil disability, his social exclusion, the laws passed by some of the non-slave States to prevent him, if free, from settling within their limits, show, beyond the possibility of doubt, that it springs from no affection for the slave."[53] Senator James Mason from Virginia similarly underscored Northern hypocrisy. "This matter of abolition is destitute of every savor of humanity, if the slave population are to be manumitted under the promise of a refuge in the free States," he observed. "See that race, the subject of so much commiseration here, because they are in slavery, dying and rotting in nakedness and filth, in the cellars and dens of your northern cities."[54] Such comments did an injustice to the significant minority of Northerners who not only opposed slavery but also demonstrated concern for free African Americans. But those remarks were a trenchant critique of the many who failed to rally to the banners of the Liberty and Free Soil parties and who rejected extending suffrage and other civil rights to African Americans.

In sum, any evaluation of the importance of the antislavery movement demands an evenhanded approach. Certainly, the activities of the abolitionists and Radicals helped change the outlook of many Northerners, particularly in New England and its westward extension. The New England states (apart from Connecticut) showed their commitment to the cause by offering at least limited civil rights to free blacks. Even in the Great Lakes region, where little progress was made in improving conditions for blacks, many advocates of free soil spoke out for the rights of African Americans. But at the same time, the support for militant antislavery remained remarkably limited. Clashes over slavery did not shake Northerners loose from their commitment to traditional parties before the mid-1850s. Antislavery candidates failed to gain more than a small percentage of Northern votes. And in most of the North, reformers made little dent in the racism that pervaded the region. Only when the Republican Party combined a broad-based economic program with opposition to slavery would the campaigns of the abolitionists and Radicals finally achieve success.

At midcentury equally far-reaching changes transformed the South, and particularly the cotton states, emboldening those who questioned the value of the Union. Along with developments in the North, these changes threatened the spirit of compromise that had tied the sections together.

—— 6 ——

# STATES' RIGHTS DIVIDES
# THE DEEP SOUTH

John C. Calhoun was deeply troubled by what he regarded as the mounting threats to his section. In December 1846 he returned to Washington, resuming his seat as senator from South Carolina. Sixty-four years old, rail thin, with eyes that seared onlookers, he seemed consumed by a fire within. He would survive little more than three years, an increasingly passionate spokesman for Southern rights, more and more convinced that secession was the only recourse for his beleaguered section. Surveying the political landscape early in 1847, Calhoun was distressed by what he saw. "Never before was the prospect so gloomy," he confided to a friend. "Both parties are distracted & divided. . . . To add to our difficulties, abolition is revived in a new and more dangerous form. It seems to be resolved on by both parties at the North that no part of the territory to be acquired by the [Mexican] war shall be for the benefit of the South." He concluded: "Thus far my worst anticipations in reference to the war would seem . . . in a fair way to be realized. It dropt a curtain between me &

the future, which, as I told my friends at the time, I could not pene-
trate, nor am I now able."[1]

Like the North, which was changed by the rise of the lake economy and the spread of antislavery, the South was transformed in the
1840s by the depletion of its once-rich soils and the frightening
prospect that its expansion had now come to an end. The response to
these changes, however, divided the Deep South. One group, whose
strength lay in the southern districts of the cotton states, saw restrictions on expansion as a threat to its very survival. These individuals
would join Calhoun in the militant factions that emerged at midcentury. An opposing group, many of whose supporters resided in the
northern districts of the Deep South, glimpsed another, more diversified path of development and was less inclined to take up arms against
the North. The clash between these groups in each of the states from
South Carolina to Texas shaped the "first secession crisis" of 1849–51.
Unlike events a decade later, no Southern state left the Union. But in
this dress rehearsal for separation, prominent politicians, state conventions, and county gatherings threatened to break up the nation if their
demands were not met.

## I.

Two concerns shaped the lines of division within the cotton states.
The first was the origins of the white settlers. One set of migrants
came from the Upper South, although many in this group could trace
their family ties back to Northern Ireland and the continent of Europe.
Typically, the ancestors of these individuals had landed in Philadelphia
and resided for a time in southeastern Pennsylvania. Over the course
of generations, these families had migrated south through the Appalachian highlands, before spreading through large areas of the South.
These settlers arrived in South Carolina and Georgia before the Rev-

olution and moved into the other Gulf States during the period of initial settlement. A second group of individuals came from a different "hearth": the tidewater region of South Carolina and Georgia. Many of these Lower South residents had ancestors who hailed from southern England.[2]

Calhoun described these two societies within South Carolina. "Our State was first settled on the coast by emigrants principally from England, but with no inconsiderable intermixture of Huguenots from France," he noted in 1846. "The portion of the State along the falls of the rivers and back to the mountains had a very different origin and settlement. Its settlement commenced long after, at a period, but little anterior to the war of the Revolution, and consisted principally of emigrants who followed the course of the mountains, from Pennsylvania, Maryland, Virginia & North Carolina. They had very little connection, or intercourse for a long time with the old settlement on the coast."[3]

These two large-scale migrations divided the Deep South into distinct areas, splitting South Carolina, Georgia, Alabama, and Mississippi into northern and southern regions. These separate groups of settlers also shaped politics in Texas and Florida. Upper South migrants dominated the northern and west-central counties of Texas, as well as the districts between the Suwannee and Apalachicola rivers in the Florida panhandle. The two sets of migrants had different outlooks, distinct family histories, and different ways of building their homes and talking to their neighbors. While there were exceptions to the rule, individuals from the Upper South became the conciliators in the sectional crisis. They retained the strongest ties of kinship and sentiment with the states to the north. Migrants from the southern reaches of South Carolina and Georgia distinguished themselves as the most ardent advocates of states' rights.[4]

The distinction between these two migrations comprised the most important cultural divide in the Lower South, but not the only one.

Several other groups stood apart from the culture and ideology of the migrants from South Carolina and Georgia. In Louisiana the Creoles and Acadians rejected the cotton planters' Southern nationalism. William Elmore reported in 1842 about Calhoun's supporters in Louisiana: "In the city of New Orleans he has a great many friends among the American democrats, but among the french and creole population his claims have not been canvassed."[5] The majority of Germans in south-central Texas opposed slavery and secession; in 1854 a group of them would convene to endorse free soil. Many Mexicans in Texas de-nounced slavery and sheltered runaway slaves. Finally, most Northern-ers, individuals who typically settled in the towns of the Deep South, decried Southern nationalism. One correspondent told Calhoun in 1849: "The cities all of them are becoming daily more & more un-sound & uncertain & all for the same reason; the infusion of North-erners & Foreigners amongst them & their influence is being felt in the interior[?]."[6]

Economic activities also split the citizenry of the Lower South, re-inforcing (for the most part) the divisions established by the conflict of cultures. To begin with, wheat cultivation, garden crops, and home manufactures gave the northern reaches of South Carolina, Georgia, Alabama, Mississippi, and Texas an economic unity that mirrored their shared culture. Wheat was grown throughout much of this region (see Map 9). The crop fostered a society of independent farmers, small milling centers, skilled craftspeople, and vigorous local exchanges. Many of these individuals nurtured a vision of more diversified development—an outlook that set them apart from the emphasis on slavery expansion that characterized landowners in the southern reaches of these states.[7]

Lines of transportation also did more to divide the Lower South than to unify it. Most of the rivers that drained these states, from the Pee Dee in South Carolina to the Pearl in Mississippi, and from the Sabine to the Nueces in Texas, served the coastal region but not the counties that lay farther inland. Only the Mississippi, Savannah, and Red rivers provided navigation that went far into the interior. The Tennessee River was the route of choice for northern Alabama. But it flowed north, joining the Ohio River near Paducah, Kentucky. Beginning in the 1820s the planters of northern Alabama lobbied for improvements to this waterway, which was obstructed at Muscle Shoals. With funds from the sale of land donated by the federal government, a canal was completed in 1831. But this route soon fell into disrepair. The state legislature refused to provide the small sum needed for its upkeep, arguing that the canal helped Tennessee more than Alabama.[8]

Railroads also failed to tie together the coastal and northern reaches of the Lower South. Before the Civil War lines were built north from Charleston, Savannah, Mobile, and New Orleans. But the impact of these railroads was mixed. The route from Charleston, which reached Atlanta by the mid-1840s, was flawed. The line did not bridge the Savannah River. While this gap inconvenienced travelers, it posed an insurmountable obstacle to the shipment of bulky goods. The Savannah line successfully spanned Georgia, entering Atlanta in 1846 and Chattanooga, Tennessee, in 1849. But in linking Georgia to the railroad terminus at Chattanooga, it strengthened the bonds between northern Georgia and the Upper South. The lines that went north from Mobile and New Orleans did not reach Tennessee until the eve of the Civil War. During the 1840s and 1850s the most important railways for northern Alabama and Mississippi traveled east-west, tying these regions to the entrepots of the Upper South. In the mid-1840s capitalists in northern Alabama completed a line that paralleled the defunct canal and allowed the shipment of goods around Muscle Shoals. The Memphis & Charleston Railroad, chartered in 1850, began in Memphis, crossed northern Mississippi and northern Alabama, and reached Chattanooga in 1857.[9]

The result of these links between the Upper South and the northern part of the cotton states was an overland trade, which would expand markedly in the 1850s. Finished goods and foodstuffs were shipped to the Deep South; bales of cotton moved northward. Hence commercial ties separated small farmers and planters in the northern reaches of the Deep South from small farmers and planters in southern parts of those states. To be sure, the landowners who shipped their goods out of the port cities were also part of a "national" economy; Northerners, typically New Yorkers, handled these transactions. But by the late 1840s these exchanges more often evoked resentment (and speeches about Northern exploitation and the need for direct trade with Europe) than any sense of national unity.[10]

The separation of the Deep South into northern and southern regions was the most important division produced by economic activities, but others may be noted. The Louisiana sugar planters, who enjoyed the protection of federal tariffs, looked favorably upon the Union. In the Bayou State crop preferences often became political allegiances. Commercial activities also tied many city and townsfolk to the North and made them less willing to entertain extreme states' rights views. Northern capital financed the sale of Southern staples and the import of finished goods into the South. Some traders, particularly in Charleston, advocated secession, but most were unionists. City dwellers were more likely to join the Whig Party, which became the party of moderation.[11]

This division of the Lower South into two societies—one that drew closer to the states lying to the north and one that looked askance at the development of a national economy—underpinned the struggles in each of the cotton states.

## II.

The division in the Deep South was also ideological. Contrasting bodies of beliefs ultimately mediated between interest and action. Many of those living in the towns, in the northern districts of South Carolina, Georgia, Alabama, and Mississippi, as well as in the Louisiana delta, north-central Florida, and the northern and western reaches of Texas questioned the need for extreme measures, even in the face of Northern intransigence. These individuals did not believe in an iron-clad link between the expansion of slave agriculture and Southern prosperity. Manufacturing and crop diversification, they asserted, would allow the region to flourish, even if free soil prevailed in the West. To be sure, these unionists condemned Northern designs on the terri-tories. But the different premises they held made them resist the fire-eaters' demands for extreme measures.

Townsfolk, whose views typically were trumpeted in Whig news-papers, often criticized the single-minded reliance on plantation agri-culture. "The most obvious principles of economy invite us to a *division of our productive labor*," the Milledgeville (Georgia) *Southern Recorder* remarked in 1843, adding, "The product of our great staple is excessive, and our lands are impoverished. Our climate, the face of our country, our copious and unfailing water power, the abundant supply of raw materials, and the cheap labor which we command, invite us to apply a portion of our labor and capital to manufactures."[12] The *Mobile Advertiser* concurred, observing in 1848 that cotton planters "instead of investing their surplus capital in negroes and lands, [should] invest it in manufactures, and draw around and among them in every neighborhood of the South an industrious, thriving, laboring white population to *consume* their surplus products and manufacture their staple."[13] The following year *The Natchez Courier* announced its pro-gram in bold letters: "The South must BRING THE LOOM TO THE COTTON—THE TANNER AND SHOEMAKER TO THE HIDES—THE MILLS TO THE GRAIN—THE FOUNDRYS TO THE IRON MINES!"[14]

Leaders in the northern districts echoed these sentiments. Few individuals were bolder or more outspoken than South Carolinian Benjamin Franklin Perry. Perry, who lived in the Greenville district, near the North Carolina border, was a courageous newspaper editor, lawyer, and politician; he roundly condemned the hotheads in the more southerly part of the state. Perry's neighbors applauded his unionism as well as his campaign for a fairer apportionment, repeatedly electing him to the state legislature. Opposing the states' rights orthodoxy was no easy task in South Carolina. Perry fought a duel with an editor who had criticized him, killing his opponent. (William Cumming, the Georgian who had battled and badly injured George McDuffie, prepared Perry for this clash.) Perry, to be sure, was no abolitionist; he owned thirteen slaves and strongly defended the institution. But he insisted that slavery would flourish in a more balanced economy. He remarked in 1854, "Let the Southern people take lessons from the Yankees, in industry, wisdom and economy, and strive to become their equals as merchants and manufacturers, as mechanics and scientific men."[15]

Perry's friend James Orr, who headed the South Carolina National Democrats, concurred. "The first step to be taken," Orr explained in an 1855 speech, "to reinvigorate our decaying prosperity, and to develop our exhaustless resources, is for our planters and farmers to invest the whole of the nett profits on agricultural capital in some species of manufacturing; the field is broad and inviting, and but little has yet been occupied. With prudence and energy there can be no failure in any branch."[16] Perry was delighted by these observations and remarked, "One such speech as this of Col. Orr's will do more good in the State than all the patriotic fustian and bombast which have been delivered in South Carolina for the last twenty years."[17]

Given their emphasis on manufacturing and diversified agriculture, these politicians were less passionate about westward expansion. In the 1840s Southern Whigs, often with roots in the towns or northern districts, opposed plans to seize Mexican territory. North Georgian Alexander Stephens, for example, sharply criticized President Polk's conduct of the Mexican War. "I am no enemy to the enlargement of our boundaries, when it can be properly done," he observed in 1847. "But free institutions never did and never will enlarge the circuit of their extent by force of arms."[18] Georgia senator John Berrien joined Stephens in opposing the war. Born and educated in New Jersey, Berrien moved to Georgia and became a lawyer in the coastal town of Savannah. Reviewing events in Mexico, Berrien condemned American efforts "to wrest from her a third of her territory." He remarked, "Such an act would be a violation of the national honor, far more to be deplored than defeat in the most sanguinary contest."[19] Stephens and Berrien, both strong supporters of Henry Clay, favored internal growth fostered by government action, rather than expansion, as the proper path of development.[20]

The citizenry in the southern part of South Carolina, Georgia, Alabama, and Mississippi, along with kindred spirits in Louisiana, Texas, and Florida, took a very different approach. They insisted that regional prosperity depended on fresh soils and a cash crop raised by slaves. They contended that other approaches to Southern development, whether based on more manufacturing or on agricultural diversification, were bound to fail.

Jefferson Davis was among the most outspoken advocates of this credo. "Without mountain slopes, and mountain streams to furnish water power," he explained in 1846, "without coal mines permanently to supply large amounts of cheap fuel at any locality, we cannot expect, in competition with those who enjoy either or both of these advantages, ever to become a manufacturing people. We must continue to rely, as at present, almost entirely upon our exports."[21] Davis often returned to this theme. During the Panic of 1857 he rejoiced in the strengths of the Southern way. "Ours was an agricultural people, and in that consisted their strength," he told an audience in Jackson, Mississippi. "Their prosperity was not at the mercy of such a commercial crisis as the one with which the country had just been visited. Our great staple was our safety."[22]

Other Southern rights leaders extolled the Southern way of life, distinguishing it from the destructive commercial spirit of the North.

In 1855 Alabama fire-eater William Lowndes Yancey expounded on the differences between the North and South: "The climate, soil and productions of these two grand divisions of the land, have made the character of their inhabitants. Those who occupy the one are cool, calculating, enterprising, selfish and grasping; the inhabitants of the other, are ardent, brave and magnanimous, more disposed to give than to accumulate, to enjoy ease rather than labor."[23] Mississippi radical John F. H. Claiborne remarked: "Sedentary and agricultural, we cherish the homesteads and laws of our ancestors, and live among the reminiscences of the past."[24]

Manufacturing played at best a minor role for these states' rights advocates. Few went as far in condemning enterprise as John Forsythe, the editor of the *Columbus* [Georgia] *Times*. In 1850 Forsythe declared: "I would to God we had fewer miles of railroad, fewer millions invested in manufactures and stocks, fewer proofs of enterprise, and thrift and money-making, and more of that chivalry of Georgia, of the olden time, which, on more than one occasion, has interposed her sovereignty to check the usurpations of the federal government."[25] Most politicians, of all persuasions, favored railroads. Some Southern rights leaders accepted a subordinate role for manufacturing; a few textile mills and armories could help the South become more self-reliant. But states' rights leaders condemned the spread of "manufacturing as a system"; industrialization neither could be nor should be the path for the South. These politicians asserted that fresh soils, not factories, were the key to continuing prosperity and that the rise of free soil demanded a militant Southern response.[26]

## III.

Given the seemingly insatiable need of slave agriculture for new land, states' rights leaders were deeply troubled by the stiffening opposition to Southern expansion. Before the late 1840s the federal government had helped the South gain new lands. In 1783 negotiators for the new nation had pushed national boundaries to the Mississippi, while twenty years later Thomas Jefferson had leaped at the opportunity to purchase Louisiana. During the following decades the federal government had acquired Florida and removed native peoples from the Gulf states. Northerners, if grudgingly, had accepted the spread of slavery into these areas. This era of expansion culminated with the annexation of Texas in 1845 and the ensuing war with Mexico—a conflict that extended the southwestern boundary to the Pacific. However, by the late 1840s the role of the federal government was changing—and decisively so. The Northern states made clear their determination to block further Southern expansion. The near-unanimous Northern support for the Wilmot Proviso, first debated in 1846, showed—as Calhoun and others were painfully aware—that gaining additional slave territories would be ever more difficult.

At the same time the demand for new soils, always a pressing concern for slave state politicians, intensified. Many planters in the southern reaches of the cotton states, and like-minded slaveholders in the Upper South, felt that their survival as a class, and even their personal safety, turned on expansion. New land was of crucial importance for three reasons. It would help preserve the balance in the Senate; it would lessen the likelihood of slave rebellions; and it would guarantee Southern prosperity by staving off the threat of soil exhaustion.

To begin with, the need for new territories to protect the South's position in the Senate seemed unquestionable. Without Western lands there could be no new slave states, and without new slave states the South would become a helpless supplicant in the upper chamber—the region's last redoubt within the federal government. Southerners noted that the North dominated the electoral college and had tightened its grip on the House of Representatives. In 1800 the free states held 54 percent of the seats in the House, while the slave states had 46 percent.

By 1848 the burgeoning North laid claim to 59 percent of the representatives, leaving the South only 41 percent. The repeated passage of the Wilmot Proviso through the House underscored this inequity. Only in the Senate, where in 1848 twenty-eight slave state senators faced twenty-eight free state lawmakers, could the South still block pernicious legislation.

Lawmakers rehearsed the horrors that would ensue once Northerners grasped all branches of government. "Where will it stop?" asked Congressman Alfred Iverson of Georgia. "The first step in this great political and fanatical drama is the one now demanded, the exclusion of slavery from the newly acquired Territories of this Republic. If the South submits, the abolition of slavery in the District of Columbia will follow in quick succession; then the overthrow of the slave trade between the States; then the application of the public treasure, drained from southern pockets by partial laws and extravagant tariffs, to the purchase of southern slaves from southern owners; and lastly, universal emancipation by act of Congress." Southern politicians pointed to that gloomy future day when free states would comprise three-fourths of the union, giving Northern politicians the power to amend the Constitution and outlaw slavery.[27]

Second, Southern rights leaders feared that slave rebellions would erupt if the growing African American population were confined to the existing states. Few uprisings had rocked the American colonies or the new nation, but even a handful of revolts and thwarted conspiracies proved an unsettling reminder of the danger that lurked in the slave quarters. African Americans had risen up en masse in New York City in 1712; in Stono, South Carolina, in 1739; and in St. John the Baptist Parish, Louisiana, in 1811. Conspiracies involving dozens of slaves shook New York City in 1741 and Richmond, Virginia, in 1800. But for many planters in the mid-nineteenth century the two most recent events—the Denmark Vesey conspiracy in Charleston in 1822 and Nat Turner's uprising in Southampton County, Virginia, in 1831—

were the most unsettling. Although historians debate the numbers involved, the court proceedings that followed Vesey's arrest painted a
graphic picture of hundreds of slaves conspiring to take over Charleston
and slaughter whites. Turner's short-lived uprising involved perhaps
seventy black rebels who killed about sixty whites. After these erup-
tions, magistrates bolstered the slave patrols, that ever-present reminder of planter anxieties. White Southerners also felt a chill when
they reflected on Saint Domingue. Slaves had risen up on that French
island in 1791, withstood Napoleon's best troops, and established a
black republic, Haiti.[28]

In public speeches and private letters, Southerners vented their
fears about rebellious servants in a constricted South. "Concentrate
the slaves where they now are," remarked Virginian James McDowell
in 1849, "and strip us by that very act of the energies and protecting
presence of the laboring white man, and the bloody process of St.
Domingo emancipation will be tried amongst ourselves—vainly, but
yet afflictingly tried."[29] Senator Robert M. T. Hunter of Virginia concurred, noting that to "confine the slave population within its present
borders . . . would dangerously diminish the relative superiority of the
white race at home."[30] Others emphasized that any setback to the
South emboldened the slaves. South Carolinian Henry Conner told
Calhoun in 1849: "Our own people many of them are desponding.
They begin to think that the Institution of Slavery is doomed. . . .
Our slaves themselves are becoming arrogant from the knowledge of
this feeling & will soon be troublesome."[31]

Militant leaders demanded new territories for a third reason: soil
exhaustion. These politicians argued that the region had to expand or
face the bone-wrenching prospect of economic decline. Anywhere
farmers harvested crops, soil depletion was a concern. In both the
North and South, landowners responded to this challenge by pulling
up stakes and moving west. But for planters, particularly in the southern districts of the Deep South, the need for new land was particularly

acute. Few felt they had the option, embraced by the best farmers of the Northeast, of remaining in place, renewing the soils, and continuing to prosper. Landowners in southeastern Pennsylvania, for example, penned livestock to provide tons of manure, rotated crops, and introduced machinery to boost productivity. These farmers benefited from a literate and motivated labor force and the willingness to spend on improvements.[32]

Most planters, however, dismissed the notion that they could renew their estates. They accepted that sometime in the future, yields would fall and they would be forced to live with less, or move. Fertilizers were too expensive for individuals whose first priority was buying slaves. As one Mississippi planter put it: "Our want is the cheapest system of enriching and preserving large plantations—for it is outrageous humbuggery to talk of hauling manure over them." Poor tools were the norm, as planters hesitated to trust uneducated, unmotivated slaves with expensive implements. "In some lots," a Northern visitor noted, "twenty Negroes with their roguish looking mules and *old time* ploughs were scratching the surface of the earth. The sight is ludicrous to one accustomed to the subsoiling of Seneca county [New York]."[33] The same problems—an apathetic workforce, a lack of capital, and a focus on a single cash crop—hampered livestock breeding. Southern pigs and cattle were scrawnier than Northern animals and produced less meat, milk, and manure.[34]

Few Southerners better understood the need for improving farming practices and the frustrations of promoting change than Virginian Edmund Ruffin. Because of his father's untimely death, Ruffin inherited a large, run-down estate on the James River before his twentieth birthday. Although barren fields, poor crops, and traditional approaches to tillage characterized much of Tidewater Virginia, Ruffin, who had been a bookish child, resolved to become a scientific farmer and a prosperous one. He read widely and experimented with marl, a shell-like deposit that countered soil acidity. To his delight, crop yields on marled land soared. Ruffin wrote up his findings first in a pamphlet and then in a 242-page book, which he published in 1832. His neighbors at first scoffed at his treatises and only gradually adopted his approach. Even in the 1850s, however, only a small percentage of Virginia planters used marl or followed Ruffin's suggestions about diversification and careful irrigation.[35]

Ruffin's frustrations and his observations on the decline of once-rich soils were not limited to Virginia. Governor James Hammond of South Carolina invited him to survey farming in that state, and Ruffin found the same deplorable conditions he had seen at home. When Ruffin arrived in Charleston in 1843, he was forty-nine years old and well known as an agricultural reformer. He was an unmistakable figure, short, with a firm, almost military posture. His long, dark brown hair, now increasingly laced with gray, fell across his shoulders in a style he had sported since he was a young man. Often shy, he spoke passionately when moved by his topic. Ruffin traveled about the state, preaching reform and recording in his journal the prevalence of rural poverty and worn-out soils. He noted along the Ashley River a "melancholy scene of abandonment, desolation & ruin" where "there seems to be no thought of doing better."[36] A few planters, and most notably Governor Hammond, experimented with marl, but most rejected Ruffin's advice. Even leading farmers, Ruffin sighed, were "ready enough to accept and to apply to themselves . . . the name of 'land killers!' "[37] He returned home "greatly disappointed," observing, "[I] am compelled to believe that the results have not yet amounted in value to the state to one-thousandth part as much as I had expected."[38]

Beginning in 1850 Ruffin embarked on a second public career—as a leading advocate of Southern rights. But he continued to lament the backward nature of Southern agriculture and, perhaps surprisingly, pointed to forced labor as part of the problem. For Ruffin, slavery was a necessary foundation for Southern society, not an efficient approach to production. He accepted that slaves, because of their "feebleness of mind and indolence of body," would "always remain unfit agents for operations which . . . would be greatly superior in effect and in profit." He stated his credo succinctly: "I would not hesitate a moment to prefer the entire existing social, domestic and industrial conditions of these slaveholding states, with all the now existing evils of indolence and waste, and generally exhausting tillage and declining fertility, to the entire conditions of any other country on the face of the globe."[39] The contradictions in Ruffin's outlook highlighted the difficulties slaveholders faced in undertaking agricultural reform.

The exhausted soils and eroded lands that Ruffin noted in Virginia and South Carolina were evident as well in the more recently settled states of the Deep South. In the 1840s a writer in the *American Agriculturalist* depicted the "common careless mode of planting" in Mississippi. A planter, he remarked, "will make for five years good crops; the next five he will make ordinary; the next five still smaller, until within less than twenty or twenty-five years he is forced to extraordinary exertions in working his land or to emigrate."[40] In 1851 an editorialist discussing the Southwest in the journal *Soil of the South* remarked, "Men not yet old, will note in the brief history of their own recollection, how the wilderness has fallen, and the gullies and barren hillsides have multiplied, under the constant wear and tear of a system of culture which has abstracted all, and returned nothing to the earth."[41] Incomes even in the newest states of the Southwest fell (relative to the national average) between 1840 and 1860.[42]

Still, for most planters, soil exhaustion appeared a far-off threat, not a present reality. It was the specter at a wedding feast, where the guests reveled in seeming abundance. All Lower South states produced more cotton in 1850 than in 1840, and more again in 1860 than in 1850. Only in South Carolina and Georgia did production fall in a cluster of counties where the fiber had been grown the longest, and then only in the 1850s. And while most planters refused to invest in fertilizers or better tools, they eagerly bought varieties of cotton seeds that resisted disease and increased output.[43]

States' rights leaders, however, conceded that these improvements only put off the day of reckoning, and most politicians recognized the need for new soils—and the grim outcome if expansion was blocked. Lawmakers underscored their concerns in the debates over the Wilmot Proviso. "What, then, will be the condition of the South?" Virginia senator James Mason asked in 1848. "With their lands worn out, and walls of circumvallation thrown around them, they will have no choice, but to abandon their property and their homes."[44] Even representatives of the prosperous Southwest feared the economic consequences of nonexpansion. "Suppose, sir, that slave labor should become unprofitable . . . in the course of time," Mississippi congressman Winfield Featherston remarked, "and that it should be profitable in New Mexico: by the adoption of this measure, known as the Wilmot proviso, the Mississippian is excluded with his slaves from this territory, and virtually deprived of this species of his property." For these lawmakers the survival of the "peculiar institution," and indeed the whole Southern way of life, depended on expansion.[45]

For many states' rights leaders, such concerns were heightened by the unmistakable decline of slavery in the Border States. By the late 1840s various observers noted that Missouri, Kentucky, Maryland, Delaware, and parts of other states were lessening their dependence on slavery. The implications for the South were unsettling. "How long will Maryland, Western Virginia, Kentucky, Eastern Tennessee and even the Western part of No. Carolina feel it is their interest to retain slaves?" Governor David Johnson of South Carolina asked in 1848. "They are already unproductive as laborers & their sympathy would not weigh a feather against their interest & their prejudices in another scale."[46] The following year South Carolinian Marcus Hammond told his brother James that Southerners should "break up" the Union before, "Ky., Md., Mo. & Tennessee draw off."[47] A Mississippi correspondent warned Calhoun that "the settlement of the slavery question ought not to be postponed. We are much stronger now, than we shall be two or five years hence." The transformation of the Border States raised the chilling specter of the collapse of the entire slave system.[48]

Because of the need to maintain a balance in the Senate, check unruly slaves, and cultivate fertile soils, many planters and small farmers—particularly those living in the southern districts of the cotton states—asserted that their survival depended on new territory. The Northern resolve to block expansion radicalized these individuals, ending the era of compromise and opening years of increasingly bitter conflict. Between 1846 (when the Wilmot Proviso was introduced) and 1858 (when politicians, North and South, recognized that Kansas would enter the Union as a free state), expansion was at the heart of the sectional debate. The battle over the West remained important during the final secession crisis. However, with Republicans preparing to take the reins of power, states' rights leaders would grow increasingly concerned about a broad range of issues that collectively (they felt) spelled the end of slavery.

## IV.

The struggle between the two groups with different interests and different visions of the future was played out in the midcentury politics of each of the cotton states. Dixon H. Lewis's career in Alabama provides a good starting point for understanding these clashes. During the 1830s and 1840s Lewis was one of the leading states' rights Democrats. Born in Georgia and educated in South Carolina, Lewis moved to Alabama soon after graduating from college. He read law but was more interested in politics, entering the state legislature in 1826. Lewis holds a distinguished place in the Southern tradition of colorful stump speakers. A massive man, he weighed 350 pounds at age twenty and at least 430 pounds at the time of his death. Both houses of Congress would build special chairs to accommodate his girth. Despite his size, Lewis was a tireless campaigner, firing up the crowds at the smallest crossroads settlements, while his opponents often remained in the larger towns. He never lost an election, serving as state assemblyman from 1826 to 1828, congressman from 1829 to 1844, and senator from 1844 to his death in 1848. In a state where the less wealthy usually voted Democratic and the more affluent Whig, Lewis joined the Democrats and, like Jefferson Davis in neighboring Mississippi, helped make Jackson's party a vehicle for Southern nationalism. An ardent states' rights leader and, on most issues, a Jacksonian, Lewis opposed the Bank of the United States, high tariffs, and internal improvements. He criticized, however, Jackson's strong stand against nullification in 1832–33.[49]

The clash between the unionists in northern Alabama and the states' rights advocates in southern Alabama shaped Lewis's actions. Lewis hailed from southern Alabama and spoke for the Southern nationalists in those districts. But in 1847, to assure his reelection to the Senate, he made a deal with his opponents in northern Alabama. He agreed to eschew any third-party efforts by states' righters and to support the candidate chosen by the Democratic national convention. Such flexibility angered Calhoun's supporters. One politician remarked: "I look upon the conduct of Lewis as the most disgraceful piece of political perfidy, truckling and time serving that has ever fallen under my observation."[50] Another Calhounite lamented the strength of the unionist districts: "The mountain democracy command the State and our politicians defer to their wishes."[51]

The quarrel between the two sections of Alabama continued in 1848. Lewis helped another southern Alabama politician, William Lowndes Yancey, draft the "Alabama Platform" and persuaded the state Democratic party to adopt this pronouncement. This Southern rejoinder to the Wilmot Proviso declared that the territory gained from Mexico should be open to slavery. After the Democratic national convention in Baltimore overwhelmingly rejected this plank, Yancey explored the creation of a states' rights party—a proposal that northern Alabama leaders roundly condemned. When Lewis died on a trip to New York City, Alabamians clashed over the selection of his successor. Governor Reuben Chapman ignited a firestorm of protest by appointing Benjamin Fitzpatrick, another southern Alabama politician. Whigs and northern Alabamians disliked Fitzpatrick far more than the genial Lewis, who had been willing to negotiate with his opponents.[52]

The conflict between regional groups intensified with the onset of the crisis of 1849–51. Alabamians split along geographical lines in the dispute over the Southern Address, which Calhoun set forth in early 1849. This strongly worded statement condemned Northern aggression. Four of the five congressmen from the southern part of Alabama endorsed the document, while the two from the northern districts did not. These actions reflected popular sentiments. "Almost all the Counties of South Alabama have responded most emphatically 'to the Southern Address' without distinction of party," one of Calhoun's correspondents explained. "North Alabama is much less interested and will be slow in her action."[53] Unionist anger over the senatorial appointment led to a new legislative ballot in 1849 and the selection of a northern Alabama politician, Jeremiah Clemens. Clemens, who was a soldier, novelist, and distant cousin of Mark Twain, began his career as a states' rights supporter. But after his election to the Senate, he moderated his views in keeping with the outlook of his northern Alabama constituency.[54]

Only gradually did tempers calm and the rift in Alabama heal. In 1850 the Democratic press divided over the Compromise: newspapers in the Tennessee Valley supported the deal, while most other journals opposed it. Despite the strength of southern Alabamians in the press and the state conventions, the congressional elections of 1851 reaffirmed ties with the Union as voters in most districts returned union Democrats or their moderate Whig allies. In 1852 a group of Alabama fire-eaters bolted from the Democratic Party, nominating George Troup for president on a states' right ticket. Although the response to this initiative was tepid, the concentration of Troup supporters in the southern counties clearly indicates the locus of states' rights fervor in Alabama (see Map 5).[55]

Georgia was similarly split between a unionist north and a states' rights south, a division evident by the early 1840s. Howell Cobb, the wealthy lawyer, slaveholder, and Democratic politician who represented northeastern Georgia, emerged as leader of the unionists. Almost from his entry into national politics, Cobb opposed Calhoun and his supporters in southern Georgia. Edward Black, a states' rights congressman, informed Calhoun in 1843: "After I returned from Washington I exerted myself to get as many of our friends from lower Georgia into the [state] Convention as possible. I went, as a member, myself, and had the satisfaction to see our labours crowned with your nomination [for President]." Black continued: "One of our members elect to Congress made every effort to defeat you. For this opposition Cobb is mainly responsible, as he sustained and directed it."[56]

The geographical division deepened during the crisis of 1849–51. In 1849 Cobb, along with other northern Georgia Democrats, rejected Calhoun's Southern Address. With Democrats so divided, the state party convention decided not to consider Calhoun's proposal. "For the sake of harmony," Herschel Johnson explained, "the subject of the Southern Address was not touched. It would have torn us to atoms."[57] The battle for Georgia only intensified during the following year. Southern nationalists denounced the Compromise of 1850 and formed Southern Rights associations in many of the counties of south and central Georgia. In response, Cobb joined with two Whig congressmen from northern Georgia—Alexander H. Stephens and Robert Toombs—to create the Constitutional Union Party. The new

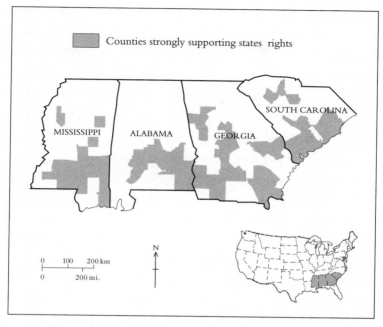

*Map 5. States' Rights Strength in the Deep South, 1851–52*

party affirmed the so-called Georgia Platform, a policy statement that accepted the Compromise of 1850 but resolved the South would suffer no further encroachments. Their opponents (who denounced the Compromise) coalesced into the Southern Rights Party.[58]

The new unionist coalition showed its strength in 1851, and then gradually dissolved in 1852 as sectional tensions eased. In 1851 the Constitutional Union Party elected Cobb governor and sent Toombs to the Senate. Unionists also won a majority of congressional seats in the fall. (Map 5 shows the states' rights strongholds in the 1851 Georgia congressional election.) Even though divisions within the Democratic and Whig parties gradually healed, the Georgia Democratic Party fielded two separate tickets in the 1852 presidential election. Votes for these slates showed the continuing division between the two regions of Georgia.[59]

South Carolina too was divided along north-south lines. But as was true during the Nullification Crisis, the States' Rights Party was stronger and the opposition weaker than in any other Southern state. The Palmetto State had long assumed the mantle of leadership in quarrels with the North. Southern nationalists dominated in South Carolina for several reasons: the remarkable concentration of large estates in the Lowcountry or "parishes"; high levels of slaveholding in most other districts; an unfair apportionment that favored the parishes; depleted soils; and the preeminence of Calhoun, who almost single-handedly guided state politics from 1830 to 1850.[60]

Still, South Carolina had dissenters from the states' rights orthodoxy. The crusty upper classes of Charleston and Columbia harbored a handful of unionists, while more significant criticism came from the districts near the North Carolina border. During the midcentury crisis, backcountry newspaper editor Benjamin Perry labeled the demands of secessionist politicians as madness, and he viewed Calhoun's passing in March 1850 as a blessing. "His death has relieved South Carolina of political despotism," Perry exclaimed. When South Carolinians continued to demand separate state action, Perry despaired, "There is a spirit of disunion abroad in South Carolina, which I am sorry to see. I love the Union & am not willing to give it up."[61]

States' rights advocates, with their strength in the parishes and the more southerly Upcountry districts, easily controlled South Carolina's course during 1849 and 1850. Local meetings applauded Calhoun's Southern Address and announced their support for separation if the North persisted in its free soil doctrines. A convention held in Columbia in May 1849 declared South Carolina ready to join with the other states and resist the adoption of the Wilmot Proviso "at every hazard." The legislature also responded quickly to Mississippi's call for a Southern Rights Convention to meet in Nashville in June 1850.[62]

However, as the conflict shifted to the issue of separate state secession, opposition to the fire-eaters of the Lowcountry gradually increased. A series of setbacks for the radicals made clear that there would be no concerted Southern resistance. Louisiana sent no representative to the June 1850 Nashville convention, and still fewer states chose delegates for the second Nashville meeting in November. Howell Cobb's triumph at the Milledgeville Convention in December showed South Carolina secessionists they would receive no support from Georgia. Lowcountry leaders, like Robert Barnwell Rhett, remained undeterred. But many other South Carolina politicians, who initially had supported vigorous steps, now considered separate state action foolish. James Orr, the congressman who would become the leader of the national Democrats in the Upcountry, was prominent in this group and helped organize the opposition. Charlestonians now supported the cause of moderation, as did many merchants in the backcountry towns. These moderates called themselves "cooperationists," indicating that they favored strong measures only if South Carolina acted in unison with the other Southern states. The new group showed its force in the October 1851 vote for delegates to a state convention (see Map 5). The Cooperationists, with their strength in the populous northern districts, won handily, 25,062 to 17,617. *The Charleston Mercury* commented: "The Co-operationists have given to their ticket a large majority, and though it will be diminished by the Parishes, it cannot be overcome."[63] In 1852 Orr and the Union Democrats supported the national Democratic candidate, Franklin Pierce, despite the sniping of the secessionists that South Carolina could not "mingle actively in the canvass without dishonor."[64]

In Mississippi, conflict between the northern and southern counties also shaped the response to the crisis of 1849–51. Tension between different regions over such issues as representation and banking had long been evident. But only with the first secession crisis did this division redefine party lines. In 1849 and 1850 northern and southern Mississippi clashed over the election of a senator. Jefferson Davis, the states' rights leader from southern Mississippi, had been appointed to the Senate in 1847. In October 1849 he toured northern Mississippi to garner support for his reelection by the legislature as well as to awaken the citizenry to the dangers of Northern aggression. But his reception was lukewarm. According to the local newspaper, Davis told the audience at Holly Springs that "he was not the senator of a section of the State, but of the whole State and that if he was more partial to one portion of the State than another, it was to the North."[65] But many in the north ignored such appeals and backed his chief rival, Roger Barton. Davis, however, garnered enough votes from the lawmakers of southern Mississippi to be reelected in February.[66]

Divisions deepened in 1850 after Mississippi's other senator, Henry Foote, endorsed Clay's Compromise. Foote was a short, brilliant, balding, pugnacious lawyer and politician. Born in Virginia, Foote settled first in Alabama, then in Mississippi. Thin-skinned and often sarcastic, he fought four duels and clashed with many individuals, including Jefferson Davis, with whom he had a fistfight in December 1847. Elected senator in 1847, Foote initially was a states' rights stalwart. However, persuaded by the arguments of the unionists and spurred by his enmity for Davis, Foote gradually distanced himself from the extremists and strengthened his ties with the moderates in northern Mississippi. His exchange with Calhoun in March 1850 illustrates the differences between the two camps in the Deep South:

CALHOUN: I appeal to the Senator from Mississippi, if he thinks that the South can remain in the Union upon terms of equality?

FOOTE: We cannot, unless the pending questions are settled; but in my opinion, these questions may be settled, and honorably settled. . . .

CALHOUN: Does the Senator think the South can remain in the Union upon terms of equality without a specific guarantee that she shall enjoy her rights unmolested?

FOOTE: I think she may, without any previous amendment of the Constitution. There we disagree.

CALHOUN: Yes, there we disagree entirely. . . . Every portion of
the North entertains feelings more or less hostile to the South.
FOOTE: I cannot think so.[67]

Within Mississippi, Governor John A. Quitman joined Davis in
denouncing Foote and the Compromise. Declared Quitman: "I believe there is no effectual remedy for the evils before us but secession."
Many lawmakers, particularly from the southern counties, agreed
with those strong sentiments. In October 1849 a state convention
called for a Southern convention to assemble in Nashville the following June. The legislature sent an official delegation to Nashville—one
of only five states to do so. Democrats from the northern districts criticized these steps, as did most Whigs, whose strength lay in the towns
and in the wealthier planting counties of northern Mississippi. Quitman scored the loyalties of the commercial classes: "With the exception of the merchants, the traders, the brokers, the millionaires, and
their dependents, the people are with us."[68]

Reflecting the regional split, Mississippians in 1851 formed new
organizations: the Union Party and the States' Rights Party. The
Union Party selected Foote as its gubernatorial candidate, and he resigned from the Senate to concentrate on his campaign. The States'
Rights Party chose Quitman, who began the campaign with several
disadvantages. He was a poor debater; he angered even some states'
rights supporters, such as Davis, with his extremism; and the tide had
clearly turned in the South against separate state action. In May a correspondent told Quitman: "Secession on the part of this state, under
the circumstances which now surround her, cannot be carried. It will
defeat the most popular man in existence."[69] Quitman withdrew from
the race in September and was replaced by Davis. Although Davis was
more popular than Quitman, he lost to Foote in the November election. The returns make clear that Davis's support lay in the southern
districts, while northern Mississippi backed Foote.[70]

The lengthy gubernatorial campaign overlapped with a second contest that divided the citizenry along north-south lines. In September 1851 voters selected delegates to a state convention, which was to determine Mississippi's response to the Compromise. The unionists, who won a decisive victory, depended on the northern districts, while the states' rights advocates clustered in the southern counties. Map 5 shows the division in the contest for convention delegates. Despite Foote's glee at the results—he memorably chanted, "Quitman and Quitmanism are dead, dead, DEAD!"—Southern nationalists suffered only a temporary setback. The Union Party was short-lived, and in 1852 the familiar split between Whigs and Democrats reemerged in Mississippi.[71]

Although Louisiana, like other Deep South states, was divided into two societies, it remained more moderate than the commonwealths to the east. Viewed in the broadest strokes, sugar planters tended to be French, unionist, and Whig, while cotton planters typically were English, Southern nationalist, and Democrat. In a state long marked by pro-Union sentiment, Whigs strongly supported the Compromise, while Democrats divided over the deal. Northern-born Democrat John Slidell noted in 1852: "In this state (and I believe, Texas) a very great majority of our party approved of the compromise; yet those who were opposed are sufficiently numerous to make our defeat certain in any contest when their support shall be withheld."[72] New Orleans, with its wealthy merchants and its Northern and French population, remained a bastion of unionism. One observer remarked: "New Orleans is almost Free soil in their opinions. The population is one half Northern agents, another 1/4 or 1/3 are Foreigners. The remnant are Creoles who cannot be made to comprehend their danger until the negroes are being taken out of the fields."[73] Indeed, few politicians from either party demanded separate state action. The *Louisiana Spectator* observed: "Except an occasional Carolinian, there [is] not a disunionist in Louisiana."[74]

In Texas, as Slidell suggested, most Democrats along with virtually all Whigs endorsed the Compromise of 1850. Texans had good reason to applaud the federal government. The United States had just roundly defeated the Mexicans, securing Texas statehood. The Compromise of 1850 allotted $5 million to fund Texas bonds at full face value. Both Democratic senators, Sam Houston and Thomas Rusk, as well as the two Democratic representatives, endorsed most components of the deal. Houston was one of only four senators to vote for all the bills that made up the Compromise. But there was dissent, even if it was not as strong as in other parts of the Lower South. Louis Wigfall, who represented the eastern, cotton-growing county of Harrison in the state legislature, condemned Houston and the Compromise. Wigfall, a transplanted South Carolinian, had campaigned for Southern rights in his native state. The lawmakers who agreed with Wigfall's views selected him as the Texas delegate to the Southern rights convention in Nashville. And while Wigfall did not attend (he nominated another Texan for the post), he drew up a set of constitutional proposals for the gathering to consider.[75]

The midcentury crisis also split Floridians, with birthplace a key factor in defining the two camps. Politicians from the Upper South headed the Whig Party and helped chart a moderate course. Virginian Edward Cabell, the state's lone representative, opposed Calhoun's Southern Address. Cabell's efforts were enthusiastically seconded by another Virginian and Whig, Governor Thomas D. Brown. Brown denounced the Nashville convention as "against the spirit if not the letter of the Constitution of the United States." Both men backed the Compromise. Still, the Southern rights opposition was strong, and pressure from Democratic districts led the legislature to send delegates to Nashville. Among the leaders of the Democrats were the West Indian–born senator David Yulee and James E. Broome, who was (according to a Whig paper) from "the strictest sect of the South Carolina separatists." Yulee, speaking as much about his own state as about the South in general, told Calhoun, "We have treacherous influences in our midst to subdue, and an indifference amounting to apathy to be overcome." Gradually the states' rights forces in Florida strengthened, in part because of the continuing influx of settlers from South Carolina and Georgia. In 1852 Broome defeated Cabell in a close vote for Florida's congressional seat. Broome's election marked the ascendance of states' rights Democrats in Florida and the end of the brief era of Whig dominance.[76]

At midcentury the Deep South was divided into two societies that held different ideas about how to deal with the sectional crisis—and the future. Planters and small farmers in the southern districts of the states from South Carolina to Mississippi, and like-minded individuals in Louisiana, Texas, and Florida, led the protests against the North. Many of these individuals contemplated secession when they reflected on their need for new land and the intensifying Northern opposition to the spread of slavery. But other residents of the Deep South criticized the fire-eaters' campaigns. These individuals, who typically resided in the northern districts of the cotton states as well as the towns, envisaged a more diversified economy. These unionists helped defuse the first secession crisis and keep the country intact. The same divisions would reemerge in 1860–61, but the outcome would be far grimmer.

Patterns of trade and production in the Border States and Upper South also evolved during these years—with important implications for the outlook of these regions and for national politics. With some exceptions, politicians in the upper tiers of the South moderated the extremism of leaders in the cotton states.

# 7

# TRANSFORMATION OF THE BORDER STATES AND UPPER SOUTH

Thomas Hart Benton, senator from Missouri, resented that lawmakers from the cotton states claimed to speak for the entire South. The issue at hand in May 1848 was opening the Oregon Territory to slavery, and Benton—although himself a slaveholder—argued for free soil. He distanced himself from those Lower South politicians who insisted that the "peculiar institution" be allowed in Oregon. "There is a law of climate, of position, and of nature herself against it," he stated. Benton roundly condemned those firebrands who felt that all Southerners shared their views. "No gentleman on this floor," he told his fellow senators, "must assume to be the representative of the fifteen slaveholding States. I assume to represent one—no more than one—and if I can satisfy my constituents, my duty is performed."[1]

In the first secession crisis of 1849–51 some individuals in the Border States and Upper South shared the views of those who counseled violent measures, but most did not. Changes in economic activities shaped the outlook of groups throughout the upper reaches of the South, and generally these developments tugged people toward unionism. Slavery became less important in many areas, while ties with the North grew stronger. The majority of small farmers and city folk felt their future lay with the United States rather than a Southern confederacy. Still, some planters (and others) stood apart from these trends and saw their destinies in very different terms. They accepted the argument that the South needed new soils to survive and that Northern intransigence threatened their way of life. The result was clashes in every state—and divisions that would reemerge during the final secession crisis.

## I.

The strong unionist leanings of the Border States during the mid-century crisis reflected the region's increasing ties with the North and the declining importance of slavery. Few individuals more fully embodied the evolving character of these states than Benton. During the 1830s and 1840s, Missouri, which Benton represented in the Senate, as well as Kentucky, Maryland, and Delaware, became less dependent on slavery and more tightly bound to the Northern economy. Changes in Benton's outlook paralleled the evolution of this region. Many observers, however, were struck most by Benton's belligerent public personality, which colored all that he did. Benton was born in North Carolina in 1782, the same year as Calhoun and Webster. At age nineteen he moved with his family to Nashville, Tennessee, where he taught school and became an attorney, state senator, and friend of Andrew Jackson. During the War of 1812 he was elected colonel of a regiment of volunteers. He also quarreled with Jackson, a dispute culminating in a barroom brawl that left Benton with five knife wounds and Jackson with a bullet lodged in his elbow. Now the general's sworn enemy, Benton moved to Missouri, convinced that his opportunities for political advancement would be greater there.

The clash with Jackson was not the last of Benton's quarrels. In 1817 he killed Charles Lucas, a political rival, in a duel. Even in 1850, when Mississippi senator Henry Foote pointed a loaded revolver at him, Benton, unarmed and sixty-eight years old, marched fearlessly up to his opponent, telling the other senators, "Stand out of the way, and let the assassin fire!" Benton was a big man, weighing two hundred pounds, with a high forehead, curly hair, and a prominent aquiline nose. He was courtly to friends and devoted to his wife and children, but a sight to behold when angered in debate. "He would rush forward," one observer remarked, "with blind fury upon every obstacle, like the huge wild buffaloes then ranging the prairies of his adopted state."[2]

The small, free farmers of Missouri comprised the bedrock of Benton's support, and their backing helped keep him in the Senate from 1820 to 1850. He delighted them with his long-standing campaign for "graduation," the demand that the federal government significantly lower the price of Western lands. He also pleased them with his efforts to restrict the circulation of paper money, and return the country to the "true currency" of gold and silver. Benton's efforts earned him the sobriquet "Old Bullion." His convictions also brought him into the newly formed Democratic Party and led to his reconciliation with Jackson.

Significantly, Benton's views on two key issues—internal improvements and slavery—evolved as the economy of Missouri and the other Border States changed. Until the 1840s, Benton believed that Missouri's trade must inevitably flow South to New Orleans, and that spending for canals or railroads to strengthen ties between St. Louis and the cities of the Northeast was foolish. In 1830 he remarked, "As to the idea of sending the products of the West across the Alleghenies, it is the conception of insanity itself! No rail roads or canals will ever carry them, not even if they do it gratis!"[3]

But as Missouri's orientation changed, so did Benton's convictions about the need to improve links with the North. By the mid-1840s the state's trade increasingly flowed northward. In 1846 a merchant remarked that while it was still somewhat cheaper to ship a barrel of flour to the east coast via New Orleans than to ship it up the Ohio River and then by canals to New York, the northern route was quicker and the flour arrived in better condition. The completion in 1848 of the Illinois and Michigan Canal, which linked Lake Michigan with the Illinois River and then the Mississippi, only accelerated this reorientation. Benton now celebrated the improvements that helped tie his state to the northern route. "I did not expect the good fortune of seeing the United States made into an island," he remarked in 1848, "by a canal connecting the waters of Lake Michigan with those of the Mississippi in my lifetime. But it has been done . . . [and] I rejoice in it."[4]

Even more noteworthy was Benton's change of heart on slavery, again reflecting the evolution of his adopted state. Benton had commanded the proslavery forces during the Missouri Controversy of 1819–21. Prohibiting bondage, he declared, was "contrary to the rights of the State." The position was a popular one and helped make Benton senator. Benton held slaves himself, and in 1829 he defended the institution in a series of newspaper articles under the name "La Salle." The essays painted the North and abolitionists as the enemies of the South and West.[5]

Gradually, Benton distanced himself from the more ardent defenders of slavery. He never freed his own slaves, and he continued to denounce abolitionists. But in the 1830s he was among the few Southerners opposing the gag rule, and he increasingly voiced his opposition to the expansion of the "peculiar institution." "The incurability of the evil is the greatest objection to the extension of slavery," he remarked.[6] In the 1840s he stood almost alone among Southern Democrats in opposing the annexation of a new slave state, Texas, and in supporting the organization of the Oregon Territory without slavery. He bitterly attacked Calhoun for threatening disunion if the North blocked Southern expansion. In 1849 one of Calhoun's St. Louis correspondents informed the South Carolinian: "Benton is canvassing the State, haranguing the people about your alleged movement to dissolve the Union, and seeking thus to arouse sympathy and assistance for himself."[7] In the debates over the Compromise of 1850 Benton took the unusual stance, for a Southerner, of supporting both the admission of California and the bill to end the slave trade in the District of Columbia.[8]

Benton's growing opposition to the expansion of slavery reflected the changing composition of the Border States, even if at times the feisty senator outpaced public opinion. Expressed as a percentage, the slave population declined in Missouri, as it did in all the Border States (see Table 7.1). Many among the swelling population of small, white farmers applauded Benton's insistence on keeping the West open to free labor. Benton also received increasing support from St. Louis, which grew from fewer than 20,000 in 1840 to 78,000 in 1850 and would reach more than 160,000 in 1860. Immigrants, who were largely from Ireland and Germany and rarely owned slaves, comprised 43 percent of the city's population in 1850 and 60 percent a decade later. Despite this growing base of support, Benton had gone beyond the views of many Missourians with his unbending opposition to slavery expansion. In January 1851 the legislature removed him from the Senate and by a vote of 80 to 55 put a Whig in his place. Undaunted, Benton campaigned for and won a seat in Congress from the first district, which included many of his strongest supporters: the workingmen of St. Louis and the yeomanry in nearby farming communities.[9]

## TABLE 7.1: SLAVES IN BORDER STATES AS PERCENTAGE OF STATE POPULATION, 1830-60

|  | 1830 | 1840 | 1850 | 1860 |
|---|---|---|---|---|
| Delaware | 4.3 | 3.3 | 2.5 | 1.6 |
| Kentucky | 24.0 | 23.4 | 21.5 | 19.5 |
| Maryland | 23.0 | 19.1 | 15.5 | 12.7 |
| Missouri | 17.9 | 15.2 | 12.8 | 9.7 |

*Source*: Inter-University Consortium for Political and Social Research: Historical Demographic, Economic, and Social Data—U.S., 1790–1970.

Like Missouri, the other three Border States—Kentucky, Maryland, and Delaware—pursued paths that drew them closer to the North and made them less dependent on slavery. These states (far more than Missouri) entertained public debates on emancipation. While none adopted even the gradual plans that reformers set forth, many observers agreed that the eventual demise of slavery in this region was inevitable.

Kentuckians expanded their trade with the North—and made clear that moderation characterized their approach to slavery. The Bluegrass State sent more and more of its products east, by canals, railroads, and the Ohio River. Tobacco shipments to New Orleans peaked in 1843. After that date, increasing quantities of Kentucky tobacco, grain, and coal were forwarded directly to New York and Philadelphia. In 1852 tobacco dealers in Cincinnati, situated across the Ohio River from Kentucky, noted that shipments to New York sent through New Orleans cost twice as much as those directed east by rail or canal. Equally significant, the journey through the Crescent City took over a month, while the trip by canal took eighteen days, and by rail six to eight days. Louisville, on the Ohio River, flourished as Kentucky's great entrepot for northern trade and became the fourth largest city in the South, after Baltimore, New Orleans, and St. Louis.[10]

Reflecting their position on the edge of the South, Kentuckians proved more flexible in dealing with forced labor than many of their Southern neighbors. In 1833 the state restricted the activities of slave traders, allowing importations only by new settlers who brought in servants for their own use. Although that measure was repealed in 1849, an effort to permit the unrestricted introduction of slaves was soundly defeated, and the lawmakers soon reimposed limits. Unlike most Southern states, Kentucky had no laws prohibiting masters from teaching slaves to read and write. And until 1860 the state did not formally restrict the freedom of press or speech.[11]

Although most Kentuckians defended slavery, several prominent individuals, along with groups in the eastern, mountainous districts, criticized the institution. In the early 1830s James G. Birney, a well-known planter and politician, became a colonizationist and then a radical abolitionist. He freed his slaves, founded the Kentucky Anti-Slavery Society, and announced plans to publish an abolitionist newspaper. But repeated threats to both his person and press persuaded Birney to move to the North, where he became the Liberty Party candidate in 1840 and 1844.[12]

Still more determined to overthrow slavery in Kentucky was Cassius Marcellus Clay, a planter and distant cousin of Henry Clay. Strong and over six feet tall, he was as ready to shoot or stab an opponent as to argue with him, all of which he did. He granted his own servants freedom, and in 1845 he launched an abolitionist paper, the Lexington *True American*, placing two four-pound cannons in the office to defend the press. Like most Border State opponents of slavery, Clay was concerned not for the blacks themselves (whom he hoped would leave the state), but for the impact of slavery on the economy. "Lawyers, merchants, mechanics, laborers, who are your consumers; Robert Wickliffe's two hundred slaves?" he asked. "How many clients do you find, how many goods do you sell, how many hats, coats, saddles, and trunks do you make for these two hundred slaves?" An injunction, secured by the angry local citizenry, closed his press after only a few months of operation. But Clay did not flee the state. He reestablished his newspaper in Louisville, and in 1849 he ran for governor on a platform that advocated gradual emancipation, receiving 5,000 votes, or about 10 percent of the total. During the 1850s he supported another antislavery newspaper and encouraged abolitionists in eastern Kentucky.[13]

In two public gatherings in 1849, Kentuckians courageously criticized slavery. In April more than 150 delegates, including both Cassius and Henry Clay, attended an Emancipation Convention at Frankfort. Speakers denounced bondage and proposed plans for freeing slaves, although no actions resulted. Delegates to the constitutional convention held at the end of the year presented similar critiques. "We have at hand a Convention to revise the Constitution," one observer told Calhoun, "& gradual emancipation reared its head with the Northern party." Again change was voted down, but most Kentuckians recognized that a vocal minority favored a legisled end to the "peculiar institution."[14]

Even more than Missouri and Kentucky, Maryland strengthened its ties with the North and veered from the mainstream of Southern development. Maryland, which shared a lengthy border with Pennsylvania (the Mason-Dixon line), had long boasted extensive connections with the free states. During the colonial era the Susquehanna River had brought Pennsylvania grain to Baltimore for milling. The Baltimore & Ohio Railroad, chartered in 1828, expanded upon long-standing canal, river, and ocean links with the North.

As a result of these ties, Baltimore grew as an industrial city. Its population soared from 81,000 in 1830, to 169,000 in 1850, to 212,000 in 1860. At midcentury it was the largest city in the South, and the second largest in the nation. Gradually, Baltimore businessmen directed their wealth from flour milling to new enterprises, including metalworking and textiles. On the west side of the city, the B&O established the Mount Clare depot and machine shops, which came to employ a thousand people. Still more operatives were involved in producing finished clothing, the city's premier industry. Ironworkers, shipbuilders, carpenters, merchants, and clerks swelled the city's population. Because Baltimore held about 30 percent of the state population by midcentury, the rise of this commercial and industrial center helped make Maryland more like the Northern states with their mix of manufacturing and agriculture, and less like the other Southern commonwealths, where industry was minimal.[15]

The impact of these changes on slavery was striking and made clear that Maryland was moving toward a free labor economy. In northern Maryland, the region that included Baltimore, many masters emancipated their servants, dramatically expanding the number of free African Americans. In 1810, 31 percent of blacks in this region were free; by 1830 it was 51 percent; and by 1850 fully 71 percent. The proportion of slaves in Baltimore declined from 6 percent in 1830 to about 1 percent in 1860. Some Baltimore slaveowners responded to the growing and varied demands for labor by leasing their slaves or allowing them to find their own employers.

These developments shaped the early life of Frederick Douglass, who spent several of his years of bondage in Baltimore. When he first came to the city at age eight in 1824, he visited the free black churches and was thrilled to see African Americans speaking out. When he returned in 1836, after laboring on a plantation, Douglass was encouraged to hire out his time. He explained his relationship with Master Hugh Auld: "I was to be allowed all my time, make all contracts with those for whom I worked, and find my own employment; and, in return for this liberty, I was to pay him three dollars at the end of each week." Douglas also used his time to plot his escape and in 1838, with the aid of a free black seaman, fled to the North.[16]

The free African American population of northern Maryland expanded, despite measures adopted by the legislature and the concerted efforts of slaveowners in southern Maryland to check this trend. An unfair apportionment gave the planters control of the assembly; in

1830 southern Maryland had 60 percent of the seats, even though it could claim only 35 percent of the white population. In 1832 the house adopted a law that declared that freed slaves must be deported and set aside $200,000 to develop a colony in Africa. Northern Maryland ignored the law, its penalties, and the incentives for colonization. Free blacks occupied too important a role in the growing economy to be exiled. They provided a flexible workforce and helped keep down the wages of white workers. Even southern Maryland slowly moved toward a free labor economy, with the proportion of free blacks rising from 20 percent in 1810 to 30 percent in 1850. No wonder that many in Maryland accepted that slavery was on the road to extinction. "I assume that we of the South," Baltimorean J. H. Alexander remarked in 1848, "are no ways desirous of extending and perpetuating Slavery *per se* and for its own sake; and that we are even ready and willing to do away with the whole Institution *if we could afford it.*"[17]

Although Delaware lacked a great trading city, its development paralleled that of its neighbor, Maryland. Delaware residents, who had close ties with both Philadelphia and Baltimore, emancipated most of their slaves. They found, as did Marylanders, that in a buoyant free labor economy, with its growing and flexible demand for workers, forced labor had grave drawbacks. In 1830 the state had 3,000 slaves and 16,000 free blacks. The small number of bondspeople were concentrated in Sussex County, the most southerly of the state's three counties and the one with the most clout in the legislature. In 1803 and again in 1847 the assembly came close to adopting a plan for gradual emancipation. Only the actions of the state senate, mirroring the wishes of Sussex County, prevented the measure from becoming law in 1847. Still, James Hammond of South Carolina could justly observe that Delaware was "no southern or slave state."[18]

As a result of strengthening ties with the North and lessening dependence on slavery, the Border States remained a voice of moderation during the midcentury crisis. In 1849 Senator David Atchison of

Missouri was the only one of thirty members of the congressional delegation from the region to sign Calhoun's Southern Address. By contrast, 17 of the 44 representatives and senators from the Upper South, and 30 of the 48 delegates from the Lower South, backed Calhoun. No Border State sent delegates to the Southern conventions in Nashville in 1850. Instead, the Border States provided the strongest support in the South for the Compromise. Four of the six Southern senators backing the admission of California came from this march land, as did five of the six Southern senators agreeing to end the slave trade in D.C. The only other exceptions to Southern unanimity were Texan Sam Houston, who accepted both pro-Northern provisions, and Tennessean John Bell, who favored admitting a free California.[19]

Finally, it must be emphasized that while most Border State politicians lauded the Union, they defended the right to own slaves. They rejected the Calhounite arguments that the slave kingdom had to expand and that the "peculiar institution" was a blessing; but they also resented Northern attacks on their way of life. The views of Green Adams, a Kentucky Whig, illustrate these crosscurrents. "I only ask of gentlemen from the free States," he explained in 1848, "to let the institution of slavery alone where it exists; if slavery is a curse, it is our misfortune, not theirs." He continued: "If they wish to confine slavery within its present limits, and, with time, ultimately to obliterate it from the Union, they had better let it alone; excitement will never effect their object."[20] During the first year of the Civil War, with the fighting focused in the border area, Lincoln took a cautious approach to these leaders who were wedded to both the Union and slavery.

## II.

The spirited but ultimately limited protests in the four Upper South states—Virginia, North Carolina, Tennessee, and Arkansas—reflected the divergent economic trends shaping the region. Most small, non-slaveholding farmers were unionists—and increasingly committed to a life without slavery. Merchants and manufacturers also called for moderation; often located in the cities, these individuals were influenced by their ever stronger links to the North. Meanwhile planters in the Upper South deepened their reliance on slavery and became more receptive to the arguments of the Southern rights leaders. These varied developments helped define the response of the Upper South to the contentious sectional issues in the aftermath of the Mexican War.

Throughout the Upper South, small farmers leaned toward unionism and helped blunt the campaigns of states' rights extremists. No one person spoke for these yeomen, some of whom were Democrats and others Whigs. Many resided in the Appalachian highlands, while in Arkansas some called the Ozarks home. But if there was a single prominent representative figure who voiced the concerns of many of these landowners, it was Andrew Johnson. Johnson was born poor in Raleigh, North Carolina, in 1808 and always remained conscious of his origins. His father, a laborer and sometime bank porter, died when Andrew was three. Andrew never went to school and learned to read only in his teenage years, while apprenticed to a local tailor. In 1826, along with his mother, stepfather, and older brother, he moved to Greeneville, in eastern Tennessee, where he opened a tailor shop—and grew increasingly interested in politics. Johnson hired a boy to read the local newspapers to him while he worked at his bench, and what he heard made him a devoted follower of his namesake, Andrew Jackson. In 1829, with strong support from the mechanics and apprentices of Greeneville, Johnson became alderman and in 1834 mayor. Despite the opposition of many of the local notables, the poorer farmers and artisans of eastern Tennessee sent Johnson to the state legislature in 1835 and to the U.S. House of Representatives in 1843.[21]

Johnson remained thin-skinned and argumentative, suspicious of the wealthy, and a resolute defender of the poorer farmers and artisans.

"The aristocracy in this district know that I am *for the people*," he announced in an 1845 election pamphlet. "The fact of a farmer or mechanic stepping out of the field or shop into an office of distinction and profit, is peculiarly offensive to an upstart, swelled headed, iron heeled, bobtailed aristocracy, who infest all our little towns and villages."[22] He was angered when Jefferson Davis, in praising the accomplishments of West Pointers, asked rhetorically whether "a blacksmith or a tailor could have secured the same results." Johnson responded that "he was not ashamed to avow that he was a mechanic, and of that class to which the gentleman alluded yesterday."[23] In discussing wartime outlays Johnson attacked the "large capitalists [who] live as drones in the hive, and feed upon the honey accumulated by the industrious bees."[24] Like his counterparts in Virginia and North Carolina, he urged democratic reforms. He called for the direct election of the president and senators, and limited terms for judges. Johnson proposed that congressional districts in Tennessee be redrawn to reflect the white population. The existing system, which used the "federal apportionment," counted each slave as three-fifths of a person and thereby overrepresented the planting class.[25]

The most significant measure Johnson advocated, and the one that tied him most closely to the aspirations of the yeomanry, was the Homestead Act. This legislation, which he first set forth in 1846, would give 160 acres to any family that agreed to settle and work the land. "Pass this bill," he told his fellow lawmakers, "and you will make a poor man's heart rejoice. Pass this bill, and their wives and children will invoke blessings upon your heads."[26] He argued that the act would create a class of prosperous taxpayers and bind these citizens to the government. But the proposal encountered opposition. Whigs wanted the sale of Western lands to continue, with the revenues devoted to education and internal improvements. Southern nationalists felt that encouraging small farmers to settle would restrict the expansion of slavery. Slave state congressmen split, 33–30, in favor of the bill when the House passed the measure in 1852. Gradually, however, they turned against the proposal once the Free Soil Party, and then the Republicans, made it part of their credo. Still, Johnson was unwavering in his support until the measure became law in 1862.[27]

An examination of the changing composition of Upper South counties with few slaves underscores the relevance of Johnson's push for a homestead act. The future for these farmers lay with free soil, not with slavery. Between 1840 and 1860, 174 Upper South counties had in at least one census year a slave population of 15 percent or less. While 21 of these counties appear only in the 1860 census, change can be tracked for the remaining 153. In more than four-fifths of the cases, the percentage of slaves in the population declined from these already low levels, or remained the same. Only in twenty-five districts (almost all in Arkansas and Tennessee) did the portion of bondspeople rise significantly. These trends undercut the dreams of states' rights leaders, who hoped that slavery would gradually spread, creating a region of like-minded individuals. Henry Wise, the mercurial Virginia politician, nurtured such hopes until he campaigned in the western counties while running for governor. He witnessed the deep-seated opposition to slave-based agriculture, remarking, "These Western people are *not Virginians* in their social or political sympathies."[28]

Johnson's sectional views, which were decidedly Southern but more moderate than the Calhounites, mirrored the outlook of these small farmers. Johnson was bitterly racist, filling his letters with disparaging comments about African Americans. Like most Southerners, he reviled abolitionists and labeled their doctrines as a danger to the Union. But Johnson was no extremist and disdained talk of secession. In 1849 he refused to sign Calhoun's Southern Address, and in 1850 he distanced himself from the Nashville Convention, which brought together states' rights advocates. "While he was a southern man," he announced in Congress, "he was an American."[29] He supported the admission of California as a free state, a position that also separated him from most Southern politicians. During the crisis of 1849–51 the yeomanry in the Appalachian highlands and Ozarks shared this moderate approach. Virginian Richard Crallé noted in 1848, "The Western portion of the State is strongly infected with the spirit of abolitionism."[30] Another writer reported to Calhoun the following year, "The state of feeling in the States I have visited, is about what you would infer it to be . . . except, that there is an obscure class of people, in humble condition, composed chiefly of emigrants [from] East and Middle, Tennessee, who do not sympathize with the Southern movement."[31]

A second significant pro-Union group in the Upper South was the commercial middle class, whose links with the free states gradually expanded. These individuals, and the politicians who spoke for them, saw their destinies intertwined with a national economy that was driven by Northern growth. Hence during the midcentury crisis they applauded efforts at compromise and decried the militant plans of the fire-eaters.

The most important group of traders and manufacturers in the Upper South resided in urban places, particularly in the towns of Virginia and Tennessee. Increasingly, the chief cities in Virginia were drawn into the Northern commercial orbit. In the late eighteenth and early nineteenth century Richmond and Norfolk were bustling independent entrepots, boasting a thriving overseas trade. In 1815, when New York accounted for 19 percent of U.S. exports, Richmond and Norfolk together shipped 12 percent of the total. However, overseas shipments from the Old Dominion dropped precipitously, so that by 1840 the two Virginia ports handled only 3 percent of all exports and in 1860 only 1 percent. The two Virginia cities lacked the financiers, merchants, and rich hinterland that allowed the great ports to flourish. (Meanwhile New York's foreign trade soared, and by 1860 had reached 36 percent of all exports.) In place of sending their goods overseas, Virginians increasingly directed their wares to Northern cities. Richmond tobacco was forwarded to New York shippers, who sent the casks to Europe and to retailers throughout the United States. Garden crops, destined for New York tables, became the chief export of Norfolk. Most flour milled at Alexandria was sent to Baltimore, Philadelphia, and New York. The industrial products produced in Wheeling, which was located on the Ohio River near Pittsburgh, were sold primarily in the North. States' rights advocate George Fitzhugh commented acidly, "Trade very easily effects now what conquest did formerly."[32]

The expansion of urban industries and commerce, fostered by broadening ties with the North, weakened slavery in Virginia cities. By 1850 almost all African Americans in Wheeling and most in Alexandria were free. In Norfolk County and several nearby districts the proportion of free blacks rose strikingly, reflecting individual decisions of masters rather than any concerted movement. Virginia cities defied the restrictive laws that the assembly had passed in the wake of the 1831 Nat Turner rebellion. Curfews were not enforced; nor was the decree that freed blacks had to leave Virginia within twelve months of their manumission. Many employers in Richmond, facing growing but erratic demands for labor, shifted from purchasing slaves to hiring them. These bondsmen often received wages and the freedom to live where they pleased, leaving observers to fret about the consequences of such liberality.[33]

Trade between the North and the Tennessee cities of Nashville and Memphis also expanded. Memphis, located on the Mississippi River just north of the state of Mississippi, was a particular bone of sectional contention. In the 1840s it lay just at the edge of the Northern commercial sphere. The 1845 Memphis Convention, a gathering of politicians and businessmen, argued for improved links between Memphis and the Southeast, with particular emphasis on rail connections. "The sooner the route from this point to the S.E. is finished," a Memphis politician wrote Calhoun in 1849, "the sooner we begin to catch a great deal of trade that now goes by us, & secure a great deal that will soon go *directly east from the Ohio valley* to N.Y. if the grand system of

R.R. projected from St. Louis to N.Y. be completed first."[34] In the 1850s rail lines were built linking Memphis both with the Northeast (through Louisville) and the Southeast (through Chattanooga).

The far-reaching impact of the Northern market shaped not only business activity in the Upper South but also the views of an influential group of unionist politicians. These individuals saw their future and that of their constituents linked to the prosperity of the free state economy. Most typically these leaders, and the commercial interests they represented, were Whigs. Virginia boasted several politicians who spoke for urban districts and disdained the visions of states' rights activists. None was more influential than John Minor Botts, who represented Richmond in the state assembly and then for three terms in the U.S. House of Representatives. Botts was a lawyer and slaveholder, a breeder of fast horses, a shaggy bear of a man, known by friends and enemies as the "Bison," and a political boss with a strong following in Richmond's working-class neighborhoods. Botts defended John Quincy Adams and attacked the gag rule, remarking that "Southern gentlemen should pursue a more liberal course than formerly." A mainstream Whig, Botts led the campaign to impeach President John Tyler, the renegade Southern rights Whig who succeeded Harrison in 1841. In the 1850s Botts was an acerbic critic of Southern nationalists, and in 1861 he became one of the few wealthy individuals in the Confederacy who remained loyal to the Union.[35]

John Bell, a prominent Tennessee Whig who made his home in Nashville, further illustrates the outlook of the Upper South Unionists. He served seven terms as representative, two terms as senator, and was also secretary of war, Speaker of the House, and in 1860 a presidential candidate. Despite this distinguished career, Bell was a singularly nondescript character in an age of colorful politicians; he was quiet and serious, with thinning hair and regular features that rarely attracted comment. He was also, thanks to the wealth of his second wife, an affluent businessman with strong ties to the North. He owned extensive coal lands in Kentucky and ironworks in Tennessee. Bell sold his products to Northerners and relied on that section for skilled labor. Although bolder than some, Bell epitomized the balance that characterized moderates in the Upper South. He held slaves and defended the "peculiar institution." But he opposed the gag rule restricting abolitionist petitions and was among the few Southerners supporting the admission of California in 1850. In 1854 he would be the lone Southern senator who denounced the Kansas-Nebraska Act.[36]

Unionist small farmers and businessmen had to contend with the Upper South's third group, the wealthy slaveholders, many of whom demanded firm resistance to Northern encroachments. To be sure, not all planters campaigned for Southern rights; nor were all firebrands slave lords. Still, the great strength of the states' rights movement in the Upper South lay in the plantation counties, and particularly in those districts dominated by wealthy Democratic slaveholders. The influence of these individuals and the lawmakers they elected was unmistakable. In all four states, representatives of the plantation districts endorsed Calhoun's Southern Address and denounced the pro-Northern provisions of the Compromise of 1850. These wealthy landowners agreed with Deep South politicians that slavery must expand or die.

Slaveholders were influential beyond their numbers in every Upper South state. As Table 7.2 indicates, while only a minority of white families owned servants, a majority of lawmakers (except in Tennessee) fell in this category. North Carolina was the most egregious case: only 25.6 percent of white families, but over 80 percent of lawmakers, held slaves. Table 7.2 also makes clear that the wealthier slaveholders, those with 20 or more servants, were overrepresented in the assemblies. In Virginia and North Carolina the framework of government helped keep the wealthy in power. Both states had a property qualification for voting as well as an unjust apportionment that gave the slaveholding east the majority of seats in the upper and lower house, even though most of the white population lay in the west. The Virginia constitu-

tional convention of 1850–51 only partially redressed these grievances. The gathering adopted universal white male suffrage and reap-
portioned the house of delegates but left the state senate in the hands
of the eastern slaveholders. In 1857 North Carolina also took a half-
step toward democracy: the state adopted full white male suffrage.
However, it left in place an unequal apportionment as well as property
qualifications for lawmakers.[37]

## TABLE 7.2: SLAVEHOLDING AMONG THE GENERAL POPULATION AND LEGISLATORS IN THE UPPER SOUTH, 1850

|  | Percentage of white families owning slaves | Percentage of lawmakers owning slaves | Percentage of white families owning 20 or more slaves | Percentage of lawmakers owning 20 or more slaves |
|---|---|---|---|---|
| Arkansas | 18.5 | 53.6 | 1.6 | 10.3 |
| North Carolina | 25.6 | 81.2 | 3.1 | 36.1 |
| Tennessee | 22.3 | 41.0 | 1.6 | 7.0 |
| Virginia | 30.8 | 67.1 | 3.2 | 22.9 |

*Source:* Marc W. Kruman, *Parties and Politics in North Carolina, 1836–1865* (Baton Rouge, La., 1983), 49–50.

In Virginia the roots of planter discontent with the North and
with nationalist programs ran deep. Virginia congressman John Randolph championed states' rights long before John Calhoun. A decidedly odd figure—short, with a shrill voice, and no beard because of an
illness he had suffered as a young man—Randolph spoke for tobacco
planters whose years of dynamic growth lay in the past. Randolph
looked disdainfully on all expansive federal programs, opposing the
War of 1812 as well as banks, tariffs, internal improvements, and military spending. He denounced all concessions to the North during the
Missouri Controversy. The poet John Greenleaf Whittier observed:

"Too honest or too proud to feign a love he never cherished / Beyond Virginia's borderline his patriotism perished."[38]

Robert M. T. Hunter, who represented the same constituency, followed in Randolph's footsteps. A large, slow-moving man, and at least early in his career a soporific speaker—another senator complained about his "drowsy, phlegmatic and over-crammed discourses"—Hunter was a disciple of Calhoun and produced a biography of the South Carolinian in 1843.[39] The planters of Tidewater Virginia sent Hunter to the state assembly in 1834 and to the U.S. House of Representatives in 1837. The Virginia legislature elevated Hunter to the Senate in 1847 along with another states' rights leader, James M. Mason, a remarkable demonstration of the power of an extremist minority. Hunter also changed his political allegiance, though not his politics. At first a states' rights Whig, he joined the Democrats in the early 1840s. This step was significant and reflected the tightening of party lines throughout the Upper South. The Whigs, with their strength among the commercial interests, emerged as the more moderate party on sectional issues. By contrast, the most outspoken advocates of Southern rights, like Hunter, gravitated to the Democrats. Party lines would be longer-lived in the Upper South than in either the North (where the rise of the lakes and abolition realigned loyalties) or the Deep South (where secessionist sentiment disrupted politics).[40]

Thanks in part to the advocacy of Senators Hunter and Mason, ten of the seventeen members of the state's congressional delegation signed Calhoun's address. Most of the ten spoke for the high-slaveholding tobacco-growing counties in eastern Virginia and comprised the largest group of signers from any state. These representatives also vigorously resisted yielding to the North during the debate over the Compromise of 1850.

North Carolina had a Southern rights tradition that paralleled Virginia's. During the early decades of the century, politician and tobacco grower Nathaniel Macon, like Randolph in Virginia, battled for limited government. North Carolina tobacco planters saw burdens, not benefits, in measures such as tariffs, banks, and internal improvements. They feared that a powerful federal state might one day limit slavery. "If Congress can make canals," Macon observed, "they can with more propriety emancipate." Like Randolph, Macon adopted a vehement pro-Southern stance during the debates over admitting Missouri.[41]

Macon died in 1837, but other politicians, who spoke for the affluent tobacco counties that lay along the Virginia border, continued his advocacy of Southern rights. Abraham Venable was the most prominent of these Democratic leaders. Born in Virginia, Venable studied both medicine and law and then moved to North Carolina, where his new neighbors elected him to Congress in 1846 and twice more after that. "I am considered as ultra on the subject of southern rights," he remarked in 1848, and his speeches affirmed that perception. He praised Calhoun for "his unwearied resistance to aggression, and the prophetic skill with which he foretold the present unhappy state of affairs." Venable decried Northern plans to "surround the slave States by a cordon of free States" and threatened disunion if the Wilmot Proviso was adopted. "Resistance before degradation," he declared, "and the hazard of all consequences to fixed political inequality."[42]

States' rights slaveowners, however, were less powerful in North Carolina than in neighboring Virginia. The North Carolina planting community was smaller than Virginia's and had less clout in state politics. Only two of the nine North Carolina congressmen, and no senators, endorsed Calhoun's Southern Address. (The two signers were Venable and John Daniel, who together represented the wealthy tobacco-growing counties.) In 1850 North Carolina was the only state, apart from Louisiana, in the Upper or Lower South not to send a delegation to the Southern Rights Convention in Nashville.[43]

Tennessee planters, with their limited influence in state politics, resembled their counterparts in North Carolina. The most outspoken leaders came from two swaths of slaveholding counties, one in western

Tennessee and one in middle Tennessee. Each belt began with tobacco-growing counties near Kentucky and ended with cotton plantations along the Mississippi and Alabama borders. But Tennessee had fewer large estates and fewer slaves than most states to the east or south. In 1850, Tennessee had only one county with an African American majority, compared to thirty-five in Virginia and eight in North Carolina. (Even Arkansas, settled far more recently, had two.) Democrat Frederick Stanton was the only one of the eleven Tennessee congressmen to approve the Southern Address. Stanton's constituency, located in the southwestern corner of the state, claimed the highest percentage of slaves and the most bales of cotton.[44]

In 1850 and 1851 mounting opposition from unionist small farmers and commercial Whigs, like John Bell, frustrated the plans of Tennessee's states' rights planters. Many slaveowners hoped the state would send an official delegation to the Southern Rights Convention scheduled for Nashville in June 1850. Unionist control of the upper house blocked that move, and ultras were forced to rely on individual counties to select representatives. Several districts did, although almost half of the 101 delegates chosen came from two slaveholding counties in middle Tennessee. Voters were still less enthusiastic about the second Southern Rights Convention, which met in Nashville in November. The state elected only fourteen delegates, and those individuals criticized the proposals set forth by representatives from the Deep South. In 1851 Tennesseans demonstrated their moderate leanings. They replaced the states' rights Democratic governor with a pro-Compromise Whig. They rejected the bid of ex-Senator Hopkins Turney, an ultra who hoped to return to Congress, and instead reelected unionist Democrats, including Andrew Johnson. Only in western Tennessee did states' rights Democrats record significant gains.[45]

Finally, Arkansas cotton planters, like Virginia tobacco lords, spearheaded a vigorous Southern rights movement. Unlike the Old Dominion, with its long tradition of states' rights, Arkansas was a nationalist stronghold before the 1840s. In the 1830s citizens cheered President Jackson, who signed the writ of statehood, and they were grateful for the federal troops sent to fight the Indians. By the late 1840s, however, the outlook of many wealthy Arkansans had changed. The rise of antislavery sentiment in the North, the declining fertility of soils, and the threat of the Wilmot Proviso persuaded many planters to question the value of the Union.[46]

Arkansas's Southern rights planters relied on their control of the state Democratic Party to keep the small farmers, with their unionist leanings, in check. A political "machine," the Conway-Sevier-Johnson clique, dominated the local Democratic Party and hence most statewide contests. The yeomanry, who occupied the counties in the north and west, found their choices limited. Before 1853, Arkansas had only one congressional representative, and that individual invariably was nominated by the ruling families. The opposing party, the Whigs, whose strength lay in the planting counties and towns, rarely gained more than 45 percent of the vote and had little attraction for yeomen who were confirmed Jacksonian Democrats. The states' rights planters could not wholly ignore the views of the small farmers, but often candidates ran on one platform and acted on another. In 1849 the entire three-man congressional delegation signed Calhoun's Southern Address, making Arkansas the only state other than Mississippi to display such solidarity. This political unanimity, however, was deceptive: in 1860–61 small landowners would break with the Democratic leadership and oppose secession.[47]

Throughout the Upper South and the Border States economic change helped shape the outlook of the citizenry. While the Border States strengthened ties with the North, the Upper South was riven by bitter conflicts. Small farmers and city folk had less and less to do with slavery, while large planters became ever more concerned about the future of their labor force. The full implications of these divisions would not be evident until the secession crisis of 1860–61. Meanwhile, equally far-reaching changes were remaking the Northern political landscape. The rise of a sectional organization, the Republican Party, transformed politics and gravely weakened the forces for national unity.

# PART THREE

# THE CLASH OF SECTIONS

# 8

# ORIGINS OF THE
# REPUBLICAN PARTY,
# 1854–56

For George Washington Julian, the challenge of creating a Republican organization in his native state of Indiana at times seemed overwhelming. Making a new party, he remarked, "was exceedingly difficult, and could not be solved in a day. . . . The dispersion of the old parties was one thing, but the organization of their fragments into a new one on a just basis was quite a different thing." A strong-minded Quaker, Julian stood out as an antislavery activist in a conservative state. He condemned the long delay before the Republican Party coalesced in Indiana and railed at the cautious platform the state party adopted. Indiana Republicans, he lamented to Salmon Chase, were "a combination of weaknesses, instead of a union of forces." To Julian's dismay, the new organization, although sending delegates to the 1856 national convention, refused to take the name *Republican*, calling itself instead the "People's Party."[1]

The Republican Party, as Julian recognized, experienced difficult birth pangs. Only gradually did it gain strength as competing groups fell by the wayside. In the seemingly chaotic months from the Kansas-Nebraska Act of 1854 to the presidential election of 1856, the impact of two far-reaching developments—the reorientation of the North around the lake economy and the spread of antislavery—became clear. Together these changes affected all political organizations and provided the basis for a new long-lived party, the Republicans.

I.

The response to the Kansas–Nebraska Act in 1854 strikingly revealed how the transformation of the economy and the growth of antislavery had reshaped Northern society. The early 1850s were quiet years politically. Although many Northerners condemned the Fugitive Slave Act of 1850, most grudgingly accepted it. To be sure, Harriet Beecher Stowe scathingly portrayed the measure in her best-selling novel, *Uncle Tom's Cabin*. But during these years only Vermont adopted legislation to assist fugitives, and the 1852 platforms of both the Democratic and Whig parties endorsed the act. The decision of the Free Soil Party to criticize the measure won it few supporters. Its proportion of the Northern vote declined from 14.5 percent in 1848 to 6.9 percent in 1852. Southern observers praised the assistance that citizens in southern Illinois and Ohio gave to slave catchers. And while African Americans and abolitionists staged several dramatic rescues, overwhelmingly fugitives brought before the courts were returned to their masters.[2]

The Kansas-Nebraska Act ended this seeming calm. The 1854 act was the final blow shattering the Second Party System of Whigs and Democrats—and the first step in the emergence of the Republican Party. At least since the late 1840s commentators north and south had noted the weakening of the old national groupings and in Stephen Douglas's words the "efforts of the extremes . . . to organize parties on geographical lines." Missourian James Wishart caught the spirit of this transformation when he remarked in 1848, "Whig and democrat exist no longer. It is north and south. Slave and free soil will now form the party lines."[3] The direction was clear, even if this epitaph was premature. Before 1854 the fiction of two national parties, with strength in both sections, continued to have a basis in fact.

The passage of the Kansas-Nebraska Act, and the angry Northern response to the measure, ended that fiction—and revealed the fault lines that ran through Northern society. Douglas, normally an astute politician, crafted the bill, and the ill success of his proposal demonstrated the weakening base for any leader who tried to bridge the sectional gap. In January 1854, Douglas faced a dilemma. He was committed to westward expansion. Ever since he moved to Illinois as a twenty-year-old law student (having abandoned his first career as a cabinetmaker), he had held fast to his belief in the country's growth. "You cannot fix bounds to the onward march of this great and growing country," he told his fellow lawmakers. "You cannot fetter the limbs of the young giant."[4] Douglas chaired the Committee on Territories, first in the House, then in the Senate. He also stood to profit personally from opening the new region, having purchased land in Chicago that could serve as the terminus for a transcontinental railroad. But his plans for organizing the Nebraska Territory were blocked by Southern lawmakers who feared the admission of another free state as well as the choice of a northern route for the railroad. In return for their cooperation, Southern senators demanded the repeal of the Missouri Compromise with its prohibition on slavery north of 36° 30'. Seeing no alternative, Douglas incorporated an explicit repeal of the 1820 line into the measure he presented January 23. His bill divided the vast territory north of Oklahoma into Kansas and Nebraska, opened the region to slavery, and left the decision about the area's fate in the hands of the settlers.

For Douglas and most other Northern Democrats, the measure was an eminently reasonable compromise that both sections should accept. They set forth three arguments: First, local decision-making was the American way. Second, the measure would end wrangling in Congress. New Jersey senator John Thomson predicted, "It will banish forever from the Halls of Congress all agitation on the exciting topic of slavery."[5] And third, Kansas would ultimately become a free state, since its soil and climate were inhospitable to slavery. "Every intelligent man knows that it is a matter of no practical importance, so far as the question of slavery is concerned," Douglas remarked. "All candid men who understand the subject admit that the laws of climate, and production and of physical geography . . . have excluded slavery from that country."[6] So the South would gain the form of a victory, the North the substance, and the nation would once again enjoy political tranquility.

Douglas, however, badly miscalculated: the act ignited a firestorm of protest across the North. Whigs, Free Soilers, and dissident Democrats immediately attacked the measure. On January 24, the day after Douglas introduced his bill, Salmon Chase, Charles Sumner, Joshua Giddings, Gerrit Smith, and two other antislavery lawmakers published the "Appeal of the Independent Democrats." The signers condemned this "gross violation of a sacred pledge" and promised to "call on the people to come to the rescue of the country from the domination of slavery."[7] In Congress speaker after speaker rose to denounce the bill and present familiar arguments about the baneful impact of slavery on the economy, the incompatibility of free and slave labor, and more generally, the evil nature of bondage. Most opponents of the act rejected Douglas's contention that slavery would fail in Kansas. "In climate, soil, and productions," Whig senator James Cooper of Pennsylvania explained, "Nebraska and Kansas differ in no respect from Missouri. They lie in nearly the same parallels of latitude, and possess a soil as fertile and varied; and yet Missouri contains nearly one hundred thousand slaves."[8] Despite such hostility, the adherence of most Northern Democrats, along with the support of a nearly solid

South, assured the act's adoption. The bill passed the Senate, 37–14, and the House, 113–100. President Pierce signed it at the end of May.

The angry response of Northern voters revealed how far the section had been changed by the growth of the lake economy and the spread of antislavery. Democrats had swept the 1852 congressional elections, winning 157 out of 234 seats in the House. In the 1854 and 1855 elections, free-state electors punished Douglas's party for opening the West to slavery. While the Democrats gave up 10 of their 67 seats in the South, they lost 64 of the 88 Northern districts they had won. The response to the Kansas-Nebraska Act changed the Democrats from a national organization to a Southern-dominated party, with minority status in the North. The pattern of losses was significant. Opposition parties drove the Democrats from a New England radicalized by antislavery. Democratic seats in the region fell from thirteen to one. In most lake districts the reaction was the same. For example, in 1852 the Michigan and Wisconsin delegations had favored Douglas's party by a margin of 7–0. Now they voted for the opposition 5–2. Democrats held sway only in the western Ohio Valley, a few cities, parts of rural Pennsylvania, and some of the poorer areas along the Canadian border. These were the districts least touched by lake commerce and the growth of antislavery sentiment. The vote in 1854 made clear that any party hoping to win the support of Northerners must unequivocally support free soil in Kansas, but it was hardly clear which group would lead that fight.[9]

## II.

During the twenty-four months after the adoption of the Kansas-Nebraska Act, three parties competed for the right to become the standard-bearer for the free soil forces. The successes and ultimate failure of the Whigs and Know Nothings provide a backdrop for the emergence and triumph of the Republicans. These partisan wars make clear how far-reaching changes were redrawing the political map of the North. They suggest that a successful party needed a base united by economic programs as well as free soil doctrines.

In spring 1854 many Whigs hoped that their party's stout resistance to Douglas's measure would revive their fortunes. Every Northern Whig congressman voted against the act, making that party for the moment the vanguard of the antislavery forces. The Nebraska bill, the Chicago *Journal* remarked, "raises up the WHIG PARTY from a season of depression and despondency and gloom to action and vigorous life." Ohio senator Benjamin Wade agreed, although he would soon quit the party. Wade predicted that "the northern wing of the Whig party, released from all southern encumbrances, will become more popular at home." Thurlow Weed, the New York political boss who guided Seward's career, was also optimistic. The Whigs, he noted, are "the most efficient and reliable organization both to resist the aggressions of Slavery and to uphold the cause of Freedom."[10]

Despite such hopes, Northern Whigs had at best limited success in 1854 and virtually disappeared by the end of 1855. In the Midwest and particularly in the districts near the lakes, most Whigs quickly abandoned the party, joining with Free Soilers and others to build antislavery coalitions. By fall 1854 the party of Clay had disintegrated in Michigan, Wisconsin, Iowa, and Indiana as well as in northern Ohio and Illinois. An Indiana politician reported in September, "The Whig party, *as a party*, are entirely disbanded." Party loyalties persisted longer in the central and southern reaches of Illinois and Ohio. Unlike their brethren in the northern districts, these Whigs rarely were passionate opponents of slavery and had not worked closely with other parties in fighting for internal improvements. Thus not until 1856 would Abraham Lincoln and his compatriots in central Illinois abandon old party ties and join the Republicans.[11]

Whigs in New England and the mid-Atlantic states tried harder to maintain their independence, but in every case the outcome was the same: the party suffered serious setbacks in 1854 and all but vanished in 1855. In Massachusetts the upstart Know Nothings trounced the Whigs in the fall 1854 elections. "Poor old Massachusetts," Robert Winthrop lamented. "Who could have believed the old Whig party would have been so thoroughly demoralized in so short a space of time?" In Pennsylvania a Whig won the 1854 gubernatorial contest, but only because he joined a Know Nothing lodge. Straight Whigs were badly beaten. In New York a Whig won the governorship by the narrowest of margins, but support for the party fell away soon after the election. An Albany politician complained in December, "I am an individual Whig, but where is my party?" During 1855 even die-hard Whigs cast their lot with other parties.[12]

Why did the Whigs, whose prospects seemed so bright in spring 1854, fade so quickly? The answer has little to do with their antislavery convictions; no less than the other Northern opposition parties, Whigs passionately denounced the Kansas-Nebraska Act. Two other reasons explain the failure of the Whigs. First, Free Soilers and antislavery Democrats made clear they had no interest in uniting under the Whig banner. Connecticut Democrat Gideon Welles, a strong antislavery partisan, explained, "The truth is there is a general feeling to throw off both the old organizations and their intrigues and machinery." Any successful organization had to be a new party. Second, the transformation of the North continued to fragment the Whig Party. Wealthy Whig merchants, with their strong links to the South, were reluctant to support any group whose priorities were antislavery rather than class-based legislation. Lake district Whigs, with their deep commitment to antislavery and internal improvements, found less and less common ground with those whose homes lay in the southern part of the North.[13]

A second party, the Know Nothings, was more successful in 1854 and 1855 and briefly appeared poised to become the dominant antislavery organization in the North. From their inception as a political force, the Know Nothings condemned both foreigners and slavery. But it is more accurate to think of the Know Nothings as an antislavery party with a nativist tinge than as a nativist party with antislavery leanings. Certainly, the flood of immigrants into the United States disturbed many Americans. Three million newcomers, chiefly from Ireland and Germany, arrived between 1845 and 1854, an influx that in proportion to population exceeded all later eras. Middle-class Protestants were distressed that most of the Irish and many of the German immigrants were Catholic and impoverished. In the mid-1840s short-lived nativist parties contested municipal elections in Philadelphia, New York, and Boston. In 1850 nativists in New York City formed the Order of the Star Spangled Banner, a secret society that would become the Know Nothing Party. It grew slowly at first, claiming only forty-three members in 1852. By early 1854 this society, whose members said they "know nothing" when asked about their activities, had perhaps fifty thousand adherents in lodges scattered through the North. Explosive growth came only after the Kansas-Nebraska Act roiled political waters.[14]

Several considerations testify to the preeminence of antislavery for the Know Nothing Party in the North. The first was the extraordinary rise and decline in membership as the Order's reputation for opposing forced labor waxed and then waned. During the early months of 1854, before the battle over Douglas's bill, the Order was a noteworthy but minor player in a society accustomed to various enthusiasms and reforms. By fall 1854 the Know Nothings boasted more than a million members and had become a powerful political force. The new party succeeded, the *Harrisburg Herald* accurately noted, because "it was clearly and unqualifiedly identified with the anti-Nebraska sentiment." After a national convention in 1855 challenged that identification, the Order's demise was equally rapid. (The party "cannot stand for an instant in New England," a New Hampshire man explained, "after its anti-slavery principles are gone.")[15]

Further underscoring the importance of antislavery in the new party was the presence of many radical reformers who had little involvement with nativism. In Massachusetts most of the Know Nothing congressmen elected in 1854 were former Free Soilers who had taken no part in antiforeign agitation. Prominent Radicals, who disdained xenophobia, either formally joined the party, as did Henry Wilson and Thaddeus Stevens, or, like Salmon Chase and William Seward, readily cooperated with it. Know Nothing leaders, if often disinclined to issue policy statements, encouraged this new following. The president of the Pennsylvania Know Nothing party labeled slavery "the greatest and most pressing issue . . . now before the people."[16]

The Know Nothings, at least initially, were ideally positioned to take advantage of the widespread hostility to the Kansas-Nebraska Act. They were a new party, with none of the baggage that dragged down the Whigs and Democrats. Remarking on the Order's success, Massachusetts senator Charles Sumner observed, "The explanation is simply this. The people were tired of the old parties & they have made a new channel."[17] While condemning Douglas's bill, Know Nothings remained moderate opponents of slavery—a position that put them in the mainstream of Northern sentiment. The secrecy characterizing Know Nothing lodges also was an advantage. It allowed individuals long associated with one of the old parties to change their allegiance without censure. Pennsylvanian E. B. Chase made that point to Democratic governor William Bigler, who had been defeated in October 1854 by Know Nothing votes. "The feeling of opposition to Nebraska here, helped give the Know Nothings strength," Chase remarked. "Those who were sour because of that were ready to jump into any organization to defeat us, and more ready to join them to strike you, because they could do so covertly."[18]

The initial success of the Know Nothings, as well as their antislavery leanings, was striking. They won their greatest victory in the fall 1854 elections in Massachusetts. Their gubernatorial candidate, Henry

Gardner, received 63 percent of the vote, while the party swept the polling for the legislature, winning all but 3 of the 365 seats and electing 7 of 11 congressmen. Know Nothings also dominated in Connecticut, New Hampshire, and Rhode Island. They were the leading group in the fusion movement in Indiana and were a force to be reckoned with in New York, Pennsylvania, Ohio, Maine, and Illinois. And while some Know Nothings lobbied for their nativist goals, most placed antislavery at the top of their agenda. Know Nothing votes helped elect antislavery senators, including William Seward in New York, John Hale and James Bell in New Hampshire, Henry Wilson in Massachusetts, and James Dixon in Connecticut.[19]

The career of Henry Wilson and his brief, intense involvement with the Know Nothings sheds light on the spectacular rise and rapid fall of the new party. Like Lincoln, Wilson ascended to high office, including Massachusetts senator and vice president under Ulysses Grant, from humble beginnings. Born in New Hampshire in 1812, he was christened Jeremiah Colbath. His father, a drunk and ne'er-do-well, bound out his ten-year-old son to a neighboring farmer—service that the boy did not complete until he was twenty-one. Once he finished his indentureship, Colbath formally changed his name to Henry Wilson, probably to distance himself from his alcoholic father. Wilson also set out on foot for Massachusetts, with hopes of becoming a cobbler.

Settling in the town of Natick, which lay midway between Boston and Worcester, Wilson rose from poverty to a measure of affluence and from obscurity to leadership in the antislavery movement. Determined to improve himself, he took courses at local academies and honed his speaking skills in the town's debating society. A trip to Washington in 1836 deepened his moral education; Wilson was horrified by the slave pens he saw and returned home a fervent opponent of slavery. He also fared well in his new profession. He learned shoemaking soon after his arrival in Natick, worked long hours, and saved his earnings. After his return from Washington, Wilson purchased a shoe manufactory, and eventually employed more than one hundred workers. He now entered politics as a Whig, championing temperance and advocating civil rights for free blacks. His background as the "Natick cobbler" and his vigorous speeches endeared him to the common folk, who sent him to the state legislature. Wilson became, along with Sumner and Charles Francis Adams, a "conscience Whig" and in 1848 a Free Soiler. Thick-skinned, he shrugged off personal insults and focused on goals rather than parties. In 1851 he reached out to the Democrats, crafting a coalition that sent Sumner to the U.S. senate. Sumner thanked him: "To yr ability, energy, determination, & fidelity our cause owes its present success. For weal or woe, you must take the responsibility of having placed me in the Senate of the U. S."[20]

After the passage of the Kansas-Nebraska Act, Wilson hunted for the right political vehicle to pursue his antislavery goals. He flirted with the idea of a reinvigorated Whig Party, then in September 1854 joined a group of Free Soilers who established the Republican Party in Massachusetts. Delighted to welcome such a prominent politician, these antislavery activists anointed Wilson as their gubernatorial candidate. But Wilson quickly realized that neither the Whigs, who were fading, nor the Republicans, who appeared to many observers simply to be the Free Soil Party under a new name, could lead a popular crusade against Douglas's act. So he bolted to the Know Nothings. He did so for the same reason that other antislavery leaders enlisted in the Order or informally cooperated with it—because during these months the new party was the strongest antislavery organization. In New York Seward successfully courted Know Nothing legislators, who made possible his reelection as senator. In Ohio, Salmon Chase urged his friends to mute their criticism of the new party, a stance that helped him broaden his base of support and win the governorship in 1855. In Indiana, antislavery leader Schuyler Colfax joined the Order, just as did Radical Thaddeus Stevens in Pennsylvania. Except for Colfax, these men rejected nativist doctrines, but all recognized the power of the new party.

Wilson's dramatic change of parties in the fall of 1854 temporarily boosted the fortunes of the Know Nothings and Wilson himself. He withdrew from the race for governor a few days before the election, assuring the victory of the Know Nothing candidate, Henry Gardner. In return, Wilson gained the Order's support for his election as senator. Republicans were enraged, as were many Know Nothings. A member of the Order remarked that Wilson "has by cunning maneuvering and adroit management succeeded in hood-winking and bamboozling the good honest native Americans of this state." Still, Wilson remained steadfast to his goal, as he told abolitionist Wendell Phillips, "to secure that cooperation by which alone the slave is to be emancipated." Wilson used his newfound prominence to push the Order into becoming more openly antislavery. On a national level the party had issued no platforms or manifestos, relying on that vagueness to attract new members in the North and South. But such indecision could not continue. When the Know Nothings came together in a national convention at Philadelphia in June 1855, Wilson urged the Northern representatives to remain true to their antislavery convictions. While many delegates agreed, the convention, dominated by Southerners and their Northern allies, rejected free soil doctrines. The new platform sounded the death knell for the Know Nothings in the North. Wilson now left the Order and threw his energies into organizing the Republicans in the Bay State.[21]

The Know Nothing parties in the free states soldiered on bravely after the national convention, but increasingly the weaknesses of these state organizations became evident. Typically, they spurned the resolutions adopted at the Philadelphia meeting and continued to pursue moderate antislavery policies. In the fall of 1855, Know Nothings decisively beat the Republicans both in New York and in Massachusetts, where Gardner was reelected governor. But the movement was fragmenting, with some leaders, like Wilson and Schuyler Colfax, defecting to the Republicans. Other individuals, particularly in the Ohio Valley, argued that the party should focus on preserving the Union rather than on checking slavery or restricting immigrants.[22]

Indeed, the problem with the Order was its lack of coherence. Like a weed on sandy soil, it had spread rapidly but sunk shallow roots. It was a catchall for many who wanted a new antislavery party and were attracted as well by its secrecy and moderate doctrines. *The New York Herald* commented in 1856, "Know Nothingism afforded a temporary lodgement to a vast body of these loose materials."[23] Analysis of votes in several states makes clear that the party was a hodgepodge and that its members were not aligned by the same economic and social divisions that underlay the more permanent parties in the North. The nomination of Millard Fillmore in February 1856 on the American Party ticket was a further blow to the Order. Fillmore's candidacy was an effort to breathe new life into the organization. But most Northern Know Nothings refused to support the Americans, who ignored free soil doctrines, downplayed nativism, and focused on the need to keep the Union intact. In November 1856 only a remnant of the once-mighty Know Nothing Party backed Fillmore.[24]

Nativists continued to be important in several states after 1856, even though the movement lost its broad following in the North. In Massachusetts after the American Party disintegrated, many of its members joined the Republican ranks, bringing with them their hostility to foreigners. In 1859 the Republican legislature in the Bay State decreed that immigrants had to wait two years before becoming voters. Nativists in Pennsylvania and Connecticut also demonstrated continuing influence, helping to shape legislation and party platforms. However, most Republicans emphatically rejected such doctrines, laboring instead to recruit foreign-born voters. State organizations rebuffed overtures from nativists, and the 1860 Republican convention declared that the party opposed "any change in our naturalization laws" and favored "giving a full and efficient protection to the rights of all classes of citizens, whether native or naturalized."[25]

## III.

By the end of 1856 the Republicans had emerged as the most successful of the three antislavery parties. Unlike the Whigs, who were fragmented by the regional realignment, or the Know Nothings, whose glory was short-lived and had few connections to these far-reaching changes, the Republicans were very much a party of the transformed North. By the November 1856 election they had developed a broad following in New England and around the lakes. Their presidential candidate, John C. Frémont, mounted a serious challenge to Democrat James Buchanan. The party's early years, however, were marked by grave setbacks as it struggled to develop the right approach to antislavery and economic issues.

The Republican parties that formed in several states in 1854 were far more radical than the mainstream of Northern opinion. A Boston newspaper accurately observed that the Republicans "are too ultra for a majority of our people to accept."[26] In the months following the adoption of Douglas's measure, the party gained a firm footing in only two Northwestern states, Michigan and Wisconsin. The Michigan platform, which illustrated the vehemence of these partisans, labeled bondage "a relic of barbarism," denounced the Fugitive Slave Act, and condemned the "slaveholding Oligarchs of the South," calling their plans "the most revolting and oppressive with which the earth was ever cursed."[27] Why only Michigan and Wisconsin in 1854? Outside of New England, these states had the highest percentage of Free Soil voters. They lacked the strong Whig parties that in New York and much of New England resisted the creation of new organizations. And unlike the Ohio Valley states, they had few Southern-born voters who might oppose the formation of such a radical party. Success in Michigan and Wisconsin gave the new party a safe haven during months when Know Nothings dominated the opposition to the Democrats. It also laid the foundation for the party's strong links to the Great Lakes economy and hinted at the Republicans' future economic program.

Apart from those two lake states, early efforts to organize Republican parties failed. Massachusetts Republicans met in September 1854 and nominated Henry Wilson for governor. A Springfield newspaper sniffed that "essentially, practically, and resultingly, it was a thoroughly Massachusetts free-soil gathering."[28] When Wilson bolted to the Know Nothings just before election day, the party quietly died. In Ohio, Radical Salmon Chase saw no reason to encourage this faction. "The Republican Party," he remarked in April 1855, "seems to me not likely to last long. It is nothing but the Freesoil Party with accessions." Ohio voters elected a few Republican congressmen, but no statewide organization emerged.[29] Efforts in 1854 in New York and Illinois were unavailing, although in Illinois a group of politicians calling themselves Republicans met and passed a spirited set of resolves. Stephen Douglas would later try to tie Lincoln to the radical resolutions of the stillborn Illinois party. Lincoln, however, doubting that the new party would survive, kept his distance from the movement.[30]

A more moderate Republican party was relaunched in the summer and fall of 1855. The times seemed more propitious for the new party. The Know Nothing convention of June 1855 showed that, at least as a national movement, the nativist party favored the South. Events in Kansas also lent credence to Republican denunciations of the Southern oligarchy: in March 1855 "border ruffians" from Missouri crossed into the territory, hoping to dominate the new government. With revolvers drawn, they established a proslavery legislature at Lecompton. Free state settlers, whose emigration was encouraged by New England agencies, countered by drafting their own constitution and setting up their own state government at Topeka.

Politicians in three key states, Ohio, New York, and Massachusetts, now fashioned Republican organizations, making certain that policies were marked by moderation. Salmon Chase, overcoming his skepticism about the new party, ran for governor of Ohio on the Republican ticket. He told a Cincinnati gathering (as reported in *The New York Times*): "He had no sympathy with the GARRISON party of the North. . . . He would not interfere with Slavery where it exists by law, but was opposed to its extension over new territories."[31] Peshine Smith, a New York politician and political economist, similarly underscored the party's limited goals in explaining its strength in western New York: "The change of name [from Whig to Republican] and the formation of a platform narrowed down to resistance to Southern domination was welcome to the West."[32]

But even with such limited agendas, Republican success in the three states was mixed. Chase, who worked hard to woo dissident Know Nothing voters, won the governorship, but Republicans lost to nativists in Massachusetts and New York. Even in states as strongly opposed to the Kansas-Nebraska Act as Massachusetts and New York, the Republicans' antislavery platform was no guarantee of success—particularly since Know Nothings also opposed slavery extension. Henry Wilson confessed that Republicans had "overestimated the power of the Anti Slavery sentiment." In New York observers noted that the Know Nothings were far better organized than the newly formed Republican Party.[33]

Early in 1856 the Republicans took steps to organize nationally and prepare for the upcoming presidential campaign. Leaders broadcast a set of modest demands, although the party's radical image proved hard to dispel. In January the chairmen of various state Republican committees put out a call for a February meeting to lay the groundwork for a nominating convention. The invitation asked for support from all who agreed that "there should be neither slavery nor involuntary servitude . . . in any of the Territories."[34] The February meeting, attended by individuals such as Joshua Giddings, Horace Greeley, and George Julian, scheduled a nominating convention for Philadelphia on June 17. By summer every Northern state had selected delegates, although in Rhode Island, New Hampshire, Pennsylvania, Illinois, and Indiana, the group typically called itself the "People's" or "Union" Party. The name *Republican* still scared off conservative voters. In some states Republicans found themselves hard pressed by the American Party, which enunciated similar antislavery doctrines. "The Americans express themselves with so much decision upon the subject," a Connecticut politician told Gideon Welles, "and come so fully up to our standard that it will be difficult to keep our party friends separated from their organization."[35]

Events both in Kansas and Washington inflamed Northern opinion, swelling Republican ranks. On May 21, 1856, Samuel Jones, the proslavery sheriff of Douglas County, Kansas, led a large, unruly posse, including many Missourians, to the free state town of Lawrence. Jones's army, although killing no one, destroyed several buildings, including the offices of two free soil newspapers. The Republican press broadcast the event as the "Sack of Lawrence." A day later Congressman Preston Brooks of South Carolina entered the Senate chamber and beat Charles Sumner with a gutta-percha cane, until the Massachusetts senator, his head bloodied, collapsed on the Senate floor. Sumner would not return to his seat for two and a half years. Together the two events shocked voters and led to an upsurge in Republican support. Lyman Trumbull, the Republican senator from Illinois, remarked to Lincoln that "the outrage upon Sumner & the occurrences in Kansas have helped us vastly."[36] Many Know Nothings now joined the Republicans. They were disappointed by the American Party's selection of Millard Fillmore, who was neither a nativist nor an antislavery partisan. A Virginian explained to a Northern Know Nothing: "Recent events in Kansas and Washington seem to be driving the masses of your people into the arms of the Republican party and forcing a coalition between them and the Americans who disapprove of Mr. F[illmore]'s nomination."[37]

The effect of the Republicans' reorganization, the attack on Sumner, and bleeding Kansas became vividly clear in Frémont's remarkable showing in the November 1856 election. He finished second in the electoral college and popular vote, winning eleven states, including all six New England commonwealths as well as Michigan, Wisconsin, Iowa, Ohio, and New York.

## IV.

The November 1856 election showed that the new party gained its strength from voters in the lake districts as well as from those who had been singed by the flames of abolitionist fervor. The largest concentrations of Republican voters resided in the counties near the lakes and in rural New England, but there were also important pockets of supporters in the middle states and Midwest (see Maps 6 and 7).

In every state former Whigs comprised the largest group of Republican voters. Lake Whigs, in particular, stood out as a key Republican constituency. They were attracted by the party's antislavery planks and its advocacy of the "improvement of rivers and harbors." New England Whigs, especially those from the small towns and rural communities, enthusiastically backed the new party. Many had long criticized the South and applauded the economic policies that Republicans now espoused. The presence of former Whigs would provide fertile soil in the coming years for those urging an active approach to development.[38]

Not all Whigs, however, rushed to the party's standard. The pattern of economic growth that divided the lake economy from the lower North affected political allegiances. Most Whigs who resided in New Jersey, along the southern border of Pennsylvania, or in the Ohio Valley disdained the Republicans and voted for Fillmore. In the major

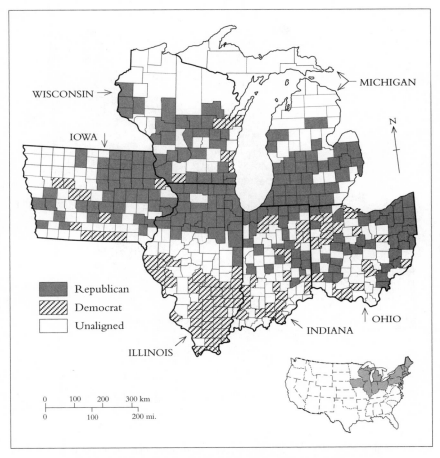

*Map 6. Republicans and Democrats in the Midwest, 1856–60*

cities wealthy merchants and manufacturers, once a mainstay of Clay's party, refused to join the new organization. Many had business ties with the South or were linked to others involved in those exchanges. Charles Dana, who assisted Greeley at the *New-York Tribune,* reported during the campaign, "The money is almost all through. The rich men here, who used to give as Whigs, are now for Fillmore or Buchanan."[39]

The next most important groups of Republican voters (among those whose loyalties can be traced) were Free Soilers and disen-

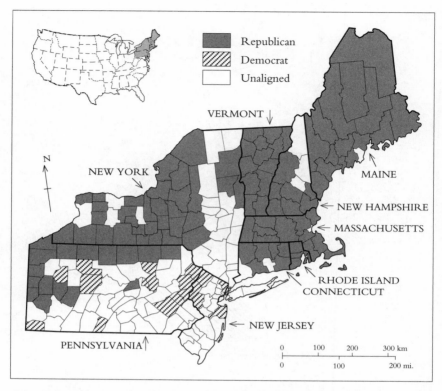

*Map 7. Republicans and Democrats in New England and the Middle States, 1856–60*

chanted Democrats. Virtually all individuals who had voted for the Free Soil Party in 1852 backed the Republicans in 1856. Some, like Henry Wilson, had sojourned among the Know Nothings but returned by 1856 to the Republican fold. In certain states, such as Massachusetts and Wisconsin, the Free Soil contingent was sizable, but in other instances it made only a minor contribution to the new party. In every state these partisans urged their fellow Republicans to broaden the attack on slavery. In the Midwest most Free Soilers resided near the lakes, but there were pockets of Free Soil—and later Republican—strength in east-central Indiana, where Quakers like George Julian had settled. Free Soil Republicans resided along both sides of the Ohio-

Pennsylvania border, where Theodore Dwight Weld and other abolitionists had proselytized. Dissident Democrats, angered by the turn
their party had taken with the Kansas-Nebraska Act, also joined the
Republicans. Many Midwestern Democrats who backed the Republicans, like Chicago politician "Long John" Wentworth, came from
lake districts. Former Democrats were especially significant in states
such as New York, Connecticut, and Ohio.

The influence of ethnicity and place of birth generally reinforced
these patterns. Inside and outside New England, Yankees favored the
Republicans. Many had been Whigs, and in the Midwest most lived
near the lakes. In Iowa they settled the northern counties, a continuation of the migration that had swelled the lake districts. By contrast,
the Southern-born individuals who populated the Ohio Valley voted
for Democrats or in some instances for the Americans. Most foreign-
born voters, and particularly Irish and German Catholics, cheered
the Democrats. Some of these foreign-born lived in cities, and along
with the wealthy they helped make most Northern towns more pro-
Democratic than the surrounding rural areas. Unlike the situation four
years later, many state Republican parties courted the Know Nothings,
an alliance that disturbed foreigners. In Illinois and Ohio, however, Republicans had a measure of success in attracting Protestant Germans.[40]

In November 1856 the Republican Party was an extraordinarily
recent creation. At the beginning of the year it had not existed in most
Northern states; by the end of the year it was the second most important party in the country. The next four years would be crucial ones
in the growth and definition of the party. Its leaders were determined
to create a long-lived organization that had strong roots and could
capture the presidency. But to do so Republicans had to work out
their differences and develop policies in two key areas: antislavery and
economic development. During the next four years they would align
the party still more fully with a North that had been transformed by
the opposition to slavery and a burgeoning regional economy.

# — 9 —

# TRIUMPH OF THE
# REPUBLICANS,
# 1856–60

Even by his own admission Horace Greeley was eccentric. He once described himself as a half-bald towheaded man, "so rocking in gait that he walks down both sides of the street at once." His clothes were often disheveled; his friend, the women's rights leader Elizabeth Cady Stanton, on occasion had to straighten his tie and push down his trouser leg before she let him walk out to the podium. He was, at times, an advocate of temperance, vegetarianism, spiritualism, women's rights, marital fidelity, and Fourier communities. Greeley was also the most influential newspaper editor of his day; his *New-York Tribune* was read throughout the North and had a circulation of almost 300,000. By 1845 he was an outspoken opponent of slavery expansion, and by the mid-1850s a leader of the newly formed Republican Party. An astute observer of the political scene, Greeley came to realize that antislavery was not enough to assure success for a candidate or a party. On the eve of the 1860 Republican convention he explained: an "Anti-Slavery man *per se* cannot be elected; but a

Tariff, River-and-harbor, Pacific Railroad, Free-Homestead man, *may* succeed *although* he is Anti-Slavery."[1]

Greeley's insight helps explain the evolution of the Republican Party in the four years after its first presidential election. Between 1856 and 1860 Republicans solidified their base of support and reached out to new voters by elaborating their antislavery and economic policies. While both sets of principles guided Republicans, the economic agenda was more important in securing a broad base of support and in setting the future course for the party.

# I.

No single person more fully embodied the antislavery policies defining the new party than Abraham Lincoln. From one vantage, the Republican Party was a "big tent" that brought together individuals ranging from Radicals like Joshua Giddings and Charles Sumner to conservatives such as Henry J. Raymond, the editor of *The New York Times*. But the party also enunciated a set of shared principles that were reflected in its national platforms and in the outlook of its leaders. Though the 1856 presidential nominee, John C. Frémont, was a soldier and adventurer who gave little thought to the challenging issues of the day, Lincoln carefully and fully enunciated his views in speeches, debates, and letters. His outlook shaped the opinions of other Republicans and (at least on issues relating to race and slavery) fully dovetailed with the platform he ran on in 1860.[2]

Lincoln's hostility to slavery had its roots in his earliest years. He remarked in 1864, "If slavery is not wrong, nothing is wrong. I can not remember when I did not so think, and feel."[3] His parents, Thomas and Nancy Hanks Lincoln, were among the minority of Kentuckians who openly rejected forced labor. They joined a small, separatist Baptist church, created by parishioners who demanded antislavery sermons. When Thomas moved the family to Indiana in 1816 (Abe was seven), the desire to farm on free soil was one of the motives, along with a dispute about land titles. Thomas's next move (in 1830) with his family was to Illinois and was simply to better his lot.[4]

Lincoln came of age in Illinois, sharing in several respects his father's disposition and outlook: like Thomas, he became a good storyteller, a supporter of Henry Clay, and a foe of slavery. Settling in the village of New Salem, he displayed a passion for self-improvement and politics. Although Lincoln had little early schooling, his determination along with the support of several friends helped him broaden his education. He began the study of law and eventually became one of the most successful lawyers in the state. Although sometimes moody, he was more often convivial and was respected for his honesty, physical strength, and intellect. When he ran for office, his neighbors strongly supported the six-foot-four young Whig politician, electing him in 1834 to the state legislature. As a lawmaker, he issued his first public protest against slavery. By a 77–6 vote, the assembly in 1837 had condemned abolitionists and affirmed that the "right of property in slaves, is sacred to the slave-holding states." Lincoln, who stood with the minority, elaborated his dissent. He agreed with the censure of abolitionists but emphasized that slavery is "founded on both injustice and bad policy."[5]

During the single term he served in the U.S. Congress, 1847–49, Lincoln's antislavery convictions deepened. Among Northern Whigs he was a moderate critic of the South. He supported the Wilmot Proviso, but unlike most Northern Whigs he voted against abolition in the District of Columbia. Influenced by Radicals like Joshua Giddings and Horace Mann, Lincoln increasingly came to see slavery as a profoundly unjust, cruel institution. Before his sojourn in Washington, Lincoln rarely spoke of the horrors of forced labor—even though he had visited the South several times as an adult. Now he told his friend Joshua Speed that the sight of shackled slaves "was a continual torment to me."[6] His new convictions proved unsettling. When he returned to Illinois, Lincoln suffered deep fits of melancholia as he wondered where his life was heading and how he could address the ills afflicting his country. He remarked to his law partner William Herndon, "How hard, oh how hard it is to die and leave one's Country no better than if one had never lived for it."[7]

With the passage of the Kansas-Nebraska Act, Lincoln made his private feelings about slavery public—a new role that lifted his spirits after several years of political inactivity. Lincoln's anger against the Kansas-Nebraska Act was inextricably entangled with his resentment of Stephen Douglas. Lincoln had known Douglas since the early 1830s; both had courted Mary Todd, the woman Lincoln married. More than once Lincoln bitterly contrasted Douglas's soaring career with his own languishing one. Now Lincoln demanded that the Democratic leader debate him, and the two had several public exchanges in 1854. With many of the same themes—and often the same words—the two men continued their dialogue during seven debates in 1858, when they were opposing candidates for the U.S. Senate.[8]

A deep moral commitment underlay Lincoln's opposition to slavery. The nub of the difference between him and Douglas, Lincoln observed, "is no other than the difference between the men who think slavery a wrong and those who do not think it wrong."[9] Lincoln pointed to the Declaration of Independence and its affirmation that "all men are created equal" as a foundation for his opposition to slavery. "Our republican robe is soiled, and trailed in the dust," he observed. "Let us repurify it. Let us turn and wash it white, in the spirit, if not the blood of the Revolution. . . . Let us re-adopt the Declaration of Independence, and with it, the practices, and policy, which harmonize with it."[10]

Lincoln grounded his view of African American rights on the Declaration's insistence that all men are entitled to "life, liberty, and the pursuit of happiness." For Lincoln, that assertion did not point to the equality of the races. Rather, it argued that all individuals should enjoy a core set of civil rights. These sentiments, which balanced racism and a concern for blacks, were widely shared by mainstream Republicans. In his first debate in 1858 with Douglas, Lincoln stated: "I, as well as Judge Douglas, am in favor of the race to which I belong, having the superior position. . . . But I hold that notwithstanding this, there is no reason in the world why the negro is not entitled to all the natural rights enumerated in the Declaration of Independence." Lincoln underscored this conviction: "I agree with Judge Douglas he ['the negro'] is not my equal in many respects—certainly not in color, perhaps not in moral or intellectual endowment. But in the right to eat the bread, without leave of anybody else, which his own hand earns, *he is my equal and the equal of Judge Douglas, and the equal of every living man.*"[11]

Because Lincoln also believed in the power of free labor, extending these fundamental rights to African Americans comprised the necessary and sufficient conditions for their rise in the world. Hard work would serve as a magical elixir. He explained to a Michigan audience in 1856, "The man who labored for another last year, this year labors for himself, and next year he will hire others to labor for him."[12] That faith in free labor would shape Republican policy in later years and discourage direct aid to the freedmen. During the war Lincoln told a group of African Americans that "success does not as much depend on external help as on self-reliance."[13]

Although committed to freedom and basic civil rights, Lincoln reassured voters that he would take no rash or unlawful steps to bring about those ends. He renounced any intention "directly or indirectly, to interfere with the institution of slavery in the States where it exists," and he put forth instead a long-term solution: halting expansion, a step that he argued would lead to slavery's "ultimate extinction." Although the process might take a century, Lincoln emphasized that it was the right path and the one that the Founding Fathers had envisioned. Emancipated slaves, Lincoln hoped, would be colonized to Africa—"their own native land."[14]

In his debates with Douglas and other addresses, Lincoln underscored his conservative approach to race and abolition. He insisted that he and his party would not repeal the Fugitive Slave Act or disturb the interstate slave trade, as some Radicals demanded. His support for ending slavery in the District of Columbia was so hedged with conditions that any bold initiative was unlikely. Lincoln insisted that a majority of citizens in the District agree to any plan; that emancipation be gradual; and that compensation be paid. Lincoln also agreed to accept new slave states in the Southwest, a possibility opened by the Compromise of 1850—although he felt such an outcome was unlikely. And he repeatedly emphasized his view that free African Americans should be second-class citizens. Lincoln remarked in 1858, "I am not nor ever have been in favor of making voters or jurors of negroes, nor of qualifying them to hold office, nor to intermarry with white people . . . and I as much as any other man am in favor of having the superior position assigned to the white race."[15]

Finally, in the last years of the 1850s Lincoln helped shift the focus of Republican oratory from "bleeding Kansas" to the dangers of slavery spreading into new areas, including the free states. By 1858 the fate of Kansas was settled: it would enter the Union, at some future date, as a free state. In 1857 settlers from Missouri and other Southern states had drawn up a proslavery frame of government, the Lecompton Constitution. Buchanan, ignoring the unrepresentative nature of the Lecompton Convention, urged Congress to accept the document and admit the new state. But the lawmakers refused; even Douglas now broke with the president, arguing the document made a mockery of popular sovereignty. In an open vote Kansans overwhelmingly rejected the frame, firmly and finally defeating the schemes of proslavery settlers. However, the Republicans now had another cause for concern: the Dred Scott decision, handed down by the Supreme Court in

March 1857. Chief Justice Roger Taney declared that no blacks, free or slave, could be citizens and that Congress could not prohibit slavery in the territories. The Kansas-Nebraska Act had repealed the Missouri Compromise line; the Dred Scott decision declared the Missouri Compromise unconstitutional.[16]

For Lincoln and for other Republicans, the Dred Scott decision, following on the heels of the Kansas-Nebraska Act, signaled an ominous sequence of events: a relentless effort to spread slavery throughout the nation. In a turn of phrase borrowed from the Bible, Lincoln intoned, "A house divided against itself cannot stand." He continued: "I believe this Government cannot endure permanently half slave and half free. . . . Either the opponents of slavery will arrest the further spread of it, and place it where the public mind shall rest in the belief that it is in the course of ultimate extinction, or its advocates will push it forward till it shall become alike lawful in all the States—old as well as new, North as well as South."[17] Noting the cooperation among leading Democrats in adopting and defending these aggressive measures, Lincoln in 1858 suggested "that there was a *tendency*, if not a conspiracy among those who have engineered this slavery question for the last four or five years, to make slavery perpetual and universal in this nation." The next Dred Scott decision, Lincoln remarked, might open the Northern states to slavery.[18]

Lincoln's mix of moral fervor, racism, and political caution made him an ideal presidential candidate. His Whiggery and his public admiration of Henry Clay ("my beau ideal of a statesman") only enhanced his standing; many of the voters the Republicans wooed were former Whigs. No wonder that Lincoln triumphed over his three opponents in the 1860 convention. Seward and Chase were considered too radical to broaden the party base, while Edward Bates of Missouri, who had supported the Know Nothings in 1855 and Fillmore in 1856, was judged too conservative.[19]

The approach most Republicans took toward slavery tracked Lin-

coln's outlook. This ideology, regarded from the vantage of abolitionists and other advocates of equality, reflected an attractive but frustrating set of beliefs. On the one hand, the Republican Party, like
Lincoln, seized the high moral ground in condemning forced labor:
both the 1856 and 1860 platforms quoted the Declaration of Independence. Republicans argued that all individuals were entitled to basic human rights and that no one should be allowed arbitrarily to
deprive African Americans of their labor or their property. On the
other hand, Republicans emphasized they would take no immediate
actions to achieve these goals, trusting to the eventual impact of free
soil policies. Republican platforms were silent on the fugitive slave
law, slavery in D.C., the interstate slave trade, civil rights for African
Americans, and of course abolition. If the Civil War had not erupted,
Republicans would have tolerated slavery for many decades to come.[20]

## II.

While Lincoln represented the mainstream of Republican opinion,
currents and eddies flowed on both sides of his views. Sizable groups
of Republicans took both more radical and more conservative approaches to change. As with economic policies, there was no enforced
uniformity of opinion. The debate within Republican ranks during
these years and later would be vigorous.

For Radicals like Charles Sumner, Salmon Chase (at least in his
private pronouncements), Joshua Giddings, Henry Wilson, George Julian, and Ben Wade, nonextension was only one aspect of a broader
program to end slavery. "How I wish that all Antislavery men could act
together," Chase remarked from Washington in 1855. "All for instance
are agreed that Congress ought (1) to prohibit Slavery in the territories; (2) to prohibit it in this District; (3) to prohibit the Slave trade in
American Vessels; (4) to prohibit the sale of persons under Federal

Process [i.e., the interstate slave trade]; (5) to repeal the fugitive slave act. Nobody doubts I presume that these things accomplished Slavery could not long survive."[21] Far more than Lincoln, Radicals demanded vigorous measures to end the "peculiar institution." Although these individuals respected the constitutional rights of the Southern states, they felt resolute action would bring quick results. "To restrict Slavery within its present limits," Greeley told the readers of the *Tribune*, "is to secure its speedy decline and ultimate extinction."[22] Wisconsin Republican Carl Schurz declared, "The clearest heads of the slave-holding States tell you openly that slavery cannot thrive, unless it be allowed to expand. . . . Well, then, . . . pent it up!"[23]

Many Radicals during these years, as earlier, took a more favorable view of civil rights for African Americans than did mainstream Republicans. Henry Wilson denounced the decision of the new state of Oregon to exclude blacks, calling the step "unconstitutional, inhuman, and unchristian," and boasted that Massachusetts recognized "the absolute and perfect equality of all men of all races." Giddings said his goal for African Americans was "not merely to protect them, but to inform, educate, refine and raise them to a moral elevation, far higher and broader" than American society had yet allowed. Republican leaders in New York and Wisconsin strongly endorsed black suffrage, although in both states voters rejected the proposals. The Wisconsin Republican Party declared itself "utterly opposed to the proscription of any man on account of birthplace, religion, or color." Such views were most strongly endorsed in the northern part of the North, and particularly in areas of Yankee settlement. They received a cooler reception in the Ohio Valley and did not become part of the national platform before the Civil War.[24]

Lincoln was also flanked by conservative Republicans who had little desire for a lofty crusade against slavery. *The New York Times* condemned abolitionist agitation, remarking in an 1858 editorial, "Ten years of absolute silence would do more than fifty of turmoil and hostility, towards a peaceful removal of the evil."[25] Simple racism drove some Republicans. A Republican orator at a New York City rally declared, "He would not speak to them on the subject of Slavery further than to say that the Republican Party was the white man's party."[26] The *New-York Tribune* accurately described the gamut of Republican opinion when it observed, "There are Republicans who are Abolitionists; there are others who anxiously desire and labor for the good of the slave; but there are many more whose main impulse is a desire to secure the new Territories for Free White Labor, with little or no regard for the interests of negroes, free or slave."[27]

## III.

Antislavery sentiments were important for the growth of the Republican Party, but ultimately their appeal was limited. By themselves they could not secure the votes required to elect a president. Those crucial votes, as most observers recognized, lay in the Lower North. The electoral math was clear. In the coming election the Republicans had to win the states they had taken in 1856, plus some combination of the other free states: Pennsylvania, New Jersey, Indiana, Illinois, and California. Pennsylvania, with its twenty-seven electoral votes, was key. Without Pennsylvania, the Republicans had to sweep the polls in the other four disputed states. "If I could see the way to get the vote of Penn for a Republican," a New York politician explained, "I should regard the road to the Presidency as plain and easy as Pennsylvania avenue."[28]

Republican emphasis on antislavery seemed to produce few favorable results in the lower North. The Pennsylvania election of 1857 was a case in point. The Republicans, calling themselves the "Union Party" (the Americans ran a separate, unsuccessful ticket), nominated David Wilmot for governor. Wilmot, the well-known antislavery leader, made nonextension of slavery and opposition to the Dred Scott decision the centerpieces of his campaign. The Democrats upbraided him as a "Free-Trade and abolition Agitator . . . who is ignorant of the business and politics of the State." When Wilmot broadened his campaign to appeal to nativists, Democrats tellingly circulated his statements among the foreign-born. Wilmot and the Union Party suffered a resounding defeat in the fall balloting. Democrats gained a majority of 63–37 in the state assembly and 20–13 in the state senate.[29]

Nor could Republicans be encouraged by the polling that took place in Illinois after the Lincoln-Douglas debates. Even with Lincoln's eloquent defense of Republican policies, the elections for the assembly reaffirmed Democratic control. The legislature predictably chose Douglas for the Senate, driving Lincoln into another fit of melancholy.[30]

A grave problem for the Republicans, who sought to distinguish themselves as the Northern antislavery party, was that the Northern Democrats also advocated free soil in the West. Douglas had argued in the debates over the Kansas-Nebraska Act that climate and soil would keep those territories free, and other Democrats repeated the same theme. A Republican politician traveling through Pennsylvania in 1856 reported, "I found that the Democracy generally evinced great hatred to the institution of slavery and particularly to the extension of Slavery but fell back on that popular delusion, 'the people ought to be allowed to decide for themselves.'"[31]

Stephen Douglas's courageous decision in December 1857 to break with President Buchanan over the Lecompton Constitution made clear that Northern Democrats, as well as Republicans, opposed extending slavery. Several Republicans, including Greeley and Henry Wilson, went so far as to suggest that all voters should back Douglas's reelection to the Senate. Illinois Republicans bitterly resented this interference and eventually persuaded Greeley and the other Eastern Republicans to endorse Lincoln. But the response of these Eastern

Republicans to Douglas demonstrates that the lines between the two parties on antislavery were sometimes blurred—and that Democrats too could attract antislavery votes. Soon after the "Little Giant" challenged Buchanan, New Yorker Peshine Smith remarked, "I hope Douglas may recede from his position, for if he adheres to it boldly and persistently he will so retrieve himself with the North as to be a very formidable candidate in 1860."[32]

Indeed, despite the vehemence of the Lincoln-Douglas debates, the outlook of the two men was often remarkably similar. Lincoln acknowledged, "There are very many of the principles that Judge Douglas has stated that I most cordially approve." Lincoln took delight in the squabbles splintering the Democratic Party but also welcomed Douglas's decision to battle the president over Lecompton.[33] The "Little Giant" professed indifference to the fate of the "peculiar institution" in the territories, but his rigorous defense of popular sovereignty placed him in the camp of the free soilers. The position to which Douglas consigned blacks in free society was not far different from the one spelled out by Lincoln. In Illinois, Douglas noted, "We have provided that the negro shall not be a slave, and we have also provided that he shall not be a citizen, but protect him in his civil rights, in his life, his person and his property, only depriving him of all political rights whatsoever, and refusing to put him on an equality with the white man. That policy of Illinois is satisfactory to the Democratic party and to me." And in fact, this stance was satisfactory to Lincoln.[34]

Finally, the Democrats' racism proved to be a strong weapon in the lower North. Douglas's speeches were filled with fear-mongering and accusations that Lincoln was forced to deny. "If you desire negro citizenship," Douglas exclaimed, "if you desire to allow them to come into the State and settle with the white man, if you desire them to vote on an equality with yourselves, and to make them eligible to office, to serve on juries, and to adjudge your rights, then support Mr. Lincoln and the Black Republican party, who are in favor of the citizenship of the negro."[35] For those voters whose outlook combined virulent racism with a desire for free soil, the Democrats were a more appealing alternative than the Republicans.

In sum, the elaboration of an antislavery ideology was important for the definition and growth of the Republican Party—but that ideology alone was not enough to turn a regional organization into a long-lived, dominant national party. The Republicans also had to become a party committed to the economic development of the North.

## IV.

Although the Republican economic agenda broadened after the Panic of 1857, many individuals advocated pro-development policies even during the party's early years. Farmers and city folk living near the lakes remained vitally concerned about the improvement of those waterways and were angered by the opposition of Democrats. A meeting of Michigan Republicans in September 1854 declared that Pierce's "recent veto [of a rivers and harbors bill] . . . and the approval by the slave Democracy is another evidence of the iron rule of slavery."[36] That same month Chicagoans made clear to Stephen Douglas their distress at the Democrats' approach to internal improvements. When Douglas tried to talk about slavery to a public meeting, the crowd demanded he discuss the rivers and harbors bill. Douglas replied, "You can't hear anything about the Harbor bill tonight. I am talking about the Nebraska Bill, and I *intend* to talk about it." The *Chicago Tribune* reported that "Douglas refused to say one word in defense of his vote against the river and harbor bill, although he was frequently requested to do so." A few days later, however, he agreed to speak to another gathering about harbor improvements—an issue, the paper noted, he had "dodged entirely on Friday night."[37]

Pierce's vetoes in 1855 and 1856 of lake improvements, along with

Republicans to Douglas demonstrates that the lines between the two parties on antislavery were sometimes blurred—and that Democrats too could attract antislavery votes. Soon after the "Little Giant" challenged Buchanan, New Yorker Peshine Smith remarked, "I hope Douglas may recede from his position, for if he adheres to it boldly and persistently he will so retrieve himself with the North as to be a very formidable candidate in 1860."[32]

Indeed, despite the vehemence of the Lincoln-Douglas debates, the outlook of the two men was often remarkably similar. Lincoln acknowledged, "There are very many of the principles that Judge Douglas has stated that I most cordially approve." Lincoln took delight in the squabbles splintering the Democratic Party but also welcomed Douglas's decision to battle the president over Lecompton.[33] The "Little Giant" professed indifference to the fate of the "peculiar institution" in the territories, but his rigorous defense of popular sovereignty placed him in the camp of the free soilers. The position to which Douglas consigned blacks in free society was not far different from the one spelled out by Lincoln. In Illinois, Douglas noted, "We have provided that the negro shall not be a slave, and we have also provided that he shall not be a citizen, but protect him in his civil rights, in his life, his person and his property, only depriving him of all political rights whatsoever, and refusing to put him on an equality with the white man. That policy of Illinois is satisfactory to the Democratic party and to me." And in fact, this stance was satisfactory to Lincoln.[34]

Finally, the Democrats' racism proved to be a strong weapon in the lower North. Douglas's speeches were filled with fear-mongering and accusations that Lincoln was forced to deny. "If you desire negro citizenship," Douglas exclaimed, "if you desire to allow them to come into the State and settle with the white man, if you desire them to vote on an equality with yourselves, and to make them eligible to office, to serve on juries, and to adjudge your rights, then support Mr. Lincoln and the Black Republican party, who are in favor of the citizenship of the negro."[35] For those voters whose outlook combined virulent racism with a desire for free soil, the Democrats were a more appealing alternative than the Republicans.

In sum, the elaboration of an antislavery ideology was important for the definition and growth of the Republican Party—but that ideology alone was not enough to turn a regional organization into a long-lived, dominant national party. The Republicans also had to become a party committed to the economic development of the North.

## IV.

Although the Republican economic agenda broadened after the Panic of 1857, many individuals advocated pro-development policies even during the party's early years. Farmers and city folk living near the lakes remained vitally concerned about the improvement of those waterways and were angered by the opposition of Democrats. A meeting of Michigan Republicans in September 1854 declared that Pierce's "recent veto [of a rivers and harbors bill] . . . and the approval by the slave Democracy is another evidence of the iron rule of slavery."[36] That same month Chicagoans made clear to Stephen Douglas their distress at the Democrats' approach to internal improvements. When Douglas tried to talk about slavery to a public meeting, the crowd demanded he discuss the rivers and harbors bill. Douglas replied, "You can't hear anything about the Harbor bill tonight. I am talking about the Nebraska Bill, and I *intend* to talk about it." The *Chicago Tribune* reported that "Douglas refused to say one word in defense of his vote against the river and harbor bill, although he was frequently requested to do so." A few days later, however, he agreed to speak to another gathering about harbor improvements—an issue, the paper noted, he had "dodged entirely on Friday night."[37]

Pierce's vetoes in 1855 and 1856 of lake improvements, along with his willingness to accept a bill to deepen the Savannah River in Georgia, further stoked this anger. A Michigan newspaper noted that Pierce "has stabbed his friends in a tender place." A Chicago newspaper called for a president who would aid "other rivers beside the political Jordan, whose waters flow only under the walls of the peculiar institution, and bear no other cargoes to market than human chattels."[38] Republicans, like other Northern representatives since the 1840s, declared that the lake improvements had a national character and deserved the full support of the federal government. Kinsley Bingham, the first Republican governor of Michigan, observed in 1855 that "the Sault St. Marie Ship Canal . . . [will] become a great national highway, connecting our richly endowed State, more intimately than at first thought would be obvious, with the ports and cities of the Eastern Hemisphere."[39]

Republicans also demanded a homestead act and a Pacific railroad by a central route. Democrat Andrew Johnson of Tennessee had been one of the earliest advocates of free tracts for settlers, and initially many in the slave states had backed this initiative. However, Southern support gradually fell away during the 1850s, as slaveholders came to see the proposal as a threat to the spread of plantations and Republicans made the issue their own. Republicans also expressed concern about Southern plans to build a railroad connecting the slave states to California. In 1854, despite Northern protests, the federal government acquired from Mexico a tract of land, the Gadsden Purchase, to facilitate such a route. Although the 1856 Republican platform did not mention the homestead act, it roundly endorsed rivers and harbors improvements "of a national character" as well as a Pacific railroad "by the most central and practicable route." According to witnesses, the applause greeting the announcement of these proposals "was only less than that which burst out when the militant Kansas plank was read."[40]

However, the most important economic issue discussed during these years was the tariff, and no Republican was a more fervent advocate of these imposts than Henry C. Carey. Carey was born in

Philadelphia in 1793, the son of Mathew Carey, an Irish immigrant, book publisher, and writer. Henry took over the family business and helped build it into the largest publishing house in the country. Unlike his convivial father, Henry was a somber if well spoken man. A contemporary remarked: "He did not shine as a conversationalist. The habit of his severe studies, and the tone of their earnestness, attached even to his common talk." In 1835 Carey retired from publishing a wealthy man and, with considerable acumen, invested his money in coal mines and Philadelphia real estate. He also turned to the study of political economy and would eventually write more than a dozen works, some several volumes in length. His earliest books trumpeted the virtues of free trade, but by the 1840s he had had nearly a complete change of heart and became the leading advocate for protection. Not incidentally, his newfound faith in the tariff dovetailed with his personal interests. As Carey was well aware, higher tariffs on iron and coal would raise the value of his holdings.[41]

For Carey, protective tariffs created the "diversity" of production that a thriving economy required, while free trade harmed a country by forcing it to concentrate on two or three products. Carey condemned England, "the great apostle of the sort of free trade we do *not* require." He praised the protective tariff of 1842 "because it had for its objects, the diversification of the demands for labor. . . . It gave us . . . the sort of [internal] free trade, that . . . we so greatly need—freedom of intercourse between man and man, town and town, county and city, State and State." Carey served up a simplified economic history of the United States, arguing that high tariffs produced prosperity while falling barriers fostered downturns. Although Carey felt that the stumbling Southern economy also required higher tariffs, he did not (until his views gradually changed in the 1850s) denounce slavery. He accepted that labor system as the most suitable for the Southern climate.[42]

Carey was not content simply to write about protection; he also proselytized for the cause and regarded the newly formed Republican

Party as the ideal vehicle for achieving his goals. In 1856 he helped the Philadelphia and state committees raise funds, a task that proved difficult, since many Southern-leaning merchants disdained the new party. "All the people who used to pay have been against us," Carey complained.[43] But above all else, Carey used the political campaign as an opportunity to promote tariff reform. He sought to persuade lawmakers with letters and pamphlets, and he recruited a cadre of speakers to drum up grassroots support. William Elder, one of these speakers (and later Carey's biographer), carried the banner of protection into towns in Pennsylvania and New England. Stopping in New Haven, Elder reported, "The Hall is a very fine one and the audience large and worthy, above 600 certainly, and the Yale College boys well represented. I gave them 10 minutes criticism upon Adam Smith, Ricardo, Malthus, Senior, Mill, Whately, and an hour exposition of the dogmas in the light of the healthy and hopeful philosophy [of protection]."[44]

However, during these early years of the party Carey encountered three grave obstacles in his effort to win over the Republicans, and the North, to a program of higher tariffs. First, the furor over Kansas absorbed the attention of Republican congressmen and constituents alike. To be sure, long-standing divisions over economic issues, such as lake improvements, helped define the constituencies of the early Republican Party. But for most individuals the top priority, as the party coalesced, was checking the spread of slavery into "bleeding Kansas." After discussing the campaign for higher imposts, New Yorker Peshine Smith told Carey in 1855, "I fear that nobody could enlist attention in this state, to any other subject than the conquest of Kansas by Missourians."[45] Ohio congressman Lewis Campbell agreed. "Our *new* members," he remarked in 1856, "generally are so much absorbed in the Kansas and kindred questions that it is difficult to attract their attention to other grave subjects with which slavery is not immediately connected."[46] Only once the battle for Kansas subsided would economic issues play a prominent role in the public debate.

Second, prosperous times and a Treasury surplus undercut the argument for a protective tariff. Before the twentieth century the tariff typically served two functions: it nurtured particular industries, and it provided the chief source of government revenue. In bountiful periods, like the months from 1854 through the first half of 1857, abundant revenues weakened the case for protection. Pennsylvania congressman James Campbell, an ardent defender of the iron and coal industry, told Carey in 1856, "The large balance in the treasury and the revenue derived from existing duties makes our position an embarrassing one."[47] Charles Dana, managing editor of Greeley's *New-York Tribune* and a committed protectonist, offered similar advice. In 1856 he cautioned the Philadelphian "that to attempt to put Protection into the platform of any party to-day would be equivalent to political suicide."[48] Indeed, before 1858 there was a strong case for a *lower* tariff, a goal realized in the Tariff of 1857. *The New York Times* remarked early in 1857: "Are we ever to have a new Tariff? . . . That our people are now heavily taxed—unnecessarily taxed—is apparent to any one who has noted the rapid accumulation of money in the Treasury, year after year. There is always more money there than the Government requires, and much more than the Government knows what to do with."[49]

Third, most New Englanders opposed higher tariffs. The vote on the Tariff of 1857, which lowered duties, cast a harsh light on divisions in the North. The representatives from Massachusetts, Connecticut, Rhode Island, and Maine favored the act, while most of the congressmen from western New York, Pennsylvania, and the Midwest (at least the districts near the lakes) opposed it. Southern votes facilitated the passage of the measure. Various observers and the testimony of the Yankee delegates themselves underscored "eastern" opposition to taxing imports. "All the Free Soil or anti Slavery people here go for Free Trade," one of Carey's Boston correspondents noted in 1856.[50] Henry Wilson concurred: "In Massachusetts, and I think I may say in New England, we desire a change in the tariff laws . . . I think American labor shall be best protected by taxing all the necessaries of life lightly."[51]

The divergence between New England and Midwestern views of the tariff signaled a broad shift in the patterns of Northern growth. New England with its textile mills had once stood in the vanguard of Northern industrial expansion. During the decades after the War of 1812 manufacturers had demanded higher duties to nurture their infant industry. But by midcentury New England factories could hold their own in world markets, and producers were concerned instead about securing cheap raw materials, particularly wool and cotton. *The New York Times* explained, "New-England has ceased to clamor for protection to her cotton and her woolen. She needs a *stable* Tariff much more than a protective Tariff."[52] By contrast, the Midwest (particularly near the lakes) and parts of Pennsylvania welcomed new enterprises, many of which were small or unable to compete with British firms and so demanded higher levels of protection.[53]

These clashes over tariff policy within the Republican Party were the opening salvos in a long dispute between Northern regions, as they embarked on different trajectories of growth. In 1850 New England accounted for 27 percent of U.S. industrial output, while six Midwestern states (Ohio, Illinois, Indiana, Wisconsin, Michigan, and Minnesota) produced only 12 percent of the total. In 1900 these percentages were nearly reversed. The Midwestern states produced 27 percent of the nation's industrial value, while New England had slid to 18 percent. New York had also declined relatively, from 23 to 17 percent of the total, while Pennsylvania (thanks to thriving industries west of the Appalachians) dipped only slightly, from 15 to 14 percent of the total.

However, differences over imposts and later currency and banking did not negate the importance of these issues for Republicans; nor did they make the party less able to adopt bold initiatives. Able leaders regularly found common ground, while in other instances the weight of numbers, typically favoring lake representatives, decided contentious questions. Moreover, virtually all Republicans agreed on measures such as the homestead act, internal improvements, and a Pacific railroad.[54]

Still, it was no wonder that in the spring of 1857 Henry Carey, discouraged by his faltering campaign for protection and by the poor showing Republicans had made in Pennsylvania, sailed to Europe for an extended visit. But when he returned late in the fall, the political scene in the North had changed. During the next three years the Republicans would commit themselves to the higher duties Carey sought as well as other related policies.

## V.

In the years leading to the outbreak of war the Republicans adopted a broad economic agenda, with a protective tariff as its centerpiece. Two developments spurred the Republicans' newfound willingness to embrace these policies. The first was the Panic of 1857, which struck the North in the fall of that year—and had a far-reaching impact on politics. Observers at the time, and since, have suggested that over-expansion in the preceding years, combined with the end of the Crimean War and declining American exports to Europe, triggered the downturn. Banks in Ohio and Pennsylvania collapsed when their customers failed. The Cleveland *Plain Dealer* posted a "List of Late bustified Banks (Corrected Hourly)."[55] The slump affected farmers and mechanics across the North, but it struck hardest in the iron and coal districts of Pennsylvania. In June 1858 one foundry owner reported, "In our own region from Harrisburg to Columbia, eleven out of fourteen furnaces are out of blast. Immediately dependent upon these for support are one thousand men with their families and very many more or less directly interested. These are entirely cut off from their means of livelihood. The coal region is even worse smitten than we are and the suspension of manufacturing has ruined half the operators."[56] Northern farmers noted improvement by the end of 1858, but iron and coal producers found recovery slower.

The downturn mightily strengthened the case for raising tariffs. Customs receipts plummeted as imports slumped from $348 million in 1857 to $263 million in 1858, the largest single-year decline to that time. The drop in revenues transformed the federal surplus into a deficit of over $40 million. Although many called for retrenchment, the government clearly needed additional funds.[57]

The second development catalyzing change was the growing awareness, on the part of many Republicans and others, that higher imposts were needed to win Pennsylvania's crucial electoral votes. The 1858 elections, held against the background of hard times, underscored that message. In the spring contest for Philadelphia mayor, opposition groups came together to demand increased duties and ousted the Democratic incumbent with relative ease. "The old line whigs were seduced on the tariff issue," an observer reported to President Buchanan. "The men out of work were told this was cause and cure for their idleness."[58] The fall congressional elections reaffirmed the importance of higher imposts. In 1857 Republican David Wilmot's focus on free soil had proven disastrous for his gubernatorial campaign. Now the Republicans (calling themselves the "People's Party") changed tactics, and emphasized "PROTECTION TO AMERICAN INTERESTS AND AMERICAN LABOR." This platform, which allowed Republicans and Americans to unite, produced a resounding victory. Coming into the election, Democrats held 15 of Pennsylvania's 25 congressional seats. In a striking reversal, voters in 1858 elected only 3 regular Democrats (along with 2 "anti-Lecompton" Democrats). Republicans took the other 20 places. Democratic losses were particularly severe in the iron and coal counties. The message was not lost on leaders in Washington. *The New York Times* reported, "The Pennsylvania election seems to have made some impression even upon the President's mind, and he would be quite willing to see a revenue Tariff so shaped as to afford incidental protection to iron."[59]

The panic and the Pennsylvania elections speeded the adoption of an economic agenda, but the Republican commitment to Northern development had deeper roots—ones that lay in the realignment of domestic trade and the rise of the lake economy. No single individual better reflected these larger developments or was more instrumental in shaping Republican economic policies than John Sherman. Born in 1823, Sherman was the eighth child (of eleven) of Mary Hoyt and Charles Sherman, a judge on the Ohio Supreme Court. When John was six, his father died, leaving his mother in difficult straits that forced her to split up the family so the younger children could be cared for and educated. Fortunately, relatives and neighbors rushed to assist. A cousin opened his home to John, while a family friend, Thomas Ewing, fostered John's older brother, William Tecumseh, the future Civil War general. The challenges John faced growing up honed his sense of responsibility and determination to succeed. After working for two years to help his mother, he returned to school, pursued law, and at the age of twenty-one was admitted to the bar. Although he had been a rather rebellious child, he became a serious young man, increasingly interested in politics. He began as a Whig but, angered by the Kansas-Nebraska Act, became one of the founders of the Republican Party in Ohio. In 1854, well before the state party coalesced, Sherman was elected as a Republican congressman from a district that bordered Lake Erie and included part of the Western Reserve.[60]

Sherman's ascent within the Republican Party was remarkable and testified to his singular abilities. Passing over more senior members, the Speaker chose Sherman and two other lawmakers in 1856 to investigate conditions in Kansas. With Sherman doing most of the work, the committee produced a 1,300-page report that excoriated the proslavery forces and provided an extraordinary source of information for Republican partisans inside and outside Congress. In the ensuing debates, Sherman distinguished himself by his opposition to the spread of slavery, his lack of partisan rancor, his clear sense of purpose, and his ability as a parliamentarian. When the 36th Congress convened in December 1859, Sherman was the overwhelming choice of Republicans for Speaker. But the Ohioan had inadvertently signed a memorial endorsing Hinton Rowan Helper's abolitionist tract, and on a series of ballots he fell three votes short of a majority. After two months of fruitless divisions, Sherman withdrew. Instead, he became chairman of the Ways and Means Committee—the second most important position in the House.[61]

Sherman helped move the Republican Party from its initial focus on nonextension to a broad program that emphasized the development of the Northern economy. Repeatedly, he made his intentions clear, setting out his views most fully in an address at Cooper Union in New York. (Lincoln had spoken there two months earlier.) Sherman explained that while stopping the spread of slavery "was the immediate purpose and aim of the Republican organization . . . it now has other purposes in view." These included a homestead act, a Pacific railroad ("the great problem of the age"), the tariff, and the "gradual colonization of the negro population."[62]

Although Sherman couched his proposals in the language of nationalism, in setting forth his plans he spoke for the North and, more particularly, the lakes. He called on the federal government to retrench, but the spending he condemned typically was focused in the South, such as the construction of Charleston and New Orleans customs houses. At the same time Sherman backed projects that fit with his vision of national development. He remarked in 1860, "I am willing to appropriate any amount necessary to aid in building a Pacific railroad."[63] Most significantly, Sherman supported spending money on the lakes and was outraged by Southern opposition and presidential vetoes. He presented lake spending as a national rather than a local concern, telling his fellow congressmen that the region would "in a short time control the destinies of this nation."[64]

Before the war Sherman's greatest accomplishment came in guiding through Congress the Morrill tariff, which secured Buchanan's assent in March 1861. Sherman liked the bill, which was drafted by Senator Justin Morrill of Vermont in close consultation with Carey and the Pennsylvania delegation. It fit the spirit of moderation that Sherman had expounded in his Cooper Union speech: "Composed as the Republican party is of Whigs and Democrats, and holding somewhat opposite creeds upon the question of the tariff, it will be prepared to consider without party bias . . . how duties or imports may be imposed sufficient to meet the necessary expenses of the Government."[65] The act raised rates moderately, replaced ad valorem with specific duties (that would not fluctuate as import prices changed), and protected iron and coal producers, wool growers, and an array of other industries. Sherman, ably assisted by Carey, kept the Republicans together through a series of votes, even though Pennsylvanians sought higher rates and many New Englanders lower ones. Although the House first approved the bill in May 1860, Southern tactics delayed final approval until just before Lincoln's inauguration.[66]

Most striking was the support for the Morrill Act in the Midwest, where many residents saw their region's future in an industrial regime supported by higher duties rather than in a purely agrarian republic. "We have in Wisconsin the finest zinc mines that are to be found, perhaps, in the world," Cadwallader Washburn reminded Congress. "They should have some protection."[67] Samuel Curtis of Iowa expressed similar sentiments: "I want to see the great Mississippi applied to mechanical use. I want to see manufactories spring up there; and I therefore want to see protection afforded by a tariff measure."[68] In most cases, Sherman and Morrill honored these requests for specific duties, helping to build a strong Midwestern bloc in favor of protection.[69]

The campaign for the Morrill tariff altered the views of many Republicans who had once been Democrats and free traders. No conversion was so striking as that of Salmon Chase, the ambitious Ohio reformer and politician. In October 1859 Chase, a longtime opponent of protection, issued a public letter setting forth his new outlook. He declared that no man "deserves the name of an American statesman who would not so shape American legislation and administration as to protect American industry."[70] Once in office as Lincoln's secretary of the treasury, Chase made Carey's disciple, William Elder, his key adviser on revenue policies. Like Chase, David Wilmot also announced his willingness to support higher imposts, as did Galusha Grow, the former Democrat who filled Wilmot's house seat. Several of Henry Carey's correspondents did a similar about-face. One Iowa politician wrote the economist: "I think it is pretty conclusively shown that a great many old Free Traders have like myself become confirmed 'Careyites.'"[71] However, not all Republicans were won over. *The New York Times*, which spoke for the liberal-minded traders of New York, disliked the higher duties, as did the *New-York Evening Post*. "The new Tariff bill," wrote the *Post*'s editor William Cullen Bryant, "effects a complete revolution in our commercial system, returning by one huge step, backward to the old doctrine of protection." Republican newspapers in the Ohio Valley and John Wentworth's *Chicago Daily Democrat* echoed these views.[72]

The platform adopted at the Republican Convention, held in Chicago in May 1860, confirmed the party's commitment to protection. The Pennsylvania and New Jersey delegations lobbied hard for a protariff plank. Bryant, viewing this activity from his free trade perspective, commented: "A deeply-laid conspiracy is in operation to pervert the Republican party to the purposes of the owners of coal and iron mines."[73] The result of such pressure was a platform that declared, "While providing revenue for the support of the general government by duties upon imports, sound policy requires such an adjustment of these imports as to encourage the development of the industrial interests of the whole country."[74] Some Republicans downplayed the importance of the statement. Gustave Koerner later remarked, "This amounted to no more than the establishment of a revenue tariff bill with incidental protection."[75] But most tariff advocates were delighted. *The New York Times* reported from Chicago, "The tariff clause gives universal satisfaction, and was received with a storm of enthusiasm seldom witnessed in any popular gathering." Another eyewitness recorded, "The scene this evening upon the reading of the 'Protection to Home Industries' plank in the platform was beyond precedent. One thousand tongues yelled, ten thousand hats, caps and handkerchiefs waving with the wildest fervor." Republicans in Pennsylvania and New Jersey also celebrated the convention's decision.[76]

Lincoln's relationship to the campaign for higher duties was complex. On the one hand, he was reluctant to support an issue that he feared would gain few votes in southern Illinois and Indiana. Asked for his views in fall 1859, he replied cautiously: "If we could have a moderate, carefully adjusted, protective tariff, so far acquiesced in, as to not be a perpetual subject of political strife, squabbles, charges, and uncertainties, it would be better for us. Still, it is my opinion that, just now, the revival of that question, will not advance the cause itself, or the man who revives it."[77] Unlike Sherman, Lincoln was in many respects an outsider in the Republican Party. He joined the party relatively late, supporting the new organization only in 1856. He came from central Illinois, well removed from the lake districts where most Midwestern Republicans resided, and did not share their passionate commitment to the development of the lake economy. He spent no time in Washington during the 1850s; nor was he privy to the debates and bargaining that underlay the development of Republican policies. Even when he was president, his knowledge of and support for tariff legislation was curiously limited. Lincoln's views may have coincided with—and helped form—the Republican consensus on slavery, but that was not the case for economic policies.[78]

On the other hand, Lincoln's Whig background helped secure his nomination as well as the support of the manufacturing districts in the presidential campaign. Pennsylvanians swung behind Lincoln at the Chicago convention because they judged he was, as his backers emphasized, "an old Clay Whig" and "right on the tariff."[79] Lincoln did not trumpet his protectionist views, but he made clear when asked that he fully supported the party platform. Republicans in Pennsylvania and New Jersey made the most of Lincoln's political roots and commitment. A Philadelphia journal noted that "Mr. Lincoln was . . . a consistent and devoted Whig, well known for his firm and unwavering fidelity to Henry Clay, and the great policy of protection to American industry."[80] New Jersey Republicans declared that "Mr. Lincoln is in favor of a protective Tariff because he earnestly desires to see all our mills and factories in successful operation, making music along our rivers and booming amid the hills."[81] Pennsylvanians reminded Lincoln about the importance of the issue in their state. Republican state chairman Alexander McClure told Lincoln that all speakers sent to Pennsylvania "should be thoroughly familiar with the Tariff question—a question, I believe, that has not been nearly so prominent in your struggles in Illinois as it has been here."[82]

As important as the tariff was, it remained only one facet of the broad economic agenda that Republicans pursued in the late 1850s. The homestead act, championed by Pennsylvania congressman Galusha Grow, was another key initiative. Northern Democrats also backed the measure but recognized that most members of their party condemned such grants. "I say it in sorrow," a Minnesota Democratic congressman remarked, "that it was to the Republican side of the House to whom we were compelled to look for support of this just and honest measure."[83] Republicans considered the homestead act as more than a means of helping settlers. It "will unquestionably aid in securing the Territories for free labor," Sherman explained in his Cooper Union address. "When the public land is open for homesteads of limited quantities there is little danger but that farms will exclude plantations and free labor exclude slave labor."[84] Congress adopted a homestead bill in 1860, but Buchanan vetoed it, declaring that it would "go far to demoralize the people and repress their noble spirit of independence." No homestead act would be adopted until after secession.[85]

Other initiatives rounded out the prewar Republican agenda and hinted at the program the party would adopt once it took power. Republicans campaigned for lake improvements, an issue that enjoyed broad support in the party. Even New Englanders like Henry Wilson, who resisted higher tariffs, endorsed the measure. Republicans also demanded federally funded agricultural colleges, with Vermont senator Justin Morrill lobbying hard for this bill. "Pass this measure," he exclaimed, "and we shall have done something to enable the farmer to raise two blades of grass instead of one." Led by a solid Republican bloc, Congress approved land grants for schools. However, in a response that was all too familiar, Buchanan rejected the bill.[86] Republicans also backed a telegraph to California, and in December 1860 Samuel Curtis, an Iowa Republican, introduced a bill for a Pacific railroad. But while virtually all Republicans agreed on the need for the road, they differed over the route and its funding. It would take several years to sort out those issues, and Curtis's proposal failed. Much of this agenda was mirrored in the 1860 platform, which was more expansive on economic issues than the 1856 resolves had been. The Chicago convention endorsed higher tariffs, a homestead act, river and harbor improvements, and a Pacific railroad.[87]

Republican advocacy of a broad economic program helped secure Lincoln's victory in November 1860. To win, Republicans had to defend their base and gain enough votes in the lower North to tip the balance in Illinois, Indiana, New Jersey, and Pennsylvania. Because few Democrats changed their loyalties, the swing constituencies were those that had backed Fillmore in 1856 and the Whig Party in earlier elections. Typically, these pivotal voters resided in the Ohio Valley, southern Pennsylvania, and New Jersey; frequently they had Southern roots; and usually they were more concerned about economic issues than about antislavery. Republicans succeeded in luring these former Whigs into their fold. Between 1856 and 1860 the proportion of Northerners voting for a Whiggish third party (American in 1856, Constitutional Union in 1860) slumped from 12 to 2 percent, with most of these voters joining the Republicans. Close analysis underscores the point. Between 1856 and 1860 Republicans increased their proportion of the vote by 25 percent or more in 79 counties. (See Map 8.) All but five of these districts were in the lower North, chiefly in Pennsylvania, Illinois, Indiana, and New Jersey. Typically, these counties had favored Fillmore and voted Whig in earlier elections. The shift of allegiances was most striking in Pennsylvania, where Republican support rose from 32 to 56 percent, while Whiggish third parties fell from 18 percent to 3 percent. The Republicans' stance on economic issues, not antislavery, swayed these individuals and allowed Lincoln to win.[88]

# VI.

Although Republicans elaborated both their antislavery and economic policies, the economic agenda was more important. To be sure, views of African Americans helped shape party membership and guided future actions. Republicans proudly trumpeted their belief in the principles of the Declaration of Independence, sentiments that attracted many in Greater New England and other "abolitionized" districts. It is also true that in the 1860 campaign Republican orators were far more likely to emphasize free soil than the tariff, which was the leading issue only in Pennsylvania, New Jersey, and scattered districts in the Midwest. Republican politician James Blaine later reflected: "To

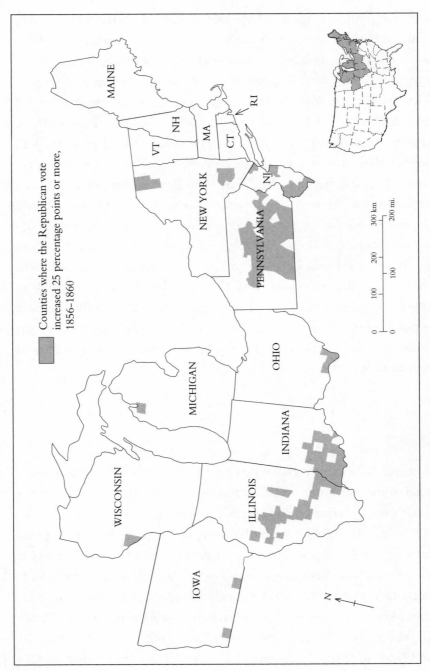

Counties where the Republican vote increased 25 percentage points or more, 1856–1860

*Map 8. Increase in Republican Vote, 1856–60*

hundreds of thousands of voters who took part in that memorable contest, the tariff was not even mentioned. Indeed this is probably the fact with respect to the majority of those who cast their suffrages for Mr. Lincoln."[89] Campaigners in much of New England, for example, overlooked the Republican tariff policies while highlighting the determined defense of free soil.

However, the case for the preeminence of economic issues is a strong one. To begin with, most Republicans viewed free soil more as an economic than an antislavery policy. When enunciated by Radicals like Charles Sumner and Salmon Chase, nonextension was one facet of a campaign to accelerate the demise of slavery. But for many others, it was simply a program to ensure that white farmers could settle the West without competition from Southern planters. Lincoln, like many Republican orators, made both arguments. In the debates with Douglas, he stated: "Now irrespective of the moral aspect of this question as to whether there is a right or wrong in enslaving a negro, I am still in favor of our new Territories being in such a condition that white men may find a home—may find some spot where they can better their condition—where they can settle upon new soil and better their condition in life."[90] Which motive attracted most Northerners to free soil? The preeminence of economic reasons is suggested by the refusal of mainstream Republicans to oppose slavery with any other steps, including ending bondage in the District of Columbia, blocking the interstate slave trade, excluding slaves from federal shipyards, or nullifying the fugitive slave act.

Furthermore, the leaders of the party that achieved victory in November 1860 were firmly committed to the economic development of the North. Republicans made their outlook clear when they organized the new Congress, which met in special session in July 1861. John Sherman, who would have been the new Speaker, helped direct economic matters in the Senate after the Ohio legislature elevated him to the upper house. In his stead, Galusha Grow, champion of the homestead act, became Speaker. Pennsylvanian Thaddeus Stevens, an ironmaster, former Whig, and longtime advocate for high tariffs, took over as chair of the Ways and Means Committee, which oversaw economic legislation in the House. Other key posts were occupied by men such as Justin Morrill, William Pitt Fessenden, and James Simmons—all strong advocates of economic legislation. The new secretary of the treasury, Salmon Chase, a convert to protection, worked closely with these individuals. The far-reaching, coherent plans for development that these leaders and other Republicans put in place after secession underscore the importance of economic programs for the party.[91]

Economic issues also were more important than antislavery in growing the Republican Party from a regional organization in 1856 to a dominant national institution after 1860. The broad-based Republican approach to Northern growth was key to winning these new voters. Free soil—which straddled the divide between antislavery and economic development—was not sufficient. To a remarkable degree, Republicans and Northern Democrats agreed on free soil. In the 1840s almost all Northern representatives had voted for the Wilmot Proviso; in 1857 Douglas had made clear his abhorrence of Southern plans to force slavery on Kansas; in 1860 Northern Democrats joined Republicans in voting for the admission of a free Kansas. The issues that separated Republicans from Northern Democrats involved the larger Republican economic program, including the tariff, agricultural colleges, and internal improvements. In the 1860 election these issues helped Republicans woo the former Whigs who had backed Fillmore—and thereby sweep the North. These new voters shared with other Republicans a common approach to the economy rather than a passion for aiding African Americans.[92]

Finally, many Republicans backed the party because particular economic programs, apart from expanding the area of free farming, appealed to them. The tariff was crucial in Pennsylvania and New Jersey. Blaine, after noting that most Republicans did not cast their vote because of the tariff plank, remarked: "It is none the less true that these hundreds of thousand of ballots . . . would have been utterly ineffectual if the central and critical contest in Pennsylvania had not resulted in a victory for the Republicans. . . . The tariff therefore had a controlling influence."[93] Henry Carey was blunter: "Protection made Mr. Lincoln president."[94] Other issues won votes for the Republicans. The lake districts had long demanded internal improvements. In 1858 the manager of a Milwaukee railroad told Simon Cameron that "Western politicians . . . will rally around anyone that may prove himself in favor of improvements of 'Rivers and Lake Harbours.'" He added that the question "will be in 1860 the prominent feature in the campaign of the West and an issue upon which the entire North West can be carried."[95] Labor leader John Commerford, speaking at a New York City rally, stated that "it was not so much by their contest with Slavery as by their Homestead bill that the Republicans achieved their victory."[96] Antislavery was unquestionably important, particularly for those who joined the party in its first years, but in many places it was only one of a set of issues that won votes for the Republicans.

Between 1856 and 1860 Republicans spelled out their antislavery and economic policies. But their views on Northern development were more important in attracting new members, determining the congressional leadership, and charting the party's future course. The Republican program also had grave repercussions for national politics. The new party's stance led many Southerners, and particularly planters in the lower reaches of the cotton states, to call for secession.

# THE COTTON STATES
# LEAVE THE UNION

**M**y father was a South Carolina nullifier, governor of the state at the time of the nullification row, and then U.S. senator. So I was of necessity a rebel born," explained Mary Chesnut in the opening pages of her Civil War diary. Like most of her friends, Chesnut was an ardent secessionist, publicly demanding bold actions. Still, she confided to her diary, "as a woman, of course, it is easy for me to be brave under the skins of other people." Her entries, in the weeks leading up to the fall of Fort Sumter in mid-April 1861, reveal the tensions that shaped Southern society and the secessionist movement. She commented on the class prejudices of her husband, who like her father had served as a U.S. senator: "One of our party <Mr. C> so far forgot his democratic position toward the public as to wish aloud, 'Oh, that we had separate coaches, as they have in England. That we could get away from these whiskey-drinking, tobacco-chewing rascals and rabble.'" Another recurrent theme is the fear of rebellious slaves. Recounting a discussion with Charlotte Wigfall, wife of Texas senator Louis Wigfall, Chesnut noted: "Mrs. Wigfall came in, and we had it out on the subject of civil war. We solaced ourselves with dwelling on all its known horrors, and then we added what we had a right to expect, with Yankees in front and negroes in the rear. 'The slave-owners must expect a servile insurrection, of course,' said Mrs. Wigfall, to make sure that we were unhappy enough."[1]

Class and racial tensions, which loom large in Chesnut's diary, helped determine the Southern response to events during 1860 and 1861. But they form only part of the explanation of how and why secession occurred. The three Southern regions—the Lower South, the Upper South, and the Border States—pursued different paths as the crisis deepened. Moreover, each region was internally divided, and these divisions (which in part fell along class lines) shaped the way secession played out. No group was more important, however, or more dynamic during the secession winter of 1860–61, than the states' rights leaders of the Lower South. Their actions set in motion events that others responded to. These individuals saw in the ascent of the Republican Party the certain, if eventual, demise of slavery. The Republicans' hostility to forced labor, affirmations of equality, willingness to use patronage, and economic policies together spelled out doom for the plantation system. For these defenders of the South, the only logical response was separation.

I.

At the heart of the secession movement, which found its strongest supporters in the states' rights districts of the cotton South, stood a clear rationale: Southerners had to leave the Union to preserve slavery or, put more broadly, their social system. Henry Benning, the secessionist commissioner whom Georgia sent to Virginia in February 1861, presented the case succinctly. "What was the reason that induced

Georgia to take the step of secession?" he asked. "This reason may be summed up in a single proposition. It was a conviction, a deep conviction on the part of Georgia, that a separation from the North was the only thing that could prevent the abolition of her slavery."[2]

No single individual or state can lay claim to originating this argument. But no politician worked longer or harder for Southern independence, or made the case for separation more forcefully, than Robert Barnwell Rhett. When South Carolina left the Union in December 1860, the Charleston correspondent for the *New-York Evening Post* reported: "This is his hour of triumph, and the triumph is more properly and peculiarly his than that of any other man now living."[3]

Political and personal reasons came together to place Rhett in the vanguard of the secession campaign. He represented a wealthy rice-growing district that claimed one of the highest concentrations of slaves and large plantations in the South. The radicalism of Lowcountry politicians like Rhett stood out even in a state known for its extremism. In addition, Rhett wrestled with the burden of measuring up to his distinguished forebears. Born Robert Barnwell Smith, he changed his name to Robert Barnwell Rhett to honor an ancestor who had been governor general of the Bahamas. Indeed, banishing "Robert Smith" entirely, he asked his friends to call him "Barnwell Rhett." Growing up in a family of only moderate means (his father had lost his rice plantation when Robert was a teenager), Barnwell became a successful lawyer and poured his money into land and slaves so he could stand shoulder to shoulder with other members of the elite.

In both the state and national legislatures Rhett made clear his hostility to any measure that threatened slave society. He urged a bold response during the Nullification Crisis of 1832–33, declaring, "Washington was a disunionist, Samuel Adams, Patrick Henry, Jefferson, Rutledge were all disunionists and traitors. . . . Shall we tremble at epithets?"[4] He came back to the same theme in 1850, when he again argued for secession. Noting his revolutionary forebears, he stated, "I have been born of Traitors, but thank God, they have ever been Traitors in the great cause of liberty, fighting against tyranny and oppression." Before the late 1850s, however, Rhett found only limited support for his goals. He recognized that denunciations of the "madness of tyranny," or of tariffs and abolitionists, would not persuade Southerners to separate as long as Northerners made a show of moderation. In 1852 he resigned his Senate seat, despairing that he could ever lead the South out of the Union.[5]

Republican victories in 1856 reinvigorated Rhett's hope for secession and convinced him that he finally had a winning issue: the survival of slave society. In 1857 Rhett and his eldest son, Robert Barnwell Rhett, Jr., purchased *The Charleston Mercury* to gain a platform for their militant views. The *Mercury* quickly became the most outspoken pro-secession paper in the South. "The issue before the country is the extinction of slavery," the Rhetts warned their readers. "No man of common sense, who has observed the progress of events, and who is not prepared to surrender the institution, with the safety and independence of the South, can doubt that the time for action has come—now or never." In speeches, letters, and editorials the Rhetts denounced not only the Republicans but also Stephen Douglas and the dangerous implications of popular sovereignty. For the many readers of the *Mercury*, the Rhetts spelled out the hardships that the Republicans would inflict on the South even before they crushed slavery.[6]

Rhett and other secessionists were not dissuaded by Republican promises to respect the South's institutions or by discussions of Southern prosperity. Such short-term concerns were beside the point. When moderates advised waiting for a hostile act before seceding, the Rhetts responded: "Although you see your enemy load his rifle with the declared purpose of taking your life, you are to wait, as a wise expedient of defense, until he makes the 'overt act'—shoots you."[7] States' rights leaders emphasized Lincoln's commitment to the "ultimate extinction" of bondage and frequently quoted his assertion that the "government cannot endure permanently half slave, half free." Secessionists were also undeterred by the unionist argument that the South was flourishing. Georgian Thomas Cobb (Howell's brother) was certain such statements would not sway his countrymen: "No, never . . . They will act as wise men before they are engulphed in the sea."[8]

Secessionists also regarded Lincoln and his party as advocates of equality and fomenters of servile insurrections. The Republicans, stated the Texas secession ordinance, proclaim "the debasing doctrine of equality of all men, irrespective of race or color—a doctrine at war with nature, in opposition to the experience of mankind, and in violation of the plainest revelations of Divine Law."[9] For the fire-eaters, the logical result of Republican doctrines was race war with all its horrors. Georgian Henry Benning explained the consequences of Republican rule. "Very soon," he noted, "a war between the whites and the blacks will spontaneously break out everywhere. It will be in every town, in every village, in every neighborhood, in every road. It will be a war of man with man—a war of extermination."[10] John Brown's attack on Harpers Ferry, Virginia, in October 1859, had heightened such concerns. Although Brown was soon captured, slave-owners shuddered at his plans to seize weapons from the federal arsenal and distribute them to African Americans. Southerners noted the lukewarm condemnations that many Northern politicians voiced after the incident.[11]

Fire-eaters listed other grievances—all of which pointed to the same unsettling conclusion: Republicans would revolutionize the South. States' rights leaders complained, as they long had, about Northern opposition to slavery expansion—and the dire consequences of that policy. If this question was not as singularly prominent between 1859 and 1861 as it had been during the preceding fourteen years, that was only because other concerns had grown more important. States' rights leaders argued that Republican patronage would raise up legions of subversive officeholders.[12] And some Southerners denounced Republican economic policies. "To plunder the South for the benefit of the North, by a new Protective Tariff," the Rhetts remarked, "will be one of their first measures of Northern sectional dominion." Republican imposts were simply another illustration of Northern measures that, over time, would destroy the slaveholders' world.[13]

Were the secessionists right when they declared that Republicans would end slavery and foster racial equality? Republicans (and sympathetic Northern Democrats) protested mightily that Lincoln's party would do neither. John Sherman was among the party leaders who expressed their willingness to back a constitutional amendment guaranteeing slavery where it existed. Garnett Adrain, a New Jersey Democratic congressman, spoke to the "groundlessness" of Southern fears. Lincoln, Adrain explained, "is opposed to all interference with slavery in the States. . . . He is in 'favor of having the superior position assigned to the white race.' . . . He is, judging him by these sentiments, a conservative man, from whom the South has nothing to fear."[14] As a national party, Republicans fought hard for economic measures, such as higher tariffs, internal improvements, and a homestead act. But they avoided all direct attacks on slavery, limiting their program to free soil, which combined economic and distant antislavery goals. They took no steps to address racial discrimination or even repeal the fugitive slave act.

Still, in a larger sense the Southern leaders who condemned the Republicans were correct. The long-term implication of the Republican ascendancy *was* the "ultimate extinction" of slavery. The rise of an industrial North, nursed by tariffs and encouraged by government outlays on rivers, harbors, and railroads, would inevitably erode the existence of bondage. The evolution of the Border States, and particularly Maryland and Delaware, illustrated the process. Secession was a rational act by a group that clearly perceived its long-term self-interest.

Is this interpretation, then, simply a restatement of the "idealistic" explanation that the South seceded to protect slavery? Only in a superficial sense. This economic interpretation emphasizes the materialist roots of secessionist ideology. It grounds the defense of slavery both *geographically* and *temporally*. For the most part, the champions of secession came from the southern reaches of the states from South Carolina to Mississippi and similar districts in the other cotton states. Typically, these Southern rights leaders had little involvement with manufacturing and took no part in the overland exchanges that were transforming the Border States, parts of the Upper South, and scattered districts in the Lower South. In his inaugural address Confederate president Jefferson Davis reminded listeners that Southerners were "an agricultural people, whose chief interest is the export of commodities required in every manufacturing country."[15] These values would be enshrined in the Confederate constitution, which prohibited tariffs "laid to promote or foster any branch of industry" and banned government outlays for internal improvements.[16] For states' rights leaders slavery was their lifeblood. Rhett, who represented a district where over 75 percent of the population was enslaved, underscored the point: "The ruin of the South, by the emancipation of her slaves, is not like the ruin of any other people. . . . It is the loss of liberty, property, home, country—everything that makes life worth having."[17]

Understanding secession temporally is also important: the wave of secession that swept across the Lower South in winter 1860–61 reflected fundamentally changed conditions, not just successful propaganda. Rhett had made the case for disunion since 1828, but only in 1860 did his arguments fall on receptive ears. Since the 1830s and early 1840s the economy of the Deep South had experienced far-reaching changes. Soils were losing their fertility; the federal government threatened to block further expansion; slavery was in decline along the Great Border; and the cotton states, once on the leading edge of economic growth, were falling further behind an increasingly populous and commercial North. These new conditions, clearly apparent during the first secession crisis of 1849–51, were intensified in 1860–61. A West without slavery was a frightening prospect to individuals who believed the South needed fresh soils to survive. "Delay is dangerous," Georgian Thomas Cobb explained in November 1860, "for ere long you will be imprisoned by walls of free States all around you. Your increasing slaves will drive out the only race that can move—the whites—and the masters who still cling to their father's graves, will, like the scorpion in a ring of fire, but sting themselves to die."[18] Now with the election of Lincoln, and grim forebodings about the impact of the Republicans' antislavery policies and their advocacy of equality, the time for action was at hand.


## II.


Not all leaders in the cotton states agreed with the secessionists' analysis. In the Deep South perhaps the most outspoken opponent of the disunionists was Alexander H. Stephens of Georgia. Slightly built, and extraordinarily sensitive to real or perceived slights (he challenged four men to duels, though none took place), Stephens was also an able and eloquent politician. During the 1850s he steered a sometimes tempestuous course between unionism and Southern rights. In 1850 Stephens angered Calhounites with his defense of the Compromise and his decision, along with two other northern Georgia politicians, Howell Cobb and Robert Toombs, to form a short-lived unionist party. States' rights activists were more pleased when "Little Aleck," as he was called, fought for the Kansas-Nebraska Act. They applauded his increasingly fervent defense of the "peculiar institution" as well as his decision to join the Democratic Party, after his long association with the Whigs. And they congratulated him in 1858 on his spirited if unsuccessful campaign to admit Kansas with the proslavery Lecompton

Constitution. But Stephens was no fire-eater. He shocked states' rights leaders in 1858 by endorsing Douglas, who had opposed Lecompton, and by campaigning fiercely for him in 1860. Stephens denounced the sectional candidates and argued that Douglas had the best chance of keeping the country together. "Should Mr. Breckinridge get the entire South," Stephens observed a month before the election, "and Lincoln the entire North no earthly power could prevent civil war."[19]

Stephens had a profoundly different outlook from most secessionists. He was optimistic about the future of the Union and unperturbed by the effects of a Republican victory—at least if extremists did not sweep the South. Stephens foresaw no catastrophe befalling the South if the North continued to grow stronger. Although he would have preferred a slave Kansas, the appearance of new free states did not trouble him. In 1859 he welcomed the admission of Oregon. "Progress is the universal law governing all things," he remarked. "I do not apprehend danger to our constitutional rights from the bare fact of increasing the number of States with institutions dissimilar to ours."[20] Rejecting dire prophecies, Stephens felt that a Republican victory hardly justified secession. "Let us not anticipate a threatened evil," he remarked after Lincoln's election. "If he violates the Constitution, then will come our time to act."[21] Even in December 1860 Stephens could remark, "All that the South has at present just cause to complain of, and the chief ground of just complaints, is the personal liberty bill[s] of some of the non-slaveholding states."[22]

For Stephens, as for other opponents of secession, the benefits of the Union far outweighed the dangers of separating. "There were many among us in 1850 zealous to go at once out of the Union," he reminded the Georgia legislature in November 1860. "Now do you believe, had the policy been carried out at that time, we would have been the same great people that we are to-day?" He marshaled statistics to show the growth of Georgia during the 1850s.[23] Stephens feared more the consequences of disunion. "I consider slavery," he noted, "much more secure in the Union than out of it."[24] Noting the outcome of the great revolutions in France and England, he observed, "Revolutions are much easier started than controlled, and the men who begin them, even for the best purposes and objects, seldom end them."[25]

Other Lower South moderates elaborated the themes that Stephens had sounded. They pointed to the flourishing state of the South and the dangers of separation. The *New Orleans Daily Picayune* remarked that "prosperity beyond example, increase in power and wealth beyond parallel, success in every department of individual and public life, but renders the shadow of coming evil the more noticeable." Secession, the editors of the *Picayune* emphasized, "is full of imminent peril to the South, not to the Union as we have been supposed to have asserted."[26] Benjamin Perry, who was one of the few who stood against the majority in South Carolina, agreed. He remarked that "the duellist may go and sacrifice his own life, and society is but little injured by it, [but] it is not so with those who stir up revolutions and civil wars."[27] These advocates did not see Lincoln's election as an immediate threat. *The New Orleans Bee* observed in November 1860, "We have no right to judge of LINCOLN by any thing but his acts, and these can only be appreciated after his inauguration."[28] Benjamin Hill, another Georgian who resisted secession, stated simply, "I believe we can make Lincoln enforce the laws."[29]

Finally, some unionist papers suggested, as had critics at mid-century, that diversification, not secession, was the solution for the South's ills. "What should we do? What remedy have we?" the *Vicksburg* [Mississippi] *Daily Whig* asked in January 1860. "Why, in the first place, let us withdraw one-third, or even one-half of our capital from agricultural operations, and invest it in the establishment of manufacturies of cotton. . . . Connected with this policy, let us encourage the mechanical arts. . . . The business of direct importation and direct exportation would, of course, build up, as if by the wand of a magician, splendid Southern cities of commercial grandeur and opulence; and thus we might become the most happy, prosperous, wealthy and intelligent people upon whom the sun has ever smiled."[30]

As the example of Alexander Stephens illustrates, immediate secessionists and their opponents shared many values. Almost all politicians defended slavery and favored its expansion. But despite common ground, the opposing sides articulated distinct worldviews. Firmly rooted in different activities and origins, unionists and disunionists advocated contrasting approaches to Southern development. These dissimilar interests and outlooks formed the basis for clashes in each of the Lower South states.

## III.

Between December 20, 1860, and March 2, 1861, all seven Deep South states seceded, and in every case conflict between opposing groups shaped the struggle to separate. Place of birth and patterns of trade were the most important factors defining the two sides within each commonwealth, while party ties and class played a secondary role.

Political and economic changes provide a background to these clashes. The ascendancy of the Republicans strengthened the case for secession and made disunionists of many who earlier had been reluctant to endorse harsh measures. Still, many held their ground against the rush to separation. These unionists were buoyed by economic trends that drew them closer to the states to the north. During the 1850s grain production soared in the northern reaches of the states from South Carolina to Mississippi as well as in northwestern Texas. The growth of this grain economy further separated these farmers from the landowners to the south. Map 9 depicts the band of grain-producing counties. Manufacturing also quickened in scattered counties near the border with the Upper South, a development that concerned some fire-eaters. "How long would it be after disunion,"

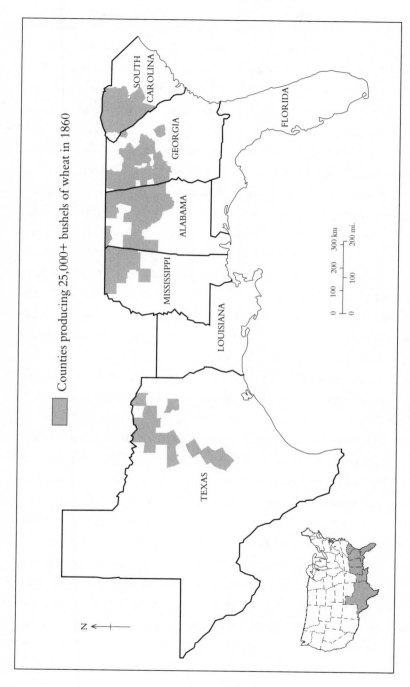

Map 9. *Wheat Growing in the Deep South, 1860*

Counties producing 25,000+ bushels of wheat in 1860

South Carolinian Daniel Hamilton observed early in 1860, "before we should have the same hungry manufacturing population infesting the upper part of So. Ca., Cherokee Georgia, Tennessee, North Carolina . . . and even the upper portion of Alabama—why not five years would elapse before they would be setting up looms on every stream in these locations."[31]

The expansion of the overland cotton trade also tied the northern districts more tightly to the Union. Estimates for 1860 for the volume shipped north by rail range from one of every eight bales used domestically to several times that proportion. A South Carolina observer remarked in March 1861, "The inland export of cotton has assumed proportions alarming to our tradesmen, injurious to the ports and a heavy [burden?] upon the incomes of tributary Rail Roads, besides there is a political significance that should challenge notice and command arrest." Although such economic changes hardly countered political developments, they did stiffen the resolve of many unionists in the upper reaches of the cotton states.[32]

While few individuals dissented when South Carolina seceded on December 20, the year began with the Palmetto State badly divided and, for once, lagging rather than leading the resistance movement. National Democrats, the faction headed by Upcountry leader James Orr, dominated the election for delegates to the Democratic national convention, scheduled to meet April 23 in Charleston. Orr's group refused to cooperate with the other Deep South states in demanding that the convention endorse the spread of slavery—or face a walkout. The line between Orr's National Democrats and their opponents reflected a long-standing geographical split. "In the up country and in Charleston the Convention party largely predominates," the *Daily South Carolinian* explained. "In the pine land belt of the interior, and in the [Lowcountry] parishes where there is a comparatively sparse [white] population, and where new ideas make slower progress, we ready assent that there the dicta of the [Rhetts'] *Mercury* is regarded as definitive of sound policy."[33]

But dissent within South Carolina was short-lived. For Northern and Southern moderates, Charleston proved the worst place to hold a national convention. Nightly rallies by Southern militants pressured wavering delegates, and when the other cotton states marched out of the Democratic convention, South Carolina joined them. The moderate majority adjourned to Baltimore, with the states' rights bolters resolving to meet in Richmond. New elections for South Carolina delegates put the extremists in control; Rhett headed up the reformed delegation. In Baltimore the mainstream Democrats selected Stephen Douglas as their candidate, while in Richmond the dissenters ratified the choice of John C. Breckinridge. Secessionists swept the balloting for the South Carolina legislature in October and for the secession convention early in December. The Rhetts boasted, "Other states are torn and divided, to a greater or less extent, by old party issues. South Carolina alone is not."[34] The convention that took South Carolina out of the Union voted for the ordinance, 159–0. Only a few prominent individuals, such as the backcountry editor Benjamin Perry and the elderly lawyer James Louis Petigru, stood against the torrent of disunion. Isolated but respected, Petigru lamented, "South Carolina is too small for a republic, but too large for an insane asylum."[35]

Three states, Mississippi, Florida, and Alabama, all marked by serious divisions, left the Union next—between January 9 and 11. Mississippi had long been a storm center of rebellion, and not surprisingly so. Other than South Carolina, it was the only state where a clear majority of the population was black and where almost half the white population held slaves (Table 10.1). While both planters and small farmers split over secession, the argument that a threat to slavery endangered the very fabric of society held more force where African Americans and slaveholding were so predominant.

## TABLE 10.1: SLAVES AND SLAVEHOLDING IN THE SOUTH, 1860

| | Slaves as % of Total Population | Slaveholding Families as % of White Families | | Slaves as % of Total Population | Slaveholding Families as % of White Families |
|---|---|---|---|---|---|
| South Carolina | 57 | 46 | North Carolina | 33 | 28 |
| Mississippi | 55 | 49 | Virginia | 31 | 26 |
| Louisiana | 47 | 30 | Arkansas | 26 | 20 |
| Alabama | 45 | 35 | Tennessee | 25 | 25 |
| Georgia | 44 | 37 | **Upper South** | **32** | **25** |
| Florida | 44 | 34 | Kentucky | 20 | 23 |
| Texas | 30 | 29 | Maryland | 13 | 12 |
| **Lower South** | **47** | **37** | Missouri | 10 | 13 |
| | | | Delaware | 2 | 3 |
| | | | **Border States** | **14** | **16** |

*Source:* 1860 U.S. Census. The percentage of slaveholding families was computed by dividing total families by the number of slaveholders.

Party loyalties in Mississippi, as elsewhere in the Deep South, played a role, if a subordinate one, in shaping views of disunion. Throughout the cotton states, supporters of the Northern Democratic candidate, Stephen Douglas, denounced immediate secession. Northern Democrats were, however, the weakest of the three parties in the Deep South. Douglas's high-water mark came in Alabama and Louisiana, where he gained 15 percent of the vote; in Mississippi he received only 5 percent. Douglas supporters clustered in areas, such as the northern districts of Mississippi, Alabama, and Georgia, where birth and trade predisposed individuals to unionism. The most ardent secessionists backed Southern Democrat John Breckinridge, who swept the electoral vote of all the Deep South states. There was, however, no one-to-one correlation between Breckinridge and separation. Many unionist farmers, particularly in northern Alabama and Georgia, persisted in old habits; they voted Southern Democrat in November 1860 and then opposed secession in January 1861. Finally, former Whigs, who now cheered John Bell and the Constitutional Union Party, tended to oppose the rush to separation. Whigs were strongest in the cities and in certain high-slaveholding districts that had reasons for favoring the Union. These areas included Louisiana's sugar parishes, which relied on federal tariffs, and the northern delta counties of Mississippi, which had familial and commercial ties with the Upper South.[36]

Far more than party, the geography of trade and settlement shaped the clash over disunion in Mississippi as elsewhere. James Alcorn's efforts to slow Mississippi's stampede to secession, his vision of growth, and the coalition that backed him illustrate these divisions. Alcorn, a wealthy planter, made his home in Coahoma, a northern delta county and a center of Whig opposition to disunion. Alcorn's rise in the world typified the ascent of many in the Southwest. Raised in Kentucky, he arrived in Mississippi on a flatboat in 1844, bringing his wife, oldest child, an elderly slave, his legal training, and a determination to seize the main chance. By 1850 he had a small plantation; by 1860 he had more than ninety slaves and an estate worth $250,000, thanks to hard work and his marriage to an Alabama heiress after his first wife died. Alcorn was a follower of Henry Clay, a believer in the American System, and in 1859 the first president of the Mississippi board of levee commissioners. Compared to many Southern Democrats, he held a more positive vision for the state's future within the United States, an outlook reflected in his campaigns for Bell and the Union.[37]

Alcorn's efforts to counter the ardent secessionists received support from several sets of Mississippi counties. The districts near Tennessee were defiantly unionist. In December 1860 a Corinth politician told

Tennessee senator Andrew Johnson, "Your own State is little less attached to the Constitution than the Northern counties of Mississippi."[38] Many planters in the northern delta counties also backed Alcorn, as did representatives of the two largest towns: Natchez (Adams County) and Vicksburg (Warren County). Finally, the secessionist stronghold of southwestern Mississippi harbored a cluster of unionist farmers. During the Civil War the southwestern county of Jones fashioned itself the "free state of Jones" and offered refuge to deserters.[39] Map 10 illustrates the division over secession.

The balloting for convention delegates indicated that most Mississippians favored disunion. Among voters whose preference is known, 45 percent favored immediate secession, 32 percent were cooperationists (a position that embraced moderate secessionists as well as unconditional unionists), and 23 percent elected delegations drawn from both camps.[40] But the Mississippi convention, like such gatherings elsewhere in the Deep South, was more strongly for disunion than were the voters. By a 74–25 vote the delegates defeated Alcorn's proposal that Mississippi follow rather than lead her sister states, then approved the ordinance of secession, 85–15. Like all the cotton states except Texas, the meeting refused to submit its work to a popular referendum.[41]

Florida, which seceded the day after Mississippi, had many cooperationists, but they did little to check the fire-eaters. In Florida, the only Deep South state not bordering on the Upper South, personal origins, more than trade or crops, dictated party lines. Secessionists were strongest in the counties, such as those in the northeast or peninsular Florida, where Georgians and South Carolinians predominated. Unionists fared better in areas populated by Virginians and North Carolinians, particularly in the counties of the western panhandle. Some of these districts were traditional Whig strongholds. Soon after the presidential election Governor Madison Perry persuaded lawmakers to call a secession convention. Echoing familiar themes, he an-

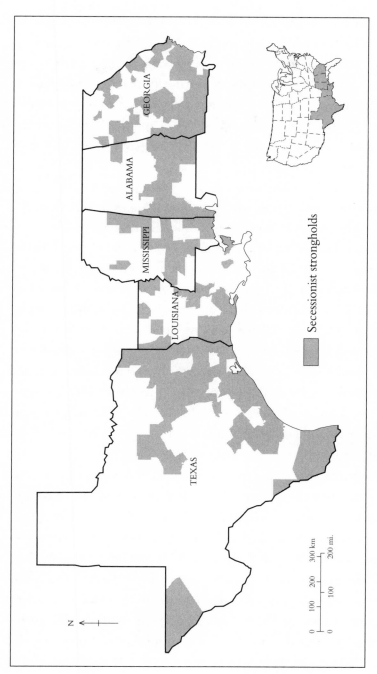

*Map 10. Secessionist Strongholds in the Deep South*

nounced that "if we wait for . . . an overt act, our fate will be that of the white inhabitants of St. Domingo." When the gathering met on January 5, about a third of the 69 delegates had been elected as co-operationists. By a 42–27 margin, the majority defeated proposals to delay its decision or allow the voters a final say. Few cooperationists stayed the course at the convention. Most approved the secession ordinance, adopted 62–7, and all but five delegates signed the final document.[42]

Alabama had the most vigorous cooperation movement of the three states that cut their ties with the United States in early January. Unionist sentiment was strongest in the northern counties and characterized both the planters of the Tennessee Valley and the small farmers in the region. Because these landowners traced their family origins to the Upper South and traded extensively with Tennessee, they had long held a different outlook than southern Alabamians. Many in the northern tier voted for Douglas in November 1860; four of the five counties he won were in this region—with the port city of Mobile the other Douglas outpost. The farmers in the northern counties trumpeted their loyalty to the Union. One prominent Douglas supporter in the Tennessee Valley remarked in October, "If the people of South Alabama should succeed in putting the State out of the Union, he favored putting the Valley out of the State."[43]

The Alabama secession convention, which met January 9, was closely divided, with 54 delegates from southern districts favoring immediate secession, while 46 individuals, almost all from the northern counties, called for "cooperation." The convention also pitted co-operationist leader Jeremiah Clemens of Huntsville against William Lowndes Yancey, the soft-spoken but occasionally violent fire-eater. (Yancey was given to fits of rage; he had, with pistol and sword in hand, attacked and killed his wife's uncle—a crime for which he served several months in jail.) The two groups agreed upon much, including the need to defend Southern rights. Clemens had earlier remarked, "We have before us the double duty of preserving the Union, & of obtaining redress for grievances."[44] By a 98–0 vote the delegates denounced the Republican credo that "slavery, in time, should be exterminated." The two sides, however, differed markedly in their tactics. By 54–45 margins, the secessionists defeated Clemens's call for a grand Southern convention and his proposal that the people ratify the convention's work. The delegates then adopted the secession ordinance, 61–39. Although large planters and small farmers were found on both sides, the disunionists were wealthier. Compared to their opponents, immediate secessionists had, on average, twice the personal property and number of slaves. The extremism of the black belt planters and the unionism of northern Alabama farmers underpinned this inequality.[45]

Widespread opposition to disunion also marked Georgia, Louisiana, and Texas, the last three Deep South states to secede. A new dynamic came into play as well: the difficulty of resisting the groundswell of disunion after four sister states had declared their independence. "Commercial relations will force Georgia out," an Augusta newspaper remarked, "for she cannot afford to have a string of custom houses on her Alabama, Florida, South Carolina, and perhaps Tennessee frontiers."[46] Still, the battle for Georgia was hard fought and divided the state roughly on geographical lines. As elsewhere, the clash of views was evident during the presidential election. Alexander Stephens campaigned vigorously for Douglas, who received 11 percent of the vote, almost entirely in the northern districts. Breckinridge won the state, but only with a plurality, not a majority as in most Deep South states.[47]

In December Georgia voters selected delegates for the secession convention, which met on January 16. The secessionists had several advantages in the contest for delegates. They campaigned hard, while unionists like Stephens and Herschel Johnson (Douglas's running mate) remained strangely subdued. Several high-profile moderates, including north Georgian Howell Cobb, joined the states' rights camp, an apostasy that delighted activists in the southern districts. "Can you find time to make two or three speeches in So. West Ga.?" one politician wrote Cobb, who hailed from northern Georgia. "You know our district has always been hostile to you. Can you not find time to remove the hostility?"[48] Still, the popular vote for delegates was close. No official tally was recorded, but modern researchers suggest a virtual dead heat, with about 42,000 votes for each side. In part because of an unfair apportionment, that equal vote translated into a secessionist majority. The delegates defeated Herschel Johnson's proposal for delay, 164–133, and then agreed in principle for secession, 166–130. The representatives approved the secession ordinance, 208–89.[49]

Analysis of the Georgia convention suggests the role played by another secondary concern: class. In Georgia, as in Alabama, wealth correlated with disunion. The counties sending secessionist delegates tended to be richer, a distinction that reflected the large contingent of poorer unionists from north Georgia as well as the secessionist leanings of the booming cotton counties. Furthermore, the 89 delegates who refused to sign the ordinance came disproportionately from the counties with the fewest slaves. Still, the geographical split defined by trade and birth remained more important than class. To begin with, for the minority of delegates born outside Georgia, place of birth mattered. South Carolinians in the convention favored disunion 25–12, while individuals from North Carolina and Tennessee voted for cooperation, 25–9. Moreover, the dissent of delegates from low slaveholding counties reflected, for the most part, the outlook of north Georgians. In the northern districts a strong majority of delegates from the low slaveholding counties opposed disunion, while an even larger proportion of representatives from the pine barrens of southern Georgia applauded secession. Similar distinctions held true in Alabama and Mississippi. In all three states the split was not between rich and poor but between landowners in the north and those in the south.[50]

Many in Louisiana also questioned the wisdom of rushing into disunion. John Winston, the secessionist commissioner sent by Alabama, reported back early in January 1861 that because of the influence of New Orleans and the dangers of disrupting Mississippi River commerce, "The State of Louisiana . . . occupies a position somewhat more complicated than any other of the Southern States."[51] Winston might also have noted the self-interest of the sugar planters. They alone of landowners in the Deep South depended on tariff protection for their prosperity. "South Carolina, Georgia, Alabama, and Mississippi are free trade states," the *New Orleans Daily Picayune* explained. "But Louisiana is scarcely prepared to abandon at once all duties upon foreign sugar. Her sugar planters are now protected by what is equivalent to $300 bonus on every $1000 worth of sugar raised."[52]

Louisianans demonstrated their moderation in the presidential election. Breckinridge won the state but with only 45 percent of the vote, his lowest percentage in the Deep South. In New Orleans he ran a dismal third, with only 24 percent of the ballots, well behind the two unionist candidates, Bell (48 percent) and Douglas (28 percent). Wealthy merchants as well as many poorer Irish and German immigrants saw little reason to break from the Union.[53]

All observers agreed that secessionist sentiment grew after Lincoln's victory, culminating in a convention and the January 26 ordinance. In some respects the contest for Louisiana was a close one. Secessionists narrowly won the January 7 election for convention delegates. Across the state disunionists polled 52 percent, while cooperationists received 48 percent, with an identical margin recorded in New Orleans. Cooperationists were particularly strong in the sugar-growing parishes; only one of the top six districts backed immediate secession. By contrast, the six richest cotton parishes all favored disunion. The close vote, however, did not translate into parity for the cooperationists, because of an unfair apportionment as well as narrow wins by disunionists. After the gathering opened January 23, the majority defeated the call for a Southern convention, 100–24, and rejected the demand for consultation with other states, 74–47. The convention then approved the secession ordinance, 113–17.[54]

Texas was the last of the Lower South states to secede, with the firm opposition of Governor Sam Houston slowing the campaign for disunion. Now sixty-seven, Houston had been a strong supporter of the Union at least since 1814, when he fought beside Andrew Jackson at the Battle of Horseshoe Bend. Undaunted by the governor's resistance, a group of prominent citizens, led by Texas Supreme Court justice Oran Roberts, seized the initiative. In December 1860 they placed announcements in several newspapers, directing all counties to elect delegates for a gathering on January 28. His hand forced, Houston convened the legislature, which despite his advice promptly approved the upcoming meeting. But in deference to Houston's wishes, the lawmakers also declared that the citizenry must ratify any decision. The January convention approved a secession ordinance, 152–6, and framed a referendum: voters would choose between "for secession" and "against secession." In preparation for the ballot, the gathering distributed a Declaration of Reasons, describing the dangers of Republican policies and underscoring the pressures on Texas. "By the secession of six of the slave-holding States," it stated, "and the certainty that others will speedily do likewise, Texas has no alternative but to remain in an isolated connection with the North, or unite her destinies with the South."[55]

In some respects the split in Texas, as revealed in the February 23 referendum, resembled the divisions elsewhere in the Deep South. The fissure between the two sides in Texas separated groups defined by place of birth and economic activities. Migrants from the Lower South populated the secessionist counties of eastern Texas, while individuals from the Upper South and Border States predominated in the unionist districts, which lay near the frontier in the northwest and west. German settlers disproportionately were unionists, even though in the plantation counties many joined their secessionist neighbors. Crops and patterns of trade reinforced these lines of division. Secessionist counties raised cotton and directed it to the Gulf ports, while unionist counties cultivated grain and sold it to the federal troops protecting the frontier. A lack of transportation, with poor roads and no railroads or rivers that reached the western districts, kept the two groups apart. But in other respects the division in Texas differed from clashes elsewhere in the cotton states. Because the decision in Texas came so late, only the most determined unionists held out against the tide engulfing the region. Voters endorsed disunion overwhelmingly, 77 to 23 percent. Also unlike most Lower South states where secession pitted planter against planter and yeoman against yeoman, in Texas the influence of birthplace and crops separated wealthy planters from smaller farmers.[56]

Across the Deep South most upper-class individuals "went with their state" once the secession ordinances were signed. However, this decision should not obscure the bitter clashes in the preceding months— nor the anguish many experienced in recasting their loyalties. Few affluent individuals emulated James Petigru in South Carolina, Jeremiah Clemens in Alabama, or Andrew Jackson Hamilton in Texas, all of whom remained loyal after war broke out. Most wealthy opponents of secession acquiesced in separation, with some accepting high positions in the new regime. Alexander H. Stephens became vice president of the Confederacy; Mississippian James Alcorn served as a brigadier general; and South Carolinian Benjamin Franklin Perry was sworn in as district attorney.

Many who had been cooperationists confessed how deeply torn they felt by their decision to support disunion. "My heart has been rent by another affliction, which I must feel more deeply than I can express as a man & a patriot," Perry exclaimed in February 1861. "It is the destruction of my country, the dismemberment of that great &

glorious Union, cemented by the blood of our fathers."[57] A representative of one of the Louisiana sugar parishes told his wife that signing the secession ordinance was the "bitterest pill I ever took."[58] A northern Alabama delegate, also writing to his wife, observed, "I have opposed this rash action of the Convention in every way I could and while I feel greatly outraged at the Convention for not submitting its action to the people for their ratification or rejection, I see no other course left but to submit to it."[59] Unconditional unionists typically came from the ranks of the small farmers, and many—about 15,000 in the Deep South—ended up joining the Northern army. Louisiana, Alabama, and Texas were the states that provided the most white soldiers to the Union army. Many counties in the Cajun regions of Louisiana, northern Alabama, and northwestern Texas boasted more troops wearing blue than gray.[60]

## IV.

This economic interpretation—the argument that separation reflected the rational interests of one group of Southerners—is not the only explanation scholars have set forth for secession. Some historians contend that paranoia, exaggerated fears, and a climate of repression led to Southern independence. "The crisis psychology of 1859," notes one scholar, "persisted and deepened in the fateful year of 1860 into a pathological condition of mind in which delusions of persecution and impending disaster flourished."[61] At first glance, contemporary testimony seems to support such an interpretation. The comments of Connecticut-born Sereno Watson are a case in point. Watson had attended Yale University, studied medicine, and briefly practiced as a doctor in the Midwest. After the Civil War he would become one of the country's leading botanists. But in the 1850s he was still searching for his calling and agreed to serve as secretary of the Planters' Insurance Company in the Alabama blackbelt town of Greensboro. Watson found the increasingly shrill demands for disunion unsettling. "The people is apparently gone crazy," he told his brother in November 1860. "I do not know how to account for it & have no idea what might be the end of it." He scored the repressive atmosphere: "It seems to be their endeavor here as elsewhere to browbeat & bully into silence those whom they cannot persuade to go with them & so to make it appear that there is but one opinion throughout the South." Unsurprisingly, Watson soon quit his position and headed north. He told his brother, "I would like to breathe free air once more,—have the privilege of speaking as I think, & feel that I am a freeman."[62]

Many in the cotton states echoed rumors of thwarted slave uprisings and abolition plots, and sharply censured those who voiced dissenting views. Vigilance committees, established in neighborhoods across the Deep South, scrutinized the activities of strangers. "The roving mendicant, the tobacco-wagoner, the whisky peddler, the sample trader," noted a South Carolina newspaper, "may be honest and reliable, but in such like disguise abolitionists have prowled about elsewhere and may do so here."[63] In the balloting for convention delegates, the pressure on voters to conform was often relentless. When independent-minded John Aughey turned up at a polling station in Choctaw County, Mississippi, he was bluntly told to back the secessionist ticket. "I thought otherwise," he later recounted, "and going to a desk, wrote out a Union ticket, and voted it amidst the frowns, murmurs, and threats of the judges and bystanders, and, as the result proved, I had the honor of depositing the only vote in favor of the Union which was polled in that precinct. I knew of many who were in favor of the Union, who were intimidated by threats, and by the odium attending it, from voting at all."[64]

While exaggerated fears and repression were evident in many communities, these qualities do not provide a satisfactory explanation for secession. To begin with, many counties in the cotton states rejected the outlook of the extremists. Polling places in northern Mississippi, Alabama, and Georgia recorded the same overwhelming majorities for the Union that precincts in the southern reaches did for separation. Uniformity within precincts and sharp differences between counties had long characterized Southern voting. Moreover, Whig and Douglas newspapers regularly dismissed the wilder accounts in the Breckinridge press. The *Vicksburg* [Mississippi] *Daily Whig* explained that stories of slave revolts were "gotten up for party purposes," while an Alabama Douglas paper remarked that "the horrid accounts of Abolition plots and incendiary and murderous designs of the Abolitionists, as at first disclosed in the Breckinridge papers, have been so frequently modified, and sometimes altogether contradicted, that we have felt a reluctance to copy them in our columns."[65] Clashes within each Southern state point to the need for an analysis that uses a narrower brush than "paranoia" or "repression" to depict motivation. A focus on economic activities and place of birth provides a more useful analysis of the differences within the Deep South states.

Furthermore, granted their premises, fire-eaters argued for secession with a reasoned brief, not a paranoid outcry. In editorials and private letters, states' rights leaders contended plausibly that the triumph of the Republicans pointed to the demise of slavery. "They refuse to recognize our rights of property in slaves, to make a division of the territory, to deprive themselves of their assumed constitutional power to abolish slavery in the Territories or District of Columbia, [or] to increase the efficiency of the fugitive slave law," Alabama secession commissioner Jabez Curry explained to the governor of Maryland. "Under an abolition government the slave-holding States will be placed under a common ban of proscription, and an institution, interwoven in the very frame-work of their social and political being, must perish gradually or speedily with the Government in active hostility to it."[66] Northerners and many Southerners challenged those premises and conclusions. But for states' rights leaders their contentions rested not on fuzzy emotional appeals but on hard, rational analysis.

Another explanation of secession focuses on the dramatic weakening of the two-party system in the Deep South (as well as its continuation in the Upper South and Border States). "There was no institutional check on extremism in the lower South," notes one historian, adding, "Democrats in the Deep South took advantage of this situation by constantly escalating their demands for the protection of slavery and Southern Rights."[67] This analysis, although incomplete, provides valuable insights. Opposing national parties had long served as the cement of union. After midcentury these bonds weakened in the cotton states, as the Whig Party (and its successors) slowly crumbled. And while the Democratic Party expanded, it became in the Lower South less a national party and more a militant pro-Southern faction. The transformation of the party of Jackson culminated in the 1860 election, when Southern Democrats nominated their own presidential candidate, John Breckinridge. Breckinridge Democrats, who comprised the leading party in every Deep South state, led the drive for separation. By contrast, the continuing vitality of a two-party system in the Upper South and Border States slowed the rush to independence. In 1860 Douglas took Missouri, while Bell won the electoral votes of Kentucky, Tennessee, and Virginia.

Still, this explanation only raises new questions. Why did the two-party system crumble in the cotton states? Why did it last longer in the upper reaches of the South? The answers bring the focus back to the changing economy of the South, and the differences between the lower tier of states and the commonwealths to the north. In the cotton states, high levels of slaveholding and the lack of alternatives to monoculture, as well as mounting concerns about soil exhaustion, expansion, and antislavery agitation, undercut the appeal of moderate parties. For these reasons, many landowners changed allegiances in the

1850s, weakening the Whig/opposition party and swelling the ranks of the Democrats. In the Upper South and Border States greater urbanization, stronger ties with the North, proportionately fewer slaves, and a more diversified approach to development fostered a different vision of the future and provided the underpinning for a robust two-party system.

Finally, many historians argue that Southerners seceded simply and primarily to defend slavery, an interpretation discussed earlier in this chapter as well as in the Introduction. This analysis overlaps in important ways with the contentions in this book. Who can disagree with Lincoln's statement that "all knew" slavery "was, somehow, the cause of the war"?[68] Former Confederates and modern neo-Confederates who contend that states' rights rather than slavery lay at the heart of the conflict stand on shaky ground. Their arguments, often part of a concerted effort to defend the motives of the secessionists, ignore the voluminous statements of the participants. And while "states' rights" remains a convenient term to describe the views of those opposing the North, it cannot be taken literally. Southern leaders had little love for states' rights when they demanded the repeal of Northern personal liberty laws, when they denounced popular sovereignty, or when they insisted that the federal government remove Indians or fight Mexicans. Maintaining and expanding slavery was the goal, states' rights a means to that end. Still, an appeal to "slavery" as the cause of secession no more explains the deep divisions in the South, or the timing of protests, than do references to repression and paranoia. A reasoned response to economic change provides a more satisfactory explanation for secession and the Civil War.[69]

The Upper South also left the Union, while the Border States remained loyal but reluctant allies of the North. Here too patterns of trade and production played a major role. The motives underlying the actions of those states and the timing of their protests suggest the striking differences between the upper tiers of slave states and the Deep South.

# 11

# SECESSION IN THE UPPER SOUTH AND BORDER STATES

The excitement is fearful. Send no troops here," Maryland governor Thomas Hicks telegraphed President Lincoln on April 18, 1861. Baltimore mayor George Brown concurred. He told Lincoln, "It is not possible for more soldiers to pass through Baltimore unless they fight their way at every step." Seemingly a unionist population in a moderate state, Baltimoreans were angered by Lincoln's decision to call up troops—and send them to Washington through their city. Jeering crowds taunted the regiments that marched through Baltimore on the eighteenth; the next day a still angrier mob awaited the recruits. Because there were no direct rail links to the capital, the troops, arriving that day from Massachusetts and Pennsylvania, had to disembark at the President Street station, travel a mile along Pratt Street through the waterfront district, and then board the Washington train at the Camden Street station. As the soldiers of the Sixth Massachusetts Regiment marched through the city, the crowd pelted them with bricks and cobblestones, then rushed them. Frightened, the troops fired back, ignoring Brown's cry, "For God's sake, don't shoot!" At the end of the melee scores were injured; thirteen soldiers and at least a dozen civilians lay dead. The unarmed Pennsylvania militia, which had remained at the President Street station, fled back to Philadelphia.[1]

As the Baltimore riot indicated, anger toward Lincoln's plans and the North in general was not limited to the Deep South. Ultimately, the four Upper South states joined the Confederacy, while the four Border States, despite a strong desire for neutrality and anger at the Union forces that Lincoln was marshaling, remained loyal. However, the Upper South seceded and the Border States protested for reasons that differed markedly from those driving independence in the Deep South. Virginia, North Carolina, Tennessee, and Arkansas left the Union not because of Lincoln's election but because they were forced to choose sides in a war between the North and the Confederacy. The riot in Baltimore came not in November, with the Republican victory, but in April, after the North decided to raise an army—and send troops through the city. A close look at the more northerly part of the South makes clear the internal conflict in these states. It also suggests the cautious outlook of the citizenry in two regions that, compared to the cotton states, had fewer slaves and closer ties to the North.

## I.

The four states of the Upper South—Virginia, North Carolina, Tennessee, and Arkansas—faced the question of separation twice. The first time came in the aftermath of Lincoln's victory, when they were pressed to decide if the election of a Republican president was just cause for secession. For the Lower South it clearly was. However, as shown by the votes taken in February and March 1861, Lincoln's election was not enough to push the Upper South to join the Confederacy. Lawmakers in these states listened to the impassioned arguments of the secessionist commissioners from the Deep South—and rejected those pleas. Virginians chose convention delegates who opposed secession by a 104–45 margin. (Edmund Ruffin grumbled, "The majority of this Convention is more basely submissive than I had supposed possible.")[2] Tennessee and North Carolina voted against even holding such a gathering. In both cases the delegates chosen, on the chance the meeting would be approved, were overwhelmingly unionist. Arkansas voters approved a convention but elected a unionist majority by a 23,626 to 17,927 margin. Compared to the Deep South, these states had a proportionately smaller black population and a lower percent of slaveholders (Table 10.1). Discussing the difference between the upper tiers of slave states and the Deep South, the Rhetts commented: "With them slavery or its abolishment is a question of expediency. . . . To us the institution is indispensable."[3]

To be sure, some politicians and editorialists in the Upper South demanded separation, echoing arguments set forth by the fire-eaters in the Deep South. A pamphlet, authored by the Arkansas senator Thomas Hindman, argued that "Republican candidates were elected upon a platform destructive of our rights, branding our institutions as infamous, decreeing the equality of the negro with ourselves and our children, and dooming us, in the end, with murderous certainty, to all the horrors of insurrection and servile war."[4] The majority in the Upper South, however, agreed with North Carolina congressman Zebulon Vance: "We have everything to gain and nothing on earth to lose by delay, but by too hasty action we may take a fatal step we can never retrace—may lose a heritage that we can never recover."[5]

During these months the mainstay of the opposition to secession came from Whig slaveholders and nonslaveholding small farmers. A Tennessee correspondent of Andrew Johnson summarized this coalition: "Men hitherto your best friends curse you—but two thirds of the old 'yeomanry' are still with you, and nearly all the Whigs." Whig behavior during these months fit with long-standing patterns. Whigs and their successors, the Americans and the Constitutional Unionists, supported the creation of a national economy. They were less likely than the Democrats to welcome disunionists into their ranks, particularly after party lines solidified in the early 1840s. Furthermore, the party's cautious approach toward Southern rights reflected, at least in part, the self-interest of its constituency. Townsfolk and, more generally, the commercial classes throughout the Upper South were Whiggish. And though the economic roots of the split between Whig and Democratic planters remain elusive, some studies suggest that Whig landowners were more open to new ventures and commercial activities than were their Democratic counterparts.[6]

The most prominent unionist in the Upper South was John Adams Gilmer of North Carolina. Gilmer had been destined for the Whig Party since birth, when his Federalist father named him after the second president. Raised on a modest farm, Gilmer had little schooling until his teenage years, when he attended and excelled at a local academy. He went on to study law, teaching school to pay for his education. A successful law practice and marriage into a wealthy family brought him land and slaves. As his practice and fortune grew, he invested in railroads and coal mines, and grew more interested in politics. Voters liked his common touch and bluff manners. Henry Winter Davis of Maryland described him as a "man of great personal popularity and ability." Gilmer was elected to Congress in 1857 and soon emerged as leader of the Southern "opposition." His principled stand against the Lecompton Constitution endeared him to Republicans, who awarded him a committee chairmanship in 1860. At Seward's urging, Lincoln offered Gilmer a cabinet post. But after much reflection, Gilmer turned it down. Instead, he urged the Republicans to compromise and open at least part of the West to slavery. This step would slake Southern anger, and the final outcome, he argued, would please Northerners. "Climate, soil, and productions," he believed, would keep the area free. Gilmer strongly cautioned against coercing the cotton states. He emphasized, "There must be no fighting, or the conservative Union men in the border slave states . . . will be swept away in a torrent of madness."[7]

Gilmer's hopes, and those of other Upper South unionists, for a compromise came to naught. Deal making failed in the winter of 1860–61, although not from want of trying. Three separate deliberative bodies met and discussed two broad plans. The Committee of Thirty-Three, appointed by the House of Representatives and headed by moderate Republicans, urged a constitutional amendment to guarantee slavery in the states where it existed. It also hoped to address the Southern need for expansion by admitting New Mexico as a slave state. Many Republicans, including Lincoln, accepted these terms. The Border State plan, drawn up by an ad hoc committee that included John Gilmer, modified a proposal first put forth by Kentucky senator John J. Crittenden. This plan approved the same constitutional amendment and addressed the territorial issue by restoring the Missouri Compromise line. The area north of the 36° 30' parallel would be free soil; the region south of it, open to slavery. A Peace Conference, which convened in Washington in February, endorsed the Border State proposal.

But the chasm separating the sections was too wide to be bridged. Many Republicans opposed any compromise. Charles Sumner denounced "any offer now, even of a peppercorn." Even moderate Republicans condemned opening the area south of 36° 30' to slavery. Southerners refused to accept the admission of New Mexico as the only territorial concession. More significantly, the impact of any of these plans seems questionable. No secessionist in the Deep South expressed an interest in these deliberations. None of the schemes would have brought the cotton states back into the Union, nor did the failure of these plans lead the Upper South to join the Confederacy. Secession came only after the outbreak of war.[8]

Along with Whig planters, many of the nonslaveholding farmers in the Upper South resisted secession. These individuals resented the large slaveholders and rejected their states' rights views. The rhetoric of class conflict often tinged the statements of these landowners and their representatives. Discussing the fire-eaters, Andrew Johnson observed, "It is not the free men of the north they are fearing most: but the free men [of the] South and now desire to have a go[vern]ment so organized as to put the institution of Slav[e]ry beyond the reach or vote of the nonslaveholder at the ballot box."[9] In large part, however, the conflict of classes was a conflict of regions within states. In a South where social conformity remained the norm, few yeomen spoke up in counties where planters dominated. Still, the small farmers of western Virginia made clear their resentment of the slaveholders of the east. "Talk about Northern oppression," one western Virginia farmer remarked, "talk about our rights being stolen from us by the North—it's all stuff, and dwindles into nothing when compared, to our situation in Western Virginia. The truth is the slavery oligarchy, are impudent, boastful and tyrannical."[10]

While most small farmers in the Appalachian highlands and in the Ozarks of northwestern Arkansas were unionists, there were exceptions to the rule. The western Virginia counties lying closest to the North Carolina border were linked by rail lines and by political persuasion to the tobacco-growing regions in eastern Virginia. When West Virginia broke off during the Civil War, these counties remained with the Old Dominion. Similarly, many residents in mountain districts of North Carolina sympathized with the Confederacy. During the 1850s the Democratic Party, which campaigned for both an expanded suffrage and states' rights, recorded strong gains in this area. Far different were the culture and politics in eastern Tennessee. Compared to the Appalachian counties of North Carolina, the Tennessee districts were more fertile, populous, and productive. They developed a strong regional culture, with Democrats and Whigs eventually uniting to oppose the secessionists in eastern and middle Tennessee. During the war eastern Tennessee flirted with the idea of forming a separate state, and eventually contributed 42,000 white troops to the Union armies. Western North Carolina boasted many fewer unionists and provided only 5,000 soldiers for the North.[11]

After the bombardment of Fort Sumter and Lincoln's call for 75,000 troops, the citizenry of the Upper South faced the issue of secession a second time. Now the question was, in a war between the North and the Deep South, which side would the Upper South choose? Neutrality was not an option. Tennessee senator A.O.P. Nicholson exclaimed, "It is no longer the negro question but a question of resistance to tyranny." Upper South unionists recognized that the ground had been cut from under them. North Carolina state senator Jonathan Worth lamented that Lincoln "could have devised no scheme more effectual than the one he has pursued to overthrow the friends of the Union here." All four states now separated by decisive margins. A Virginia convention meeting in April declared for secession, a decision ratified by the voters. The next month conventions in Arkansas and North Carolina severed ties with the Union, as did the Tennessee legislature.[12]

The opposition of Whig planters to secession melted away, revealing a new alignment: one that pitted the high slaveholding districts against those with fewer servants. (See Map 11.) In Arkansas, for example, the pro-Confederate plantation counties of the southeast faced off against the poorer districts of the northwest. A map of secessionist strength in Tennessee clearly delineates the slaveholding belts in the middle and western parts of the state. Before the outbreak of fighting, wealthy Whigs in middle Tennessee had joined with the small farmers of the east to keep the state loyal. Now these Whigs sided with slaveholders in the west to vote Tennessee out of the Union. The eastern slaveholding counties in Virginia and North Carolina also favored joining the Confederacy. By contrast, the Appalachian highland counties of western Tennessee and northwestern Virginia remained true to the Union. On June 11 West Virginians met in convention to begin a process that would lead to the creation of a new state.

As in the months before the outbreak of fighting, exceptions modified these larger patterns of loyalty. In North Carolina, where states' rights forces had gained strength during the 1850s, support for the Confederacy extended well beyond the area of high slaveholding. In eastern Virginia, there were noteworthy defections from the secessionist camp. Norfolk and the nearby counties voted for the Union, reflecting their strong commercial ties with the North. The Virginia counties near the Potomac also resisted secession. These districts, which tended to be more Whig than Democratic and to grow more grain than tobacco, had long displayed their independence. Still, as a rule the planting counties of the Upper South led the campaign for secession, while the regions dominated by nonslaveholders clung to the Union.[13]

## II.

Like the Upper South, the Border States—Missouri, Kentucky, Maryland, and Delaware—faced the question of secession twice. With a lower proportion of slaves and stronger ties to the North, the commonwealths of the Great Border resolved on both occasions to remain in the Union. Still, in each state save Delaware, unionists had their work cut out for them. Although secessionists were a distinct minority, many citizens, particularly in Kentucky and Maryland, demanded neutrality. In the end, federal troops were needed to secure the loyalty of the Great Border.

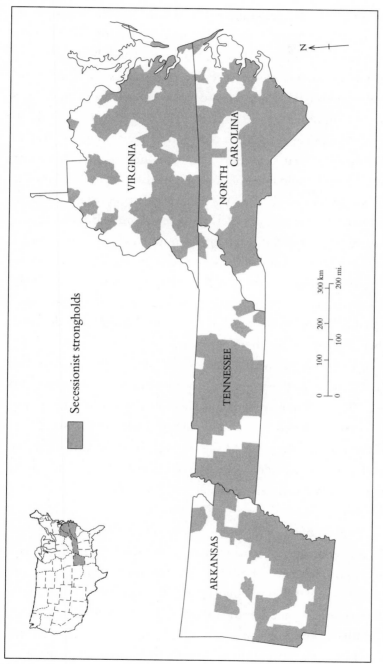

Map 11. Secessionist Strongholds in the Upper South

In the months between Lincoln's election and the outbreak of fighting, the Border States made clear their opposition to secession. Like Upper South lawmakers, Border States legislators heard and then dismissed the arguments of the secessionist commissioners. Missouri was the only one of the four states to hold a convention, and voters there selected unionists by a 110,000 to 30,000 margin. The Kentucky legislature spurned calls for a convention, frustrating the plans of the state's pro-Southern governor, Beriah Magoffin, who hoped an independent body would take the state out of the Union. In Maryland the unionist governor, Thomas Hicks, refused to convene the legislature, effectively checking the designs of extremists. Both houses of the Delaware legislature affirmed their loyalty. Nonetheless, a small group in every state clamored for immediate secession, while others announced that if fighting occurred, their sympathies were with the South. "The cause of South Carolina is the cause of all the slaveholding States," Missouri congressman Thomas Anderson declared. "Strike her, and you strike them."[14]

In part, the divisions within the Border States fell along familiar lines. Most citizens in the three great border cities—Louisville (population 68,000), St. Louis (population 160,000), and Baltimore (population 212,000)—favored the Union. Strong ties with the North and low levels of slaveholding shaped the outlook of these urbanites. No county in Kentucky provided as many volunteers for the Union army as Jefferson, which contained Louisville. St. Louis also showed its loyal colors, electing a free soil congressman in 1856 and a Republican in 1860 and giving a plurality of votes to Lincoln. A German editor remarked, "St. Louis has the character of a free state, a virtual enclave in this region of slavery."[15] Baltimore too set itself against secession. Businessmen signed two pro-Union petitions, one in December 1860 with 1,300 names, and another the following January with 5,000 names.

Still, both St. Louis and Baltimore had sizable pro-Southern minorities and business communities divided by patterns of commerce.

Although most merchants traded with the North and championed the Union, those focusing on the South often sympathized with the Confederacy. The working class in the two cities also split, mirroring ethnic lines and long-standing partisan battles. Typically the Irish, who competed with blacks for menial jobs, denounced Republicans and their African American allies. Germans, and particularly the Protestant Germans (who often brought a more liberal cast of mind from Europe), usually favored the crusade against slavery.[16]

Larger slaveowners typically sympathized with the South. Although the Delaware lower house unanimously expressed its "unqualified disapproval" of secession, the senate concurred only by a 5–3 vote. The negatives came from the three slaveholding senators. In Maryland the tobacco-growing counties near the Potomac harbored the most vehement advocates of separation. In the Missouri convention the average slaveholding of the southern rights group was significantly higher than that of the unionists: 10.5 slaves compared to 4.1. However, in Kentucky, a state with many small slaveholders and few large ones, there was no strong correlation between slaveholding and views of secession.[17]

Conversely, nonslaveholders generally opposed the Confederacy. Those sympathies were evident in the cities as well as in the counties along the northern borders of Kentucky, Maryland, and Delaware. "The time is not far distant when the counties in Kentucky bordering on the Ohio river will have no slaves in them," the *Louisville Daily Courier* remarked, noting their disdain for the Southern cause.[18] Still, many poor whites in these states sympathized with the South. The Missouri districts near Kansas were a hotbed of Confederate sympathizers. In the 1850s "border ruffians" from this area had invaded Kansas, and during the secession crisis these counties again made clear their Southern leanings. In Kentucky the nonslaveholding counties in the Southwest, as well as several mountain districts that traditionally voted Democratic, favored the South. In Maryland many farmers in the Eastern Shore counties shared the states' rights views of the planters whose homes lay across Chesapeake Bay.[19]

Party loyalties also helped shape behavior, with Democrats favoring secession more than did Whigs—much as was the case in the rest of the South. In Maryland political allegiances reinforced geographical divisions. The tobacco-growing counties near the Potomac were Democratic and Southern-leaning, while Baltimore and the northern districts were Whiggish and favored the Union. Partisan divisions showed a similar north–south split in Delaware. In Kentucky the Whig-Democratic split better explains behavior than does slaveholding. Within the assembly, Whig counties opposed aiding the Confederacy by a 40–8 margin, while the Breckinridge districts divided 18–14 in favor of states' rights. In Missouri, however, the links between parties and sectional loyalties are less clear.

Unlike the rest of the South, the Border States boasted a few Republicans, but they were exotic flowers that bloomed here and there in harsh, unwelcoming soils. Their numbers were sparse outside of Delaware, whose two northernmost counties and largest city, Wilmington, were closely linked to the free states. In 1860 Lincoln received 23.7 percent of the votes cast in Delaware; but he garnered only 0.9 percent in Kentucky, 2.5 percent in Maryland, and 10.3 percent in Missouri. These votes came from the counties along the northern borders of these states, as well as from the cities, particularly St. Louis. Despite this poor showing, individual Republicans achieved prominence in a party that claimed to speak for the entire country.

No one family of Border State Republicans was more influential than the Blairs. Their careers and views shed light on the outlook of party members in the region. Francis Preston Blair, Sr., and his sons, Montgomery and Francis Preston, Jr., were active in the politics of Maryland and Missouri as well as nationally. Francis Sr., often called Preston, was born in Virginia, came of age in Kentucky, and eventually moved to an estate in Silver Springs, Maryland, where he often entertained Washington lawmakers. (Charles Sumner recuperated at Blair's home after Congressman Brooks's attack.) Among other honors, Preston chaired the 1856 Republican national convention. His older son, Montgomery, who made his home in Maryland, served as lead counsel in the Dred Scott case and would enter Lincoln's cabinet as postmaster general after John Gilmer turned down the "Southern" seat. Francis Jr., usually called Frank, was a lawyer, a soldier, and a prominent St. Louis politician.

One reason the Blairs joined the Republican Party was their nationalism—they applauded a party that stood its ground against Southern hotheads. Preston had been an outspoken nationalist at least since his service with Andrew Jackson, who had brought him to Washington to manage a pro-administration newspaper. Preston approved Jackson's unflinching response to South Carolina's threats in 1832–33, and his sons maintained that tradition. In the 1850s they condemned secessionist threats, labeling the Southern Democrats as "the progeny of Calhoun doctrines." During the first months of 1861, Frank organized militia companies to counter the growing Confederate presence in Missouri, while Montgomery showed his firmness as an adviser to Lincoln. Montgomery was the only cabinet member who unequivocally urged Lincoln to retain Fort Sumter as the crisis in Charleston deepened.

The Blairs also judged the Republican Party the organization most in harmony with their strongly held, sometimes contradictory, views on race and western settlement. The Blairs were slaveholders who favored the end of slavery. They were also free soilers, whose desire to settle white farmers in the West reflected their racist vision of America. The Blairs' aim was a nation free of blacks. Preston remarked in 1858 that "it is certainly the wish of every patriot that all within the limits of our Union should be homogeneous in race and of our own blood." Their views led them to endorse the Free Soil Party in 1848, condemn the Kansas-Nebraska Act in 1854, and join the Republican

Party by 1856. They helped to write the state party platforms in Maryland and Missouri. These documents denounced "free negro equality" and declared the goal in the Western state was "Missouri for white men and white men for Missouri." Other Border State Republicans, such as Cassius Clay of Kentucky and Edward Bates, whom the Blairs supported for president in 1860, agreed.

The Blairs reconciled their dedication to free soil, their opposition to slavery, and their dislike of blacks by leading the campaign for colonization. Frank explained, "The idea of liberating the slaves and allowing them to remain in the country, is one that never will be tolerated." Although colonization never became official Republican doctrine, the prominence of the Blairs, their position in the crucial Border States, and the intensity with which they made their case persuaded many in the party to back resettlement. Looking ahead, the Blairs would abandon the Republican Party soon after the war; they could not feel at home in a party that campaigned for black rights. In 1868 Frank Blair became the Democratic vice presidential candidate.[20]

Like the Upper South, the Border States faced renewed demands for secession after Lincoln called for troops on April 15. While the four states remained loyal, the path to that outcome was not a straight one. To be sure, secessionist movements were weak across the region. Years of increasing trade with the North and low levels of slaveholding had tugged these commonwealths into the orbit of the free states. But only in Delaware were unionists strong enough to guarantee the state's allegiance. Elsewhere, outspoken secessionists and the clamor for neutrality left the result in doubt. In the end, firm action by the new administration kept these commonwealths loyal.

Of the four Border States, Missouri had the strongest secession movement—and even then only about a fourth of the citizenry backed the rebels. Dating back to the Compromise of 1819–21, Missouri had a long history of harboring states' rights advocates. Although Senator Thomas Hart Benson had opposed Calhoun, the state's other senator, David Atchison, had been one of the South Carolinian's most loyal supporters. In the 1850s, Missourians, particularly from the western counties, had spearheaded the proslavery forces in Kansas.

During the secession crisis pro-Southern sentiments were evident even before Lincoln's call for troops. Early in 1861 secessionists began training a small group of militiamen at the Berthold mansion in St. Louis. In response Frank Blair mustered several companies, drawing recruits from the Wide Awakes, the young men who had campaigned for Lincoln. This force (totaling about 750 men) drilled in secret, using abandoned breweries, foundries, and halls for their musters. Sawdust on the floors muffled the maneuvers, while blankets over the windows kept out prying eyes. For both sides, the immediate prizes to be grasped were the $400,000 in gold deposited in the vaults of the assistant treasurer in St. Louis, and the 60,000 rifles and 90,000 pounds of powder in the federal arsenal. Unionist forces received a boost when Captain Nathaniel Lyon, a veteran soldier, arrived with a contingent of regular troops. Lyon reinforced the arsenal while troops from New York secured the treasury.

Conflict escalated in mid-April, when Lincoln asked Governor Claiborne Jackson to raise four infantry regiments. Jackson, an ardent secessionist, spurned this demand. "Your requisition," he replied, "is illegal, unconstitutional, and revolutionary, in its object, inhuman and diabolical, and cannot be complied with."[21] Instead, Jackson turned to Jefferson Davis for weapons and assembled a force of seven hundred men, bivouacking them in "Camp Jackson" on the outskirts of St. Louis. Meanwhile Frank Blair promised to raise the troops Lincoln needed, even without the governor's permission. Early in May Captain Lyon, disguised as Frank Blair's mother-in-law, surveyed the Confederate camp. With revolvers in his basket and a "thickly veiled sun-bonnet" hiding his red beard, he rode through the compound. The next day, well informed about the enemy's disposition, Lyon, Blair, and seven thousand troops captured the Confederate forces. Although Camp Jackson was taken without a shot, riots ensued when the prisoners were marched to jail. The clashes, which left over thirty dead, revealed the divisions in the city. Before order was restored, pro-Southern Irish militiamen battled with unionist German volunteers.

The fall of Camp Jackson began an era of open warfare in which the Union forces dominated but never completely controlled the state. After the Confederate camp was overrun, the governor fled to the capital, Jefferson City, burning the bridges behind him. About a fourth of the members of the convention joined Jackson in establishing a pro-Southern government, and eventually about a fourth of the 150,000 Missourians who took up arms fought on the side of the Confederacy. Union forces, initially led by Blair and Lyon, soon drove the governor out of the capital and, by the end of the year, out of the state. Missouri was secured for the North, but bitter guerrilla warfare plagued the state for the next four years.[22]

Delaware's loyalty was never in question, but for Maryland and Kentucky the issue of allegiance was more complicated. In both states the strongest resistance came not from secessionists but from advocates of neutrality. To some Northern eyes, neutrality was treason. It was not. Neither state had a strong secessionist movement. Both states, however, were crucial to the war effort. How Lincoln dealt with them reflected their different strategic positions.

Securing the loyalty of Maryland was the most immediate problem for Lincoln and the new Republican government. The route to Washington, whether for soldiers or lawmakers, lay through Maryland. Lincoln was made painfully aware of the need to control the state in February 1861, when he learned of a plot to assassinate him as he passed through Baltimore on his way to Washington. Accepting the counsel of his advisers, Lincoln squeezed into a small berth as the "invalid brother" of a Pinkerton detective and changed trains in Baltimore in the middle of the night of February 22, well before the presidential coach was scheduled to reach the city. Later that day more than ten thousand people spilled into Baltimore's streets, many furious that Lincoln had rushed through the town in secret.[23]

Anger against Republican rule and the Union army escalated once fighting began in April. On April 18 and 19 citizens rioted when troops from Massachusetts, despised as the breeding ground of abolitionists, attempted to march between train stations in Baltimore. Irish laborers as well as clerks and merchants involved in trade with the South led the attacks. The city government also denounced the incursion of Northerners. It ordered the bridges leading to Baltimore destroyed, and called for a militia force fifteen thousand strong to defend the city. Republican editor Horace Greeley declared that Baltimore's "government was in the hands of the Breckinridge Democracy . . . and the leaders of the Democracy were deep in the counsels of treason."[24] Compounding the state's sins in the eyes of the Republicans, Governor Hicks, although a unionist, delayed recruiting the soldiers Lincoln demanded. Meanwhile many Marylanders crossed over into Virginia to fight for the Confederacy. Perhaps a third of the white Marylanders taking up arms fought for the South.

Despite these actions, Marylanders remained more neutralists than secessionists. State officials called for an "armed neutrality" rather than an alliance with either side. Many in the Baltimore business community made clear their support for the Union. John W. Garrett, head of the Baltimore & Ohio Railroad, placed his railroad at the service of the national government. Lincoln called Garrett "the right arm of the Government in the aid he rendered the authorities in preventing the Confederates from seizing Washington."[25]

Neutrality could not be tolerated in a state that lay astride such a crucial supply route, and the federal government took firm steps to secure this vital link. The army agreed to a new route for its soldiers. Instead of passing through Baltimore, Washington-bound troops would travel by steamer to Annapolis and board trains there for the capital. Late in April General Benjamin Butler, paunchy, balding, and self-important, landed his small fleet at Annapolis and took over the town. Mustering a thousand troops, he next descended on Baltimore and secured that city. He removed the mayor and police chief and arrested Ross Winans, a wealthy secessionist and member of the legislature. "I . . . thought that if such a man, worth $15,000,000 were hanged for treason," Butler explained, "it would convince the people of Maryland, at the least, that the expedition we were upon was no picnic." Lincoln, however, ordered Winans released.[26]

Gradually the unionist majority, bolstered by the presence of Northern troops, reasserted itself. Even before Butler marched into Baltimore, Mayor Brown disbanded the city defense force and Governor Hicks began raising the regiments Lincoln had requested. In May the legislature resolved that "it is not expedient to call a sovereign convention of the state . . . or to take any measures for the immediate reorganization and arming of the militia."[27] Lincoln took still stronger steps. Fearing secessionist plots, he ordered thirty-one Southern-leaning assemblymen jailed in September. While most were released after several months, the arrests stifled dissent and assured a resounding unionist victory in the November state elections.[28]

Lincoln adopted a more cautious approach to Kentucky, which like Maryland sought to remain on the sidelines in the fratricidal war. Although the secessionist movement gained little traction, many Kentuckians cheered the Confederacy. Perhaps 40 percent of white Kentuckians who took up arms fought for the Confederacy. Thousands joined regiments formed in Tennessee, while others enlisted in the pro-secessionist "state guard." Governor Beriah Magoffin firmly rejected the president's request for soldiers. "Kentucky will furnish no troops," he told Lincoln, "for the wicked purposes of subdueing her sister Southern States."[29] And while the majority favored the Union, the strongest sentiment was the hope that Kentucky could remain outside the fray. "Any attempt at coercion," a Louisville newspaper warned, "can only end in the calamities of war and produce nothing but evil. This sentiment is universal in this State, and not a man can be had for this fight."[30]

Lincoln understood the delicacy of the situation and initially sent no troops to Kentucky. In April he informed unionist Garrett Davis that if the state "made no demonstration of force against the United States, he would not molest her."[31] But Lincoln allowed his commanders in Ohio to recruit Kentuckians, and they did so actively. Responding to the pleas of Kentuckian William Nelson, he also quietly directed arms to Louisville and other towns to supply the "home guard," which was the loyal counterpart to Magoffin's "state guard."[32]

Gradually the unionist majority asserted itself, and Lincoln undertook bolder measures. Three elections made clear that most voters rejected the counsels of the secessionists. In May unionists elected virtually all the delegates to a Border State convention. In June Kentuckians chose pro-Northern congressmen in nine of the state's ten districts; only the counties of the southwest sent a states' rights politician to Washington. Unionists prevailed again in the August balloting for the state legislature, establishing majorities of 76–25 in the lower house and 27–11 in the senate. Lincoln responded to these affirmations of loyalty with increasingly firm steps. After the August elections he banned trade between Kentucky and the Confederacy, and he encouraged William Nelson to establish an army base, Camp Dick Robinson, near Lexington. After opening the encampment, Nelson recruited several regiments among the unionists of eastern Kentucky. Northern commanders also readied soldiers at Cairo, Illinois, for an invasion of the Bluegrass State.

On September 5, days after Confederate troops marched into southwestern Kentucky, Union forces under Ulysses S. Grant crossed into Kentucky. Angered by the Southern advance but not by the Northern response, the legislators resolved that all Confederate troops must leave the state. When Governor Magoffin rejected this decree, the lawmakers overrode his veto and raised the American flag over the capitol in Frankfort. The legislature declared that "the attempt to destroy the Union of these States we believe to be a crime, not only against Kentucky, but against all mankind." Fighting would continue in Kentucky in 1861 and 1862, but the state remained firmly in Union hands.[33]

Had the entire South resembled the Border States, or even the Upper South, there would have been neither secession nor Civil War. The citizenry in these states did not like Lincoln's election, but they did not consider the Republican victory as cause for dissolution. Only when these northerly regions were drawn into the vortex of war did the large slaveholders of the Upper South, over the protests of many small farmers, lead their states out of the Union. Meanwhile the Border States, despite dissension and a professed desire for neutrality, remained loyal commonwealths.

More broadly, the different paths taken by the Border States, Upper South, and cotton states show that the South went to war not simply to defend slavery but because of larger social and economic concerns. To be sure, planters in the lower reaches of the Deep South took up arms in defense of their institutions. In Lincoln's ascent they heard the death knell of their society. But their vision reflected more than a commitment to preserve forced labor. It was also shaped by fears of soil exhaustion, by high concentrations of slaves in their states, by their family origins, and by their distance from the overland exchanges that helped knit other parts of the South into the national fabric. The more cautious response of the northern tiers of states suggests that trade, place of birth, class, and levels of slaveholding—not just the desire to defend a social system—determined who seceded and when.

# PART FOUR

# THE WAR
# AND BEYOND

—— 12 ——

# REPUBLICANS
# IN POWER:
# THE WAR YEARS

S enator William Pitt Fessenden of Maine was proud of the
work of the wartime Congress. Since birth Pitt, as he was
called, had seemed destined for greatness. He was named for
Britain's Tory prime minister, who died in 1806, the year Fessenden
was born. An able lawyer and lawmaker, handsome and always impec-
cably dressed, Fessenden rose steadily in the world, serving as state assemblyman, congressman, and senator. Early in his career Fessenden
decided that the best government was one that promoted economic
growth and checked the slave power. In keeping with his convictions,
he moved from the National Republicans to the Whigs and finally to
the Republicans. Widely respected, Fessenden chaired the Senate Finance Committee and worked long hours to fund the war. It was from
this insider's vantage that he reflected on the Republicans' accomplishments. The lawmakers, he knew, had transformed the government and the nation. "With all its faults and errors, this has been
a great and self-sacrificing Congress," he told a friend in 1863. "If

the rebellion should be crushed, Congress will have crushed it. We have assumed terrible responsibilities [and] placed powers in the hands of the government possessed by none other on earth short of a despotism."[1]

Understanding the Republicans' achievements after they took power helps explain the powerful new party that stood up to the South, refused to compromise, and (along with the secessionists of the Deep South) precipitated the Civil War. In the years after the outbreak of fighting, as before the war, Republicans were driven both by their commitment to the rights of African Americans and by their determination to develop the Northern economy. Although their efforts to help blacks began slowly, Republicans implemented a remarkable series of measures, including emancipation and enfranchisement. Still, less than a dozen years after Lincoln assumed the presidency, that commitment flagged in the face of white Southern resistance. The stronger continuity in Republican actions lay with their broad-based economic program, measures that fell under the rubric of "nationalism." Lawmakers laid the foundations for a rapidly growing industrial state, and drew ever closer to the industrialists and financiers who came to dominate the business life of the nation. Economic development, not the empowerment of African Americans, would be the true legacy of the Republican Party.

## I.

Beginning hesitantly in 1861 and culminating with the adoption of the Thirteenth Amendment in 1865, Republicans attacked slavery. They acted both because they agreed with Lincoln that African Americans were "entitled to all the natural rights enumerated in the Declaration of Independence" and because of the dramatically changed circumstances brought on by the war. That any measures were taken in 1861 to check slavery is perhaps surprising. Despite their opposition to forced labor, Republicans entered the war firmly committed to respecting slavery where it existed. In the 1860 presidential campaign and again in the bargaining that marked the secessionist winter, they promised not to disturb the institution in the South. Party members reaffirmed that stance in July 1861 when, overwhelmingly, they supported a resolution put forth by John Crittenden of Kentucky. It declared that "this war is not prosecuted . . . for any purpose of conquest or . . . interfering with the rights or established institutions of those [Southern] States." The House approved the statement, 117–2, while the Senate concurred, 30–5.[2] Moreover, the commanding general in the Virginia theater, George McClellan, reassured civilians he would not interfere with their servants. "We will, on the contrary," he stated, "with an iron hand, crush any attempt at insurrection on their part." When General (and former presidential candidate) John Frémont announced that in Missouri slaves belonging to rebels would be freed, Lincoln countermanded the order and relieved Frémont of his post.[3]

Still, Republicans took the first steps against slavery in 1861, responding to a new set of pressures. Most significantly, slaves themselves transformed the nature of war as more and more of them fled to Union lines. One of the unlikely heroes in this saga was Benjamin Butler, the short, balding, overweight federal general with drooping eyes. No one doubted Butler's audacity. In April 1861 he had secured the railhead at Annapolis, allowing federal troops to travel to Washington unmolested, and then—without specific orders—took over rebellious Baltimore. But few could have predicted his willingness to welcome fugitive slaves at his next command, Fortress Monroe, a citadel near Hampton, Virginia. Before the war Butler had been an outspoken Democrat, as well as an enthusiastic backer of James Buchanan in 1856 and Southern Democrat John Breckinridge in 1860. Butler supported the Kansas-Nebraska Act, long after most Northerners rejected the measure. The war, however, radicalized the general, beginning with the decisions he made at Fortress Monroe. In late May 1861 he set three slaves to work on the fortifications after they surrendered to his men. When a local Confederate commander protested, Butler replied: "I shall hold them as contraband of war. You were using them against the Government: I proposed to use them in favor of it." By summer almost a thousand slaves had entered Fortress Monroe.[4]

Butler's actions, which Secretary of War Simon Cameron accepted, sounded the tocsin for what some historians have called the great Civil War slave rebellion. Courageously, first hundreds and then thousands of African Americans arrived at the Union camps. For example, Harry Jarvis of Northampton County, Virginia, escaped a master he called "the meanest man on all the Eastern shore." Jarvis was shot at, took to the woods, stole a canoe, and then paddled thirty-five miles to Fortress Monroe. In other cases, slaves presented themselves to Union commanders after their masters fled. In November 1861, when Union forces captured Port Royal, South Carolina, about ten thousand "contrabands" came under federal protection. The arrival of African Americans in Union camps, and the services they provided to hard-pressed commanders, suggested that lawmakers should change the rules. Well before the Emancipation Proclamation, blacks made Union troops an army of liberation.[5]

Outspoken Radical Republicans comprised another force for change. These principled individuals, like Charles Sumner, George Julian, Owen Lovejoy (whose brother Elijah had been killed in 1837 defending his abolition press), and Henry Wilson, had long crusaded against slavery and for black rights. They agreed that war could shorten a timetable once measured in decades.[6]

Along with Sumner, who led the militants in the Senate, the most influential Radical was Congressman Thaddeus Stevens of Pennsylvania. He chaired the powerful Ways and Means Committee and was floor leader for much of the Reconstruction-era legislation. From the beginning of the war until his death in August 1868 Stevens remained a force to be reckoned with. His power came as much from his personality as from his position. Stevens was in equal measure sharp-tongued and caring, an ideologue and a practical politician.

Stevens's difficult early years helped shape his seemingly contradictory nature, which combined an acerbic wit with a deep compassion for the less fortunate. He was born in Vermont in 1792 into challenging circumstances. Thaddeus, like his older brother, came into the world with a clubfoot. The condition lamed him and led other children, and later opposing politicians, to mock him. Stevens quickly learned the power of his finely honed, cutting replies. (A newspaper later called him "a skirmisher, rather than a regular debater . . . a great master of sarcasm and unsparing in his use of it.") Stevens's father, who was a drunk and a bankrupt, compounded the woes of these early years. Only Thaddeus's mother stood by her son, encouraging his education at a local academy and then at Dartmouth College. Though he eventually grew rich from his law practice, Stevens never forgot his origins or lost his concern for the poor and mistreated. He gave generously to charities, often helping strangers in need.[7]

After Dartmouth, Stevens moved to Pennsylvania, became an attorney and politician, and grew increasingly effective in working for the causes he believed in. He learned to compromise and build coalitions, a skill that helped him lead a successful campaign for free public schools. His success in establishing a system of public education was a remarkable achievement in a conservative state. Stevens's flexibility was also evident in his willingness to change parties. He started as an Antimason, became a Whig, briefly joined the Know Nothings (despite his dislike of their nativist doctrines), and then helped found Pennsylvania's Republican Party. His abilities, however, were sorely tested in his efforts to promote antislavery and black rights, causes that became his principal focus after 1837. That year Stevens, desperately but vainly, tried to persuade the delegates to the Pennsylvania constitutional convention to retain the limited black suffrage then in place. In 1848 and 1850 he was elected to Congress, where he attacked Calhoun's followers and helped coordinate the opposition to the slavoc-racy. "Our enemy has a general now," remarked Georgian Howell Cobb. In 1858 Stevens was once again chosen congressman, a position he held until his death. Stevens's empathy for African Americans was also evident in his personal life. Beginning in 1848 he lived with a mu-latto woman, Lydia Smith, and generously provided for her in his will.[8]

Stevens had still another dimension that shaped his actions: he was an economic nationalist. His ownership of several ironworks con-tributed to his expansive outlook. He began investing in the iron in-dustry in the 1820s and built successively larger furnaces in 1831 and 1837. A Confederate raid in 1863 destroyed his ironworks, an attack that he judged cost him $75,000. Stevens's involvement with the iron industry helped make him an advocate of railroad construction, higher tariffs, and an expanded currency.

With the outbreak of war, Stevens, like other Radicals, demanded strong steps against slavery. He abstained in the vote on the Crittenden resolve (as did Sumner), and several days later explained his refusal to vote with the majority: "I, for one, shall never shrink from saying, when these slaves are conquered by us, 'Go and be free.' God forbid that I should ever agree that they should be returned to their masters!"[9] In December Stevens proposed that all slaves who reached Union lines be liberated. During the winter and first half of 1862, he and other militants lobbied the president. "Stevens, Sumner and Wilson, simply haunt me with their importunities for a Proclamation of Emancipa-tion," Lincoln informed Missouri senator John Henderson. "Wherever I go and whatever way I turn, they are on my train, and still in my heart, I have the deep conviction that the hour has not yet come."[10]

In 1861 the result of these pressures was one limited piece of leg-islation: the First Confiscation Act. This measure, adopted in August, sanctioned at least in part what Butler and other generals had done: it allowed Union commanders to harbor those slaves who had been di-rectly employed by Confederate forces. But it left the question of freedom up to the courts and offered no protection to other African Americans now behind Union lines.

In 1862 Republicans intensified their attack on slavery, driven by a mix of heartfelt convictions and wartime practicalities. The forces for change evident during the first year of war had strengthened. Still more African Americans came under Union control with the capture of New Orleans in April. Radical politicians such as Sumner and Stevens, orators like Wendell Phillips, and newspaper editors like Horace Greeley demanded emancipation ever more insistently, reflecting the views of important constituencies, particularly in the northern part of the North. Furthermore, in 1862 politicians came to realize that the war would be a prolonged one. Leaders in the North, like their counterparts in the South, had assumed the fighting would be brief, concluded in six months or at most a year. Now Republicans recognized that the conflict would be protracted and fought in the "sickly" climate of the South, where it was felt blacks had a natural resistance to illness. (The immunities conferred by the sickle cell trait, a condition affecting certain African Americans, provide some substance for these beliefs.)[11]

The response to these new circumstances was a series of heated debates in Congress and the landmark antislavery legislation adopted between March and July 1862. The most prolonged exchanges examined two related questions: Should Congress hasten emancipation with another confiscation act? Should Northern armies enlist black soldiers? With few exceptions Democrats as well as Unionists, who were particularly strong in the Border States and had backed the Bell-Everett ticket, opposed these actions. They argued that the Constitution prohibited such steps; that stern measures betrayed Republican promises; and that rash moves could provoke servile insurrection. "The voice of the conservative masses must be heard," declared Indiana Democrat William Holman. Other politicians warned that with emancipation, hordes of illiterate blacks would march north. Democrat

Samuel Cox of Ohio asked whether his state's troops would "fight at all, if the result shall be the flight and movement of the black race by millions northward to their own State?"[12]

Republicans rejected such reasoning and made the case for attacking slavery by pointing both to military necessity and to their belief in the equality of all men. Only when yoked together did these two reasons drive change. Military pressures alone cannot explain the steps taken to free African Americans. Although most Northern Democrats and Unionists shared the Republicans' determination to defeat the Confederacy, they spurned all "unconstitutional" measures. At the same time, despite their convictions, most Republicans respected the rights of slaveholders during the first year of fighting.

In arguing for these measures, the more radical Republicans emphasized principle, while the more conservative party members underscored expediency. George Julian, long one of the more outspoken antislavery crusaders in the party, declared, "Nothing can possibly sanctify the trials and sufferings through which we are called to pass but the permanent establishment of liberty and peace. If this is not a war of ideas, it is not a war to be defended."[13] By contrast, James R. Doolittle, the cautious Republican senator from Wisconsin, remarked: "It is conceded upon all hands that there is no ground upon which we can set free the slaves of rebels, but on that of military necessity."[14]

Most Republicans, while acknowledging the importance of moral arguments, expanded on the need for black support in what was becoming a prolonged contest. "They build fortifications for the rebels. Why not for us?" William Windom, a Minnesota Republican, observed. "They relieve rebel soldiers from nearly all the fatigue duties of war. Why should they not aid ours? They man rebel batteries. Why not ours? The sickly season at the South is rapidly approaching, when exposure and toil will be almost certain death to northern soldiers. Why not employ the services of those who are acclimated, and save the lives of our friends and neighbors?"[15] New Yorker Charles Sedgwick reasoned, "You go through a forest with a black man, and meet a beast of prey, you do not ask him to stand aside behind a tree while you alone fight the ferocious animal; you are willing that he should take his club and deal such blows as he can."[16]

The result of this changed climate of opinion was a series of measures that struck at slavery without demanding abolition. In March Congress forbade army officers from returning fugitive slaves. In April lawmakers banned slavery in the District of Columbia; in June they ended bondage in the territories. In July Lincoln signed the Second Confiscation Act, as well as a militia law allowing the army to enroll "persons of African descent." The value of the Confiscation Act, however, was more symbolic than real. While it freed the slaves of rebels and sanctioned what generals had been doing for over a year, it relied on the courts for enforcement and was restricted by the explanatory resolution Lincoln demanded. This proviso limited the forfeiture of property to the life of the individual rebel.

Lincoln too was changing on the issue of emancipation, guided as were other Republicans by his convictions and by new circumstances. Lincoln had long abhorred slavery, but he also had a strong respect for private property and a clear set of priorities that put saving the Union ahead of ending bondage. His words and deeds place him closer to the conservatives than to the radicals in his party. During 1861 and most of 1862 Lincoln hoped that blacks and whites would voluntarily travel the road to freedom. For Lincoln, the first stage of the journey was compensated emancipation, and the next the colonization of the freed people. Few, however, were willing to march down that highway. Border State representatives rebuffed overtures for compensated emancipation, underscoring their opposition again in July 1862, when Lincoln invited lawmakers from those states to meet with him. African Americans similarly rejected Lincoln's pleas for colonization. In August a gathering of black leaders (the first such meeting ever in the White House) spurned his arguments for a new homeland.[17]

During summer 1862 Lincoln began ever more seriously to contemplate presidential emancipation. "I view the matter as a practical war measure," he told a group of visitors, "to be decided upon according to the advantages or disadvantages it may offer to the suppression of the rebellion." Pressure from Congress; from the growing number of fugitive slaves whose status in Union camps remained uncertain; from the army with its increasing needs for manpower; from editors and governors who demanded firmer action; and even from foreign governments threatening to recognize the Confederacy if the moral issues remained blurred—all drove Lincoln toward action. The Border States (particularly Kentucky), which he feared would be alienated by a decree, had gradually become more secure thanks to gains made by the Union armies.[18]

Responding to these pressures and emboldened by the victory at Antietam, Lincoln issued his Preliminary Emancipation Proclamation on September 22. Although he knew the announcement would raise a firestorm of protest in the Border States, Lincoln tried to assuage these unionists. Loyal areas were excluded from decree. The proclamation also reaffirmed Lincoln's support for compensated emancipation and colonization, and it promised legislation to reimburse slaveholding loyalists "for all losses by acts of the United States." The document remained silent on the morality of slavery. Polish-born Count Adam Gurowski, who worked as a translator for the State Department, accurately described the decree as written in the "most dry routine style; not a word to evoke a generous thrill." Like a lawyer's brief, it recited precedents, including the Second Confiscation Act and the congressional resolve prohibiting army officers from returning fugitive slaves. Lincoln declared he would promulgate a final version on January 1, 1863.[19]

The final Emancipation Proclamation, like the preliminary one, breathes the air of practicality rather than passion. Emphasizing "military necessity," Lincoln justified the step as a "fit and necessary war measure for suppressing said rebellion." Like the preliminary proclamation, the document freed the slaves only in the areas still under Confederate control. Still, whether prose or poetry, the Emancipation Proclamation had a breathtaking impact, and Lincoln was justly proud of what he had accomplished. "If my name ever goes into history," he remarked, "it will be for this act."[20] The proclamation was not dependent on the courts as the Confiscation Acts were. Announced to fugitives in the camps, it unmistakably set them free. As the Union forces moved south, Lincoln's decree was proclaimed to African Americans. "After the reading," future black leader Booker T. Washington recollected, "we were told that we were all free, and could go when and where we pleased." Although few Republicans initially had anticipated or even advocated such an outcome, the Civil War had become a war for freedom.[21]

Lincoln similarly changed his position on recruiting African Americans. Reluctant to take such a bold step and fearing the anger of the Great Border, Lincoln had initially opposed enlisting blacks. Although the Second Confiscation Act and the Militia Act (both adopted July 1862) empowered the president to raise black troops, Lincoln refused to do so. In August, when an Indiana delegation volunteered two regiments of black soldiers, Lincoln responded that he "would employ all colored men offered as laborers, but would not promise to make soldiers of them."[22] The Preliminary Emancipation Proclamation made no mention of black soldiers. However, serious shortfalls in Northern recruiting; the demands of Sumner, Stevens, and other Radicals; and the activities of several generals, such as Butler, who had begun mustering black companies, led Lincoln to change his mind. The final Emancipation Proclamation welcomed African American soldiers, and by spring 1863 Lincoln strongly encouraged enlistments. Eventually about 179,000 black men fought in the war and comprised 10 percent of the Union army.[23]

Republicans, who had come to accept emancipation as the embodiment of their principles and a wise wartime measure, endorsed the Thirteenth Amendment with virtual unanimity. This initiative, which would enshrine freedom in the Constitution, was needed because once peace returned, the legal status of the Emancipation Proclamation was uncertain. The amendment also addressed the issue of slavery in the states not covered by Lincoln's decree. Despite unmistakable evidence that slavery would not survive the war, Democrats and Union Party members opposed this step, and for many weeks they were able to deny Republicans the two-thirds majority in the House needed to send the amendment to the states. However, hard lobbying by Lincoln and Secretary of State Seward gained the needed votes, and on January 31, 1865, the House joined the Senate in approving the amendment.[24]

Although most Republicans in 1860 had confidently expected slavery to continue for many decades, the war gave them an unexpected opportunity to realize their commitment to freedom. Republican willingness to free the slaves and make them soldiers changed the shape of the war and the nation. Another set of measures, dealing with the economy, would do so as well.

## II.

Nationalism was the hallmark of the economic legislation Republicans adopted during the war. This outlook, which dated back to the late 1840s and 1850s, had its roots in the demands of lake representatives and their New England allies for internal improvements. Unlike earlier incarnations of nationalism (such as Henry Clay's American System), this ideology catered to the self-interest of the North, and particularly to the needs of those who formed the Republican coalition. This view shaped the 1860 platform, with its call for a protective tariff, a homestead act, a transcontinental railroad, and internal improvements—all measures that the triumphant Republicans would enact. The same ideology guided other legislation drafted in response to the pressures of war. To be sure, party members at times differed on these economic programs. Representatives of the rapidly growing "West" clashed with lawmakers from the more established "East." But with few exceptions, Republicans agreed on the need for a strong central government that promoted development—and had expressed those views well before the outbreak of fighting.

Financing the war was the most pressing economic problem the Republicans faced and the one that gave rise to the most extensive and innovative set of nationalist measures. Once fighting erupted, the traditional source of emergency funds—the sale of government bonds to bankers—dried up. Financiers were reluctant to extend loans to a government under siege. There was a desperate need for new sources of revenue: in July 1861 Secretary of the Treasury Salmon Chase estimated government expenses for the next fiscal year at $320 million— over five times the average federal budget in the 1850s.[25]

One recourse was higher tariffs, an initiative that conveniently combined economic development and revenue generation. Democrats and a few (but hardly all) New England Republicans resisted this measure. When Massachusetts senator Charles Sumner argued that such a step might offend England, William Pitt Fessenden of Maine, who chaired the Finance Committee, stormed, "What right has a foreign country to make any question about what we choose to do." With input from political economist Henry Carey and his circle, Congress increased duties in summer 1861 and again in 1862 and 1864.[26]

Another financial expedient—a popular loan—also broadened the role of government. After bankers spurned his appeals, Chase determined to sell bonds directly to the citizenry. The secretary found his ideal partner in Jay Cooke, a financier who had been involved in marketing securities for railroads and state governments. Cooke was so successful in 1861 that Chase made him general subscription agent for the whole country. Cooke advertised the bonds widely and appointed

2,500 subagents to promote their sale throughout the North, from the great cities to mining camps. After the war Cooke noted that "out of three million subscribers to our various public loans, over nine-tenths are of the class called *the people*." Where government finance had once been the province of the few, now a broad swath of citizens linked their fortunes to those of the government.[27]

Two other financial measures adopted in 1861 suggest the far-reaching programs that the Republicans would pursue. Congress authorized $50 million in Treasury notes but refused to make them legal tender for all debts—leaving their status uncertain. And urged on by Senator Fessenden, who hoped to minimize government borrowing, the lawmakers also agreed to levy an income tax, with collections to begin the next year.

In 1862 Republicans in the House, led by Stevens's Ways and Means Committee, broke new ground with a series of measures to pay for the war—and not incidentally create a stronger central government. The demand for funds had only intensified; Chase informed lawmakers in December 1861 that expenditures would outpace his earlier estimates by nearly 70 percent. One answer was the creation of a national currency. Many Republicans urged the government to print paper money, arguing that the notes would help finance the war as well as assist businesses interested in the national market. The Treasury bills would replace the existing system, with its innumerable state bank-notes that circulated at full face value only in one city or county.[28]

In January 1862 Elbridge Spaulding, a member of the House Ways and Means Committee, proposed a legal tender paper currency, boldly defending the plan with a paean to a consolidated nation-state. Spaulding, a former Whig, was a well-chosen spokesman. He was a banker, but one who hailed from western New York rather than from any of the eastern centers where financiers feared measures limiting the prerogatives of their profitable local institutions. Spaulding called upon the lawmakers to issue $100 million in legal tender Treasury notes and to support the bills with heavy taxes. "In . . . putting down the rebellion it is necessary to bring into exercise all the sovereign power of the Government to sustain itself," he exclaimed. "The war power must be exercised to its full extent . . . The tax-gatherer will be an unwelcome visitor to most people, but his face must soon be familiar."[29] John Sherman led the fight for the bill in the Senate. In both houses some Republicans, largely from the Northeast and often linked to state banks, opposed the measure, as did many Democrats, who still adhered to hard money policies. But most Republicans, particularly those from western New York, Pennsylvania, and the Midwest, backed the legislation. Lincoln signed the Legal Tender Act in February 1862. Eventually the government issued $432 million in Treasury notes or "greenbacks," as they were called (because of the green ink used in printing them). Congress taxed local banknotes out of existence, although the efforts of northeastern Republicans delayed this levy until the end of the war.[30]

Stevens's committee also introduced a comprehensive income tax, building on the legislation adopted in 1861 and helping to bring the citizenry into a new, more intimate relationship with the federal government. The bill created the Internal Revenue Bureau and unleashed an army of inspectors to oversee enforcement. Lincoln approved the measure in July 1862.[31]

In 1863 the Republicans approved the National Banking Act, the keystone in their plan to finance the war and build a prosperous, more unified country. The bill established a network of stable national banks with substantial reserves, held in the form of federal securities. These institutions could also issue a currency, "national banknotes," that had the same value across the country. Thus the measure tied the wealthy to the government, sold bonds, created a sound banking infrastructure, and provided a currency that had none of the drawbacks of local notes. The United States now had two uniform currencies: greenbacks and national banknotes. Sherman and Spaulding underscored the nationalist arguments for adopting the bill. Sherman stated: "It will make a community of interest between the stockholders of banks, the people and the Government . . . Every stockholder, every mechanic, every laborer who holds one of these notes will be interested in the Government." Sherman continued, elaborating his credo: "The policy of this country ought to be to make everything national as far as possible; to nationalize our country, so that we shall love our country."[32] A few days later Spaulding made a similar appeal in the House, noting: "It is now most apparent that the policy advocated by Alexander Hamilton, of a strong central Government, was the true policy." He concluded: "This is our country. Let it have one national Government—one destiny."[33]

Along with these financial measures, the Republicans passed during the war years three other major acts designed to foster American development. First, in May 1862 Republicans secured a homestead act, a measure they long had advocated. A few party members from the Northeast, and particularly New England, grumbled that during wartime land should be sold to help the cash-strapped government. Speaker Galusha Grow stifled that dissent when he stepped down from his chair to defend the measure. The "real wealth" of a nation, he explained, "consists not in the sums of money paid into its Treasury, but in its flocks, its herds, and cultivated fields, and, above all, in the comfort of its laboring classes; not in the mass of its wealth, but in its diffusion."[34]

Second, in July 1862 Justin Morrill of Vermont persuaded his fellow lawmakers to back the creation of land-grant agricultural colleges. In this instance, complaints came from Midwestern states that feared losing control of their public lands. Still, Morrill's arguments, which struck familiar nationalist chords, proved persuasive. "There . . . can be no mode," he remarked, "by which the resources of a country can be so fully developed as by educating the vast numbers who are to devote their lives to agricultural employments as tillers or owners of the soil."[35]

Third, also in July Lincoln signed into law the Pacific Railroad Act, fulfilling a promise set forth in the 1856 and 1860 Republican platforms. The route selected served Chicago and the Republican heartland, the northern part of the North. Stevens promoted the undertaking as necessary for America's rise. "I believe few will doubt its utility as a great national work," he observed. "This is not a western measure, and ought not to be defended as such. The western soil is but a platform on which to lay the rails to transport the wealth of the furthest Indies to Philadelphia, New York, Boston, and Portland [Maine]." For Stevens, as for most Republicans, "national" did not include the South, even once the country was reunited. He urged immediate passage of the act, fearing that once the South returned to the Union it would demand a Southern route or multiple roads.[36]

Thus by 1865 Republicans had adopted a wide-ranging series of economic measures that reflected their commitment to a "nationalism" that catered to the North. With higher tariffs, a system of national banks, two national currencies, an income tax, the homestead act, land-grant colleges, and a transcontinental railroad, they laid the foundation for a new era of growth. Economists debate the connection between this legislation and the rise of big business during the last third of the century. But what seems clear is the determination of leading Republicans to replace a society of local institutions and laissez-faire policies with one marked by a national marketplace and an assertive central government.[37]

Republican wartime accomplishments in civil rights and in economic development were remarkable, but these gains only heightened the challenges that came with peace. Difficult years lay ahead as Republicans sought to bring the South back into the nation, while pursuing their long-held goals. The era of Reconstruction would show that for Republicans, building a stronger economy was more important than protecting African American rights.

# REPUBLICANS IN POWER:
# BUILDING THE
# INDUSTRIAL STATE

To understand the priorities of the Republican Party in the decades after the war, follow the movement of the federal commanders and their troops. Generals O. O. Howard and Winfield S. Hancock, two heroes of the Civil War, were both posted to the South after the conflict and ordered to assist with Reconstruction. Howard headed the Freedmen's Bureau; Hancock supervised federal forces in Texas and Louisiana. These assignments were brief; along with many of their troops, both generals were soon sent west to fight the Indians. In 1877, while Howard was chasing the Nez Percé, Hancock received another posting. The War Department directed him to oversee the federal campaign against the strikers threatening the nation's railroads. Soldiers who a year earlier had defended the Louisiana statehouse swelled his forces. Former president Ulysses Grant was struck by this turn of events. My critics, Grant remarked, "thought it horrible to keep U.S. troops stationed in the Southern States . . . to protect the lives of negroes. . . . Now, however there is no hesitation about exhausting the whole power of the government to suppress a strike on the slightest intimation that danger threatens."[1]

The determination of the federal government (and the Republicans who guided it) to protect the rights of blacks was short-lived. Although Lincoln's party adopted landmark legislation, by the early 1870s it backed away from its commitment to the freed people. By contrast, government resolve to corral native peoples onto reservations, suppress labor agitation, and more broadly, build the industrial economy was sustained and enthusiastic. The years after the war were a testing time for Republicans. In 1865 they remained committed to their long-held goals of defending basic African American rights and expanding the Northern economy. But to stay the course on both issues they had to overcome external obstacles and internal divisions. The gravest difficulty lay with unreconstructed Southerners who were intent on frustrating Republican hopes of assisting blacks. In the end, this resistance proved overwhelming. Still, had the resolve been there, the problems in the South would have been no more insurmountable than challenges Republicans faced elsewhere. These years made clear the nature of the Republican Party and showed that fostering growth, not empowering African Americans, lay at the heart of the new party's outlook.

## I.

In the decade after the war the Republicans first advanced, then retreated in their campaign to ensure blacks basic rights—and ended by abandoning the field to the remnants of the old slavocracy. The willingness of mainstream Republicans to enact bold measures in the late 1860s testifies to their commitment to those fundamental rights. However, their readiness, beginning in the early 1870s, to abandon their black allies shows the limits of that resolve.

The reconstruction programs put forward by Lincoln and Congress during the war demonstrate the initial, limited scope of Republican concern for African Americans. Lincoln's "10 Percent Plan," announced in December 1863, required that one-tenth of 1860 voters swear an oath of future loyalty and accept abolition. These newly minted unionists would then proceed to establish state governments. Critics noted that the proclamation made no provision for black voting or even legal equality. Abolitionist Wendell Phillips remarked that it "frees the slave and ignores the negro." Lincoln's proposal also placed no restrictions on former Confederates. Congressional Republicans responded in July 1864 with the Wade-Davis Bill, which took a sterner approach to those who had been disloyal. This measure insisted that a majority of white voters swear their future loyalty, while allowing only those who had remained true to the Union to write the new constitutions. The congressional plan demanded equality before law for African Americans as well as abolition, but it too rejected universal manhood suffrage. Lincoln pocket-vetoed the Wade-Davis Bill, making clear that the president, not Congress, would control the initial stage of Reconstruction.

Although excluded for the moment from directing Reconstruction, Republican lawmakers showed their measured support for African Americans by creating the Freedmen's Bureau in March 1865. The new agency would distribute food and clothing and oversee the first steps to freedom. Republicans envisioned a short-lived organization and granted a mandate for only a single year. They believed that free labor—not government handouts—would allow blacks to rise in the world. Congress provided no funding for the bureau, which had to draw its personnel and resources from the War Department.[2]

The defiance of Southern whites during 1865 and the early months of 1866 gradually convinced Republicans that they had to adopt firmer policies to protect blacks—and prevent die-hard Confederates from regaining power. After Lincoln's death on April 15,

Radicals pinned their hopes on the new president, Andrew Johnson. The Tennessean had never loved Southern aristocrats, and his plan of reconstruction, announced in May, banned Confederate officials and those with more than $20,000 worth of property from participating in the new governments. But Johnson quickly undid the severity of his decree. Driven by his virulent Negrophobia, his susceptibility to the pleas of wealthy Southern supplicants, and his dislike of the monied and commercial classes of the North, Johnson issued pardons to more than seven thousand supplicants and ordered their estates restored.[3]

Johnson's policies allowed former Confederates to retain power across the South—with consequences that were deeply disturbing for Republicans. A tidal wave of violence struck the newly freed people. White Southerners, who had lost the war but not their beliefs in caste and class, resented outspoken blacks and their demands for land, education, and an open labor market. Too often the revolver and the rope defined the white response. One witness claimed that in 1865 "over two thousand colored people" were murdered near Shreveport, Louisiana. In May 1866 a Memphis race riot left forty-six blacks dead. In July a rampage against blacks in New Orleans killed thirty-four African Americans and three whites. Meanwhile across the South, state after state adopted "black codes," laws designed to compel the freed people to labor on the plantations. The codes granted blacks a minimal set of rights, including the right to marry, hold property, and make contracts. But they also prohibited African Americans from working in occupations other than farmer or laborer, and they established penalties for those without written proof of employment. As if these indignities were not enough, Southerners chose slates of ex-Confederates to represent them in the 39th Congress, which convened in December 1865.[4]

In the face of this challenge, Republicans responded decisively and with virtual unanimity, reaffirming their belief that all individuals were entitled to a set of fundamental rights. The steps that mainstream Republicans took between December 1865 and July 1866 reveal the strengths—and shortcomings—of a party that was determined to affirm the values of the Declaration of Independence but was not yet ready to move beyond those principles. The Republicans began their campaign by rejecting the delegations from the eleven former Confederate states. A broad spectrum of party members approved this decision. Two moderate Republican senators, William Pitt Fessenden of Maine, who chaired the Joint Committee on Reconstruction, and Lyman Trumbull of Illinois, who headed the Judiciary Committee, guided the lawmakers during these months.

Trumbull, a Connecticut Yankee who moved to southern Illinois in the 1830s, embodied both the commitment and the caution of many Republicans. A tall, fair-haired man, somewhat ill at ease in the rough-and-tumble of Western society, Trumbull entered politics in the 1840s as a Democrat. He pleased many voters with his tirades against banks and his espousal of Jacksonian policies. But his constituents, many of whom had emigrated from the South, were less enthusiastic about his attacks on slavery. In 1855 Trumbull proved to be the ideal compromise candidate for senator. The legislature, torn between Douglas Democrats and antislavery Whigs, sent Trumbull, an antislavery Democrat, to Washington. He joined the Republicans in 1856. During the war he ardently backed emancipation, and after 1865 insisted with equal fervor that blacks be guaranteed their basic rights. But Trumbull was reluctant to move beyond the narrow bounds of legal equality, placing him firmly among the moderate Republicans. He also never abandoned his Jacksonian roots or his critical approach to big business. In the early 1870s Trumbull would leave the Republicans, condemning them as the corrupt servants of corporations, and would become, by turns, a Liberal Republican, a Democrat, and, in the 1890s, a Populist.[5]

During the first months of 1866 Trumbull introduced two key pieces of legislation. First, he called for the renewal of the Freedmen's

Bureau. The outrages committed against blacks made clear that this agency, headed by General O. O. Howard, had much left to do. Republicans, who approved this seemingly modest step, were shocked when Johnson vetoed the measure. Next, Trumbull proposed a Civil Rights Act, legislation that fully embodied the Republican commitment to protecting blacks. It declared that everyone (except native Americans) born in the United States was a citizen and was entitled to the "full and equal benefit of all laws and proceedings for the security of person and property." The measure nullified laws that used race to deprive individuals of those rights. The judicial system and the Freedmen's Bureau were to enforce the act.

The Civil Rights Act was important for what it did and did not do. While the measure attacked the discriminatory provisions of the black codes, it was silent on such "privileges" as voting or jury service. The act also cast the problems afflicting Southern blacks in narrow, legalistic terms. For Trumbull and others, the repeal of unjust statutes was the key to establishing a more equitable society. Trumbull explained: "When it comes to be understood in all parts of the United States that any person who shall deprive another of any right . . . in consequence of his color or race will expose himself to fine and imprisonment, I think such acts will soon cease."[6] Virtually all Republicans backed Trumbull's initiative; they passed the act, and when Johnson negatived the measure, they overrode the veto.

Along with the Freedmen's Bureau Act (which Congress repassed in July, defying the president) and the Civil Rights Act, the Republicans' third major piece of legislation was the Fourteenth Amendment. The Joint Committee on Reconstruction introduced this legislation. In part, the amendment repeated the provisions of the Civil Rights Act, enshrining them in the Constitution. Without such an amendment, Thaddeus Stevens warned, "the first time that the South with their copperhead allies obtain the command of Congress" they would repeal all protective legislation.[7] Like the Civil Rights Act, the amendment created birthright citizenship and banned discriminatory state laws. The amendment also addressed the problem of representation. With freedom, blacks counted as full persons rather than as three-fifths of a person for the apportionment of congressmen. There was a danger than an unreconstructed South might return to Congress with more seats. The amendment penalized any state denying males the vote, by proportionately reducing its representation. Finally, the amendment repudiated the Confederate debt and barred Confederate officeholders from holding any position in national or state governments.[8]

Radicals and outspoken moderates pointed to the grave limitations of these measures. They condemned these initiatives for not extending suffrage to Southern blacks. "Without it [the ballot]," George Julian observed, "the freedom of these people is a delusion and a lie."[9] Although never a Radical, James Garfield, the Ohio congressman and future president, agreed. He observed that the right to vote, while "not indeed one of the natural rights of all men, is so necessary to the protection of their natural rights as to be indispensable, and therefore equal to the natural rights."[10]

Critics underscored a second problem: the failure of Congress to distribute land to the freed people. Radicals argued that only property could provide African Americans with the security they needed to flourish in a hostile South. "In my judgement," remarked Thaddeus Stevens, "we shall not approach the measure of justice until we have given every adult freedman a homestead on the land where he was born and toiled and suffered."[11] Without land, Julian noted, "the loyal masses . . . are thus reduced to a condition of servitude and helplessness."[12] African Americans across the South in conventions, churches, and local meetings raised the same demands. Few estates, however, were seized, and those initially taken from Confederate planters were restored. General William Sherman, in the waning days of the war, distributed abandoned coastal lands in South Carolina, Georgia, and Florida to the freed people, but only some of those tracts would remain in black hands. In June 1866 Congress adopted a Southern Homestead Act, proposed by Julian and Stevens; however, the limited public lands available provided homes for only about four thousand families. The result was that overwhelmingly, Southern blacks remained landless. They rejected gang labor, despite the strictures of the Black Codes. But that victory proved hollow. By the end of the 1860s most African Americans were forced to sharecrop, grow cotton, and accept a life of poverty and white control.[13]

The legislation adopted during the first half of 1866 mapped out the hopeful vision of race relations that Lincoln and others had long advocated. It defended the blacks' right to "life, liberty, and the pursuit of happiness," although it stopped far short of true equality. Republicans dreamed that equal laws and free labor would allow blacks to rise in the world. That optimistic program, however, was not to be realized. Sharecropping negated free labor, while racist state governments blocked legal equality—and defeated the moderate reconstruction plan of 1866. Between October 1866 and February 1867 ten of the eleven former Confederate states, encouraged in their defiance by President Johnson, rejected the Fourteenth Amendment. Only Tennessee ratified the amendment, and was readmitted to the Union.

Southern resistance forced the Republicans to take still stronger steps and propelled them into unknown terrain. "The last one of the sinful ten," James Garfield observed, "has at last with contempt and scorn, flung back into our teeth the magnanimous offer of a generous nation. It is now our turn to act."[14] Republicans, both moderate and radical, felt they had little choice but to create new state governments—and enfranchise blacks. During the first months of 1867 speaker after speaker reminded Congress of the deplorable conditions in the South. "What real progress has been made?" asked Illinois representative Ebon Ingersoll. "The condition of things there has been growing worse from day to day since the day of their surrender. Crime is holding a high carnival there; industry is in a great measure paralyzed;

[and] the Congress is repudiated and denounced as an unconstitutional body."[15]

The new Republican program, which drew many moderates outside their zone of comfort, was embodied in the Reconstruction Act of March 1867. This legislation, as clarified by subsequent Reconstruction Acts, divided the South into five military districts, enfranchised the freedmen, and barred former Confederate officials from voting. Every state was to ratify the Fourteenth Amendment, write a constitution, and elect a new government. Republicans agreed that black voters were the only effective counterweight to the recalcitrant white population. "The ballot in the hands of the negro," Senator Lot Morrill of Maine explained, "became as much the necessity of reconstruction of republican States and their restoration as the bayonet in his hands was the necessity of the war."[16] Unlike the measures put forth during the first half of 1866, the Reconstruction Acts moved well beyond the position taken by most mainstream Republicans. Significantly, blacks were enfranchised in the South before that right was extended to African Americans in the North. During the debates over the Reconstruction Act, moderates acknowledged the necessity for the bill but expressed their discomfort in working so closely with the Radicals. These qualms raised questions about how long the program would last if the seas ahead proved stormy.[17]

Although many of the Republican regimes now formed in the South were short-lived, their accomplishments were impressive. Blacks were elected to state legislatures across the South, and a few were sent to Congress. In several towns they became mayors, and in plantation counties, sheriffs. Assemblies established school systems, hospitals, and asylums, often for the first time. Lawmakers integrated public conveyances, protected tenants, extended rights to women, and encouraged economic development, frequently funding railroad construction. These regimes, which offered the hope of a truly "new

South," rested on a fragile coalition of blacks, Northern interlopers (or "carpetbaggers"), and sympathetic local whites. This last group, sneered at as "scalawags," typically drew its support from individuals and districts that had resisted secession.[18]

Even though some Republicans spurned the new regimes as early as 1870, the majority continued to back them during 1871 and 1872. Supporting these governments meant countering the waves of violence that surged across the South. Between the advent of peace in 1865 and the removal of the last troops in 1877, three eras of white terror can be discerned. Each killed thousands of blacks and their sympathizers. The first, which lasted from the end of the war until 1868, was unorganized and directed at individuals who questioned the efforts of the former slave lords to restore old ways. The Ku Klux Klan, the Knights of the White Camelia, and similar organizations led the second wave, which targeted the new Republican governments. The third era, which began in about 1873, was marked by armed bands that paraded openly and were determined to unseat the remaining Republican governors.

The success Republicans had in stopping Klan violence, although limited to a few states and particular years, suggests what the party might have achieved had it remained resolute in opposing terror. Firm action by determined executives achieved impressive results. In Arkansas, Governor Powell Clayton declared martial law in 1868, mustered a state militia composed of blacks and whites, and expelled the Klan. In Texas, Governor Edmund J. Davis deployed an integrated state police unit that arrested more than six thousand lawbreakers and provided security for voters. Washington also took effective if sporadic steps to end white terror. Congress passed a series of enforcement acts in the early 1870s, culminating in the Ku Klux Klan Act of April 1871. These measures banned groups that disguised themselves, and empowered public officials to jail lawbreakers and supervise elections.

Backed by federal troops, marshals made hundreds of arrests in South Carolina, North Carolina, and Mississippi between 1871 and 1873. These efforts dealt a lethal blow to the Klan.[19]

However, even while voting for the enforcement acts, many Republicans raised doubts about the path the party was pursuing—and some abandoned the party altogether. Voting rights had never been part of the Republican credo in the way that legal equality and free labor had been. In 1870 Lyman Trumbull urged black leaders not to focus on voting but to teach their followers about "sobriety, industry, and the importance of having a home that they may call their own."[20] Other moderates expressed grave concerns about the exceptional measures needed to suppress violence in the South. "We are working on the very verge of the Constitution," James Garfield remarked, "and many of our members are breaking over the lines."[21]

Perhaps the most significant—and surprising—defection from Republican ranks came with the Liberal Republican revolt of 1872. Among the supporters of this movement were former antislavery crusaders such as Charles Sumner, George Julian, Salmon Chase, Charles Francis Adams, Lyman Trumbull, and Carl Schurz. Horace Greeley was the new party's presidential candidate. The Liberal Republicans fused with the Democrats and endorsed a campaign that called for ending Reconstruction. Their platform demanded "universal amnesty," so that Confederate officials could vote again, and "local self-government," shorthand for removing all troops from the South. Southern blacks were shocked by the apostasy of these reformers. One correspondent told Sumner, "If I go, sir, into a hotel here in the South where they have hung up . . . portraits of Horace Greeley and [vice presidential candidate] Gratz Brown . . . I am [told]: 'Go out of here, this is no place for niggers!' "[22]

What explains this strange turn of allegiances? Some moderates like Lyman Trumbull, who had grown increasingly dissatisfied with Republican policies toward the South, viewed the Liberal Republican

Party as a logical next step. But others, like Sumner and Julian, had not abandoned their belief in equal rights. Rather, for most Liberal Republicans, economic concerns now trumped race relations. Sumner and other critics condemned the mainstream Republicans for their corruption and ties to big business. Julian scored the "mercenary element" that had taken over Lincoln's party and urged "the radical reform of its Tariff and Land Policy, and its emancipation from the rule of great corporations and monopolies."[23] Henry Adams, who shared the views of his father, Charles Francis Adams, remarked that "the day is at hand when corporations far greater than [the] Erie [Railroad] . . . will ultimately succeed in directing government itself."[24] Grant's victory in 1872 dashed the hopes of reformers as well as of the Democrats who joined them. Grant won every state save six. Some reformers drifted back into the Republican Party, but with few exceptions the issues they pursued involved "clean" government, not African American rights.[25]

More generally, in the early 1870s antislavery activists left the Republican Party, either through death or defection. They no longer felt at home in a party that catered to big business and lacked the resolve to protect black rights. Reformers sounded a sad litany of declension. Abolitionist Theodore Tilton commented in 1871 that the party had "lost the manly mettle of its early youth. . . . It does not sow new seed—it is only garnering its former harvest."[26] In 1875 George Julian toured the Western Reserve of Ohio and visited the monument to Joshua Giddings, who had died in 1864. Julian noted in his diary: "The abolition element has almost died out in that old stronghold of radicalism, as it has in so many others throughout the country, and the few antislavery pioneers who remain seem to feel lonely and lost."[27]

Republicans, including many militants, now retreated from their defense of black rights. Former Radical Ben Wade observed: "A thing may be right in the abstract, and yet not be expedient, because public sentiment will not tolerate or accept the full application of the principle."[28] Although lawmakers adopted new enforcement laws, they restricted the funds of the agencies implementing those statutes. Congress capped the outlays for the judiciary despite the demands of prosecuting thousands of Klansmen and Knights. Republicans also cut troop strength in the South from about 12,000 in 1868 to 3,400 in 1873, stretching forces far too thin for the demands placed on them. General Sherman noted that "we subject our soldiers to dangers worse than an ordinary battle." Republicans displayed a far stronger commitment to the West, where by the 1870s most of the army's 27,000 soldiers were engaged fighting Indians. Furthermore, after 1870 and the adoption of the Fifteenth Amendment, which gave the vote to all African Americans, Republican concern to protect black voting increasingly focused on the North, where these ballots could make the difference in close elections.

The weakening commitment of Northern Republicans, coupled with continuing violence and Democratic appeals to "scalawags," the whites backing the radical governments, soon led to the demise of most of the new regimes in the South. By the end of 1874 Republican executives survived only in South Carolina, Mississippi, Louisiana, and Florida. In the states where Democrats resumed power, conditions worsened for blacks. Lawmakers repealed progressive legislation, cut funding for schools, and adopted repressive labor laws.[29]

The presidency of Ulysses S. Grant fully reflected the rise and fall of the Republicans' support for the radical state governments. Grant had his shortcomings, which detractors readily pointed out. He was physically unimpressive, and many who first met him underestimated the man. During the war one colonel described Grant as "stumpy, unmilitary, slouchy, and western looking; very ordinary, in fact." In the 1850s Grant drank to excess. The thirty-year-old captain had trouble, after the excitement of the Mexican War, adapting to the peacetime army and then, after his resignation in 1854, earning a living as a civilian. While the charge of drunkenness would dog him in later years, ci-

gars, not alcohol, were his vice after 1860. His willingness to give sub-
ordinates a free hand in carrying out their orders, while a virtue in the
"fog of war," often proved a poor policy in peacetime. Although
Grant was personally honest, his administration was scandal-ridden;
his attorney general and secretaries of interior and war resigned in
disgrace.

These shortcomings were balanced by Grant's exceptional abilities.
He was more politically astute than many detractors suggested. His
skill in dealing with other Union commanders was good training for
the years immediately after the war, when he was able to work with a
Congress and president who stood at sword's point. In key areas Grant
grew and changed. He became an outstanding military leader, always
learning from his own mistakes and accomplishments as well as from
the campaigns of other generals. His close relationship with Lincoln
during the war deepened his understanding of politics. Grant was un-
flappable under fire ("Ulysses don't scare worth a damn," a soldier
noted when a shell landed near the general) and willing to defend his
convictions. Above all, his deep confidence in himself and in victory
inspired those around him and made the difference in close-fought
battles. After grave reverses at Shiloh, a colonel asked, "Shall I make
preparations for retreat?" "Retreat?" Grant replied. "No. I propose to
attack at daylight and whip them." These qualities of leadership were
evident not only during the war but also in the years that followed.[30]

The Civil War changed Grant's politics and his views of African
Americans. Before the conflict he was nominally a Democrat, voting
for Buchanan in 1856, although rarely voicing his opinions on sectional or political matters. Still, he was no supporter of slavery; in
1859, despite being financially hard pressed, Grant emancipated rather
than sell a servant left to him by his father-in-law. During the war
Grant readily complied with Chief of Staff Henry Halleck's request to
help recruit black troops. Grant told Halleck, "I never was an abolitionist, nor even what could be called anti-slavery. [But] you may rely

upon it I will give . . . all the aid in my power." He refused a prisoner exchange with Robert E. Lee when he learned that African American soldiers would not be treated the same as their white comrades.

By war's end Grant was a defender of black rights. Sent on a fact-finding tour of the South in 1865, he informed President Johnson that continuing the Freedmen's Bureau was "an absolute necessity until civil law is established and enforced securing to the freedmen their rights and full protection." Despite Johnson's efforts to recruit him as an ally, Grant gradually distanced himself from the president and in 1867 supported congressional efforts to extend the vote to blacks. Republicans eagerly nominated him for president in 1868, and with no hesitation he assumed the highest office.[31]

As president, Grant initially took a firm stance against Klan violence, facing down not only Southern whites but also dissidents within his own party. He reassured those, like William Chandler, the head of the Republican National Committee, who argued the task was hopeless. Chandler remarked in 1869, "We are bound to be overwhelmed by the new rebel combinations in every southern state."[32] Grant appointed Amos Akerman attorney general and Benjamin Bristow solicitor general—two men determined to prosecute the Klan. In 1871 Grant made a rare appearance on the Hill to secure passage of the Ku Klux Klan Act. He told lawmakers that there was "no other subject on which I would recommend legislation during the current session."[33]

But like a growing number of Republicans, Grant eventually tired of the seemingly endless battles needed to protect black voting and Republican governments in the South. Steadfast commander though he was, Grant recognized that not every breastwork could be stormed—particularly if the battalions were lacking. With Congress cutting troop strength and failing to provide for the attorneys and marshals needed for prosecutions, Grant realized the futility of carrying on the struggle. Violence surged in the four remaining Republican states—South Carolina, Louisiana, Florida, and Mississippi. This time the adversaries that local Republicans faced were not masked men but well-armed white vigilante groups. Grant made desultory attempts to suppress this lawlessness, particularly in Louisiana. But he acknowledged in 1875: "The whole public are tired out with these annual autumnal outbreaks in the South . . . [and] are ready now to condemn any interference on the part of the Government." When the new president, Rutherford Hayes, removed the remaining troops from the South in 1877, he only completed a retreat that Grant began several years earlier.[34]

Despite heartrending pleas, Republicans abandoned Southern blacks. Speaking to the 1876 Republican convention, Frederick Douglass summarized the party's strengths and failings: "You say you have emancipated us. You have; and I thank you for it. You say you have enfranchised us. You have; and I thank you for it. But what is your emancipation?—what is your enfranchisement? What does it all amount to, if the black man, after having been made free by the letter of your law, is unable to exercise that freedom, and, having been freed from the slaveholder's lash, he is to be subject to the slaveholder's shot-gun?" Congress had briefly seized an advanced position, promising blacks full participation in the state governments as well as a fundamental set of rights. In retreating, Republicans not only abandoned those privileges but also backed away from their support for the most basic rights. To be sure, until the 1890s blacks continued to vote in the South— although poll taxes and intimidation reduced their numbers. A few still held office, but everywhere their power was reduced. Congress gradually repealed the enforcement legislation, while Supreme Court decisions undercut constitutional protections.[35]

Ironically, given the fanfare of Reconstruction legislation, the most enduring gains for African Americans came in the North. Republicans came to value Northern black voters, who had been enfranchised by the Fifteenth Amendment and could make the difference in close elections. During these years most Northern states ended discrimination on public conveyances; Chicago, Cleveland, and Milwaukee even integrated their schools. However, 90 percent of African Americans lived in the South. These individuals suffered because Republicans never considered protecting black rights to be as important as assisting the business community.

## II.

After the war, and particularly after 1870, Republicans turned their attention to growing the Northern economy. The pursuit of this goal led lawmakers to expand upon wartime legislation, create a flexible money supply, reject Southern demands for assistance, and abandon the idealism that leavened party ideology before 1865. Increasingly this dominant party catered to the needs of the big businesses that loomed ever larger in American society.

Republicans built on the measures they had put in place during the Civil War, more often helping the wealthy than the common folk. For example, the expansion of the National Banking System enlarged the community of financiers closely tied to the government. The number of national banks grew from 467 in 1864, to 2,076 by 1875, to more than 7,000 by the early twentieth century. Meanwhile, the roster of state banks shrank, at least temporarily, reaching a low point of 277 in 1873. Republicans also encouraged industrialists by keeping high "wartime" tariff rates in place until the twentieth century. Even the party's land policy, with the Homestead Act as its centerpiece, had mixed results for small farmers. Although thousands took up free tracts, latecomers found that the best land was in private hands. Fraudulent transactions, grants to railroads, and a series of measures in the 1870s (such as the Timber-Culture Act and the Timber and Stone Act) allowed corporations to grab vast expanses. Between the Civil War and 1900 only one acre in five of new farmland came from homesteading. The repeal of the Income Tax Act also reflected the rightward drift of the party. Congress, responding in 1870 to the pleas of northeastern lawmakers, removed this levy, which had been the one truly progressive wartime tax.[36]

The Pacific Railroad Act, which Republicans had pushed through in 1862, led to the completion of the transcontinental railroad in 1869—and produced fortunes for well-placed investors. As track was laid, the act transferred millions of acres to the Union and Central Pacific railroads. The irony of bestowing these fiefdoms on corporations while denying freedmen forty-acre plots was not lost on Radical Republicans or Southern blacks. Anthony Wayne, who had been a slave in Texas, asked, "Whilst Congress appropriated land by the million acres to pet railroad schemes . . . did they not aid poor Anthony and his people starving and in rags?" The answer was no.[37]

For many observers the injustice of these grants was only compounded by the extraordinary corruption that accompanied the building of the railroad. The directors of the Union Pacific created a company, the Crédit Mobilier of America, and gave it the exclusive right to lay track. The new enterprise, owned by the railroad's inner circle, profited handsomely by charging the Union Pacific exorbitant rates and drawing on government subsidies to cover these costs. The railroad men also distributed shares to lawmakers who turned a blind eye to this malfeasance. The scandal broke only in 1872 after the corruption had gone too far.

Republicans also devoted much energy to creating a flexible money supply that could help the new industrialists as they grew their enterprises. Between the late 1860s and 1900 no single issue, including race, played a more important role in national politics—or was more contentious. While ostensibly about currency, the debates that roiled state and federal politics were really about class and economic development.

On the money issue, the Republican majority reflected the interests of the "West," including the merchants, manufacturers, and wealthier farmers of the lake districts and the iron and steel producers of Pennsylvania. Their optimistic vision of America called for an expansive currency that fostered growth—but not inflation. A minority within the Republican Party, however, voicing the concerns of the Northeast and particularly the banking centers, favored a more stately pace of expansion and a more stable money supply. At the other extreme stood the poorer farmers, who typically supported the Democratic Party and championed inflationary policies. They favored growth but wanted to weaken the vise grip they felt creditors and monopolists had on the economy.

Beginning right after the war and continuing until the end of the century, the Republican majority carved out a middle path between the banking interests of the East and the poorer farmers of the South and West. Leading this majority was John Sherman, head of the Senate Finance Committee and later secretary of the treasury. Sherman fought a war on two fronts. He condemned the cautious bankers, whose spokesman after the war was Treasury Secretary Hugh McCulloch. McCulloch sought to contract the money supply by sharply reducing the number of greenbacks in circulation. Sherman resisted the plan, making clear his beliefs: "I say the future for this country is hopeful, buoyant, joyous. . . . I do not wish now to cripple the industry of the country by adopting the policy of the Secretary of the Treasury, as he calls it, by reducing the currency."[38] Sherman, with strong support from Congress, moderated McCulloch's plans.

At the same time Sherman and the Republican majority had no interest in the inflationary schemes proposed by Democrats. In December 1868 they passed a resolution affirming that public creditors would be paid in specie or a solidly backed currency, like national banknotes, rather than in depreciated greenbacks. When Johnson vetoed this bill, Republicans reaffirmed their position. "An Act to Strengthen the Public Credit of the United States" became the first measure Grant signed after entering office.

To the delight of his supporters in the "West" and particularly the corporate magnates, Sherman continued to steer a middle course between contraction and inflation. He charted a steady route despite strong winds that blew from greenbackers and silverites on the one side and conservative bankers and goldbugs on the other. The coordinates that marked this path included the "Crime of 1873," which demonetized silver; the 1875 decision to keep $300 million of greenbacks in circulation; the Bland–Allison Act of 1878, which partially reversed the 1873 "Crime"; the resumption of specie payments in 1879; the Sherman Silver Purchase Act of 1890; and finally, the repeal of the Purchase Act, which had proved too inflationary. Sherman's course more resembled a ship tacking against contrary winds than a straight line. But the overall direction remained clear and helped provide the growing nation with a stable but expanding money supply.[39]

Throughout this era the Republicans' "nationalism" excluded the South. In 1866 Thaddeus Stevens set the tone for the ensuing years when he spurned Southern requests for flood relief. Venting his anger against the former rebels, he announced: "Let them build their own levees. . . . I would not be in favor of hanging them, but I do not think I should interfere if the Lord should choose to drown them out."[40] The national party remained tightfisted even after the Southern states established new regimes and sent Republicans to Washington. Northern Republicans excluded their Southern counterparts from choice committee assignments, and offered little funding to Southern state parties.

The Confederate states received few appropriations despite the devastation they had suffered. In the 41st Congress (1869–71) only 15 percent of the spending on internal improvements was allotted to the South, and much of that sum went to railroads with Northern investors. While Congress repealed the income tax, which burdened the Northeast, it kept the excise on whiskey, which hurt Southern mountain communities. Cotton state politicians noted the foolishness of these policies for a party hoping to nurture loyal supporters in the region. "Prosperity to the South, aided by a generous policy of internal improvements," an Alabama Republican remarked in 1870, "will more firmly cement and bind us in the family of States." Only in the late 1870s, after Democratic gains in Congress, did outlays for the South rise. Even then Congress directed much of the spending to improving the navigation of the Mississippi, an initiative that also helped Northerners.[41]

After 1870 the Republican Party increasingly gravitated toward big business. The defection of abolitionists (who despaired of ever reforming the South), along with the revolt of Liberal Republicans (who were angered by the spread of corruption), left the party in the hands of those whose chief concern was encouraging the growth of the industrial state. Since the earliest days of the Republic, political parties had cultivated rich men. What was new in this era was the unprecedented wealth and power of the captains of industry and the influence they gained in the political process. Jay Cooke and other business leaders gave generously to Grant. But the relationship between the new tycoons and the Republicans blossomed with James Garfield's successful run for the presidency in 1880. Garfield solicited funds from a broad cross section of the newly wealthy, including railroad tycoon Jay Gould, oil baron John D. Rockefeller, and Chauncey Depew, who oversaw affairs for the Vanderbilt family, owners of the New York Central Railroad.

Mark Hanna, a Cleveland shipping, mining, and steel magnate, perfected the ties between business and the Republican Party. Hanna observed, "All questions of government in a democracy were questions of money," and he acted on that dictum. Managing William McKinley's 1896 campaign, Hanna raised a war chest, variously estimated from $3.5 million to $16 million. Rockefeller's firm, Standard Oil, provided $250,000, as did the nation's leading banker, J. P. Morgan. The four great Chicago meat-packing houses together contributed a reported $400,000.[42]

The business community received fair value for its contributions from a party that had long since abandoned its radicalism and its hostility to affluent men. The Supreme Court, filled with Republican appointees, regularly struck down state laws restricting corporations. Republican presidents and governors, and Democratic officials who shared the same views (and who typically came from the conservative, eastern wing of that party), marshaled troops to break up strikes. Republican lawmakers and like-minded Democrats adopted measures that deflected the anger of Western and Southern farmers—but did little to check corporations. The Interstate Commerce Act of 1887 was a good example of such an initiative. It did more to protect railroads from angry state lawmakers than to address the needs of farmers and shippers. A Republican senator accurately described it as "an empty menace to great interests, made to answer the clamor of the ignorant and the unreasoning." The Sherman Anti-Trust Act of 1890, sponsored by John Sherman, came from the same mold. Couched in murky language, it relied on the courts for enforcement. "The whole effort," a lawmaker remarked, "has been to get some bill headed: 'A Bill to Punish Trusts' with which to go to the country." Since its earliest days the Republican Party had focused on developing the North, but now the "North" it catered to was a society dominated by monopolies and oligopolies.[43]

## III.

This work argues that more than any other concern, the evolution of the Northern and Southern economies explains the Civil War. During the 1820s, 1830s, and 1840s North-South patterns of trade, the strong growth of the cotton kingdom, and parties rooted in class rather than geographical divisions kept the country together, despite contentious sectional issues. After midcentury the rise of the Great

Lakes economy along with the spread of antislavery sentiment transformed the North. In the South, the disappearance of fresh soils and concerns about the long-term survival of slavery altered the outlook of the cotton planters. The result was the emergence of two hostile camps, each unwilling to compromise. Civil war came from these changed conditions and, more particularly, from the triumph of the Republicans and the heightened concerns of the cotton planters that their way of life was doomed.

Such an economic interpretation is hardly fashionable. Americans, like the citizens of most nations, prefer to view their history as a series of comforting myths. Thus most commentators contend that the American Revolution pitted freedom-loving colonists against the tyrannical British. Similarly, many writers argue that the Civil War was all about freeing the slaves. (Southerners, in the most recent recasting of the myth, were on the wrong side of the moral issue but displayed lesser virtues such as bravery, nobility, and loyalty to their comrades.) Seen in the same rosy light, World War I was fought to make the world "safe for democracy"; the United States intervened in Vietnam to protect freedom; and more recently, it fought two wars with Iraq to spread laudable American values.[44]

These myths endure because they portray Americans favorably and because they all contain an element of truth. As this account makes clear, Republicans were not simply concerned with fostering Northern growth; they also abhorred slavery and sought to secure fundamental rights for African Americans. But such idealism, important though it was, does not explain the events, divisions, and party platforms of these years. Nor does it show why the Republicans strongly supported the industrial state but were willing to abandon African Americans in the 1870s. Ultimately, myths are luxuries that no nation can afford. Economics more than high moral concerns produced the Civil War.

# NOTES

ABBREVIATIONS USED IN NOTES

AC      *Annals of Congress*

ANB      *American National Biography*

CG      *Congressional Globe*

HSP      Historical Society of Pennsylvania, Philadelphia, Pa.

LC      Library of Congress, Washington, D.C.

SHC      Southern Historical Collection, Chapel Hill, N.C.

NOTES FOR MAPS

*Map 1*

National Geographical Society, *Historical Atlas of the United States* (Washington, D.C., 1988), 186–89, provides information on canals.

## Maps 2, 3, and 4

These maps draw on data for the four presidential elections, 1840–52. Counties were labeled Whig, Democrat, or Unassigned based on three criteria: (1) A party could claim any county where it had an absolute majority in three of the four elections. (2) Since the presence of third parties often rendered that test too restrictive, counties were assigned to the party that claimed 45 percent or more of the votes in a district in all four elections. (3) The few counties where the first two criteria created conflicts were grouped with the Unassigned. Election returns as well as manufacturing and agricultural data (originally from the 1850 U.S. Census) are drawn from *The Great American History Machine*, version 2.0, CD-ROM, Academic Software Development Group, University of Maryland, 1995.

## Map 5

*For South Carolina:* John Barnwell, *Love of Order: South Carolina's First Secession Crisis* (Chapel Hill, N.C., 1982), 198–99, presents votes for the 1851 convention. *For Georgia: Great American History Machine* provides the 1851 congressional vote. The map shows counties voting 49 percent or more for the States' Rights Party. *For Alabama: Great American History Machine* details the support for the States' Rights Party in 1852. The map displays counties where the party received 5 percent or more of the vote. *For Mississippi:* John McCardell, "John A. Quitman and the Compromise of 1850 in Mississippi," *Journal of Mississippi History* 37 (1975): 266, shows the vote for the 1851 convention.

## Maps 6 and 7

A county was assigned to the Republican or Democratic party if it gave a majority vote to one of those parties in both elections of 1856 and 1860. Counties not fitting that criterion were judged Unaligned. *Great American History Machine* provides these data.

## Map 8

Map based on voting data for 1856 and 1860 elections in *Great American History Machine*.

## Map 9

U.S. Bureau of the Census, *Agriculture of the United States in 1860* (Washington, D.C., 1864).

## Map 10

*For Georgia:* Consult Ralph A. Wooster, *The Secession Conventions of the South* (Princeton, N.J., 1962), 81. The map shows the counties where the entire delegation supported immediate secession. *For Alabama and Mississippi:* William L. Barney, *The Secessionist Impulse: Alabama and Mississippi in 1860* (Princeton, N.J., 1974), 317–20, presents returns. The map indicates the counties where secessionists received 65 percent or more. *For Louisiana:* Charles B. Dew, "Who Won the Secession Election in Louisiana," *Journal of Southern History* 36 (1970): 26–29, provides data. The map shows the districts where secessionists received 65 percent or more. *For Texas:* Consult Joe T. Timmons, "The Referendum in Texas on the Ordinance of Secession, February 23, 1861: The Vote," *East Texas Historical Journal* 11 (Fall 1973): 15–16. The map shows all counties where 85 percent or more of the voters supported the secession ordinance. The percentage is set so high because Texans seemed to have little choice: they voted after all other states in the Lower South had seceded.

*Map 11*

For Arkansas: James M. Woods, *Rebellion and Realignment: Arkansas's Road to Secession* (Fayetteville, Ark., 1987), 190–96. *For Tennessee:* Thomas Perkins Abernethy, *From Frontier to Plantation in Tennessee* (Chapel Hill, N.C., 1932), 343; Wooster, *Secession Conventions,* 174; Daniel W. Crofts, *Reluctant Confederates: Upper South Unionists in the Secession Crisis* (Chapel Hill, N.C., 1989), 343. *For North Carolina:* J. Carlyle Sitterson, *The Secession Movement in North Carolina* (Chapel Hill, N.C., 1939), 246–48; North Carolina, *Journal of the Convention . . . of 1861* (Raleigh, N.C., 1862), 3–5, 12–14. *For Virginia:* Wooster, *Secession Conventions,* 138.

## INTRODUCTION: RETHINKING THE ORIGINS OF THE CIVIL WAR

1. James M. McPherson, *Battle Cry of Freedom: The Civil War Era* (New York, 1988), esp. vii–viii, 202–35, quote from the *Richmond Examiner* on p. 232; "The Heart of the Matter," *New York Review of Books,* Oct. 23, 1997. McPherson presents similar views in *Ordeal by Fire: The Civil War and Reconstruction* (New York, 1992), passim, and esp. 125–26 (with the same *Richmond Examiner* quote); and in *This Mighty Scourge: Perspectives on the Civil War* (New York, 2007), 3–19.

2. Richard N. Current, *Lincoln's Loyalists: Union Soldiers from the Confederacy* (Boston, 1992), 89–104, 213–15.

3. Lincoln to Horace Greeley, Aug. 22, 1862, in *The Collected Works of Abraham Lincoln,* ed. Roy P. Basler, 8 vols. (New Brunswick, N.J., 1953–55), 5:388.

4. Charles A. and Mary R. Beard, *The Rise of American Civilization,* 2 vols. (New York, 1927, 1930).

5. Lincoln to Albert Hodges, Apr. 4, 1864, in *Collected Works,* 7:281–82.

6. Beard, *Rise of American Civilization,* quotes from 1:628, 663; 2:7.

## CHAPTER 1: FOUNDATIONS

1. Clay, Feb. 6, 1850, *CG,* 31st Cong., 1st sess., App., pp. 126, 127.

2. Douglas, Mar. 14, 1850, *CG,* 31st Cong., 1st sess., App., p. 375.

3. Charles W. Dahlinger, "The *New Orleans*, Being a Critical Account of the Beginning of Steamboat Navigation on the Western Rivers of the United States," *Pittsburgh Legal Journal* 59, no. 2 (Oct. 21, 1911): 570–91, quotes Fulton, Web document, www.myoutbox.net/nr59plj.htm. (accessed Mar. 10, 2008); H. W. Dickinson, *Robert Fulton: Engineer and Artist* (London, 1913), chap. 9.

4. Erik F. Haites, James Mak, and Gary M. Walton, *Western River Transportation: The Era of Early Internal Development, 1810–1860* (Baltimore, 1975), 59–73, 129–33.

5. Calhoun toast, Nov. 8, 1845, Calhoun to James E. Colhoun, Dec. 14, 1845, in *The Papers of John C. Calhoun*, ed. Robert L. Meriwether et al., 28 vols. (Columbia, S.C., 1959– ), 22:271, 343–44; Dwight L. Dumond, "The Mississippi: Valley of Decision," *Mississippi Valley Historical Review* 36 (1949): 6.

6. Douglas, Mar. 13, 1850, *CG*, 31st Cong., 1st sess., App., p. 365; Douglas to Citizens of Chicago, Oct. 1850, June 19, 1851, in *The Letters of Stephen A. Douglas*, ed. Robert W. Johannsen (Urbana, Ill., 1961), 197, 221–26; Clay, Feb. 6, 1850, *CG*, 31st Cong., 1st sess., App., p. 127.

7. Lewis Cass, July 7, 1856, *CG*, 34th Cong., 1st sess., App., p. 741.

8. John D. Barnhart, "The Southern Influence in the Formation of Indiana," *Indiana Magazine of History* 33 (1937): 261–76; Glover Moore, *The Missouri Compromise, 1819–1821* (Lexington, Ky., 1953), 52–54, 62, 204–6, 281–83.

9. *Boston Whig*, Dec. 11, 1847, quoted in Frank Otto Gatell, "Palfrey's Vote, the Conscience Whigs, and the Election of Speaker Winthrop," *New England Quarterly*, 31 (1958): 223n; Reinhard H. Luthin, "Abraham Lincoln and the Massachusetts Whigs in 1848," *New England Quarterly* 14 (1941): 619–32.

10. Robert G. Albion, *The Rise of New York Port, 1815–1960* (New York, 1939), 95–121.

11. Joseph G. Baldwin, *The Flush Times of Alabama and Mississippi: A Series of Sketches* (New York, 1854), 82–83.

12. Alexis de Tocqueville, *Democracy in America*, trans. George Lawrence (1840; rpt., New York, 1988), vol. 1, part 2, chap. 10, pp. 372–73.

13. Paul David, "The Growth of Real Product in the United States Before 1840: New Evidence, Controlled Conjectures," *Journal of Economic History* 27 (1967): 151–97; Marvin Town and Wayne Rasmussen, "Farm Gross Product and Gross Investment in the 19th Century," in National Bureau of Economic Research, *Trends in the American Economy in the 19th Century*, Studies in Income and Wealth, vol. 24 (Princeton, N.J., 1960): 244–312; Marc Egnal, *Divergent Paths: How Culture and Institutions Have Shaped North American Growth* (New York, 1996), 3–20.

14. Tocqueville, *Democracy in America*, vol. 2, part 2, chap. 13.

15. Harriet Martineau, *Society in America*, 3 vols. (1837; rpt., New York, 1966), 2: 360–61.

16. Ibid., 2:204, 205.

17. George W. Pierson, *Tocqueville and Beaumont in America* (New York, 1938), 242–45, quote on pp. 584–85.

18. J. H. Ingraham, *The South-west by a Yankee*, 2 vols. (1835; rpt. New York, 1968), 2:171–72.

19. Sean Wilentz, *Chants Democratic: New York City & the Rise of the American Working Class, 1788–1850* (New York, 1984), 3–142; Paul E. Johnson, *A Shopkeeper's Millennium: Society and Revivals in Rochester, New York, 1815–1837* (New York, 1978), 15–61; Paul G. Faler, *Mechanics and Manufacturers in the Early Industrial Revolution: Lynn, Massachusetts, 1780–1860* (Albany, N.Y., 1981).

20. Jan. 30, 1824, *AC*, 18th Cong., 1st sess., p. 1313.

21. Robert V. Remini, *Henry Clay: Statesman for the Union* (New York, 1991), 2–272, 382; Daniel Walker Howe, *The Political Culture of the American Whigs* (Chicago, 1979), 123–49.

22. Clay, Mar. 31, 1824, *AC*, 18th Cong., 1st sess., pp. 1977, 1966.

23. Clay, Mar. 31, 1824, ibid., pp. 1970, 1987, 1999, 1986.

24. Clay, Feb. 14, 1824, ibid., pp. 1036, 1978; Remini, *Henry Clay*, 225–30; Howe, *Political Culture*, 137–39.

25. Remini, *Clay*, 234–72; Paul C. Nagel, "The Election of 1824: A Reconsideration Based on Newspaper Opinion," *Journal of Southern History* 26 (1960): 315–29.

26. Clay to Benjamin W. Crowninshield, Mar. 18, 1827, in *The Papers of Henry Clay*, ed. Mary W. M. Hargreaves and James F. Hopkins, 10 vols. (Lexington, Ky., 1959–92), 6:320.

27. Clay to Edward Everett, Apr. 5, 1827, ibid., 6:401.

28. Ephraim Pentland to Clay, Feb. 18, 1827, Nathaniel Dike and others to Clay, June 16, 1827, Sidney Breese to Clay, July 21, 1827, ibid., 6: 208, 690, 807–808.

29. Jackson to William B. Lewis, May 7, 1824, in *The Papers of Andrew Jackson*, ed. Harold D. Moser, David R. Hoth, George H. Hoemann (Knoxville, Tenn., 1996), 5:404.

30. Thomas Perkins Abernethy, *From Frontier to Plantation in Tennessee* (University, Alabama, 1932), 228–45; Marquis James, *Andrew Jackson: Portrait of a President* (Indianapolis and New York, 1937), 21–30.

31. *Papers of Jackson*, 5:371–72; Marquis James, *Andrew Jackson: The Border Captain* (Indianapolis and New York, 1933), 120–25, quote on p. 121.

32. Jackson to John Coffee, June 18, 1824, in *Papers of Jackson*, 5:416.

33. Quoted in James, *Jackson: Portrait of a President*, 66–67.

34. James, *Jackson: Border Captain*, 122–25, quote on p. 125.

35. Jackson to Jacob Call, Oct. 9, 1824, in *Papers of Jackson*, 5:446.

36. Jackson to John Coffee, Feb. 15, 1824, ibid., 5:357.

37. John McFarland to Jackson, Aug. 14, 1824, ibid., 5:436.

38. Marquis Barnett to Clay, Feb. 22, 1827, in *Papers of Clay*, 6:220; James, *Jackson: Portrait of a President*, 86.

39. Donald J. Ratcliffe, *The Politics of Long Division: The Birth of the Second Party System in Ohio, 1818–1828* (Columbus, Ohio, 2000), p. 160; Simon Cameron to Clay, c. July 26, 1827, in *Papers of Clay*, 6:822.

40. Van Buren to P. N. Nicholas, Nov. 1826, quoted in Robert V. Remini, *Martin Van Buren and the Making of the Democratic Party* (New York, 1970), 120.

41. Jackson to George W. Campbell, Feb. 14, 1828, in *Correspondence of Andrew Jackson*, vol. 3: *1820–1828*, ed. John Spencer Bassett (Washington, D.C., 1928), 390.

42. Jackson to James Hamilton, Jr., June 29, 1828, memorandum in Jackson's handwriting, Dec. 9, 1828, ibid., 3:412, 452.

43. Edward Ingersoll to Clay, Mar. 11, 1827, in *Papers of Clay*, 6:282.

44. Sidney Breese to Clay, July 21, 1827, ibid., 6:809.

45. Remini, *Van Buren*, quotes on pp. 1, 81–82, and see also 120–22.

46. Ibid., 170–85; George Dangerfield, *The Era of Good Feelings* (New York, 1952), 405–409; Remini, "Martin Van Buren and the Tariff of Abominations," *American Historical Review* 63 (1958): 903–17.

47. Van Buren, Dec. 20, 1825, *Register of Debates*, 19th Cong., 1st sess., p. 20; Martin Van Buren, *Inquiry into the Origin and Course of Political Parties in the United States* (1867; rpt., New York, 1967), 1–2; Remini, *Van Buren*, 126.

48. Van Buren, *Inquiry into the Origin*, 4–6; Charles S. Sydnor, "The One-Party Period of American History," *American Historical Review* 51 (1946): 443–48.

49. Remini, *Van Buren*, 143–44, quote on pp. 130–31.

50. Van Buren, Dec. 20, 1825, *Register of Debates*, 19th Cong., 1st sess., p. 20; Remini, *Van Buren*, 53–54.

51. Richard B. Latner, "A New Look at Jacksonian Politics," *Journal of American History* 61 (1975): 955–61, quote on p. 955; Remini, *Van Buren*, 103.

52. Richard P. McCormick, "New Perspectives on Jacksonian Politics," *American Historical Review* 65 (1960): 288–301; McCormick, *The Second American Party System: Party Formation in the Jacksonian Era* (Chapel Hill, N.C., 1966); Michael F. Holt, *The Rise and Fall of the American Whig Party: Jacksonian Politics and the Onset of the Civil War* (New York, 1999), 27–30, 105–11. Several Web sites provide state-by-state election data; see www.multied.com/elections (accessed Mar. 10, 2008).

## CHAPTER 2: RICH MAN, POOR MAN

1. Varina B. Howell to Margaret K. Howell, Dec. 19, 1843, in *The Papers of Jefferson Davis*, ed. Haskell M. Monroe, Jr., and James T. McIntosh, 10 vols. (Baton Rouge, La., 1971–99), 2:52–53; V. Howell's *Memoirs* cited ibid., 2:57n; William J. Cooper, Jr., *Jefferson Davis, American* (New York, 2000), 96–100.

2. Louise H. Tharp, *The Appletons of Beacon Hill* (Boston, 1973), 219; Marc Egnal, *Divergent Paths: How Culture and Institutions Have Shaped North American Growth* (New York, 1996), 91–99.

3. Robert Rich, "'A Wilderness of Whigs': The Wealthy Men of Boston," *Journal of Social History* 4 (1971): 263–76.

4. Frank Otto Gatell, "Money and Party in Jacksonian America: A Quantitative Look at New York City's Men of Quality," *Political Science Quarterly* 82 (1967): 235–52, quote on p. 246.

5. For example, see the data in Dixon Ryan Fox, *The Decline of Aristocracy in the Politics of New York, 1801–1840* (New York, 1919), 409–49.

6. Stephen A. Douglas, "Autobiographical Sketch," Sept. 1, 1838, in *The Letters of Stephen A. Douglas*, ed. Robert W. Johannsen (Urbana, Ill., 1961), 57–58.

7. Alexandra U. McCoy, "Political Affiliations of American Economic Elites: Wayne County, Michigan, 1844, 1860, as a Test Case" (Ph.D. diss., Wayne State University, 1965); Kenneth J. Winkle, "The Second Party System in Lincoln's Springfield," *Civil War History* 44 (1998): 267–84; Paul E. Johnson, *A Shopkeeper's Millennium: Society and Revivals in Rochester, New York, 1815–1837* (New York, 1978), 197–200; Kathleen Smith Kutolowski, "The Social Composition of Political Leadership, Genesee County, New York, 1821–1860" (Ph.D. diss., University of Rochester, 1973).

8. John Michael Rozett, "The Social Bases of Party Conflict in the Age of Jackson: Individual Voting Behavior in Greene County, Illinois, 1838–1848" (Ph.D. diss., University of Michigan, 1974), 83–87; Paul Goodman, "The Social Basis of New England Politics in Jacksonian America," *Journal of the Early Republic* 6 (1986): 23–58. Goodman found that the poorest individuals, typically servants, often voted as their masters did. Also in several of the eighteen communities there was no connection between wealth and allegiance. More generally, rural voters were far more numerous than urban ones. In 1840 over 86 percent of Northerners lived on farms or in communities of fewer than 2,500 persons.

9. Walsh, Jan. 17, 1854, *CG*, 33rd Cong., 1st sess., App., p. 1220; Robert Ernst, "The One and Only Mike Walsh," *New York Historical Society Quarterly* 26 (1952): 43–65, quote on p. 48; Arthur M. Schlesinger, Jr., *The Age of Jackson* (New York, 1945), 408–10; Sean Wilentz, *Chants Democratic: New York City and the Rise of the American Working Class, 1788–1850* (New York, 1984), 327–35.

10. Wilentz, *Chants Democratic*, quote on p. 332; Gatell, "Money and Party," 240–46.

11. Rozett, "Social Bases of Party Conflict," 18–35, 83–156.

12. Michel Chevalier, *Society, Manners, and Politics in the United States: Letters on North America*, ed. John William Ward (1839; rpt., Gloucester, Mass., 1961), 106–107.

13. Quotes from Frances Trollope, *Domestic Manners of Americans*, ed. Donald Smalley (New York, 1949), 301–302; and Thomas Hamilton, *Men and Manners in America*, 2 vols. (1842; rpt., New York, 1968), 2:283–84; Egnal, *Divergent Paths*, 87–101; Ford quoted in Rozett, "Social Bases of Party Conflict," 155; Eric Foner, *Free Soil, Free Labor, Free Men: The Ideology of the Republican Party Before the Civil War* (New York, 1970), 48–50.

14. Rozett, "Social Bases of Party Conflict," 157–97; Paul Goodman, "The Social Basis of New England Politics in Jacksonian America," *Journal of the Early Republic* 6 (1986): 23–58.

15. Lincoln to Zachary Taylor, June [15?], 1849, in *The Collected Works of Abraham Lincoln*, ed. Roy P. Basler, 8 vols. (New Brunswick, N.J., 1953–55), 2:54; Karl Raitz, "The Face of the Country," in *The National Road*, ed. Karl Raitz (Baltimore, 1996), 45–72; Billy Joe Peyton, "Surveying and Building the Road," ibid., 123–58; Gregory S. Rose, "Extending the Road West," ibid., 159–92.

16. Neither the northern Whig belt nor the Ohio Valley Whig belt in the Midwest had the economic diversity evident in the midstate Whig belt, and both were smaller. The northern Whig belt held only 11 percent of the population in Whig counties, while the Ohio Valley Whig belt contained 23 percent of the population in Whig counties. The Ohio Valley Whig counties were preeminent (at least in Illinois and Indiana) in the value of slaughtered animals. In Illinois and Ohio the northern Whig belt stood second only to the Whig midstate belt in per capita farm value. The Ohio Valley Whig counties were preeminent (at least in Illinois and Indiana) in the value of slaughtered animals. However, the northern Whig counties were not high in the value of slaughtered animals, while the Ohio Valley Whig counties had only average farm values. The note for Map 2 discusses the sources for these data.

17. Richard H. Brown, "The Missouri Crisis, Slavery, and the Politics of Jacksonianism," *South Atlantic Quarterly* 65 (1966): 55–70; Sean Wilentz, *The Rise of American Democracy: Jefferson to Lincoln* (New York, 2005), 114–16, 294–96; Noble E. Cunningham, Jr., *The Jeffersonian Republicans: The Formation of Party Organization, 1791–1801* (Chapel Hill, N.C., 1957), 8–19, 33–49.

18. Claiborne quoted in William G. Shade, "Society and Politics in Antebellum Virginia's Southside," *Journal of Southern History* 53 (1987): 163.

19. U.S. Bureau of the Census, *Historical Statistics of the United States, Colonial Times to 1970,* 2 vols. n.p. (Washington, D.C., 1975), 1:22–37; Egnal, *Divergent Paths,* 72–73, 87–101.

20. Quoted in Charles Bolton, *Poor Whites of the Antebellum South: Tenants and Laborers in Central North Carolina and Northeast Mississippi* (Durham, N.C., 1994), 124–25.

21. Quoted in Christopher J. Olsen, *Political Culture and Secession in Mississippi: Masculinity, Honor, and the Antiparty Tradition, 1830–1860* (New York, 2000), 102–103.

22. Daniel W. Crofts, *Old Southampton: Politics and Society in a Virginia County, 1834–1869* (Charlottesville, Va., 1992), 126–31; Paul Bourke and Donald DeBats, "Identifiable Voting in Nineteenth-Century America: Toward a Comparison of Britain and the United States Before the Secret Ballot," *Perspectives in American History* 11 (1977): 259–88; Anthony Gene Carey, *Parties, Slavery, and the Union in Antebellum Georgia* (Athens, Ga., 1997), 105–31; J. Mills Thornton III, *Politics and Power in a Slave Society: Alabama, 1800–1860* (Baton Rouge, La., 1978), 158–59; William G. Shade, *Democratizing the Old Dominion: Virginia and the Second Party System, 1824–1861* (Charlottesville, Va., 1996), 150; Paul H. Bergeron, *Antebellum Politics in Tennessee* (Lexington, Ky., 1982), 9–34; Bolton, *Poor Whites,* 113–38.

23. Shade, *Democratizing the Old Dominion,* 121–22; Harry L. Watson, *Jacksonian Politics and Community Conflict: The Emergence of the Second American Party System in Cumberland County, North Carolina* (Baton Rouge, La., 1981), 234–35, 298–303, 312–13; Shade, "Society and Politics," 163–93; Crofts, *Old Southampton,* 134–35, 149–51; Christopher Waldrep, "Rank-and-File Voters and the Coming of the Civil War, Caldwell County, Kentucky, as a Test Case," *Civil War History* 35 (1989): 60–66.

24. Randolph Campbell, "The Whig Party of Texas in the Elections of 1848 and 1852," *Southwestern Historical Quarterly* 73 (1969–70): 25–28; Frank Towers, *The Urban*

*South and the Coming of the Civil War* (Charlottesville, Va., 2004), 78–79; Roger W. Shugg, *Origins of Class Struggle in Louisiana: A Social History of White Farmers and Laborers During Slavery and After, 1840–1875* (Baton Rouge, La., 1939), 134–38; William H. Adams, "The Louisiana Whigs," *Louisiana History* 15 (1975): 217; Lacy K. Ford, Jr., *Origins of Southern Radicalism: The South Carolina Upcountry, 1800–1860* (New York, 1988), 167–70; Gene W. Boyett, "Quantitative Differences Between the Arkansas Whig and Democratic Parties, 1836–1850," *Arkansas Historical Quarterly* 34 (1975): 221–22. The situation appears similar in neighboring Missouri. St. Louis County supported the Whigs in the presidential elections, 1840–48, while the state went Democratic. Data from *Great American History Machine* (CD-ROM produced by Academic Software Development Group, College Park, Md.), version 2.0. Thomas E. Redard, "The Election of 1844 in Louisiana: A New Look at the Ethno-cultural Approach," *Louisiana History* 22 (1981): 419–33; John M. Sacher, "The Sudden Collapse of the Louisiana Whig Party," *Journal of Southern History* 65 (1999): 221–48; David N. Young, "The Mississippi Whigs, 1834–1860" (Ph.D. diss., University of Alabama, 1968), 85–86.

25. Quoted in Paul Horton, "The Culture, Social Structure, and Political Economy of Antebellum Lawrence County, Alabama," *Alabama Review* 41 (1988): 260.

26. Wallace Hettle, *The Peculiar Democracy: Southern Democrats in Peace and Civil War* (Athens, Ga., 2001), 85.

27. Thornton, *Politics and Power*, 28–58, quote on p. 42; Daniel Walker Howe, *The Political Culture of the American Whigs* (Chicago, 1979), 131–32, 142.

28. Quoted in William J. Evitts, *A Matter of Allegiances: Maryland from 1850 to 1861* (Baltimore, 1974), 22. The same logic shaped the choices of Mississippi politician Wiley Harris, who confessed: "I found myself a democrat without being able to explain why I was of that party. My uncle was a staunch Jackson man and I adopted his preferences without examination." Quoted in Olsen, *Political Culture*, 102.

29. Michael J. Dubin, *United States Presidential Elections, 1788–1860: The Official Results by County and State* (Jefferson, N.C., 2002), 9–11, provides the 1800 voting data.

30. Crofts, *Old Southampton*, 187–91.

31. Ford, *Southern Radicalism*, 99–144, 183–85, 281–307; John Barnwell, *Love of Order: South Carolina's First Secession Crisis* (Chapel Hill, N.C., 1982), 3–31; Herbert J. Doherty, Jr., *The Whigs of Florida, 1845–1854* (Gainesville, Fla., 1959), 63–72; Lincoln, Speech in United States House of Representatives, January 12, 1848, in *Collected Works*, 1:440; Walter L. Buenger, *Secession and the Union in Texas* (Austin, Tex., 1984), 24–25; Terry G. Jordan, "The Imprint of the Upper and Lower South on Mid-nineteenth-century Texas," *Annals of the Association of American Geographers* 57 (1967): 667–74. Significantly, South Carolina and Georgia planters dominated Jefferson County, the only wealthy Democratic district in Middle Florida.

32. Marc Kruman, *Parties and Politics in North Carolina, 1836–1865* (Baton Rouge, La., 1983); Peter D. Levine, *The Behavior of State Legislative Parties in the Jacksonian Era: New Jersey, 1829–1844* (Rutherford, N.J., 1977); Herbert Ershkowitz and William G. Shade, "Consensus or Conflict? Political Behavior in the State Legislatures During the Jacksonian

Era," *Journal of American History* 58 (1971): 591–621; Thornton, *Politics and Power*, 463–71; James Roger Sharp, *The Jacksonians Versus the Banks: Politics in the States After the Panic of 1837* (New York, 1970), 242–46; Michael F. Holt, *The Rise and Fall of the American Whig Party: Jacksonian Politics and the Onset of the Civil War* (New York, 1999), 72–73; Melvin P. Lucas, "The Period of Political Alchemy: Party in the Mississippi Legislature, 1835–1846" (M.A. thesis, Cornell University, 1981), 136–83.

33. Glyndon G. Van Deusen, *William Henry Seward* (New York, 1967), 3–104, 233, 255–63; Seward, Speech at Syracuse, July 18, 1844, Senate Speech, Mar. 11, 1850, in *The Works of William H. Seward*, ed. George E. Baker, 3 vols. (1853; rpt., New York, 1972), 1:74, 3:252.

34. Seward, Annual Message to Legislature, Jan. 1, 1839, Address to Sunday-School Celebration, July 4, 1839, in *Works of Seward*, 2:189, 3:209–10; Van Deusen, *Seward*, 45–46, 102–4, 203–5, quote on p. 103.

35. Seward, "The Election of 1844," July 13, 1844, in *Works of Seward*, 3:252–53.

36. Seward, Speech at a Whig Mass Meeting, Oct. 29, 1844, ibid., 3:261.

37. Seward, "The Election of 1848," Oct. 26, 1848, ibid., 3:299.

38. Stephens, Aug. 7, 1848, *CG*, 30th Cong., 1st sess., App., pp. 1106–107.

39. Stephens, Apr. 6, 1848, ibid., p. 588; "Alexander H. Stephens," *ANB*; Daniel Walker Howe, *The Political Culture of the American Whigs* (Chicago, 1979), 238–62.

40. Cobb to a Committee of Citizens in Charleston, S.C., Nov. [4?], 1848, in *The Correspondence of Robert Toombs, Alexander H. Stephens and Howell Cobb*, ed. Ulrich B. Phillips (1913; rpt., New York, 1970), 134–35; John E. Simpson, *Howell Cobb: The Politics of Ambition* (Chicago, 1973), 1–36; "Howell Cobb," *ANB*.

41. R. P. Brooks, "Howell Cobb and the Crisis of 1850," *Mississippi Valley Historical Review* 4 (1917): 279–98, quote on p. 283.

42. James Buchanan to Howell Cobb, Dec. 29, 1849, in *Toombs, Stephens and Cobb Correspondence*, 180–81; Dec. 3, 1849, *CG*, 31st Cong., 1st sess., p. 2, provides several of the ballots for Speaker. For votes on the Fugitive Slave Act, see Holman Hamilton, *Prologue to Conflict: The Crisis and Compromise of 1850* (New York, 1964), 195–200. For the vote on the slave trade in the District of Columbia, Jan. 31, 1849, see *CG*, 30th Cong., 2nd sess., p. 416.

## CHAPTER 3: DEAL MAKING

1. Tallmadge, Feb. 16, 1819, *AC*, House, 15th Cong., 2nd sess., p. 1204. For the emergence of sectional views before 1819, see Mathew Mason, *Slavery and Politics in the Early American Republic* (Chapel Hill, N.C., 2006).

2. Glover Moore, *The Missouri Controversy, 1819–1821* (Lexington, Ky., 1953), 33–52; "James Tallmadge," *ANB*.

3. Clagett, Feb. 1, 1820, *AC*, House, 16th Cong., 1st sess., pp. 1040–41.

4. Darlington, Feb. 16, 1820, ibid., p. 1375.

5. Taylor, Feb. 15, 1819, *AC*, House, 15th Cong., 2nd sess., p. 1176.

6. Charles Pinckney, Feb. 14, 1820, *AC*, House, 16th Cong., 1st sess., p. 1325; "Charles Pinckney," *ANB*; William Pinckney, Feb. 15, 1819, *AC*, Senate, 16th Cong., 1st sess., p. 39.

7. Walker, Jan. 19, 1820, ibid., p. 175.

8. Ruggles, Jan. 27, 1820, ibid., p. 287.

9. John D. Barnhart, "The Southern Influence in the Formation of Indiana," *Indiana Magazine of History* 33 (1937): 261–76; Moore, *Missouri Controversy*, 52–54, 62–64.

10. "Ninian Edwards," "William Henry Harrison," *ANB*; Moore, *Missouri Controversy*, 88–90.

11. Otis to William Sullivan, Feb. 13, 1820, in Samuel Eliot Morison, *Harrison Gray Otis, 1765–1848: The Urban Federalist* (Boston, 1969), 428.

12. Moore, *Missouri Controversy*, 197–201, quotes Mason and Christopher Gore on pp. 106, 199.

13. Irving H. Bartlett, *John C. Calhoun: A Biography* (New York, 1993), 20–63, quotes on pp. 46, 47; Merrill D. Peterson, *The Great Triumvirate: Webster, Clay, and Calhoun* (New York, 1987), 18–27.

14. Bartlett, *Calhoun*, quote on p. 82.

15. U.S. Bureau of the Census, *Historical Statistics of the United States, Colonial Times to 1970*, 2 vols. consec. pagin. (Washington, D.C., 1975), 209.

16. Bartlett, *Calhoun*, 44–45, 122–25, 268–85.

17. Calhoun to Charles Tait, Oct. 26, 1820, in *The Papers of John C. Calhoun*, ed. Robert L. Meriwether et al., 28 vols. (Columbia, S.C., 1959–2003), 5:413.

18. Moore, *Missouri Controversy*, 111–15, 243–45, quotes on pp. 115, 219, 244.

19. Reid, Feb. 1, 1820, *AC*, House, 16th Cong., 1st sess., pp. 1032–33; Elliot, Jan. 17, 1820, *AC*, Senate, 16th Cong. 1st sess., p. 133; Tyler, Feb. 17, 1820, *AC*, House, 16th Cong., 1st sess., pp. 1391–93.

20. Morril, Jan. 17, 1820, *AC*, Senate, 16th Cong., 1st sess., p. 148; Lowrie, Jan. 20, 1820, *AC*, Senate, 16th Cong. 1st sess., p. 208; Burrill, Jan. 20, 1820, *AC*, Senate, 16th Cong., 1st sess., p. 218; Sergeant, Feb. 9, 1820, *AC*, House, 16th Cong., 1st sess., pp. 1206–10.

21. Moore, *Missouri Controversy*, 91–120; Barbour, Feb. 10, 1820, *AC*, House, 16th Cong., 1st sess., p. 1241; Macon, Jan. 10, 1820, *AC*, Senate, 16th Cong., 1st sess., p. 226; Smith, Jan. 26, 1820, *AC*, Senate, 16th Cong., 1st sess., p. 267.

22. Richard Walsh and William Lloyd Fox, eds., *Maryland: A History, 1632–1974* (Baltimore, Md., 1974), 156–238; Moore, *Missouri Controversy*, 94–95, 102–3, 111–13, 147–64.

23. Calhoun to James Edward Colhoun, May 4, 1828, quoted in Barlett, *Calhoun*, 142; *Historical Statistics*, 209; J. P. Ochenkowski, "The Origins of Nullification in South Carolina," *South Carolina Historical Magazine* 83 (1982): 138–45; William W. Freehling, *Prelude to Civil War: The Nullification Controversy in South Carolina, 1818–1836* (New York, 1966), 25–48.

24. James Brewer Stewart, "'A Great Talking and Eating Machine': Patriarchy, Mobilization and the Dynamics of Nullification in South Carolina," *Civil War History* 37 (1981): 199–204; Lacy K. Ford, *Origins of Southern Radicalism: The South Carolina Upcountry, 1800–1860* (New York, 1988), 106–107.

25. Whitemarsh Seabrook, Jan. 23, 1828, quoted in Freehling, *Prelude to Civil War*, 35–36. Before 1833 Lowcountry society was marked by more political diversity than it would be in later years. Many of the planters were cosmopolitan individuals who had been schooled in the North and who summered in Northern retreats such as Newport, Rhode Island. Some remained unionists throughout the Nullification Crisis.

26. Ibid., 90–175; Bartlett, *Calhoun*, 114–74.

27. Calhoun to Virgil Maxcy, Sept. 11, 1830, quoted in Freehling, *Prelude to Civil War*, 257.

28. Hamilton to John Taylor et al., Sept. 14, 1830, quoted ibid., 256.

29. S. C. Jackson, Dec. 14, 1832, quoted ibid., 264; Jane H. Pease and William H. Pease, "The Economics and Politics of Charleston's Nullification Crisis," *Journal of Southern History* 47 (1981): 335–62; Stewart, "Great Talking and Eating Machine," 214–19; Ford, *Origins of Southern Radicalism*, 127–44.

30. Richard B. Latner, "The Nullification Crisis and Republican Subversion," *Journal of Southern History* 43 (1977): 19–38; Bartlett, *Calhoun*, 177–201; Freehling, *Prelude to Civil War*, 260–97; Andrew Jackson, Proclamation Regarding Nullification, Dec. 10, 1832, www.yale.edu/lawweb/avalon/presiden/proclamations/jack01.htm (accessed Jan. 6, 2008).

31. J. Mills Thornton III, *Politics and Power in a Slave Society: Alabama, 1800–1860* (Baton Rouge, La., 1978), 27–30; Lucie R. Bridgforth, "Mississippi's Response to Nullification, 1833," *Journal of Mississippi History* 6 (1983): 8–20, quotes on pp. 8, 20; Charles M. Wiltse, *John C. Calhoun: Nullifier, 1829–1839* (Indianapolis, Ind., 1949), 121–29; Freehling, *Prelude to Civil War*, 203.

32. Governor Roman, 1833, quoted in John M. Sacher, *A Perfect War of Politics: Parties, Politicians, and Democracy in Louisiana, 1824–1861* (Baton Rouge, La., 2003), 54; Ulrich B. Phillips, *Georgia and State Rights* (1902; rpt., Yellow Springs, Ohio, 1968), 133–34; Alabama and Georgia legislatures quoted in Freehling, *Prelude to Civil War*, 265.

33. William Carroll to Jackson, Dec. 18, 1832, quoted in Jonathan M. Atkins, *Parties, Politics, and the Sectional Conflict in Tennessee, 1832–1861* (Knoxville, Tenn., 1997), 28; Paul H. Bergeron, "Tennessee's Response to the Nullification Crisis," *Journal of Southern History* 39 (1973): 23–44.

34. Virginia legislature, 1833, quoted in Freehling, *Prelude to Civil War*, 290.

35. William W. Freehling, *The Road to Disunion*, vol. 1: *Secessionists at Bay, 1776–1854* (New York, 1990), 308–36; William Lee Miller, *Arguing About Slavery: The Great Battle in the United States Congress* (New York, 1996), 28–112.

36. Freehling, *Road to Disunion*, 336; Miller, *Arguing About Slavery*, 115–298; Dec. 21, 1837, *CG*, 25th Cong., 2nd sess., p. 45.

37. Freehling, *Road to Disunion*, 337–51; Miller, *Arguing About Slavery*, 310–454; Dec. 10, 1844, *CG*, 28th Cong., 2nd sess., p. 18.

38. Wilmot, Aug. 3, 1846, *CG*, 29th Cong., 1st sess., p. 1185; Eric Foner, "The Wilmot Proviso Revisited," *Journal of American History* 56 (1969): 262–79; Arthur M. Schlesinger, Jr., *The Age of Jackson* (New York, 1945), 450–52.

39. Clarke, July 24, 1848, William Collins, July 28, 1848, *CG*, 30th Cong., 1st sess., App., pp. 1149, 920; Chaplain W. Morrison, *Democratic Politics and Sectionalism: The Wilmot Proviso Controversy* (Chapel Hill, N.C., 1967), 3–37; David M. Potter, *The Impending Crisis, 1848–1861* (New York, 1976), 18–23, examines the divisions in August 1846. See the votes, Aug. 8, 1846, *CG*, 29th Cong., 1st sess., pp. 1217–18. On the first division (p. 1217) eight Northern representatives voted for tabling the measure. But on the next division (p. 1218) only the four representatives from Illinois persisted in their opposition. Three of the opponents now voted for the measure, and one abstained.

40. Collamer, July 27, 1848, *CG*, 30th Cong., 1st sess., App., p. 968.

41. Corwin, July 24, 1848, ibid., p. 1161; Lawrence, June 12, 1848, ibid., p. 678.

42. Bradbury, July 26, 1848, *CG*, 30th Cong., 1st sess., App., p. 1192; Smith, July 31, 1848, ibid., p. 1072.

43. Mason, July 6, 1848, ibid., p. 883.

44. Wallace, July 26, 1848, ibid., p. 955.

45. Keitt to Calhoun, Jan. 14, 1849, in *Papers of Calhoun*, 26:215.

46. Resolution of Sumter District, Mar. 5, 1849, ibid., 26:343.

47. Proceedings of a public meeting, Accomack County, Va., Mar. 26, 1849, ibid., 26:360.

48. Lillian A. Kibler, *Benjamin F. Perry: South Carolina Unionist* (Durham, N.C., 1946), 239–59, quote on p. 240; Resolutions of the Mississippi Convention, Oct. 3, 1849, in *Papers of Calhoun*, 27:72.

49. Richard Crallé to Calhoun, Feb. 2, 1849, in *Papers of Calhoun*, 26:266–67. Crallé wrote "goarded," which I have corrected.

50. James Hammond to Calhoun, Feb. 19, 1849, ibid., 26:294–95.

51. William Duval to Calhoun, Feb. 13, 1849, ibid., 15:289; Calhoun to James Hammond, Feb. 14, 1849, to Henry Foote, Aug. 3, 1849, ibid., 26:291, 27:9.

52. Kirk H. Porter and Donald B. Johnson, eds., *National Party Platforms, 1840–1964* (Urbana, Ill., 1966), 13–14, quote on p. 14.

53. Holman Hamilton, *Prologue to Conflict: The Crisis and Compromise of 1850* (1964; rpt., New York, 1966), 162, 191–200.

54. Philip S. Foner, *Business and Slavery: The New York Merchants and the Irrepressible Conflict* (New York, 1941), 16–33, quotes on pp. 25, 31; Hamilton, *Prologue to Conflict*, 68, 82, 102, 122–23, 130–32.

55. Webster, Mar. 7, 1850, *CG*, 31st Cong., 1st sess., pp. 476–84, quotes on pp. 476, 480–81; Merrill D. Peterson, *The Great Triumvirate: Webster, Clay, and Calhoun* (New York, 1987), 27–38, 96–105, 175–76, 236–45, 290–94, 370–95, 462–90.

56. Foner, *Business and Slavery*, 26–29, quotes on p. 27; Hamilton, *Prologue to Conflict*, 81, 121.

57. Houston, Feb. 8, 1850, *CG*, 31st Cong., 1st sess., App., pp. 97–102, quote on p. 99; "Samuel Houston," *ANB*.

## CHAPTER 4: RISE OF THE LAKE ECONOMY

1. Mentor L. Williams, "The Chicago River and Harbor Convention, 1847," *Mississippi Valley Historical Review* 35 (1949): 607–26; Madison Kuhn, "Economic Issues and the Rise of the Republican Party in the Northwest" (Ph.D. diss., University of Chicago, 1940), 69–71, quote on p. 69.

2. J.D.B. DeBow, "The Chicago and Memphis Conventions," *DeBow's Review* 4, no. 1 (Sept. 1847): 122–27, quotes on pp. 123, 126.

3. Giddings, Feb. 17, 1851, *CG*, 31st Cong., 2nd sess., p. 559; James B. Stewart, *Joshua Giddings and the Tactics of Radical Politics* (Cleveland, 1970), 4–32.

4. Giddings, Jan. 12, 1844, *CG*, 28th Cong., 1st sess., App., p. 289.

5. Don E. Fehrenbacher, *Chicago Giant: A Biography of "Long John" Wentworth* (Madison, Wis., 1957), 3–52, 66–69, 151–75.

6. Wentworth, Feb. 10, 1846, *CG*, 29th Cong., 1st sess., App., pp. 450–55, quotes on pp. 452, 453. For other testimony on the value of trade on the lakes, see Buel, Feb. 17, 1851, *CG*, 31st Cong., 2nd sess., p. 567; Cass, July 22, 1852, *CG*, 32nd Cong., 1st sess., p. 1881; Cass, July 7, 1856, *CG*, 34th Cong., 1st sess., p. 748; Goodwin, May 31, 1858, *CG*, 35th Cong., 1st sess., p. 480; Cameron, June 15, 1860, *CG*, 36th Cong., 1st sess., p. 3018; John C. Clark, *The Grain Trade in the Old Northwest* (Urbana, Ill., 1966), 117, 281. These figures all show strong growth but present different estimates for the value and volume of trade.

7. Clark, *Grain Trade*, 59–88; Feb. 10, 1846, *CG*, 29th Cong., 1st sess., App., p. 452; U.S. Bureau of the Census, *The Seventh Census of the United States, 1850* (Washington, D.C., 1853), 705; Richard Yates, Apr. 23, 1852, *CG*, 32nd Cong., 1st sess., App., p. 473.

8. U.S. Bureau of the Census, *Statistical Abstract of the United States, 1936* (Washington, D.C.: U.S. Government Printing Office, 1936), 371; Clark, *Grain Trade*, 217–27; Erik F. Haites, James Mak, and Gary M. Walton, *Western River Transportation: The Era of Early Internal Development, 1810–1860* (Baltimore, 1975), 124–28; William Cronon, *Nature's Metropolis: Chicago and the Great West* (New York, 1991), 64–70; George Rogers Taylor, *The Transportation Revolution, 1815–1860* (New York, 1951), 75–103.

9. Tonnage sent from the Midwest down the Mississippi to New Orleans doubled in the 1840s and again in the 1850s. Shipments sent east, however, increased even more rapidly. See Haites et al., *Western River Transportation*, 124–28; *Cleveland Daily Leader*, Sept. 27, Dec. 5, 1859, Feb. 21, 1860; U.S. Bureau of the Census, *Historical Statistics of the United States, Colonial Times to 1970*, 2 vols., consec. pagin. (Washington, D.C., 1975), 26–37; William T. Hutchinson, *Cyrus Hall McCormick*, 2 vols. (1930; rpt., New York, 1968), 1:318–25.

10. Cass, July 29, 1854, *CG*, 33rd Cong., 1st sess., App., p. 1170.

11. Brinkerhoff, Aug. 3, 1846, *CG*, 29th Cong., 1st sess., p. 1186.

12. Toombs, May 27, 1858, *CG*, 35th Cong., 1st sess., App., p. 477.

13. Douglas, May 24, 1858, ibid., p. 2349; Douglas to Charles H. Lanphier, Nov. 11, 1853, to Joel Matteson, Jan. 2, 1854, Autobiographical Notes [Sept.–Oct. 1859?], in

*The Letters of Stephen A. Douglas,* ed. Robert W. Johannsen (Urbana, Ill., 1961), 268, 272–82, 472.

14. Stuart, July 28, 1854, *CG,* 33rd Cong., 1st sess., App., p. 1159.

15. Cass, July 29, 1854, ibid., App., p. 1171.

16. Thompson, Mar. 13, 1846, *CG,* 29th Cong., 1st sess., p. 496; Brinkerhoff, Feb. 25, 1846, ibid., p. 429.

17. Wade, May 10, 1852, *CG,* 32nd Cong., 1st sess., p. 1303; H. L. Trefousse, *Benjamin Franklin Wade: Radical Republican from Ohio* (New York, 1963), 17–80.

18. Buel, Feb. 17, 1851, *CG,* 31st Cong., 2nd sess., p. 568; Cass, July 22, 1852, *CG,* 32nd Cong., 1st sess., pp. 1880–81; Conger, Aug. 24, 1852, *CG,* 32nd Cong., 1st sess., App., pp. 1061–65.

19. Cass, July 7, 1856, *CG,* 34th Cong., 1st sess., App., p. 749; *Ashtabula Sentinel,* Nov. 16, 1854, Jan. 25, 1855; Schenck, Dec. 15, 1847, *CG,* 30th Cong., 1st sess., p. 37; *Cleveland Morning Leader,* Apr. 1, Nov. 16, 1859.

20. William W. Freehling, *Prelude to Civil War: The Nullification Controversy in South Carolina, 1816–1836* (New York, 1966), 144–47, quote on p. 146; "George McDuffie," *ANB.*

21. McDuffie, Mar. 3, 1845, *CG,* 28th Cong., 2nd sess., p. 392.

22. Davis, Mar. 16, 1846, *CG,* 29th Cong., 1st sess., App., pp. 434–35.

23. Polk, vetoes, Aug. 3, Dec. 15, 1846, *CG,* 29th Cong., 1st sess., pp. 1181–83; *CG,* 30th Cong., 1st sess., pp. 30–32, quote p. 30.

24. McMullen, Feb. 17, 1851, *CG,* 31st Cong., 2nd sess., p. 566; Rhett, Aug. 3, 1846, *CG,* 29th Cong., 1st sess., p. 118.

25. Votes, Aug. 4, 1846, Feb. 18, 1851, *CG,* 29th Cong., 1st sess., p. 1189; *CG,* 31st Cong., 2nd sess., p. 594; Kuhn, "Economic Issues," 92–96. The results in the text tabulate the votes in the eleven Southern states that would join the Confederacy.

26. McClernand, Jan. 10, 1848, *CG,* 30th Cong., 1st sess., App., pp. 77–78.

27. Gordon, March 10, 1846, *CG,* 29th Cong., 1st sess., App., pp. 341–42.

28. Robinson, Feb. 17, 1851, *CG,* 31st Cong., 2nd sess., p. 562.

29. Douglas, March 13, 1846, *CG,* 29th Cong., 1st sess., p. 497.

30. Douglas, Aug. 3, 1846, ibid., p. 1184.

31. Douglas, July 31, 1854, *CG,* 33rd Cong., 1st sess., App., p. 1185.

32. Stuart, July 28, 1854, ibid., p. 1159.

33. Stuart, July 3, 1852, *CG,* 32nd Cong., 1st sess., App., p. 868; Cass, July 7, 1856, *CG,* 34th Cong., 1st sess., App., p. 741.

34. Brinkerhoff, Aug. 3, 1846, *CG,* 29th Cong., 1st sess., p. 1186.

35. Wentworth, Feb. 10, 1846, ibid., p. 455.

36. Toombs, July 28, 1854, *CG,* 33rd Cong., 1st sess., App., p. 1154.

37. Smith, July 21, 1848, *CG,* 30th Cong., 1st sess., App., p. 811.

38. Cass, Aug. 24, 1852, *CG,* 32nd Cong., 1st sess., App., p. 1156.

39. Cass, Aug. 18, 1852, ibid., p. 984.

40. Green included in his letter copies of letters he had sent to F. H. Elmore, May 29, and Richard Crallé, May 30, 1847. Duff Green to Calhoun, May 31, 1847, in *The*

*Papers of John C. Calhoun*, eds. Robert L. Meriwether et al., 28 vols. (Columbia, S.C., 1959–2003), 24:386–88; "Duff Green," *ANB*.

41. Calhoun to Green, June 10, 1847, in *Papers of Calhoun*, 24:396–97.

42. McClelland, Feb. 26, 1846, *CG*, 29th Cong., 1st sess., App., p. 329.

43. Wentworth, Jan. 6, 1854, *CG*, 33rd Cong., 1st sess., p. 139.

44. Goodwin, May 31, 1858, *CG*, 35th Cong., 1st sess., p. 480.

45. Chandler, Feb. 6, 1860, *CG*, 36th Cong., 1st sess., App., p. 670.

46. Smith, Aug. 23, 1852, *CG*, 32nd Cong., 1st sess., App., pp. 1135–37; "Truman Smith," *ANB*.

47. Davis, Aug. 18, 1852, *CG*, 32nd Cong., 1st sess., App., p. 985; "John Davis," *ANB*.

48. Hale, Aug. 18, 1852, *CG*, 32nd Cong., 1st sess., App., p. 989.

49. Calhoun, Speech at a Meeting of Citizens of Charleston, Mar. 9, 1847, Speech on Slavery Resolutions, Feb. 20, 1847, in *Papers of Calhoun*, 24: 249–50, 24:186.

50. Davis to Malcolm D. Haynes, Aug. 18, 1849, in *The Papers of Jefferson Davis*, ed. Haskell M. Monroe, Jr., and James T. McIntosh, 10 vols. (Baton Rouge, La., 1971–99), 4:27.

51. Davis, Speech in Congress, Apr. 14, 1848, ibid., 3:297; Alexander Bowie to Calhoun, Apr. 13, 1846, in *Papers of Calhoun*, 24:315.

## CHAPTER 5: THE CAMPAIGN AGAINST SLAVERY

1. Douglass to Sidney Howard Gay, Aug. 1847, in *The Life and Writings of Frederick Douglass: Early Years, 1817–1849*, ed. Philip S. Foner (New York, 1950), 256–59. Douglass refused to spell out the racial epithet in his account.

2. Walter M. Merrill, *Against Wind and Tide: A Biography of William Lloyd Garrison* (Cambridge, Mass., 1963), 3–50, quote on p. 45; "William Lloyd Garrison," *ANB*.

3. Garrison to Henry E. Benson, July 30, 1831, to Gerrit Smith, Mar. 7, 1835, to Hannah Webb, Mar. 1, 1843, in *The Letters of William Lloyd Garrison*, ed. Walter M. Merrill, 6 vols. (Cambridge, Mass., 1971–81), 1:124, 458, 3:131.

4. Betram Wyatt-Brown, *Lewis Tappan and the Evangelical War Against Slavery* (Cleveland, 1969), 1–97.

5. Ibid., 121–32; Gilbert H. Barnes, *The Anti-Slavery Impulse, 1830–1844* (New York, 1933), 64–87, 100–108; Dorothy Sterling, *Ahead of Her Time: Abby Kelley and the Politics of Antislavery* (New York, 1991), quote on p. 40.

6. Barnes, *Anti-Slavery Impulse*, 79–87, quote on p. 83; Leonard L. Richards, *"Gentlemen of Property and Standing": Anti-Abolition Mobs in Jacksonian America* (New York, 1970), 4–45; James B. Stewart, *Holy Warriors: The Abolitionists and American Slavery* (New York, 1976), 58–65.

7. Fitzwilliam Byrdall to Calhoun, Apr. 9, 1848, in *The Papers of John C. Calhoun*, ed. Robert L. Meriwether et al., 28 vols. (Columbia, S.C., 1959–2003), 25:307; Gerald Sorin, *The New York Abolitionists: A Case Study of Political Radicalism* (Westport, Conn.,

1971), 99–118; Stewart, *Holy Warriors*, 65; Bruce Levine, *Half Slave and Half Free: The Roots of Civil War* (New York, 1992), 154.

8. Barnes, *Anti-Slavery Impulse*, 88–91.

9. Bertram Wyatt-Brown, "The Abolitionists' Postal Campaign of 1835," *Journal of Negro History* 50 (1965): 227–38, quote on p. 228; Stewart, *Holy Warriors*, 69–71; Kendall quoted in William Lee Miller, *Arguing About Slavery: The Great Battle in the United States Congress* (New York, 1996), 102.

10. Stewart, *Holy Warriors*, 82–83; Levine, *Half Slave*, 154.

11. Sterling, *Ahead of Her Time*, 32–34, quote on p. 33.

12. Ibid., 13–19, 32–36, quotes on p. 35.

13. Ibid., 37–106, quote on p. 51.

14. Richard H. Sewell, *Ballots for Freedom: Antislavery Politics in the United States, 1837–1860* (New York, 1976), 26–40; Leon F. Litwack, *North of Slavery: The Negro in the Free States, 1790–1860* (Chicago, 1961), 214–46; Lawrence J. Friedman, *Gregarious Saints: Self and Community in American Abolitionism, 1830–1870* (New York, 1982), 129–95.

15. Levine, *Half Slave*, 168–70; Stewart, *Holy Warriors*, 109.

16. Wallace, July 26, 1848, *CG*, 30th Cong., 1st sess., App., p. 954.

17. Iverson, July 26, 1848, ibid., p. 962.

18. Kirk H. Porter and Donald B. Johnson, eds., *National Party Platforms, 1840–1864* (Urbana, Ill., 1966), 4–8; John Stauffer, *The Black Hearts of Men: Radical Abolitionists and the Transformation of Race* (Cambridge, Mass., 2002), 16–17.

19. Fitzwilliam Byrdall to Calhoun, Apr. 9, 1848, in *Papers of Calhoun*, 25:307; Gerald Sorin, *The New York Abolitionists: A Case Study of Political Radicalism* (Westport, Conn., 1971), 99–118.

20. Smith, Apr. 6, 1853, *CG*, 33rd Cong., 1st sess., App., p. 528; Stauffer, *Black Hearts*, 135–57, 174–79, 195–99, 239–67.

21. Calhoun, Speech, Mar. 9, 1847, in *Papers of Calhoun*, 24:252.

22. David H. Donald, *Charles Sumner and the Coming of the Civil War* (New York, 1960), 70–97, quote on p. 83; Speech, Nov. 6, 1850, in *Charles Sumner: His Complete Works*, intro. George F. Hoar, 20 vols. (1900; rpt., New York, 1969), 3:146–47; "Charles Sumner," *ANB*.

23. Sumner, Speech, July 4, 1845, in *Sumner: Complete Works*, 1:8; Donald, *Sumner*, 106–11, quote on p. 106; Sumner to Wendell Phillips, Feb. 4, 1845, in *The Selected Letters of Charles Sumner*, ed. Beverly W. Palmer, 2 vols. (Boston, 1990), 1:145.

24. Donald, *Sumner*, 110–29.

25. Sumner to Robert C. Winthrop, Oct. 25, 1846, in *Sumner: Complete Works*, 1:327.

26. Sumner, Speech, June 28, 1848, ibid., 2:233.

27. Philip S. Foner, *Business and Slavery: The New York Merchants and the Irrepressible Conflict* (New York, 1941).

28. Martin Duberman, *Charles Francis Adams, 1807–1886* (Stanford, Calif., 1960), 87–138; Donald, *Sumner*, 134–77.

29. *National Party Platforms*, 13; Sumner, Speech, Aug. 22, 1848, in *Sumner: Complete Works*, 2:295.

30. Kevin Sweeney, "Rum, Romanism, Representation, and Reform: Coalition Politics in Massachusetts, 1847–1853," *Civil War History* 22 (1976): 116–37; Frank Otto Gatell, "'Conscience and Judgement': The Bolt of the Massachusetts Conscience Whigs," *Historian* 21 (1958): 18–45; Sewell, *Ballots for Freedom*, 148–67, 219–23; Donald, *Sumner*, 160–204.

31. John Niven, *Salmon P. Chase: A Biography* (New York, 1995), 1–27; "Salmon P. Chase," *ANB*.

32. Chase to Charles D. Cleveland, Aug. 29, 1840, in *The Salmon P. Chase Papers*, vol. 2: *Correspondence, 1823–1857* (Kent, Ohio, 1994), 71; Niven, *Chase*, 21–66, quote on p. 48; Albert B. Hart, *Salmon Portland Chase* (New York, 1899), 46–47.

33. Chase to Joshua Giddings, Aug. 15, 1846, in *Chase Papers*, 2: 126; "Salmon P. Chase," *ANB*; Niven, *Chase*, 74–113.

34. Chase to Sarah Chase, Dec. 20, 1848, Horace Greeley to Chase, Apr. 16, 1852, in *Chase Papers*, 2:205, 346; Stephen E. Maizlish, *The Triumph of Sectionalism: The Transformation of Ohio Politics, 1844–1856* (Kent, Ohio, 1983), 121–46; Niven, *Chase*, 115–23.

35. Sewell, *Ballots for Freedom*, 148–72.

36. Chase to John Hale, June 2 [5], 1848, in *Chase Papers*, 2:174; Sumner to Joshua Giddings, July 5, 1848, in *Selected Letters*, 1:235.

37. Sumner to Charles Francis Adams, July 30, 1848, in *Selected Letters*, 1:239.

38. Chase to Charles Sumner, Sept. 19, 1849, in *Chase Papers*, 2:259; Judah B. Ginsberg, "Barnburners, Free Soilers, and the New York Republican Party," *New York History* 57 (1975): 474–500; Dale Baum and Dale T. Knobel, "Anatomy of a Realignment: New York Presidential Politics, 1848–1860," *New York History* 65 (1984): 61–81; Herbert D. Donovan, *The Barnburners: A Study of the Internal Movements in the Political History of New York State and of the Resulting Changes in Political Affiliation, 1830–1852* (New York, 1925), 84–120; "Martin Van Buren," *ANB*.

39. Chase to Van Buren, Aug. 21, 1848, in *Chase Papers*, 2:186–87; *National Party Platforms*, 14; "John Hale," *ANB*.

40. Chase to Charles Sumner, Apr. 13, 1850, in *Chase Papers*, 2: 287. For the twelve Free Soil representatives, see Sewell, *Ballots for Freedom*, 168n. By the next Congress the twelve were reduced to only five; ibid., 240–41. On earlier Radical victories, see ibid., 47.

41. Julian to Colored Citizens of Illinois, Sept. 17, 1853, quoted in Sewell, *Ballots for Freedom*, 172.

42. Sewell, *Ballots for Freedom*, 177–82; Litwack, *North of Slavery*, 91.

43. Fawn M. Brodie, *Thaddeus Stevens: Scourge of the South* (New York, 1959), 30–31, 64–69; Litwack, *North of Slavery*, 76–77, 84–87.

44. John L. Stanley, "Majority Tyranny in Tocqueville's America: The Failure of Negro Suffrage in 1846," *Political Science Quarterly* 84 (1969): 412–35; Eric Foner, "Politics and Prejudice: The Free Soil Party and the Negro, 1849–1852," *Journal of Negro History* 50 (1965): 239–56; James T. Adams, "Disfranchisement of Negroes in New England," *American Historical Review* 30 (1925): 543–47; Litwack, *North of Slavery*, 77–91; Sewell, *Ballots for Freedom*, 172–77.

45. John M. Rozett, "Racism and Republican Emergence in Illinois, 1848–1860: A Re-evaluation of Republican Negrophobia," *Civil War History* 22 (1976): 101–15; Litwack, *North of Slavery*, 66–71, 93–94, 114–37; Sewell, *Ballots for Freedom*, 180–81.

46. Litwack, *North of Slavery*, 72–73, 97–102, 155–63.

47. Sumner, Argument before Supreme Court of Massachusetts, Dec. 4, 1849, in *Sumner: Complete Works*, 3:99.

48. Litwack, *North of Slavery*, 104–11, 143–49; Sewell, *Ballots for Freedom*, 183–86; Speech, Buffalo, Sept. 18, 1851, in *The Frederick Douglass Papers, Series One: Speeches, Debates, and Interviews*, ed. John W. Blassingame, 5 vols. (New Haven, Conn., 1979– ), 2:85; Litwack, *North of Slavery*, 104–10; Sewell, *Ballots for Freedom*, 183–86.

49. Sewell, *Ballots for Freedom*, 6–40; Stewart, *Holy Warriors*, 97–120.

50. Smith, July 31, 1848, *CG*, 30th Cong., 1st sess., App., p. 1072.

51. Quoted in Niven, *Chase*, 106. In fact, Greeley after much vacillation ended up backing Taylor rather than Van Buren for president. Greeley later claimed that Whig support for higher tariffs was the deciding factor. See Glyndon G. Van Deusen, *Horace Greeley: Nineteenth-Century Crusader* (New York, 1953), 123–25.

52. Wilmot quoted in Sewell, *Ballots for Freedom*, 173; Wilmot, Aug. 3, 1848, *CG*, 30th Cong., 1st sess., App., p. 1076; Trumbull quoted in Eric Foner, *Free Soil, Free Labor, Free Men: The Ideology of the Republican Party Before the Civil War* (New York, 1970), 266; Foner, *Politics and Ideology in the Age of the Civil War* (New York, 1980), 83.

53. Jefferson Davis, July 12, 1848, *CG*, 30th Cong., 1st sess., App., p. 913.

54. James Mason, July 6, 1848, ibid., p. 886.


## CHAPTER 6: STATES' RIGHTS DIVIDES THE DEEP SOUTH

1. Calhoun to Henry W. Conner, Jan. 14, 1847, in *The Papers of John C. Calhoun*, ed. Robert L. Meriwether et al., 28 vols. (Columbia, S.C., 1959–2003), 24:69.

2. David Hackett Fischer, *Albion's Seed: Four British Folkways in America* (New York, 1989), 605–782, 817–18; Rupert Vance, *Human Geography of the South: A Study in Regional Resources and Human Adequacy* (Chapel Hill, N.C., 1932), 110; D. W. Meinig, *The Shaping of America: A Geographical Perspective on 500 Years of History*, vol. 2: *Continental America, 1800–1867* (New Haven, Conn., 1993), 221–40, esp. the map on p. 233.

3. Calhoun to James L. Orr et al., Nov. 1846, in *Papers of Calhoun*, 23:512.

4. Herbert J. Doherty, Jr., *The Whigs of Florida, 1845–1854* (Gainesville, Fla., 1959), 63–72; Henry Glassie, *Pattern in the Material Folk Culture of the Eastern United States* (Philadelphia, 1968), 78–117; Gordon R. Wood, *Vocabulary Change: A Study of Variation in Regional Words in Eight of the Southern States* (Carbondale, Ill., 1971), 325–52, esp. the maps on pp. 3–5, 358–59.

5. William A. Elmore to Robert Barnwell Rhett, Nov. 10, 1842, Robert Barnwell Rhett Papers, SHC; D.L.A. Hackett, "Slavery, Ethnicity, and Sugar: An Analysis of Vot-

ing Behaviour in Louisiana, 1828–1844," *Louisiana Studies* 13 (1974): 73–118; Thomas F. Redard, "The Election of 1844 in Louisiana: A New Look at the Ethno-cultural Approach," *Louisiana History* 22 (1981): 419–33; Roger W. Shugg, *Origins of Class Struggle in Louisiana: A Social History of White Farmers and Laborers during Slavery and After, 1840–1875* (Baton Rouge, La., 1939), 145–50.

6. Augustus Fisher[lue?] to Calhoun, Sept. 24, 1848, Henry Conner to Calhoun, Jan. 12, 1849, Joseph W. Lesesne to John C. Calhoun, Sept. 12, 1847, in *Papers of Calhoun*, 26:63, 211, 24:552; Laura Wood Roper, "Frederick Law Olmsted and the Western Texas Free-Soil Movement," *American Historical Review* 56 (1950): 58–64; Wendell G. Addington, "Slave Insurrections in Texas," *Journal of Negro History* 35 (1950): 408–34; Robin E. Baker and Dale Baum, "The Texas Voter and the Crisis of the Union, 1859–1861," *Journal of Southern History* 53 (1987): 395–420; J. Mills Thornton III, *Politics and Power in a Slave Society: Alabama, 1800–1860* (Baton Rouge, La., 1978), 42; D. Clayton James, *Antebellum Natchez* (Baton Rouge, La., 1968), 164–65. Despite their antislavery sentiments, most Mexicans in Texas voted for secession during the first months of 1861. See Walter L. Buenger, *Secession and the Union in Texas* (Austin, Tex., 1984), 80–81, 88–89.

7. Steven Hahn, "The 'Unmaking' of the Southern Yeomanry: The Transformation of the Georgia Upcountry, 1860–1890," in *The Countryside in the Age of Capitalist Transformation: Essays in the Social History of Rural America*, ed. Steven Hahn and Jonathan Prude (Chapel Hill, N.C., 1985), 180–85, 197; David F. Weiman, "The Economic Emancipation of the Non-Slaveholding Class: Upcountry Farmers in the Georgia Cotton Economy," *Journal of Economic History* 45 (1985): 71–93; Wilma A. Dunaway, *The First American Frontier: Transition to Capitalism in Southern Appalachia, 1700–1860* (Chapel Hill, N.C., 1996), 225–26, 231–45. Sam B. Hilliard, *Atlas of Antebellum Southern Agriculture* (Baton Rouge, La., 1984), 58–62, illustrates the evolution of this wheat–growing area.

8. Daniel Dupre, "Ambivalent Capitalists on the Cotton Frontier: Settlement and Development in the Tennessee Valley of Alabama," *Journal of Southern History* 56 (1990): 215–40; Thornton, *Politics and Power*, 107–108; Charles C. Bolton, *Poor Whites of the Antebellum South: Tenants and Laborers in Central North Carolina and Northeast Mississippi* (Durham, N.C., 1994), 86–90.

9. R. S. Cotterill, "Southern Railroads and Western Trade, 1840–1850," *Mississippi Valley Historical Review* 3 (1917): 427–41; Cotterill, "Southern Railroads, 1850–1860," *Mississippi Valley Historical Review* 10 (1924): 396–405. This argument linking lines of transportation with divergent views on secession parallels the case made in Kenneth W. Noe, *Southwest Virginia's Railroad: Modernization and the Sectional Crisis* (Urbana, Ill., 1994).

10. Gordon B. McKinney, "Economy and Community in Western North Carolina, 1860–1865," in *Appalachia in the Making: The Mountain South in the Nineteenth Century*, ed. Mary Beth Pudup et al. (Chapel Hill, N.C., 1995), 163–84; John C. Inscoe, *Mountain Masters, Slavery, and the Sectional Crisis in North Carolina* (Knoxville, Tenn., 1989), 25–53, esp. map on p. 42, showing patterns of trade; Dunaway, *First American Frontier*, 132–45, 200–208; Vicki Vaughan Johnson, *The Men and the Vision of the Southern Commercial Conventions, 1845–1871* (Columbia, Mo., 1992), 87–165.

11. William A. Elmore to Robert Barnwell Rhett, Nov. 10, 1842, Robert Barnwell Rhett Papers, SHC; Shugg, *Origins of Class Struggle*, 152–54, 157; Charles G. Sellers, Jr., "Who Were the Southern Whigs?" *American Historical Review* 59 (1954): 335–46.

12. Milledgeville *Southern Recorder*, Aug. 29, 1843, quoted in Larry Keith Menna, "Embattled Conservatism: The Ideology of the Southern Whigs" (Ph.D. diss., Columbia University, 1991), 173.

13. *Mobile Advertiser*, Nov. 27, 1848, quoted in Larry K. Menna, "Southern Whiggery and Economic Development: The Meaning of Slavery in a National Context," in David Roediger and Martin H. Blatt, eds., *The Meaning of Slavery in the North* (New York, 1998), 64.

14. *Natchez Courier*, Apr. 13, 1849, quoted in Menna, "Embattled Conservatism," 230.

15. Lillian A. Kibler, *Benjamin F. Perry: South Carolina Unionist* (Durham, N.C., 1946), 302–303.

16. James L. Orr, "Development of Southern Industry," *DeBow's Review* 19, no. 1 (July 1855): 1–22, quote on pp. 11–12; Marc Egnal, *Divergent Paths: How Culture and Institutions Have Shaped North American Growth* (New York, 1996), 63–68.

17. Kibler, *Perry*, 303.

18. Stephens, Feb. 12, 1847, *CG*, 29th Cong., 1st sess., App., p. 353; Michael F. Holt, *Rise and Fall of the American Whig Party: Jacksonian Politics and the Onset of the Civil War* (New York, 1999), 252–53, 311, 464; William W. Freehling, *The Road to Disunion*, vol. 1: *Secessionists at Bay, 1776–1854* (New York, 1990), 456–57; John H. Schroeder, *Mr. Polk's War: American Opposition and Dissent, 1846–1848* (Madison, Wis., 1973), 17, 26–29, 76–77, 86–88.

19. Berrien, Feb. 5, 1847, *CG*, 29th Cong., 1st sess., p. 329.

20. "Alexander Stephens," "John Berrien," *ANB*.

21. Davis to the People of Mississippi, July 13, 1846, in *The Papers of Jefferson Davis*, ed. Haskell M. Monroe, Jr., and James T. McIntosh, 10 vols. (Baton Rouge, La., 1971–99), 3:5.

22. Davis, Speech at Jackson, Nov. 4, 1857, ibid., 6:157.

23. Yancey, Speech at Columbus, Georgia, 1855, in John W. DuBose, *The Life and Times of William Lowndes Yancey*, 2 vols. (1892; rpt., New York, 1942), 1:301.

24. J.F.H. Claiborne, *Life and Correspondence of John A. Quitman*, 2 vols. (New York, 1860), 2:273; Egnal, *Divergent Paths*, 21–32, 87–101.

25. John Forsythe to "Gentlemen of Charleston," Sept. 12, 1850, in DuBose, *Yancey*, 2:426.

26. Eugene D. Genovese, *The Political Economy of Slavery: Studies in the Economy and Society of the Slave South* (New York, 1965), 180–239; William H. Pease and Jane H. Pease, *The Web of Progress: Private Values and Public Styles in Boston and Charleston, 1828–1843* (New York, 1985), 18–20, 40–53, 222–24.

27. Iverson, July 26, 1848, *CG*, 30th Cong., 1st sess., App., p. 962; Address of the Southern Delegates in Congress to Their Constituents, Jan. 22, 1849, in *Papers of Calhoun*, 26:239–40.

28. Sally E. Hadden, *Slave Patrols: Law and Violence in Virginia and the Carolinas* (Cambridge, Mass., 2001), 41–70, 137–66; "*Forum:* The Making of a Slave Conspiracy, part 1,"

with essays by Robert A. Gross and Michael P. Johnson, *William and Mary Quarterly* 58, no. 4 (2001): 913–76, and "*Forum:* The Making of a Slave Conspiracy, part 2," with articles by Edward A. Pearson, Douglas R. Egerton, David Robertson, Philip D. Morgan, Winthrop D. Jordan, James Sidbury, Robert L. Paquette, and Michael P. Johnson, *William and Mary Quarterly* 59, no. 1 (2002): 135–202, provides a vigorous exchange on the extent—or existence—of the Vesey conspiracy; Herbert Aptheker, *American Negro Slave Revolts* (New York, 1943); Eugene D. Genovese, *Roll, Jordan, Roll: The World the Slaves Made* (New York, 1974), 587–97.

29. McDowell, Feb. 23, 1849, *CG*, 30th Cong., 2nd sess., App., p. 217.

30. Hunter, July 11, 1848, *CG*, 30th Cong., 1st sess., App., p. 904.

31. Henry W. Conner to Calhoun, Jan. 12, 1849, in *Papers of Calhoun*, 26:211.

32. Gavin Wright, *Old South, New South: Revolutions in the Southern Economy Since the Civil War* (New York, 1986), 24–26; James Oakes, *The Ruling Race: A History of American Slaveholders* (New York, 1982), 73–81; Donald F. Schaefer, "A Statistical Profile of Frontier and New South Migration: 1850–1860," *Agricultural History* 59 (1985): 563–67; Schaefer, "A Model of Migration and Wealth Accumulation: Farmers at the Antebellum Southern Frontier," *Explorations in Economic History* 24 (1987): 130–57; Richard H. Steckel, "Household Migration and Rural Settlement in the United States, 1850–1860," *Explorations in Economic History* 26 (1989): 198–218: Steven Stoll, *Larding the Lean Earth: Soil and Society in Nineteenth-Century America* (New York, 2002), 17–82; Avery O. Craven, *Soil Exhaustion as a Factor in the Agricultural History of Virginia and Maryland, 1606–1860* (1926; rpt., Gloucester, Mass., 1965), 11–24, 122–64.

33. John Hebron Moore, *The Emergence of the Cotton Kingdom in the Old Southwest: Mississippi, 1770–1860* (Baton Rouge, La., 1988), quotes on pp. 36, 44; Genovese, *Political Economy*, 43–105, 124–79.

34. Stoll, *Larding the Lean Earth*, 73–82; Genovese, *Political Economy*, 106–23.

35. Betty L. Mitchell, *Edmund Ruffin: A Biography* (Bloomington, Ind., 1981), 1–44; "Edmund Ruffin," *ANB*; Edmund Ruffin, "Incidents of My Life, Volume 2," 1851, reprinted in *Incidents of My Life: Edmund Ruffin's Autobiographical Essays*, ed. David F. Allmendinger, Jr. (Charlottesville, Va., 1990), 17–48.

36. Stoll, *Larding the Lean Earth*, 121; Mitchell, *Edmund Ruffin*, 4–5; William M. Mathew, *Edmund Ruffin and the Crisis of Slavery in the Old South: The Failure of Agricultural Reform* (Athens, Ga., 1988), 44–45.

37. Mathew, *Ruffin*, 40.

38. Ruffin, *Incidents of My Life*, 68.

39. Mathew, *Edmund Ruffin*, 56–61, quotes on p. 57, 60.

40. Moore, *Cotton Kingdom*, 30.

41. Stoll, *Larding the Lean Earth*, 202.

42. Jefferson Davis, Speech at Oxford, Miss., July 15, 1852, in *Papers of Davis*, 4:277; Richard A. Easterlin, "Regional Income Trends, 1840–1950," in *The Reinterpretation of American Economic History*, ed. Robert W. Fogel and Stanley L. Engerman (New York, 1971), 38–49. With U.S. income equal to 100, personal income per capita declined in all

sections of the South from 1840 to 1860. In the South West Central (LA, AK) the drop was 144 to 115; East South Central (MS, AL, TN, KY) from 73 to 68; South Atlantic (DE, MD, VA, NC, SC, GA, FL) 70 to 65. *Real* income rose throughout the South. But as soils grew less fertile, the pace of this growth slowed, and as these figures illustrate, the South failed to keep up with the brisk expansion in the North.

43. Alan L. Olmstead and Paul W. Rhode, "'Wait a Cotton Pickin' Minute!' A New View of Slave Productivity," Working Paper, April 2005; Moore, *Cotton Kingdom*, quote on p. 12.

44. Mason, July 6, 1848, *CG*, 30th Cong., 1st sess., App., p. 886.

45. Featherston, June 26, 1848, ibid., p. 764; Davis, July 12, 1848, ibid., p. 911.

46. David Johnson to Calhoun, Oct. 18, 1848, in *Papers of Calhoun*, 26:98.

47. Marcus Hammond to James Hammond, Dec. 17, 1849, quoted in Freehling, *Road to Disunion*, 1:474.

48. Caswell R. Clifton to Calhoun, Jan. 30, 1849, in *Papers of Calhoun*, 26:257.

49. Thornton, *Politics and Power*, 22–26; Thomas P. Abernethy, *The Formative Period in Alabama: 1815–1828* (1922, rpt., Tuscaloosa, Ala., 1990), 135–51, quote on p. 151; "Dixon H. Lewis," *ANB*; Thomas M. Williams, *Dixon Hall Lewis* (Auburn, Ala., 1910).

50. Joseph W. Lesesne to Calhoun, Jan. 30, 1848, in *Papers of Calhoun*, 25:156.

51. John A. Campbell to Calhoun, Dec. 20, 1847, ibid., 25:22–23.

52. George S. Houston to Cobb, June 26, Aug. 10, 1849, in *The Correspondence of Robert Toombs, Alexander H. Stephens and Howell Cobb*, ed. Ulrich B. Phillips (1913; rpt., New York, 1970), 166, 173; Thornton, *Politics and Power*, 181–83.

53. Hilliard M. Judge to Calhoun, Apr. 29, 1849, in *Papers of Calhoun*, 26:385.

54. Thornton, *Power and Politics*, 3–4, 201–203; "Jeremiah Clemens," *ANB*.

55. Thornton, *Politics and Power*, 182–84, 192–200, 262–65; Holt, *Rise and Fall*, 616.

56. Edward J. Black to Calhoun, Sept. 1, 1843, in *Papers of Calhoun*, 17:389–90.

57. Herschel Johnson to Calhoun, July 20, 1849, ibid., 26:509; Howell Cobb to James Buchanan, June 17, 1849, in *Toombs, Stephens and Cobb Correspondence*, 164; Calhoun, "The Address of the Southern Congressmen," January 1849, in *Works of John C. Calhoun*, ed. Richard K. Crallé, 6 vols. (New York, 1874–88), 6:290–313; Richard H. Shryock, *Georgia and the Union in 1850* (1926; rpt., New York, 1968), 178–216.

58. Absalom H. Chappell to Howell Cobb, July 10, 1850, in *Toombs, Stephens, and Cobb Correspondence*, 193; Holt, *Rise and Fall*, 610–13; Shryock, *Georgia and the Union*, 264–342, and particularly the map facing p. 320, which shows the vote for the state convention.

59. Horace Montgomery, *Cracker Parties* (Baton Rouge, La., 1950), 26–52.

60. Lacy K. Ford, Jr., *Origins of Southern Radicalism: The South Carolina Upcountry, 1800–1860* (New York, 1988), 99–144, 183–85, 281–307; John Barnwell, *Love of Order: South Carolina's First Secession Crisis* (Chapel Hill, N.C., 1982), 3–31. On soil depletion, see Sam B. Hilliard, *Atlas of Antebellum Southern Agriculture* (Baton Rouge, La., 1984), 67–71; *DeBow's Review* 11, no. 6 (Dec. 1851): 617–21; Genovese, *Political Economy*, 85–105; Gavin Wright, *The Political Economy of the Cotton South: Households, Markets, and Wealth*

*in the Nineteenth Century* (New York, 1978), 15–17. The terminology ("Backcountry/ Lowcountry"), which contemporaries used and which appears here in the text to describe the regional division, only approximates the north-south split in the state. In fact, the northern districts in the Lowcountry—Marion and Horry—often sided with the unionists. Some of the southern districts in the Backcountry (particularly Barnwell and Orangeburg) frequently favored the secessionists. See the map in Barnwell, *Love of Order,* xi.

61. Kibler, *Perry,* 239–59, quotes on pp. 243, 245; J. M. Rutland to B. F. Perry, March 17, 1851; J. R. Poinsett to B. F. Perry, March 28, 1851, Perry Papers, SHC; William W. Freehling, *Prelude to Civil War: The Nullification Controversy in South Carolina, 1816–1836* (New York, 1966), 252–53; "Benjamin Franklin Perry," *ANB.*

62. Kibler, *Perry,* 240; Ford, *Southern Radicalism,* 183–96.

63. Barnwell, *Love of Order,* 121–90, quote on p. 181; Kibler, *Perry,* 260–77; Robert W. Barnwell to James L. Orr, Aug. 26, 1851, Orr-Patterson Papers, SHC.

64. Ford, *Southern Radicalism,* 212–14, quote on p. 213.

65. Davis, "Speech at Holly Springs," Oct. 25, 1849, in *Papers of Davis,* 4:50; John McCardell, "John A. Quitman and the Compromise of 1850 in Mississippi," *Journal of Mississippi History* 37 (1975): 240–41; James R. Sharp, *The Jacksonians versus the Banks: Politics in the States after the Panic of 1837* (New York, 1970), 68, 86–108; Bolton, *Poor Whites,* 117–20.

66. Davis to William R. Cannon, Jan. 8, 1850, in *Papers of Davis,* 4:55, and see note on p. 57.

67. Calhoun-Foote exchange, Mar. 5, 1850, CG, 31st Cong., 1st sess., p. 463; this dialogue is also reprinted in *Papers of Calhoun,* 27: 213–14; "Henry Foote," *ANB*; Jon L. Wakelyn, *Confederates Against the Confederacy: Essays on Leadership and Loyalty* (Westport, Conn., 2002), 53–75. The *ANB* says the fistfight with Davis was in 1849, but Wakelyn more convincingly dates it in 1847.

68. Quitman to J. J. McRae, Sept. 28, 1850, in Claiborne, *Quitman,* 2:44, 46; "Henry Stuart Foote," *ANB.* Ferdinand L. Claiborne told Davis that Natchez was a "Hot bed of Whiggery." Feb. 27, 1848, in *Papers of Davis,* 3:274.

69. Unknown to Quitman, May 20, 1851, in Claiborne, *Quitman,* 121; Davis to David L. Yulee, July 18, 1851, in *Papers of Davis,* 4:218–19; McCardell, "Quitman," 251–64.

70. For the gubernatorial vote, see McCardell, "Quitman," 265–66; *Papers of Davis,* 4: endpaper.

71. McCardell, "Quitman," 264.

72. John Slidell to Howell Cobb, Jan. 28, 1852, in *Toombs, Stephens and Cobb Correspondence,* 276; James K. Greer, "Dissension Among the Democrats and Acceptance of the Compromise of 1850," *Louisiana Historical Quarterly* 12 (1929): 570–89.

73. Henry Conner to Calhoun, Jan. 12, 1849, in *Papers of Calhoun,* 26:211.

74. Quoted in Shugg, *Origins of Class Struggle,* 158; James D. B. DeBow to Calhoun, Apr. 23, Dec. 6, 1847, E. Warren Moise to Henry W. Conner, July 18, 1847, in *Papers of Calhoun,* 24:334, 25:42–43, 24:472; Holt, *Rise and Fall,* 617.

75. Buenger, *Secession and Union,* 24–25; Terry G. Jordan, "The Imprint of the Upper and Lower South on Mid-nineteenth-century Texas," *Annals of the Association of*

American Geographers 57 (1967), 667–74; David M. Potter, *The Impending Crisis, 1848–1861* (New York, 1976), 111–12; Eric H. Walther, *The Fire-Eaters* (Baton Rouge, La., 1992), 169–71; Holman Hamilton, *Prologue to Conflict: The Crisis and Compromise of 1850* (1964; rpt., New York, 1966), 179–81, 191–200; Louis T. Wigfall to Calhoun, Jan. 4, 1849, in *Papers of Calhoun*, 26:201; Alvy L. King, *Louis T. Wigfall: Southern Fire-eater* (Baton Rouge, La., 1970), 3–60.

76. Herbert J. Doherty, *The Whigs of Florida, 1845–1854* (Gainesville, Fla., 1959), 18–62, quotes on pp. 38, 52; Dorothy Dodd, "The Secession Movement in Florida, 1850–1861," *Florida Historical Quarterly* 12 (1933): 3–24; David Levy Yulee to Calhoun, July 10, 1849, in *Papers of Calhoun*, 26:500.

## CHAPTER 7: TRANSFORMATION OF THE BORDER STATES AND UPPER SOUTH

1. Benton, May 31, 1848, *CG*, 30th Cong., 1st sess., App., pp. 685–86.

2. William Nisbet Chambers, *Old Bullion Benton: Senator from the New West* (Boston, 1956), passim, quotes on pp. 146, 361; "Thomas Hart Benton," *ANB*.

3. Benton, Feb. 2, 1830, *Register of Debates*, 21st Cong., 1st sess., pp. 115–16.

4. Benton, May 3, 1848, *CG*, 30th Cong., 1st sess., App., p. 536; George Rogers Taylor, *The Transportation Revolution, 1815–1860* (New York, 1951), 161–66.

5. Chambers, *Old Bullion*, 92–100, 158–59, quote on p. 93.

6. Benton, June 10, 1850, *CG*, 31st Cong., 1st sess., App., p. 681.

7. Samuel Treat to Calhoun, June 17, 1849, in *The Papers of John C. Calhoun*, ed. Robert L. Meriwether et al., 28 vols. (Columbia, S.C., 1959–2003), 26:438.

8. Chambers, *Old Bullion*, 366–68.

9. Frank Towers, *The Urban South and the Coming of the Civil War* (Charlottesville, Va., 2004), 7, 75, 95; Chambers, *Old Bullion*, 317, 352–53, 369–84.

10. Taylor, *Transportation Revolution*, 161–75; R. C. Taylor, *Statistics of Coal*, 2nd ed. (Phila., 1855), 477–81.

11. Clement Eaton, *Freedom of Thought in the Old South* (Raleigh, N.C., 1940), 129–30, 189–94; William W. Freehling, *The Road to Disunion*, vol. 1: *Secessionists at Bay, 1776–1854* (New York, 1990), 464–67.

12. "James G. Birney," *ANB*; Eaton, *Freedom of Thought*, 175–78.

13. "Cassius M. Clay," *ANB*; Freehling, *Road to Disunion*, 1:464–73; David L. Smiley, *The Lion of White Hall: The Life of Cassius M. Clay* (Madison, Wis., 1969), 82–111; Eugene D. Genovese, *The Political Economy of Slavery: Studies in the Economy and Society of the Slave South* (New York, 1965), 173.

14. Nathan Gaither to Calhoun, Dec. 2, John Custis Darby to Calhoun, Dec. 4, 1848, in *Papers of Calhoun*, 26:145, 155; Freehling, *Road to Disunion*, 1:467–71.

15. Towers, *Urban South*, 8, 22–24, 39–60, 95; Barbara J. Fields, *Slavery and Freedom on the Middle Ground: Maryland During the Nineteenth Century* (New Haven, Conn., 1985),

40–62; Marc Egnal, *Divergent Paths: How Culture and Institutions Have Shaped North American Growth* (New York, 1996), 14–18.

16. Frederick Douglass, *Narrative of the Life of Frederick Douglass* (New York, 1995), 61; "Frederick Douglass," *ANB*; Freehling, *Road to Disunion*, 1:201–206; Fields, *Slavery and Freedom*, 1–39.

17. J. H. Alexander to Calhoun, July 31, 1848, in *Papers of Calhoun*, 25:643; Freehling, *Road to Disunion*, 1:197–202.

18. Freehling, *Road to Disunion*, 1:197, 207–209, quote on p. 473.

19. Holman Hamilton, *Prologue to Conflict: The Crisis and Compromise of 1850* (1964; rpt., New York, 1966), 191–200; Southern Address, Jan. 22, 1849, in *Papers of Calhoun*, 26:242–43.

20. Adams, July 28, 1848, *CG*, 30th Cong., 1st sess., App., p. 1045; "David Rice Atchison," *ANB*.

21. Hans L. Trefousse, *Andrew Johnson: A Biography* (New York, 1989); Robert W. Winston, *Andrew Johnson: Plebeian and Patriot* (New York, 1928), 15–33; "Andrew Johnson," *ANB*.

22. Johnson, To the Freemen of the First Congressional District of Tennessee, Oct. 15, 1845, in *The Papers of Andrew Johnson*, ed. Leroy P. Graf and Ralph W. Haskins, 15 vols. (Knoxville, Tenn., 1967– ), 1:220–75, quotes on pp. 270, 271.

23. Trefousse, *Johnson*, 64.

24. Johnson, Speech on the Tariff and Oregon, June 20, 1846, in *Papers of Johnson*, 1:324.

25. Trefousse, *Johnson*, 78–79; Johnson, To the Freemen of the First Congressional District of Tennessee, Oct. 15, 1845, Johnson, Resolution for Constitutional Amendments on Presidential, Senatorial, and Judicial Elections, Feb. 21, 1851, in *Papers of Johnson*, 1:254–57, 604–607.

26. Johnson, July 25, 1850, *CG*, 31st Cong., 1st sess., App., pp. 952, 1449–50.

27. Johnson, Remarks on the Homestead Bill, Feb. 28, 1851, to Horace Greeley, Dec. 15, 1851, in *Papers of Johnson*, 1:609–10, 632; Trefousse, *Johnson*, 63, 72, 76–77, 80.

28. Craig M. Simpson, *A Good Southerner: The Life of Henry A. Wise of Virginia* (Chapel Hill, N.C., 1985), 106–14, quote on p. 113. Data for the low slavery counties are drawn from the censuses of 1840, 1850, 1860 as presented in the *Great American History Machine*, version 2.0, CD-ROM, Academic Software Development Group, University of Maryland, 1995. A "significant increase" is defined as two percentage points or more. That is, a county that had slaves as 5 percent of its population in 1840 and 7 percent in 1850 would record that 2 percent "significant increase." An increase from 0 to just under 2 percent was defined as remaining the same.

29. Johnson, Speech on the Admission of Oregon, Jan. 31, 1845, in *Papers of Johnson*, 1:286; Trefousse, *Johnson*, 71–76.

30. Richard K. Crallé to Calhoun, Nov. 6, 1848, in *Papers of Calhoun*, 26:125.

31. Joseph W. Woodward to Calhoun, Sept. 7, 1849, ibid., 27:48.

32. David R. Goldfield, *Urban Growth in the Age of Sectionalism: Virginia, 1847–1861* (Baton Rouge, La., 1977), xi–xxiv, 2–21, 182–201, 228–47, quote on p. 235.

33. Ibid., 123–35.

34. John T. Trezevant to Calhoun, June 7, 1849, in *Papers of Calhoun*, 26:427.

35. Simpson, *Good Southerner*, 100, 127–28; William A. Link, *Roots of Secession: Slavery and Politics in Antebellum Virginia* (Chapel Hill, N.C., 2003), 15–16, 21–22, 145–48; Botts, Jan. 20, Aug. 30, 1842, Jan. 10, 1843, *CG*, 27th Cong. 2nd sess., pp. 182, 974, *CG*, 27th Cong., 3rd sess., p. 144, for quote, Jan. 16, 1840, *CG*, 26th Cong., 1st sess., p. 126.

36. Joseph H. Parks, *John Bell of Tennessee* (Baton Rouge, La., 1950), 6–7, 202–8, 278–79, 339–41; "John Bell," *ANB*; Bell, Feb. 2–3, 1848, July 3, Sept. 14, 1850, *CG*, 30th Cong., 1st sess., App., pp. 189–201, *CG*, 31st Cong., 1st sess., App., pp. 1088–1106, 1668–70; Jonathan M. Atkins, *Parties, Politics, and the Sectional Conflict in Tennessee, 1832–1861* (Knoxville, Tenn., 1997), 147–48.

37. Freehling, *Road to Disunion*, 1:169–70, 176–77, 512–14; Link, *Roots of Secession*, 23–25; Marc W. Kruman, *Parties and Politics in North Carolina, 1836–1865* (Baton Rouge, La., 1983), 12–13, 49, 86–92, 102–103; Richard P. McCormick, "Suffrage Classes and Party Alignment: A Study in Voter Behavior," *Mississippi Valley Historical Review* 46 (1959): 398–403; Max R. Williams, "The Foundations of the Whig Party in North Carolina: A Synthesis and a Modest Proposal," *North Carolina Historical Review* 47 (1970):122–24.

38. Simpson, *Good Southerner*, 91–93, quote from Henry Foote on p. 93.

39. "Robert M.T. Hunter," *ANB*.

40. Hunter, *CG*, 30th Cong., 1st sess., App., pp. 272–78.

41. "Nathaniel Macon," *ANB*; Arthur M. Schlesinger, Jr., *The Age of Jackson* (New York, 1945), 26–28.

42. Venable, July 29, Aug. 7, 1848, Feb. 26, 1849, *CG*, 30th Cong., 1st sess., App., pp. 1063–64, *CG*, 30th Cong., 2nd sess., App., p. 165.

43. Southern Address, Jan. 22, 1849, in *Papers of Calhoun*, 26:242–43; Kruman, *Parties and Politics*, 126–28. In contrast to North Carolina's two signers, seven Virginia congressmen and both senators endorsed Calhoun's address.

44. Atkins, *Sectional Conflict in Tennessee*, 161–62; U.S. Bureau of the Census, *The Seventh Census of the United States, 1850* (Washington, D.C., 1853). Senator Hopkins Turney, from a slaveholding district in Middle Tennessee, also signed the Southern Address.

45. Paul H. Bergeron, *Antebellum Politics in Tennessee* (Lexington, Ky., 1982), 7–8, 102–105; Atkins, *Sectional Conflict in Tennessee*, 168–77.

46. Brian G. Walton, "The Second Party System in Arkansas, 1836–1848," *Arkansas Historical Quarterly* 28 (1969): 127–28; James M. Woods, *Rebellion and Realignment: Arkansas's Road to Secession* (Fayetteville, Ark., 1987), 35–37.

47. Gene W. Boyett, "Quantitative Differences Between Arkansas Whig and Democratic Parties, 1836–1840," *Arkansas Historical Quarterly* 34 (1975): 214–26; Walton, "Second Party System," 120–55; Wood, *Rebellion and Realignment*, 17–26, 35–51; Johnson, June 7, 1850, *CG*, 31st Cong., 1st sess., App., pp. 715–18.

## CHAPTER 8: ORIGINS OF THE REPUBLICAN PARTY, 1854–56

1. George W. Julian, *Political Recollections, 1840 to 1872* (1884; rpt., New York, 1970), quotes on pp. 143, 155; "George W. Julian," *ANB*; William E. Gienapp, *The Origins of the Republican Party, 1852–1856* (New York, 1987), 285.

2. Stanley W. Campbell, *The Slave Catchers: Enforcement of the Fugitive Slave Law, 1850–1860* (Chapel Hill, N.C., 1968, 1970), 87–92.

3. Douglas, Mar. 14, 1850, *CG*, 31st Cong., 1st sess., App., p. 375; James Wishart to Calhoun, Dec. 6, 1848, in *The Papers of John C. Calhoun*, ed. Robert L. Meriwether et al., 28 vols. (Columbia, S.C., 1959–2003), 26:156.

4. Robert W. Johansen, *Stephen A. Douglas* (New York, 1973), 431; Michael F. Holt, *The Rise and Fall of the American Whig Party: Jacksonian Politics and the Onset of the Civil War* (New York, 1999), 459–520; "Stephen A. Douglas," *ANB*.

5. John R. Thompson, Feb. 28, 1854, *CG*, 33rd Cong., 1st sess., App., p. 257.

6. Douglas to Editor of Concord, N.H., *State Capitol Reporter*, Feb. 16, 1854, in *Letters of Stephen A. Douglas*, ed. Robert W. Johannsen (Urbana, Ill., 1961), 289.

7. "Appeal of the Independent Democrats," written Jan. 19, published Jan. 23, 1854, online at www.teachingAmericanHistory.org/library/index.asp?document=945 (accessed Mar. 12, 2008).

8. James Cooper, Feb. 27, 1854, *CG*, 33rd Cong., 1st sess., App., p. 507; Bishop Perkins, May 10, 1854, ibid., p. 647; Galusha Grow, May 10, 1854, ibid., p. 975; Andrew Stuart, May 20, ibid., p. 843. Significantly, many Southern leaders also were optimistic, in their private correspondence, about the possibility of slavery gaining a foothold in Kansas. William W. Freehling, *The Road to Disunion*, vol. 1: *Secessionists at Bay, 1776–1854* (New York, 1990), 550–51.

9. David M. Potter, *The Impending Crisis, 1848–1861* (New York, 1976), 165–75; Kenneth C. Martis and Ruth A. Rowles, *The Historical Atlas of Political Parties in the United States Congress, 1789–1989* (New York, 1989). Democrats also retained two seats in California.

10. Gienapp, *Republican Party*, 82–86, quotes Weed on p. 83; Wade, May 25, 1854, *CG*, 33rd Cong., 1st sess., App., p. 764; Holt, *Rise and Fall*, 836.

11. John Law to William Marcy, Sept. 25, 1854, quoted in Michael F. Holt, *The Political Crisis of the 1850s* (New York, 1978), 150; Gienapp, *Republican Party*, 105–22; Holt, *Rise and Fall*, 861–71; Stephen B. Oates, *With Malice Toward None: A Life of Abraham Lincoln* (New York, 1977, 1994), 112–13, 123–25.

12. Gienapp, *Republican Party*, 129–277, quotes Winthrop, p. 137; Daniel D. Barnard to Hamilton Fish, Dec. 21, 1854, quoted in Holt, *Rise and Fall*, 910, and see pp. 871–950.

13. Gideon Welles quoted in Holt, *Political Crisis*, 165.

14. Tyler Anbinder, *Nativism and Slavery: The Northern Know Nothings and the Politics of the 1850s* (New York, 1992), 3–43; Gienapp, *Republican Party*, 92–101. For contrasting perspectives on the Know Nothing Party, see Michael Holt, "The Politics of Impatience: The Ori-

gins of Know Nothingism," *Journal of American History* 60 (1973): 309–31; Holt, *Political Crisis*, 162–73; Gienapp, *Republican Party*, 92–99; William G. Bean, "An Aspect of Know Nothingism—The Immigrant and Slavery," *South Atlantic Quarterly* 23 (1924): 319–34.

15. *Harrisburg Herald*, Dec. 24, 1854, Aaron H. Cragin to Thurlow Weed, June 15, 1855, both quoted in Anbinder, *Nativism and Slavery*, 99.

16. Speech by Otis Tiffany, quoted ibid., 181.

17. Charles Sumner to Julia Kean Fish, Nov. 15, 1854, in *The Selected Letters of Charles Sumner*, ed. Beverly W. Palmer, 2 vols. (Boston, 1990), 1:422.

18. E. B. Chase to William Bigler, Oct. 10, 1854, quoted in Gienapp, *Republican Party*, 147; Julian, *Political Recollections*, 140–41. Know Nothings typically called for the restoration of the Missouri Compromise, rather than the end of all slavery in the territories. Unlike a few of the more radical Republican state parties, they shunned any denunciation of the fugitive slave law.

19. Ernest McKay, *Henry Wilson, Practical Radical: A Portrait of a Politician* (Port Washington, N.Y., 1971), 91–92; Anbinder, *Nativism and Slavery*, 75–99; Gienapp, *Republican Party*, 136–65.

20. Charles Sumner to Wilson, Apr. 25, 1851, in *Selected Letters*, 1:325–26; McKay, *Wilson*, 6–74; "Henry Wilson," *ANB*.

21. McKay, *Wilson*, 86–103, quotes *Boston Know Nothing*, 89, and Wilson letter to Phillips, 99; Salmon Chase to John Paul, Dec. 27, 1854, to James M. Ashley, Jan. 21, 1855, to Edward S. Hamlin, Jan. 22, Feb. 9, 1855, in *The Salmon P. Chase Papers*, ed. John Niven, 2 vols. (Kent, Ohio, 1993– ), 2:392–94, 396, 397–99, 401–402; "Schuyler Colfax," *ANB*; Gienapp, *Republican Party*, 174–87.

22. Anbinder, *Nativism and Slavery*, 180–81, 187–93.

23. Ibid., 183–201; *New York Herald*, June 27, 1856, quoted in Gienapp, *Republican Party*, 436, and see pp. 209–23.

24. Anbinder, *Nativism and Slavery*, 202–41. For maps and an analysis of Know Nothing votes, see ibid., 34–43, 64, 85, 94, 127–35; Gienapp, *Republican Party*, 160, 212, 232, 419–46, 506–46.

25. Anbinder, *Nativism and Slavery*, 246–70; John R. Mulkern, *The Know-Nothing Party in Massachusetts: The Rise and Fall of a People's Movement* (Boston, 1990), 155–73; Kirk H. Porter and Donald B. Johnson, eds., *National Party Platforms, 1840–1964* (Urbana, Ill., 1966), 33.

26. *Boston Bee*, Oct. 1, 1855, quoted in Anbinder, *Nativism and Slavery*, 190.

27. Platform quoted in Holt, *Political Crisis*, 153–54.

28. Quoted in McKay, *Wilson*, 90.

29. Chase to James W. Grimes, Apr. 13, 1855, in *Chase Papers*, 2:405.

30. Gienapp, *Republican Party*, 122–23, 287–89.

31. *New York Times*, Aug. 23, 1855.

32. Smith to Henry Carey, Nov. 13, 1855, Carey Papers, HSP.

33. Wilson quoted in Anbinder, *Nativism and Slavery*, 192; Smith to Henry Carey, Nov. 13, 1855, in Carey Papers, HSP.

34. *New York Times*, Jan. 18, 1855.

35. Charles English to Gideon Welles, May 8, 1856, quoted in Holt, *Political Crisis*, 170; Eric Foner, *Free Soil, Free Labor, Free Men: The Ideology of the Republican Party Before the Civil War* (New York, 1970), 201; Gienapp, *Republican Party*, 239–71.

36. Trumbull to Lincoln, Jun. 15, 1856, quoted in Holt, *Political Crisis*, 195; Gienapp, *Republican Party*, 273–303.

37. T. M. Monroe to Daniel Ullman, June 13, 1856, quoted in Holt, *Political Crisis*, 195.

38. *National Party Platforms*, 28.

39. Charles Dana to Henry Carey, June 14, 1856, Carey Papers, HSP.

40. Gienapp, *Republican Party*, 413–48; William Gienapp, "Nativism and the Creation of a Republican Majority in the North before the Civil War," *Journal of American History* 72 (1985): 529–59; Dale Baum, *The Civil War Party System: The Case of Massachusetts, 1848–1876* (Chapel Hill, N.C., 1984), 8–54; Joel H. Silbey, "The Surge of Republican Power: Partisan Antipathy, American Social Conflict, and the Coming of the Civil War," in *Essays on American Antebellum Politics, 1840–1860* (Arlington, Tex., 1982), 199–229; Michael F. Holt, *Forging a Majority: The Formation of the Republican Party in Pittsburgh, 1848–1860* (New Haven, Conn., 1969), 123–219; Paul Kleppner, *The Third Electoral System, 1853–1892* (Chapel Hill, N.C., 1979), 49–74.

## CHAPTER 9: TRIUMPH OF THE REPUBLICANS, 1856–60

1. Glyndon Van Deusen, *Horace Greeley: Nineteenth-Century Crusader* (New York, 1953), passim, quote on p. 56; Horace Greeley to R. M. Whipple, April [?] 1860, quoted in James L. Huston, *The Panic of 1857 and the Coming of the Civil War* (Baton Rouge, La., 1987), 237; "Horace Greeley," *ANB*.

2. William E. Gienapp, *The Origins of the Republican Party, 1852–1856* (New York, 1987), 316–29.

3. Lincoln to Albert G. Hodges, Apr. 4, 1864, in *The Collected Works of Abraham Lincoln*, ed. Roy P. Basler, 8 vols. (New Brunswick, N.J., 1953–55), 7:281.

4. Stephen B. Oates, *With Malice Toward None: A Life of Abraham Lincoln* (New York, 1977, 1994), 5–16; Richard J. Carwardine, *Lincoln* (London, 2003), 3–18.

5. Lincoln, Protest in Illinois Legislature on Slavery, Mar. 3, 1837, in *Collected Works*, 1:74–75; Oates, *With Malice Toward None*, 16–39, 95. In important ways, however, Lincoln was unlike his father. Abraham rejected his father's occupation, farming, and became estranged from Thomas and did not attend his funeral.

6. Lincoln to Joshua Speed, Aug. 24, 1855, in *Collected Works*, 2:320. Compare his earlier description of the same episode in Lincoln to Mary Speed, Sept. 27, 1841, ibid., 1:260.

7. David Herbert Donald, *Lincoln* (New York, 1995), 130–37, 162–70, and quote on p. 162; Richard N. Current, *The Lincoln Nobody Knows* (New York, 1958), 215–19; Phillip

Shaw Paludan, "Lincoln and Negro Slavery: I Haven't Got Time for the Pain," *Journal of the Abraham Lincoln Association* 27, no. 2 (Summer 2006): 1–57.

8. Lincoln, Speech at Peoria, Oct. 16, 1854, Speech at Chicago, July 10, 1858, in *Collected Works*, 2:282, 492; Oates, *With Malice Toward None*, 26–27, 52–55.

9. Lincoln, Sixth Debate with Douglas, Oct. 13, 1858, in *Collected Works*, 3:254.

10. Lincoln, Speech at Peoria, Oct. 16, 1854, ibid., 2:276.

11. Lincoln, First Debate with Douglas, Aug. 21, 1858, ibid., 3:16, italics in original.

12. Lincoln, Speech at Kalamazoo, Aug. 27, 1856, ibid., 2:364.

13. Lincoln, Address on Colonization to a Deputation of Negroes, Aug. 14, 1862, ibid., 5:374; Eric Foner, *Free Soil, Free Labor, Free Men: The Ideology of the Republican Party Before the Civil War* (New York, 1970), 20–23, 29–30; Gabor S. Borritt, *Lincoln and the Economics of the American Dream* (Urbana, Ill., 1978, 1994), 155–85, 217–21.

14. Lincoln, First Debate with Douglas, Aug. 21, 1858, ibid., 3:15–18; Foner, *Free Soil*, 267–80.

15. Lincoln, Fourth Debate with Douglas, Sept. 18, 1858, ibid., 3:145–46.

16. David M. Potter, *The Impending Crisis, 1848–1861* (New York, 1976), 267–327.

17. Lincoln, Sixth Debate with Douglas, Oct. 13, 1858, in *Collected Works*, 3:265.

18. Lincoln, First Debate with Douglas, Aug. 21, 1858, ibid., 3:20.

19. Lincoln, First Debate with Douglas, Aug. 21, 1858, ibid., 3:29; Doris Kearns Goodwin, *Team of Rivals: The Political Genius of Abraham Lincoln* (New York, 2005), 170–256.

20. Lincoln, First Debate with Douglas, Aug. 21, 1858, in *Collected Works*, 3:20; Kirk H. Porter and Donald B. Johnson, eds., *National Party Platforms, 1840–1964* (Urbana, Ill., 1966), 27–28, 31–33. Neither platform, however, mentioned one of Lincoln's pet projects, colonization.

21. Chase to Sydney H. Gay, Jan. 3, 1855, in *The Salmon P. Chase Papers*, ed. John Niven, 2 vols. (Kent, Ohio, 1993), 2:394.

22. *New-York Tribune*, Oct. 15, 1856, quoted in Foner, *Free Soil*, 116.

23. Schurz, Speech of Sept. 1858, quoted ibid., 116.

24. Ibid., quotes Wilson, p. 289; Richard H. Sewell, *Ballots for Freedom: Antislavery Politics in the United States, 1837–1860* (New York, 1976), 323–37, quotes Giddings p. 329, and Wisconsin Republicans p. 335.

25. *New York Times*, Nov. 24, Dec. 1, 1858, quoted in Sewall, *Ballots for Freedom*, 349.

26. *New York Times*, Nov. 1, 1860.

27. *New-York Tribune*, Oct. 15, 1856, quoted in Foner, *Free Soil*, p. 61.

28. E. Peshine Smith to Henry Carey, Apr. 3, 1856, Carey Papers, HSP. In 1860 Northern states held 176 of the 296 votes in the electoral college. Republicans needed 149 votes for a majority and had received 114 in 1856. They needed 35 more from some combination of Pennsylvania (27), Indiana (13), Illinois (11), New Jersey (7), and California (4). See Gienapp, *Republican Party*, 378 and note.

29. John F. Coleman, *The Disruption of Pennsylvania Democracy, 1848–1860* (Harrisburg, Pa., 1975), 103–10, quote on p. 108.

30. Donald, *Lincoln*, 227–29.

31. L. Clephane to Henry Carey, Oct. 20, 1856, Carey Papers, HSP.

32. E. Peshine Smith to Henry Carey, Dec. 6, 1857, Carey Papers, HSP; Van Deusen, *Greeley*, 225–28.

33. Lincoln, Third Debate with Douglas, Sept. 15, 1858, in *Collected Works*, 3:116.

34. Lincoln, First Debate with Douglas, Aug. 21, 1858, ibid., 3:10.

35. Douglas, First Debate with Lincoln, Aug. 21, 1858, ibid., 3:9.

36. Oakland County *Pontiac Gazette*, Sept. 16, 1854, quoted in Madison Kuhn, "Economic Issues and the Rise of the Republican Party in the Northwest" (Ph.D. diss., University of Chicago, 1940), 120.

37. Quotes from *Chicago Journal* and *Chicago Tribune*, ibid., 120–21.

38. Quotes from *Niles Republican* and *Chicago Daily Tribune*, ibid., 128.

39. Bingham to Senate and House of Representatives of Michigan, Jan. 4, 1855, in *Messages of the Governors of Michigan*, ed. George N. Fuller, 4 vols. (Lansing, Mich., 1925–26), 2:300.

40. Quoted in Kuhn, "Economic Issues," 129; *National Party Platforms*, 27–28.

41. George W. Smith, *Henry C. Carey and American Sectional Conflict* (Albuquerque, N.M., 1951), 7–57; "Henry C. Carey," *ANB*; William Elder, *A Memoir of Henry C. Carey* (Philadelphia, 1880), 31–36, quote on p. 34. Congressman George Scranton informed Carey, "If we can carry the Tariff Bill *through*, you may safely mark up your coal interests." Apr. 30, 1860, Carey Papers, HSP.

42. Henry Carey, *Letters to the President on the Foreign and Domestic Policy of the Union: And Effect, as Exhibited in the Condition of the People and the States* [1858], quotes on pp. 65, 169; Huston, *Panic of 1857*, 72–77; Arthur M. Lee, "The Development of an Economic Policy in the Early Republican Party" (Ph.D. diss., Syracuse University, 1953), 46–50.

43. Carey to Horace Binney, Oct. 7, 1856, quoted in Smith, *Carey*, 47.

44. William Elder to Carey, Feb. 12, 1856, Carey Papers, HSP. Elder is referring to a group of British economists: Adam Smith, David Ricardo, Rev. Thomas Malthus, Nassau Senior, John Stuart Mill, and Richard Whately.

45. Smith to Carey, June 8, 1855, ibid.

46. Lewis D. Campbell to Carey, July 9, 1856, ibid.

47. James H. Campbell to Carey, Dec. 4, 1856, ibid.

48. Charles A. Dana to Carey, undated, 1856, ibid.

49. *New York Times*, Feb. 4, 1857.

50. James L. Baker to Carey, Jan. 15, 1856, Carey Papers, HSP.

51. Henry Wilson, Mar. 1, 1855, *CG*, 33rd Cong., 1st sess., App., p. 371.

52. *New York Times*, Dec. 8, 1858.

53. William Cronon, *Nature's Metropolis: Chicago and the Great West* (New York, 1991), 311–40.

54. Data for manufacturing is from the published U.S. census, accessed online at fisher.lib.virginia.edu/collections/stats/histcensus/ (accessed Mar. 13, 2008). On change

in the Midwest, see Nicole Etcheson, *The Emerging Midwest: Upland Southerners and the Political Culture of the Old Northwest, 1787–1861* (Bloomington, Ind., 1995); and Allan R. Pred, *The Spatial Dynamics of U.S. Urban-Industrial Growth, 1800–1914: Interpretative and Theoretical Essays* (Cambridge, Mass., 1966).

55. Huston, *Panic of 1857*, 1–34, quote on p. 16.

56. Henry McCormick to Simon Cameron, June 5, 1858, Cameron Papers, LC.

57. U.S. Bureau of the Census, *Historical Statistics of the United States, Colonial Times to 1970* (Washington, D.C., 1975), 885, 1106, 1114; Sherman, May 7, 1860, *CG*, 36th Cong., 1st sess., p. 1946.

58. Richard Vaux to Buchanan, May 16, 1858, quoted in Huston, *Panic of 1857*, 140.

59. *New York Times*, Dec. 8, 1858; J. [Casey?] to Joseph Barrett, Sept. 19, 1859, Cameron Papers, LC; Simon Cameron to Henry Carey, June 3, 1858, Carey Papers, HSP; Huston, *Panic of 1857*, 152–72, quote on p. 156.

60. John Sherman, *Recollections of Forty Years in the House, Senate and Cabinet: An Autobiography*, 2 vols. (Chicago, 1895), 1:1–86; "John Sherman," *ANB*; Marc Egnal, "Explaining John Sherman," *Ohio History* 114 (2007), 105–17. Surprisingly, there is no modern biography of John Sherman. Two older works, Theodore Burton, *John Sherman* (Boston, 1906), and Winfield S. Kerr, *John Sherman: His Life and Public Services*, 2 vols. (Boston, 1907), are badly out of date.

61. Sherman, July 9, 1862, *CG*, 37th Cong., 2nd sess., p. 3199; Gienapp, *Republican Party*, 295–96; Sherman, *Recollections*, 1:114–35, 168–80.

62. The Cooper Union Speech was reported in both the *New-York Tribune* and *The New York Times* for Apr. 14, 1860. I have drawn on both accounts (they differed slightly). Lee, "Economic Policy," 127, quotes the *Tribune* version. See also Sherman, Dec. 8, 1856, Jan. 20, 1860, *CG*, 34th Cong., 3rd sess., App., p. 85, *CG*, 36th Cong., 1st sess., App., p. 85.

63. Sherman, May 7, 1860, *CG*, 36th Cong., 1st sess., p. 1947.

64. Sherman, May 27, 1858, *CG*, 35th Cong., 1st sess., p. 2431, Jan. 18, 1858, 35th Cong., 1st sess., p. 326; Howell Cobb to Sherman, Jan. 5, 1858, Sherman Papers, LC.

65. *New-York Tribune* quoted in Lee, "Economic Policy," 127.

66. Heather Cox Richardson, *The Greatest Nation of the Earth: Republican Economic Policies During the Civil War* (Cambridge, Mass., 1997), 103–12.

67. Cawallader C. Washburn, May 7, 1860, *CG*, 36th Cong., 1st sess., p. 1983.

68. Samuel R. Curtis, May 9, 1860, ibid., p. 2021.

69. Thomas M. Pitkin, "Western Republicans and the Tariff in 1860," *Mississippi Valley Historical Review* 27 (1940): 401–20.

70. *New York Times*, Jan. 21, 1860, quotes Chase's letter of Oct. 25, 1859; William Elder to Carey, Feb. 15, Mar. 21, June 20, 1861, Carey Papers, HSP.

71. W. G. Hammond to Carey, Dec. 28, 1860, W. W. Davis to Carey, Feb. 18, 1860, Carey Papers, HSP; Grow, May 8, 1860, *CG*, 36th Cong., 1st sess., p. 1954; Lee, "Economic Policy," 76–77.

72. Pitkin, "Western Republicans," 419; Lee, "Economic Policy," 196–202, quotes the *New-York Evening Post*, Mar. 1, 1861; *New York Times*, Sept. 28, 1860, Feb. 14, 15, Mar. 26, 1861; E. Peshine Smith to Carey, Feb. 7, 1861, Carey Papers, HSP.

73. Lee, "Economic Policy," 120, quotes *New-York Evening Post*, Mar. 1, 1860.

74. *National Party Platforms*, 33.

75. Lee, "Economic Policy," 177, quotes Koerner; Reinhard J. Luthin, "Abraham Lincoln and the Tariff," *American Historical Review* 49 (1944): 616.

76. *New York Times*, May 18, 1860; Lee, "Economic Policy," 178; Pyrus Elder to Carey, June 16, 1860, Carey Papers, HSP; Luthin, "Lincoln and the Tariff," 617, quotes William Onahan's diary.

77. Lincoln to Edward Wallace, Oct. 11, 1859, in *Collected Works*, 3:487; Luthin, "Lincoln and the Tariff," 609–29.

78. Lincoln, Speech at Pittsburgh, Pa., Feb. 15, 1861, in *Collected Works*, 4:214; Hans L. Trefousse, *The Radical Republicans: Lincoln's Vanguard for Racial Justice* (Baton Rouge, La., 1968), 137–304.

79. Luthin, "Lincoln and the Tariff," 613, quotes Joseph Medill.

80. Ibid., 618–21; Pitkin, "Western Republicans," 408–409, quotes Philadelphia *North American*, May 19, 1860.

81. Luthin, "Lincoln and the Tariff," 622.

82. Huston, *Panic of 1857*, 250, quotes McClure.

83. James Cavanaugh, Jan. 20, 1859, *CG*, 35th Cong., 2nd sess., p. 505.

84. *New York Times*, Apr. 14, 1860.

85. The 1860 homestead bill was in fact a watered–down compromise between the two houses of Congress. It would have charged settlers twenty-five cents an acre. Lee, "Economic Policy," 153, quotes Buchanan; Hans L. Trefousse, *Andrew Johnson: A Biography* (New York, 1989), 119–20; Sherman, May 7, 1860, *CG*, 36th Cong., 1st sess., p. 1949; Benjamin H. Hibbard, *A History of the Public Land Policies* (New York, 1924), 370–83.

86. Henry Wilson, Mar. 1, 1855, Morril, Apr. 20, 1858, Trimble, May 5, 1860, *CG*, 33rd Cong., 1st sess., App., p. 371, 35th Cong., 1st sess., p. 1696, 36th Cong., 1st sess., App., p. 301; Huston, *Panic of 1857*, 128–29, 192; Hibbard, *Public Land Policies*, 328–33; cf. vote, Mar. 7, 1860, *CG*, 36th Cong., 1st sess., pp. 1024–25; *New York Times*, Jan. 3, 1859.

87. Richardson, *Greatest Nation*, 172–75; *National Party Platforms*, 31–33; vote on telegraph, May 24, 1860, *CG*, 36th Cong., 1st sess., pp. 2328–29; L.F.S. Foster to Henry Carey, Jan. 9, 1861, Carey Papers, HSP.

88. William Montgomery, Feb. 21, 1859, *CG*, 35th Cong., 2nd sess., App., p. 183; William E. Gienapp, "Who Voted for Lincoln?" in *Abraham Lincoln and the American Political Tradition*, ed. John L. Thomas (Amherst, Mass., 1986), 50–97; Gienapp, "Nativism and the Creation of a Republican Majority in the North before the Civil War," *Journal of American History* 72 (1985): 529–59; Joel H. Silbey, "The Surge of Republican Power: Partisan Antipathy, American Social Conflict, and the Coming of the Civil War," in *Essays on American Antebellum Politics, 1840–1860* (Arlington, Tex., 1982), 199–229; Paul Kleppner, *The Third Electoral System, 1853–1892* (Chapel Hill, N.C., 1979), 49–74; Ray

M. Shortridge, "The Voter Realignment in the Midwest During the 1850s," *American Politics Quarterly* 4 (1976): 193–222; Shortridge, "Voting for Minor Parties in the Antebellum Midwest," *Indiana Magazine of History* 74 (1978): 117–34; Robert P. Swierenga, "The Ethnic Voter and the First Lincoln Election," *Civil War History* 11 (1965): 27–43.

89. James Blaine, *Twenty Years of Congress*, quoted in Huston, *Panic of 1857*, 267.

90. Lincoln, Seventh Debate with Douglas, Oct. 15, 1858, in *Collected Works*, 3:312.

91. Richardson, *Greatest Nation*, 8–15.

92. See the following votes: Subtreasury, June 12, 1858, *CG*, 35th Cong., 1st sess., pp. 3015–16; agricultural colleges, Feb. 16, 1859, Mar. 7, 1860, *CG*, 35th Cong., 2nd sess., pp. 1066–67, 36th Cong., 1st sess., pp. 1024–25; tariff, Feb. 26, 1859, May 10, 1860, *CG*, 35th Cong., 2nd sess., pp. 1411–12, 36th Cong., 1st sess., p. 2056; St. Clair Flats, Mar. 2, 1859, *CG*, 35th Cong., 2nd sess., p. 1598; Treasury notes, Mar. 3, 1859, *CG*, 35th Cong., 2nd sess., pp. 1680–81; loan bill, June 21, 22, 1860, *CG*, 36th Cong., 1st sess., pp. 3221–22, 3254–55; telegraph to Pacific, May 24, 1860, *CG*, 36th Cong., 1st sess., pp. 2328–29; admission of Kansas, Apr. 12, 1860, *CG*, 36th Cong., 1st sess., p. 1672. On tariff and loan bills, Pennsylvania Democrats typically defected to the Republican side.

93. James Blaine, *Twenty Years of Congress*, quoted in Huston, *Panic of 1857*, 267.

94. Lee, "Economic Policy," 629, quotes Carey to Noah H. Swayne, Feb. 4, 1865.

95. Hiram Calkins[?] to Simon Cameron, Aug. 7, 1858, Cameron Papers, LC.

96. *New York Times*, Nov. 9, 1860.

## CHAPTER 10: THE COTTON STATES LEAVE THE UNION

1. C. Vann Woodward, ed., *Mary Chesnut's Civil War* (New Haven, Conn., 1981), 4, 28, 43–44; Isabella D. Martin and Myrta Avary, eds., *A Diary from Dixie* (New York, 1905). 3. As Woodward makes clear in his introduction (pp. xv–lvii), his edition is only a selection from the many notebooks Chesnut filled. Martin and Avary provide material that is not in Woodward.

2. Henry Benning, secessionist commissioner of Georgia, to Virginia convention, Feb. 18, 1861, online at members.aol.com/jfepperson/benningva.htm (accessed Apr. 17, 2007).

3. *New-York Evening Post*, Dec. 13, 21, 1860, quoted in Laura A. White, *Robert Barnwell Rhett: Father of Secession* (1931; rpt., Gloucester, Mass., 1965), 181–82.

4. Ibid., 4–25, quote on pp. 20–21; "Robert Barnwell Rhett," *ANB*. I have modernized the punctuation of this quote, adding a question mark.

5. Rhett quoted in White, *Rhett*, 24, 109; Eric H. Walther, *The Fire-Eaters* (Baton Rouge, La., 1992), 142–48.

6. *Charleston Mercury*, Nov. 3, 1860, quoted in *Southern Editorials on Secession*, ed. Dwight L. Dumond (1931; rpt., Gloucester, Mass., 1964), 204; White, *Rhett*, 135–90; Walther, *Fire-Eaters*, 147–56; Robert Barnwell Rhett, Jr., to William Porcher Miles, Apr. 7, 1858, Jan. 29, Mar. 28, Apr. 17, 1860, William Porcher Miles Papers, SHC.

7. *Charleston Mercury*, Dec. 3, 1860, in *Southern Editorials*, 292.

8. Thomas R. R. Cobb, Secessionist Speech, Nov. 12, 1860, in *Secession Debated: Georgia's Showdown in 1860*, ed. William W. Freehling and Craig M. Simpson (New York, 1992), 27–28; Benjamin Wade, Mar. 7, 1860, *CG*, 36th Cong., 1st sess., p. 150.

9. Texas Declaration of Reasons for Seceding, Feb. 2, 1861, online at www.yale.edu/lawweb/avalon/csa/texsec.htm (accessed Mar. 12, 2007).

10. Benning, Secessonist Speech, Nov. 19, 1860, in *Secession Debated*, 120.

11. William L. Barney, *The Secessionist Impulse: Alabama and Mississippi in 1860* (Princeton, N.J., 1974), 165–66, 197, 228; David M. Potter, *The Impending Crisis, 1848–1861* (New York, 1976), 378–84.

12. Dew, *Apostles of Disunion*, 101–102; Lauren Keitt to William Porcher Miles, Oct. 3, 1860, William Porcher Miles Papers, SHC; *Charleston Mercury*, Oct. 11, 1860, in *Southern Editorials*, 179.

13. *Charleston Mercury*, Oct. 11, 1860, in *Southern Editorials*, 179; see also same, July 25, 1860, ibid., 153; *New Orleans Daily Crescent*, Jan. 21, 1861, ibid., 408.

14. Adrain, Jan. 15, 1861, *CG*, 36th Cong., 2nd sess., pp. 393–94.

15. Davis, Inaugural Address, Feb. 18, 1861, online at www.yale.edu/lawweb/avalon/csa/csainau.htm (accessed Mar. 12, 2007).

16. Constitution of the Confederate States, Mar. 11, 1861, online at www.yale.edu/lawweb/avalon/csa/csa.htm (accessed Mar. 12, 2007).

17. *Charleston Mercury*, Oct. 11, 1860, in *Southern Editorials*, 181.

18. Cobb, Secessionist Speech, Nov. 12, 1860, in *Secession Debated*, 29. On secessionist concerns about the disappearance of arable lands, see Barney, *Secessionist Impulse*, 3–23.

19. Stephens to J. Henly Smith, Oct. 13, 1860, in *The Correspondence of Robert Toombs, Alexander H. Stephens, and Howell Cobb*, ed. Ulrich B. Phillips (1913; rpt., New York, 1970), 501; Thomas E. Schott, *Alexander H. Stephens of Georgia: A Biography* (Baton Rouge, La., 1988), 19–22, 122–322; Daniel Walker Howe, *The Political Culture of the American Whigs* (Chicago, 1979), 238–55.

20. Stephens, Feb. 12, 1859, *CG*, 35th Cong., 2nd sess., App., p. 124.

21. Stephens, Unionist Speech, Nov. 14, 1860, in *Secession Debated*, 56.

22. Stephens to J. Henly Smith, Dec. 31, 1860, in *Toombs, Stephens, and Cobb Correspondence*, 526.

23. Stephens, Unionist Speech, Nov. 14, 1860, in *Secession Debated*, 66–68.

24. Stephens to J. Henly Smith, July 10, 1860, in *Toombs, Stephens, and Cobb Correspondence*, 487.

25. Stephens to Unknown, Nov. 25, 1860, ibid., 504.

26. *New Orleans Daily Picayune*, Oct. 31, Nov. 4, 1860, in *Southern Editorials*, 199, 217.

27. Perry quoted in Lacy K. Ford, Jr., *Origins of Southern Radicalism: The South Carolina Upcountry, 1800–1860* (New York, 1988), 370.

28. *New Orleans Bee*, Nov. 8, 1860, in *Southern Editorials*, 222.

29. Benjamin Hill, Unionist Speech, Nov. 15, 1860, in *Secession Debated*, 98.

30. *Vicksburg Daily Whig*, Jan. 18, 1860, *Southern Editorials*, 14–15.

31. For example, in fifteen counties in northwestern Georgia wheat output nearly tripled during the decade from 258,000 to 748,000 bushels, while population increased only 10 percent. *U.S. Census: Agriculture, 1860*; Daniel H. Hamilton to William Porcher Miles, Jan. 23, 1860, William Porcher Miles Papers, SHC;. Robert E. Bonner, *Colors and Blood: Flag Passions of the Confederate South* (Princeton, N.J., 2002), 102–105; "William Porcher Miles," *ANB*; Walther, *Fire-Eaters*, 270–96; Wilma A. Dunaway, *The First American Frontier: Transition to Capitalism in Southern Appalachia, 1700–1860* (Chapel Hill, N.C., 1996), 157–94.

32. B. G. Wilkins to Miles, Mar. 13, 1861, William McBurney to Miles, Feb. 21, 1861, William Porcher Miles Papers, SHC. George Rogers Taylor, *The Transportation Revolution, 1815–1860* (New York, 1951), 169, estimates one in eight bales. But see the much higher figures in Philadelphia *North American and United States Gazette*, Jan. 30, 1861, in *Northern Editorials on Secession*, ed. Howard C. Perkins, 2 vols. (1942; rpt., Gloucester, Mass., 1964), 1:583. These figures are for bales sent to the North; that trade, in turn, accounted for only perhaps one-fourth of the cotton produced. The rest was sent abroad, chiefly to England.

33. Columbia *Daily South Carolinian*, quoted in Steven A. Channing, *Crisis of Fear: Secession in South Carolina* (New York, 1974), 193; ibid., 159–203; Robert Barnwell Rhett, Jr., to William Porcher Miles, Jan. 29, Mar. 28, Apr. 17, 1860, William Henry Trescott to Miles, Mar. 10, 1860, D. H. Hamilton to Miles, Apr. 26, 1860, William Porcher Miles Papers, SHC.

34. *Charleston Mercury*, Nov. 3, 1860, in *Southern Editorials*, 204; Channing, *Crisis of Fear*, 204–50; Ford, *Origins of Southern Radicalism*, 366–70; J. D. Ashmore to James Orr, May 23, 1860, Orr-Patterson Papers, SHC; Alfred Huger to William Porcher Miles, June 1, 1860, William Porcher Miles Papers, SHC.

35. Petigru quoted in Ford, *Origins of Southern Radicalism*, 371; James Petigru to Benjamin Perry, Oct. 8, 1860, Benjamin F. Perry Papers, SHC.

36. Presidential votes from Walter Dean Burnham, *Presidential Ballots 1836–1892* (Baltimore, 1955); Thomas B. Alexander and Peggy J. Duckworth, "Alabama Black Belt Whigs During Secession," *Alabama Review* 17 (1964): 181–97. In the blackbelt counties, some Whigs who seemingly had the same holdings and activities as their Southern Democratic neighbors proved more reluctant to endorse militant action.

37. Lillian A. Pereyra, *James Lusk Alcorn: Persistent Whig* (Baton Rouge, La., 1966), 3–44.

38. James M. Jones to Andrew Johnson, Dec. 29, 1860, quoted in Percy L. Rainwater, *Mississippi: Storm Center of Secession, 1856–1861* (1938; rpt., New York, 1969), 196n.

39. Rudy H. Leverett, *Legend of the Free State of Jones* (Jackson, Miss., 1984).

40. On the convention vote, see Rainwater, *Mississippi*, 200. The total vote was 41,656. Of this, 40.5 percent favored immediate secession, 29.3 percent were cooperationists, 20.7 percent voted for coalition tickets, and 9.5 percent were unknowns. I divided the coalition votes to get the figures in the text. Also see Barney, *Secessionist Impulse*, 77–88, 319–20.

41. Rainwater, *Mississippi*, 202–12; Ralph A. Wooster, *The Secession Conventions of the South* (Princeton, N.J., 1962), 26–47. Natchez—and Adams County, where it was

located—was another center of cooperationist strength. See D. Clayton James, *Antebellum Natchez* (Baton Rouge, La., 1968), 133–34.

42. John F. Reiger, "Secession of Florida from the Union—A Minority Decision?" *Florida Historical Quarterly* 46 (Apr. 1968): 358–68, quotes Perry, p. 362; Dorothy Dodd, "The Secession Movement in Florida, 1850–1861, Part II," *Florida Historical Quarterly* 12 (Oct. 1933): 45–66; Wooster, *Secession Conventions*, 67–79. Divisions in the convention are illustrated by the votes in *Journal of the Proceedings of the Convention of the People of Florida, Begun and Held in the Capitol in the City of Tallahassee, on Thursday, January 3, A.D. 1861* (Tallahassee, 1861). The 1870 census provides information, by county, on the states of origin for Florida citizens. *Census of the United States, 1870.*

43. S. D. Cabaniss to Governor Andrew Moore, quoted in Ollinger Crenshaw, *The Slave States in the Presidential Election of 1860* (1945; rpt., Gloucester, Mass., 1969), 255–56; Frank Towers, *The Urban South and the Coming of the Civil War* (Charlottesville, Va., 2004), 208.

44. Clemens to William B. Wood, Nov. 26, 1860, quoted in Barney, *Secessionist Impulse*, 200; "William Lowndes Yancey," *ANB*.

45. J. Mills Thornton III, *Politics and Power in a Slave Society: Alabama, 1800–1860* (Baton Rouge, La., 1978), 373–461, quote on p. 416; Wooster, *Secession Conventions*, 49–66.

46. Augusta *Daily Constitutionalist*, Dec. 30, 1860, in *Southern Editorials*, 380; Michael P. Johnson, *Toward a Patriarchal Republic: The Secession of Georgia* (Baton Rouge, La., 1977), 111.

47. Schott, *Stephens*, 295–322.

48. A. Hood to Howell Cobb, Dec. 19, 1860, in *Toombs, Stephens, and Cobb Correspondence*, 524.

49. Michael P. Johnson, "A New Look at the Popular Vote for Delegates to the Georgia Secessionist Convention," *Georgia Historical Quarterly* 56 (1972): 259–75; Johnson, *Patriarchal Republic*, 116–21; Wooster, *Secession Conventions*, 89–92.

50. Wooster, *Secession Conventions*, 80–100; Peyton McCrary, Clark Miller, and Dale Baum, "Class and Party in the Secession Crisis: Voting Behavior in the Deep South, 1856–1861," *Journal of Interdisciplinary History* 8 (1978): 429–57. The table below examines the eighty-nine delegates who refused to sign the Georgia secession ordinance. In the "low slaveholding" counties, slaves accounted for less than 30 percent of their population. Typically, counties sent two delegates to the convention, though the most populous were permitted three.

| | Low slaveholding counties in north | Low slaveholding counties in south | High slaveholding counties | Total |
|---|---|---|---|---|
| Nonsigning delegates | 46 | 9 | 34 | 89 |
| Total counties | 35 | 15 | 82 | 132 |

Percy S. Flippin, *Herschel V. Johnson of Georgia: States' Rights Unionist* (Richmond, Va., 1931), 190, provides the names and counties of the nonsigners.

51. John A. Winston, Alabama secessionist commissioner, to Governor A. B. Moore, Jan. 2, 1861, online at members.aol.com/jfepperson/AL–La.htm (accessed Apr. 15, 2007).

52. *New Orleans Daily True Delta*, Nov. 3, 1860, *New Orleans Daily Picayune*, Dec. 8, 1860, in *Southern Editorials*, 211–12, 310.

53. Towers, *Urban South*, 192–97; Burnham, *Presidential Ballots*; Roger W. Shugg, *Origins of Class Struggle in Louisiana: A Social History of White Farmers and Laborers During Slavery and After 1840–1875* (Baton Rouge, La., 1939), 157–68; John M. Sacher, *A Perfect War of Politics: Parties, Politicians, and Democracy in Louisiana, 1824–1861* (Baton Rouge, La., 2003), 259–90.

54. Charles B. Dew, "The Long Lost Returns: The Candidates and Their Totals in Louisiana's Secession Election," *Louisiana History* 10 (1969): 353–69; Dew, "Who Won the Secession Election in Louisiana?" *Journal of Southern History* 36 (1970): 18–32; Towers, *Urban South*, 197–201; Wooster, *Secession Conventions*, 101–20; Sacher, *Perfect War of Politics*, 290–99.

55. Texas Declaration of Reasons for Seceding, Feb. 2, 1861, online at www.tsl.state.tx.us/ref/abouttx/secession/2feb1861.html (accessed Mar. 21, 2008); Walter L. Buenger, *Secession and Union in Texas* (Austin, 1984), 120–32; Wooster, *Secession Conventions*, 121–24.

56. Joe T. Timmons, "The Referendum in Texas on the Ordinance of Secession, February 23, 1861: The Vote," *East Texas Historical Journal* 11 (Fall 1973): 12–28; Dale Baum, "Pinpointing Apparent Fraud in the 1861 Texas Secession Referendum," *Journal of Interdisciplinary History* 22 (1991): 201–21; Laura Wood Roper, "Frederick Law Olmsted and the Western Texas Free-Soil Movement," *American Historical Review* 56 (1950): 58–64; Robin E. Baker and Dale Baum, "The Texas Voter and the Crisis of Union, 1859–1861," *Journal of Southern History* 53 (1987): 395–420; Terry G. Jordan, "The Imprint of the Upper and Lower South on Mid-nineteenth-century Texas," *Annals of the Association of American Geographers* 57 (1967): 667–90; Richard B. McCaslin, "Voices of Reason: Opposition to Secession in Angelina County, Texas," *Locus* 3 (1991): 177–94; Buenger, *Secession and Union*, 64–71, 133–56; Wooster, *Secession Conventions*, 125–35; Buenger, *Secession and Union*, 88–89.

57. Perry quoted in Lillian A. Kibler, *Benjamin F. Perry: South Carolina Unionist* (Durham, N.C., 1946), 340, 349.

58. Andrew McCollam to Ellen McCollam, Jan. 27, 1861, quoted in Sacher, *Perfect War of Politics*, 297.

59. Thomas McClellan to wife, Jan. 14, 1861, quoted in Barney, *Secessionist Impulse*, 303.

60. Richard N. Current, *Lincoln's Loyalists: Union Soldiers from the Confederacy* (Boston, 1992), 89–104, 213–15.

61. C. Vann Woodward, *The Burden of Southern History*, 3rd ed. (Baton Rouge, La., 1993), 67.

62. Sereno Watson to Henry Watson, Nov. 17, 1860, quoted in Barney, *Secessionist Impulse*, 213–14; John M. Coulter, "Sereno Watson," *Botanical Gazette* 17 (May 1892): 137–41.

63. *Yorkville Enquirer*, Sept. 20, 1860, quoted in Ford, *Origins of Southern Radicalism*, 367.

64. Quoted in Barney, *Secessionist Impulse*, 269.

65. Quoted ibid., 177–78.

66. J.L.M. Curry to Governor Hicks of Maryland, Dec. 28, 1860, online at members.aol.com/jfepperson/AL-MD.htm (accessed July 18, 2007).

67. Michael F. Holt, *The Political Crisis of the 1850s* (New York, 1978), 236.

68. Lincoln, Second Inaugural Address, Mar. 4, 1865, in *Collected Works of Abraham Lincoln*, ed. Roy P. Basler, 8 vols. (New Brunswick, N.J., 1953–55), 8:332.

69. Charles B. Dew, *Apostles of Disunion: Southern Secession Commissioners and the Causes of the Civil War* (Charlottesville, Va., 2001), 1–21, discusses both Confederate and neo-Confederate views of the conflict.


CHAPTER 11: SECESSION IN THE UPPER SOUTH
AND BORDER STATES


1. Frank Towers, *The Urban South and the Coming of the Civil War* (Charlottesville, Va., 2004), 166–70; William J. Evitts, *A Matter of Allegiances: Maryland from 1850 to 1861* (Baltimore, 1974), 176–82, quotes on pp. 178, 180.

2. *Diary of Edmund Ruffin*, quoted in Daniel W. Crofts, *Reluctant Confederates: Upper South Unionists in the Secession Crisis* (Chapel Hill, N.C., 1989), xviii.

3. *Charleston Mercury*, Mar. 10, 1860, in Dwight L. Dumond, ed., *Southern Editorials on Secession* (New York, 1931), 52; Jonathan M. Atkins, *Parties, Politics, and the Sectional Conflict in Tennessee, 1832–1861* (Knoxville, Tenn., 1997), 226–44; Marc W. Kruman, *Parties and Politics in North Carolina, 1836–1865* (Baton Rouge, La., 1983), 200–19; Edward L. Ayers, *In the Presence of Mine Enemies: The Civil War in the Heart of America, 1859–1863* (New York, 2003), 119–34; William A. Link, *Roots of Secession: Slavery and Politics in Antebellum Virginia* (Chapel Hill, N.C., 2003), 213–39; James M. Woods, *Rebellion and Realignment: Arkansas's Road to Secession* (Fayetteville, Ark., 1987), 113–48.

4. Hindman quoted by Samuel S. Cox, Jan. 14, 1861, *CG*, 36th Cong., 2nd sess., p. 374.

5. Vance quoted in John C. Inscoe, *Mountain Masters, Slavery and the Sectional Crisis in North Carolina* (Knoxville, Tenn., 1989), 230.

6. Charles L. Lufkin, "Divided Loyalties, Sectionalism in Civil War McNairy County, Tennessee," *Tennessee Historical Quarterly* 47 (1989): 169–77; Burton W. Folsom II, "The Politics of Elites: Prominence and Party in Davidson County, Tennessee, 1835–1861," *Journal of Southern History* 39 (1973): 359–78; Richard N. Current, *Lincoln's Loyalists: Union Soldiers from the Confederacy* (Boston, 1992).

7. Gilmer, Jan. 26, 1861, *CG*, 36th Cong., 2nd sess., pp. 580–83; Crofts, *Reluctant Confederates*, 13, 34–35, 68, 74–75, 124–28, 198–206, 221–25, 245–47, 255–59, 273, 310, 336–40, quotes on pp. 36, 258; "John A. Gilmer," *ANB*.

8. Crofts, *Reluctant Confederates*, 195–287, Sumner quote on p. 230; David M. Potter, *The Impending Crisis, 1848–1861* (New York, 1976), 529–54.

9. Andrew Johnson to Sam Milligan, Jan. 13, 1861, in *The Papers of Andrew Johnson*, vol. 4: *1860–1861*, ed. Leroy P. Graf and Ralph W. Haskins (Knoxville, Tenn., 1976), 160.

10. Henry Dering to Waitman Willey, Mar. 19, 1861, quoted in Crofts, *Reluctant Confederates*, 163.

11. Crofts, *Reluctant Confederates*, quotes William Speer, p. 158. See also pp. 132–91 for a discussion of the different interests of Whigs and Democrats; Kenneth W. Noe, *Southwest Virginia's Railroad: Modernization and the Sectional Crisis* (Urbana, Ill., 1994); Sam B. Hilliard, *Atlas of Antebellum Southern Agriculture* (Baton Rouge, La., 1984); Wilma A. Dunaway, *The First American Frontier: Transition to Capitalism in Southern Appalachia, 1700–1860* (Chapel Hill, N.C., 1996), 123–55; Kruman, *Parties and Politics*, 140–98; Inscoe, *Mountain Masters*, 211–56.

12. Crofts, *Reluctant Confederates*, 315–60, quotes on pp. 336, 351; Atkins, *Parties, Politics, and the Sectional Conflict*, 244–58; Kruman, *Parties and Politics*, 219–21; Ayers, *In the Presence of Mine Enemies*, 135–40; Link, *Roots of Secession*, 240–53; Woods, *Rebellion and Realignment*, 148–64. In June Tennessee voters ratified the decision of the legislature.

13. Crofts, *Reluctant Confederates*, 164–94; Marc Egnal, *A Mighty Empire: The Origins of the American Revolution* (Ithaca, N.Y., 1988), 87–101; Hilliard, *Atlas*; Joseph C. Sitterson, *The Secession Movement in North Carolina* (Chapel Hill, N.C., 1939). U.S. Bureau of the Census, *The Seventh Census of the United States: 1850* (Washington, D.C., 1853), presents data on religion.

14. Anderson, Jan. 15, 1861, *CG*, 36th Cong., 2nd sess., p. 399; Ralph A. Wooster, *The Secession Conventions of the South* (Princeton, N.J., 1962), 207–15, 225–38, 242–48, 252–55; Wilson P. Shortridge, "Kentucky Neutrality in 1861," *Mississippi Valley Historical Review* 9 (1923): 286–94; William T. McKinney, "The Defeat of the Secessionists in Kentucky in 1861," *Journal of Negro History* 4 (1916): 381–85; Evitts, *Matter of Allegiances*, 154–75; Jean H. Baker, *The Politics of Continuity: Maryland Political Parties from 1858 to 1870* (Baltimore, 1973), 47–53; *Kentucky Statesman*, Nov. 13, 1860, in *Southern Editorials*, 234.

15. Quoted in Towers, *Urban South*, 188.

16. Towers, *Urban South*, 170–78, 185–92; Evitts, *Matter of Allegiances*, 170–71.

17. Wooster, *Secession Conventions*, 233–38, 252–54, quote on p. 254; Evitts, *Matter of Allegiances*, 137–41.

18. *Louisville Daily Courier*, Dec. 20, 1860, in *Southern Editorials*, 360.

19. Paul C. Nagel, *Missouri: A Bicentennial History* (New York, 1977), 130–36; Wooster, *Secession Conventions*, 216–21; Will D. Gilliam, Jr., "Party Regularity in Three Kentucky Elections and Union Volunteering," *Journal of Southern History* 16 (1950): 511–18; James R. Robertson, "Sectionalism in Kentucky from 1855 to 1865," *Mississippi Valley Historical Review* 4 (1917): 60; McKinney, "Defeat of the Secessionists," 381–82.

20. Elbert B. Smith, *Francis Preston Blair* (New York, 1980), 216–43, 256–74, quote on p. 233; Frank Blair, June 6, 1860, *CG*, 36th Cong., 1st sess., App., p. 396; "Francis Preston Blair, Sr.," "Montgomery Blair," "Francis Preston Blair, Jr.," *ANB*; Eric Foner, *Free Soil, Free Labor, Free Men: The Ideology of the Republican Party Before the Civil War* (New York, 1970), 63–65, 176–79, 267–81, quotes on pp. 178, 269, 270.

21. Quoted in William E. Smith, *The Francis Preston Blair Family in Politics*, 2 vols. (New York, 1933), 2:37.

22. Doris Kearns Goodwin, *Team of Rivals: The Political Genius of Abraham Lincoln* (New York, 2005), 388–89, with quote on 389; James M. McPherson, *Battle Cry of Freedom: The Civil War Era* (New York, 1988), 290–93.

23. Stephen B. Oates, *With Malice Toward None: A Life of Abraham Lincoln* (New York, 1977), 210–12, quote on p. 212; Towers, *Urban South*, 165–66; Evitts, *Matter of Allegiances*, 172–74.

24. Towers, *Urban South*, 169–79, quote on p. 179.

25. Evitts, *Matter of Allegiances*, 171–77, quote on p. 171.

26. Robert S. Holzman, *Stormy Ben Butler* (New York, 1954), 42–49, quote on p. 34; Evitts, *Matter of Allegiances*, 183–84.

27. Evitts, *Matter of Allegiances*, quotes on p. 188.

28. McPherson, *Battle Cry of Freedom*, 284–90, 293; Towers, *Urban South*, 180–81; Evitts, *Matter of Allegiances*, 185–91; Baker, *Politics of Continuity*, 54–58, 70–73.

29. Governor Magoffin to Lincoln, Apr. 17, 1861, quoted in Shortridge, "Kentucky Neutrality," 294n.

30. Ibid., 293–97, quote on 294n; McPherson, *Battle Cry of Freedom*, 293; McKinney, "Defeat of the Secessionists," 384–87.

31. Lincoln to Garrett Davis, Apr. 26, 1861, quoted in McPherson, *Battle Cry of Freedom*, 294.

32. E. Merton Coulter, *The Civil War and Readjustment in Kentucky* (Chapel Hill, N.C., 1926), 88–93.

33. Shortridge, "Kentucky Neutrality," 297–301, quote on 300n; Coulter, *Civil War*, 93–105; McPherson, *Battle Cry of Freedom*, 293–96; McKinney, "Defeat of the Secessionists," 387–91. Dick Robinson was a unionist landowner who offered his 3,200-acre estate as a training ground.

## CHAPTER 12: REPUBLICANS IN POWER: THE WAR YEARS

1. Fessenden to Unknown, Mar. 1863, quoted in Leonard P. Curry, *Blueprint for Modern America: Nonmilitary Legislation of the First Civil War Congress* (Nashville, Tenn., 1968), 251–52; "William Pitt Fessenden," *ANB*; Charles A. Jellison, *Fessenden of Maine: Civil War Senator* (Syracuse, N.Y., 1962), 1–9, 112–13, 127–91.

2. Lincoln, First Debate with Douglas, Aug. 21, 1858, in *Collected Works of Abraham*

*Lincoln*, ed. Roy P. Basler, 8 vols. (New Brunswick, N.J., 1953–55), 3:16; Jul. 22, 1861, *CG*, 37th Cong., 1st sess., pp. 222–23, quote on p. 257.

3. Fawn M. Brodie, *Thaddeus Stevens: Scourge of the South* (1959: rpt., New York, 1966), quote on p. 164; "John C. Frémont," *ANB*.

4. Robert S. Holzman, *Stormy Ben Butler* (New York, 1954), 32–55, quote on p. 42; "Benjamin F. Butler," *ANB*; Steven Hahn, *A Nation Under Our Feet: Black Political Struggles in the Rural South from Slavery to the Great Migration* (Cambridge, Mass., 2003), 69–71.

5. Hahn, *Nation Under Our Feet*, 70; James M. McPherson, *Battle Cry of Freedom: The Civil War Era* (New York, 1988), 370–71.

6. Michael Les Benedict, *A Compromise of Principle: Congressional Republicans and Reconstruction, 1863–1869* (New York, 1974), 21–58.

7. Brodie, *Stevens*, 17–31, quote on pp. 24–25; "Thaddeus Stevens," *ANB*.

8. Stevens, June 10, 1851, *CG*, 31st Cong., 1st sess., App., p. 767; Brodie, *Stevens*, 23–151, quote on p. 110.

9. Stevens, Aug. 2, 1861, *CG*, 37th Cong., 1st sess., pp. 414–15.

10. Stevens, Dec. 3, 1861, ibid., p. 6; Brodie, *Stevens*, quote on pp. 157–58.

11. Glyndon Van Deusen, *Horace Greeley: Nineteenth-Century Crusader* (New York, 1953), 284–90; McPherson, *Battle Cry of Freedom*, 494–500.

12. Holman, May 23, 1862, Cox, June 3, 1862, *CG*, 37th Cong., 2nd sess., App., pp. 153, 242–43.

13. Julian, May 23, 1862, *CG*, 37th Cong., 2nd sess., App., p. 185.

14. Doolittle, May 2, 1862, ibid., p. 137.

15. Windom, May 20, 1862, ibid., p. 2246.

16. Sedgwick, May 23, 1862, ibid., p. 2326.

17. David H. Donald, *Lincoln* (New York, 1995), 362–67; McPherson, *Battle Cry of Freedom*, 496–506.

18. Lincoln, "Reply to Emancipation Memorial Presented by Chicago Christians of All Denominations," Sept. 13, 1862, in *Collected Works*, 5:421.

19. Donald, *Lincoln*, 375, quotes Gurowski; Lincoln, Preliminary Emancipation Proclamation, Sept. 22, 1862, in *Collected Works*, 5:436.

20. Lincoln, Emancipation Proclamation, Jan. 1, 1863, Lincoln to Albert G. Hodges, Apr. 4, 1864, in *Collected Works*, 6:30, 7:282; Stephen B. Oates, *With Malice Toward None: A Life of Abraham Lincoln* (New York, 1994), 333.

21. Booker T. Washington, *Up from Slavery* (1901; rpt., New York, 1968), 27.

22. Lincoln, Remarks to Deputation of Western Gentlemen, Aug. 4, 1862, in *Collected Works*, 5:357.

23. David H. Donald, Jean H. Baker, and Michael Holt, *The Civil War and Reconstruction* (New York, 2001), 341–42.

24. George W. Julian, *Political Recollections, 1840 to 1872* (1884; rpt., Westport, Conn., 1970), 251; McPherson, *Battle Cry of Freedom*, 303, 706, 712–16, 805, 838–40; Donald et al., *Civil War and Reconstruction*, 344–45.

25. Curry, *Blueprint for Modern America*, 149–50; Heather Cox Richardson, *The Greatest Nation on Earth: Republican Economic Policies During the Civil War* (Cambridge, Mass., 1997), 33–36; U.S. Bureau of the Census, *Historical Statistics of the United States, Colonial Times to 1970*, 2 vols. consec. pagin. (Washington, D.C., 1975), 2:1104; Bray Hammond, *Sovereignty and an Empty Purse: Banks and Politics in the Civil War* (Princeton, N.J., 1970), 37–98.

26. Richardson, *Greatest Nation*, 114–15, 134–35, quote on p. 114; Curry, *Blueprint for Modern America*, 159–62.

27. Richardson, *Greatest Nation*, 37, 43, 50–64, quote on p. 64.

28. Brodie, *Stevens*, 72–73.

29. Spaulding, Jan. 28, 1862, *CG*, 37th Cong., 2nd sess., p. 524.

30. Robert P. Sharkey, *Money, Class, and Party: An Economic Study of Civil War and Reconstruction* (Baltimore, 1967), 16, 38–44; Curry, *Blueprint for Modern America*, 184–97.

31. Curry, *Blueprint for Modern America*, 164–80; Richardson, *Greatest Nation*, 116–21.

32. Sherman, Feb. 10, 1863, *CG*, 37th Cong., 3rd sess., p. 843; Curry, *Blueprint for Modern America*, 198–206; Richardson, *Greatest Nation*, 86–91.

33. Spaulding, Feb. 19, 1863, *CG*, 37th Cong., 3rd sess., pp. 1115, 1117; David F. Weiman and John A. James, "The Political Economy of the US Monetary Union: The Civil War as a Watershed," *AEA Papers and Proceedings* 97 (May 2007): 271–75.

34. Grow, Feb. 21, 1862, *CG*, 37th Cong., 2nd sess., p. 910; Richardson, *Greatest Nation*, 141–55; Curry, *Blueprint for Modern America*, 103–8.

35. Morril, June 6, 1862, *CG*, 37th Cong., 2nd sess., App., p. 258; Richardson, *Greatest Nation*, 154–61; Curry, *Blueprint for Modern America*, 108–14.

36. Stevens, May 6, 1862, *CG*, 37th Cong., 2nd sess., pp. 1949–50; Curry, *Blueprint for Modern America*, 119–34.

37. David Gilchrist and W. David Lewis, eds., *Economic Change in the Civil War Era* (Greenville, Del., 1965); Ralph L. Andreano, ed., *Economic Impact of the American Civil War*, 2nd ed. (Cambridge, Mass., 1967); Douglas A. Irwin, "Tariff Incidence in America's Gilded Age," *Journal of Economic History* 67 (2007): 582–607.

## CHAPTER 13: REPUBLICANS IN POWER: BUILDING THE INDUSTRIAL STATE

1. Grant to Daniel Ammen, Aug. 28, 1877, quoted in William Gillette, *Retreat from Reconstruction, 1869–1879* (Baton Rouge, La., 1979), 348; Eric Foner, *Reconstruction: America's Unfinished Revolution, 1863–1877* (New York, 1988), 582–87; Jerry M. Cooper, *The Army and Civil Disorder: Federal Military Intervention in Labor Disputes, 1877–1900* (Westport, Conn., 1980), 47–52, 61–82; Robert M. Utley, *Frontier Regulars: The United States Army and the Indian, 1866–1891* (New York, 1973), 296–321; "Oliver O. Howard," "Winfield S. Hancock," *ANB*.

2. Foner, *Reconstruction*, 35–48, 60–69, quote on p. 36.

3. Kenneth M. Stampp, *The Era of Reconstruction, 1865–1877* (New York, 1965), 50–82, quotes on pp. 58, 63; Foner, *Reconstruction*, 176–90, quote on p. 180; Michael Perman, *Reunion Without Compromise: The South and Reconstruction, 1865–1868* (New York, 1973), 122–31.

4. Wilson, Mar. 2, 1866, *CG*, 39th Cong., 1st sess., App., p. 140; Fawn M. Brodie, *Thaddeus Stevens: Scourge of the South* (New York, 1959), 229–30; Foner, *Reconstruction*, 119–23, 181–96; George C. Rable, *But There Was No Peace: The Role of Violence in the Politics of Reconstruction* (Athens, Ga., 1984), 17–32; Thomas J. Brown, ed., *Reconstructions: New Perspectives on the Postbellum United States* (New York, 2006), 40–65.

5. Ralph J. Roske, *His Own Counsel: The Life and Times of Lyman Trumbull* (Reno, Nev., 1979), passim; Mark M. Krug, *Lyman Trumbull: Conservative Radical* (New York, 1965), passim, quote on p. 14; "Lyman Trumbull," *ANB*.

6. Trumbull, Jan. 29, 1866, *CG*, 39th Cong., 1st sess., pp. 474–76; Civil Rights Act, Apr. 9, 1866, online at www.africanamericans.com/CivilRightsActof1866.htm (accessed Mar. 7, 2008); Foner, *Reconstruction*, 228–43.

7. Stevens, May 8, 1866, *CG*, 39th Cong., 1st sess., p. 2459.

8. Fourteenth Amendment, ratified 1868, online at www.law.cornell.edu/constitution/constitution.amendmentxiv.html (accessed Mar. 7, 2008).

9. Foner, *Reconstruction*, 253; Julian, Jan. 29, 1866, *CG*, 39th Cong., 1st sess., App., p. 57.

10. Garfield, May 8, 1866, *CG*, 39th Cong., 1st sess., p. 2462.

11. Stevens, May 8, 1866, *CG*, 39th Cong., 1st sess., p. 2459.

12. Julian, Feb. 4, 1868, *CG*, 40th Cong., 2nd sess., App., p. 119; Eric Foner, *Politics and Ideology in the Age of the Civil War* (New York, 1980), 128–49; Michael Les Benedict, *A Compromise of Principle: Congressional Republicans and Reconstruction 1863–1869* (New York, 1974), 258–59; Brodie, *Thaddeus Stevens*, 231–32.

13. Foner, *Reconstruction*, 70–71, 104–6, 246, 374–77; Brodie, *Thaddeus Stevens*, 303–304.

14. Garfield quoted in Brodie, *Thaddeus Stevens*, 289–90; Foner, *Reconstruction*, 256–73.

15. Ingersoll, Feb. 7, 1867, *CG*, 39th Cong., 2nd sess., App., p. 89; Benedict, *Compromise of Principle*, 210–43.

16. Morril, Feb. 5, 1868, *CG*, 40th Cong., 2nd sess., App., p. 114; Foner, *Reconstruction*, 271–91.

17. For examples of moderates who reluctantly supported these steps, see Miller, Jan. 19, Rice, Feb. 13, Davis, Feb. 13, 1867, *CG*, 39th Cong., 2nd sess., App., pp. 80–83, 120–23, 151–53; Foner, *Reconstruction*, 222–23.

18. Foner, *Reconstruction*, 281–307, 316–33, 346–411.

19. Ibid., 439–59; Gillette, *Retreat from Reconstruction*, 46–54, 168–69; Rable, *But There Was No Peace*, 91–112.

20. Trumbull, Apr. 19, 1870, *CG*, 41th Cong., 2nd sess., App., pp. 293.

21. Gillette, *Retreat from Reconstruction*, 52, quotes Garfield.

22. Foner, *Reconstruction*, 500–509, quote on p. 507; Kirk Porter and Donald B. Johnson, eds., *National Party Platforms, 1840–1964* (Urbana, Ill., 1966), 44.

23. George W. Julian, *Political Recollections, 1840 to 1872* (1884; rpt., New York, 1970), 331, 333.

24. Andrew L. Slap, *The Doom of Reconstruction: The Liberal Republicans in the Civil War Era* (New York, 2006), 100, quotes both Charles Francis, Jr., and Henry Adams.

25. Foner, *Reconstruction*, 500–509; Matthew Josephson, *The Politicos, 1865–1896* (New York, 1938), 160; Martin Duberman, *Charles Francis Adams, 1807–1886* (Stanford, Calif., 1960), 38; *National Party Platforms*, 44–45.

26. Tilton, writing in *Golden Age*, Sept. 9, 1871, quoted in Hans L. Trefousse, *The Radical Republicans: Lincoln's Vanguard for Racial Justice* (Baton Rouge, La., 1968), 441.

27. Julian, diary entry, Oct. 10, 1875, quoted in Gillette, *Retreat from Reconstruction*, 238 (punctuation has been added).

28. Wade quoted in ibid., p. 256.

29. Foner, *Reconstruction*, 412–59; Gillette, *Retreat from Reconstruction*, 26–46, quote on p. 35; Rable, *But There Was No Peace*, 81–121; Michael Perman, *The Road to Redemption: Southern Politics, 1869–1879* (Chapel Hill, N.C., 1984); Utley, *Frontier Regulars*, 10–67.

30. Jean Edward Smith, *Grant* (New York, 2001), passim, quotes on pp. 306, 348, 200.

31. Ibid., 259–60, 381–87, 429–30, quotes on pp. 259, 421.

32. William Chandler to Benjamin Butler, Aug. 10, 1869, quoted in Foner, *Reconstruction*, 451.

33. Smith, *Grant*, 542–52, quote on p. 546; Gillette, *Retreat from Reconstruction*, 46–50, 90–97; Foner, *Reconstruction*, 456–59.

34. Foner, *Reconstruction*, 524–63, quote on p. 560; Gillette, *Retreat from Reconstruction*, 31–52, 182, 275–95; Smith, *Grant*, 553–68.

35. Gillette, *Retreat from Reconstruction*, 300–34, quote on p. 304; Foner, *Reconstruction*, 591–99; Heather Cox Richardson, *The Death of Reconstruction: Race, Labor, and Politics in the Post–Civil War North, 1865–1901* (Cambridge, Mass., 2001), 150–55.

36. Gary M. Walton and Hugh Rockoff, *History of the American Economy*, 6th ed. (New York, 1990), 298–303, 407–10.

37. Anthony Wayne to Charles Sumner, Sept. 2, 1872, quoted in Foner, *Reconstruction*, 467; Walton and Rockoff, *American Economy*, 409, presents the number of banks. State banks had a resurgence in the 1890s, when they surpassed the number of national banks.

38. Sherman, Apr. 9, 1866, *CG*, 39th Cong., 1st sess., p. 1850; Robert P. Sharkey, *Money, Class, and Party: An Economic Study of the Civil War and Reconstruction* (Baltimore, 1959, 1967), 56–80; Irwin Unger, *The Greenback Era: A Social and Political History of American Finance, 1865–1879* (Princeton, N.J., 1964), 41–46.

39. Richard H. Timberlake, Jr., "Repeal of Silver Monetization in the Late Nineteenth Century," *Journal of Money, Credit and Banking* 10 (1978): 27–45; Allen Weinstein, "Was There a 'Crime of 1873'? The Case of the Demonetized Dollar," *Journal of American History* 54 (1967): 307–26; Walter T. K. Nugent, *The Money Question During Reconstruction* (New York, 1967), 52–101; Sharkey, *Money, Class, and Party*, 81–140. After the war the majority of Democrats abandoned their support of hard money and advocated inflation. Both positions—although seemingly contradictory—reflected the interests of a

debtor class. The relentless spread of the market economy made more money rather than less appear to be the answer to the woes of these less affluent individuals.

40. Stevens, July 27, 1866, *CG*, 39th Cong., 1st sess., p. 4255.

41. Terry L. Seip, *The South Returns to Congress: Men, Economic Measures, and Intersectional Relationships, 1868–1879* (Baton Rouge, La., 1983), 112–70, 219–68, quote on p. 223.

42. Josephson, *Politicos*, 276–315, 636–61, quote on p. 641; "Marcus Alonzo Hanna," *ANB*.

43. Josephson, *Politicos*, 386–92, 454–66, quotes on pp. 389, 460; John Sherman, *Recollections of Forty Years in the House, Senate and Cabinet: An Autobiography*, 2 vols. (Chicago: 1895), 1:110–250; Gabriel Kolko, *Railroads and Regulation, 1877–1916* (Princeton, N.J., 1965), 30–83; Richard F. Bensel, *The Political Economy of American Industrialization, 1877–1900* (New York, 2000), 130n, 307–49; Elizabeth Sanders, *Roots of Reform: Farmers, Workers, and the American State, 1877–1917* (Chicago, 1999), 179–95, 269–78.

44. Edward L. Ayers, *What Caused the Civil War? Reflections on the South and Southern History* (New York, 2005), 103–30. For the economic origins of the American Revolution, see Marc Egnal, *A Mighty Empire: The Origins of the American Revolution* (Ithaca, N.Y., 1988); Marc Egnal and Joseph A. Ernst, "An Economic Interpretation of the American Revolution," *William and Mary Quarterly*, 3d ser., 29 (1972): 3–32.

# ACKNOWLEDGMENTS

More than I could have imagined when I started this project, *Clash of Extremes* turned out to be a collaborative work. The chapter-by-chapter critiques presented by the individuals thanked below led me time and again to rethink my arguments. Paragraphs, sections, and even whole chapters disappeared or were reworked in ways that set the final copy many removes from the early drafts. Much of the pleasure I have had in working on the book during the past dozen years emerged from these dialogues. Michael Holt and Daniel Crofts were there from the beginning. They read every chapter and provided me with the benefit of their remarkable knowledge of nineteenth-century U.S. history. Other individuals examined particular chapters or groups of chapters and offered commentaries that on occasion were almost as long as the drafts I sent them. These readers include Edward Ayers, William Barney, Michael Les Benedict, Stanley Engerman, Eric Foner, James Huston, Bruce Levine, James McPherson, Michael Perman, Craig Simpson, John

Stauffer, Margaret Storey, Frank Towers, and David Weiman. In some cases, as changes were made, we persuaded each other of the validity of our points of view; in other cases, not. But all these historians will see the imprint of their contentions in this book.

I've been most fortunate in the editorial support I received at Hill and Wang. Thomas LeBien and his assistant, Elizabeth Maples, commented on multiple drafts, guiding me in matters large and small. Indeed, I selected Hill and Wang because of Thomas's presence there; he oversaw my two previous books at Oxford University Press.

I'm also grateful for the assistance provided by the Faculty of Arts at York University and the Social Sciences and Humanities Research Council of Canada. Funds from these organizations helped me broaden my research. They paid for archival trips and the services of research assistants. Carolyn King of the York Cartographic Office created the eleven maps.

Finally, my wife, Judith Humphrey, and sons, Barton and Benjamin, deservedly have a page of their own. Their support and love have sustained me through my many years of work on the Civil War. This book is affectionately dedicated to them.

# INDEX